The Hidden Structure of Violence

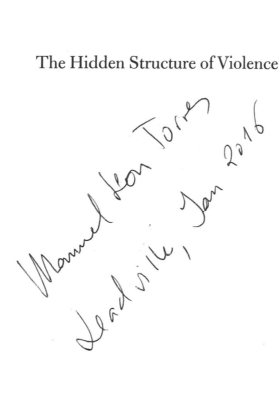

THE HIDDEN STRUCTURE
OF VIOLENCE

Who Benefits from Global Violence and War

by MARC PILISUK *and* JENNIFER ACHORD ROUNTREE

MONTHLY REVIEW PRESS

New York

Library of Congress Cataloging-in-Publication Data
Pilisuk, Marc.
  The hidden structure of violence : who benefits from global violence and
war / by Marc Pilisuk and Jennifer Achord Rountree.
     pages cm
  Includes bibliographical references and index.
  ISBN 978-1-58367-542-7 (pbk. : alk. paper) — ISBN 978-1-58367-543-4
(cloth : alk. paper) 1. Violence. 2. War, Cost of. 3. War. I. Rountree,
Jennifer Achord. II. Title.
  HM886.P57 2015
  303.6—dc23
                          2015014106

Complete bibliographic information for this title is available
on our website.

Monthly Review Press
146 West 29th Street, Suite 6W
New York, New York 10001
www.monthlyreview.org

Typeset in Bulmer 11/14

5 4 3 2 1

Contents

PREFACE

THIS BOOK IS A SUBSTANTIALLY REVISED edition of our earlier work, *Who Benefits from Global Violence and War*. The earlier version represented the work of many people who helped to locate the information, synthesize and draft summaries of diverse materials, and edit portions of the manuscript. For the first edition they include Danial Durazo, Peter Christiansen, Jillian Marks, Donna Nassor, Wanda Woodward, Emmauelle Julien-Sinclair, Herb Diamond, Scott Field, JoAnne Zazzi, Anthony Marsella, and William Domhoff. For the current edition we recognize dedicated and tireless work by Chris Boyd, Pohsuan Zaide, Jenni McConnell, James Reeds, Gianina Pellegrini, Monica Ajer, Ines-Lena Mahr, Lael Curtis, and Carole Patrick. The authors are grateful to the Saybrook University librarians, Noah Lowenstein and Joe Marino, and to Laurens DeHaans for tech support. We are deeply indebted to alternative media for providing information not readily reported in the mainstream and particularly to Amy Goodman of *Democracy Now*. We are indebted to the scholars, journalists, and professional activists who look beneath the blanket of distracting facades to the voices of the casualties of a violent social order and into the back rooms of powerful planners who orchestrate a continuing culture of violence and manipulation. Here we must thank the Corporate Accountability Project, OxFam, Global Exchange, Food First, Peace Action, Amnesty International, the American Civil Liberties Union, Fairness and Accuracy in Reporting, Project Censored, and the Psychologists for Social Responsibility, among myriad sources of information and hope. The scholarship of two of Marc's own mentors, Anatol Rapoport and Kenneth

Boulding, reverberates through the themes of this book as do the words of psychologists JoAnna Macy and Mike Wessells. The inspiration we continue to find in the words and deeds of Dr. Martin Luther King Jr. encourage us to believe that a better world is possible—which is the main reason for this book.

Finally we appreciate deeply the contribution of our families. Marc's parents, Louis and Charlotte, provided him with the chance to grow up in an environment in which social justice was truly valued. His wife, Phyllis, has listened and shared the ideas and dilemmas in writing this book. He thanks her for her understanding of long hours at work that made him less of a caregiver than he might have been as her multiple sclerosis progressed. Jennifer thanks her husband, Shane, for his ongoing encouragement, and her son Levi for his patience—many hours of playing with stuffed animals and Legos were delayed.

As parents and grandparents and practitioners working for those most in need in our communities, we want our offspring to live in a world in which love and interdependence find the resources needed to assure peace, sustainability, and justice. We hope this book will be a resource to that end.

Introduction

During times of universal deceit, telling the truth becomes
a revolutionary act.

—GEORGE ORWELL

The trouble is that once you see it, you can't un-see it. And once you've seen
it, keeping quiet becomes as political an act as speaking out. There's no
innocence. Either way, you're accountable.

—ARUNDHATI ROY

NO SOCIAL SCIENTIST IS VALUE-FREE. We write from a deep belief that
life is not only complex but also precious. Each individual is part of a web of
connections to others and to the surrounding ecology, a marvelous design that
sustains this delicate balance that is life. We believe also that this complex master-
piece is in danger that is largely the result of how many humans think and behave.
For life, particularly human life, to continue there must be a balance between
how we use our interconnections for our own needs and how we nurture these
connections so that the entire web of life can continue. If we abuse, exploit, and
conquer the world about us, we dishonor the gift of life and jeopardize the future.
If we care for the web and nurture it, then the world will nourish us.

This book is about contemporary global violence. When we wrote the original edition, the United States was heavily engaged in two undeclared wars in
Iraq and Afghanistan. Neither has ended; neither has brought peace nor added

to the security of people in any country. New military involvements have begun in Syria and Yemen with no hope of bringing a just peace. Such acts of war provide one of the many examples of the ways that humans inflict harm upon one another. The continuing cost for the United States of war in Iraq has surpassed $3 trillion. It is an amount that we cannot imagine, but we do know that the same money might have addressed such serious problems as world hunger; the AIDS epidemic; housing for homeless people; quality health care and education for everyone; alternative energy research to combat global warning; cleanup of carcinogenic wastes from our environment; adequate warning and response systems for such natural disasters as hurricanes, floods, and earthquakes; research to prevent or heal and to rehabilitate sickness and disability; and guarantees of social security. More than 8,000 U.S. and coalition forces have died in these two wars as have more than 650,000 Iraqis, and, of course, the Iraq war is only one part of the violence happening around the globe. If we humans are to take charge of our destiny, we will have to understand why such violence, at such a cost, recurs so often.

Violence is evident where any life is harmed or ended through the behavior or the negligence of other people. It takes many forms. We will concentrate on two of these: military violence (or war) and economic violence in which the requirements for life and livelihood are taken away or destroyed. Violence may be direct, as when one uses a gun or bomb to destroy others, or structural, as when patterns of land ownership and land use by distant corporate entities result in the starvation of children who live on that land. In this book we look first, in painful detail, at what military violence with modern weapons is inflicting and what it is able to inflict. Military violence is our most profound threat but is not, at this time, our most lethal killer. On a daily basis, even without the casualties of direct military violence, we live in ways that result in the violent deaths of vulnerable people, particularly children, as a consequence of how we exploit, consume, and dispose of the environment that sustains human life. These patterns of investment and exploitation already contribute to a loss of life greater than all wars. Moreover, the persistence of widespread violence causes us to live in a world of fear—fear of being unable to protect ourselves or those we love. It is also a world of denial that the suffering can be so great or that the danger can be so imminent. Even among those who acknowledge the problem, we find widespread disbelief that existing corporate or governmental institutions can address current problems or that ordinary people have the power or the wisdom to transform this world into a better place.

It is not pleasant to look at the larger picture of the violence of war and economic and environmental exploitation. But to avoid seeing the danger will remove all chances of ending it. To see how the parts fit together and what propels this dance of death is, we believe, a first step to reversing it. When we humans see instances of violence, we are often quick to respond, sometimes with efforts to assist the victims, often with efforts to punish the perpetrators. It is important that we are able to feel the pain of each individual case. It is equally important to find out why there are so many cases. For this to take place it is important to examine what common underlying levers are causing the human family to engage in such protracted and recurrent violence. This is painful. It has surely been painful for us to deal with this subject over the years it takes to write such a book. Who wants to be reminded of the extent of destruction and killing? But as distressing as such an examination may be, that look into a dysfunctional system is our best hope to guide our actions to create a better way.

Lessons from the Past

We have much to learn from our national history. Throughout this book we provide examples of the consequences of violence—in its direct, cultural, and structural forms. As we will demonstrate, the U.S. military-industrial complex is surpassed by no other nation in the world; as such, it is important to acknowledge our country's role in facilitating and condoning violence in the present and the past—including during our nation's infancy. The history of U.S. federal policy toward the more than five hundred Native nations across the United States demonstrates the intergenerational effect these policies and their legacy of violence continue to have on these communities to this day.

The "discovery" and takeover of the Americas was driven by Western European monarchs seeking to expand their empires. The claims to these new and foreign lands were justified by the Doctrine of Discovery—a series of papal bulls issued in the fifteenth and early sixteenth centuries—that divided the world into those who were civilized (Christian) and those who were savages (non-Christian). The central message of the Doctrine was that Christian European power had dominion over the lands and the peoples they discovered.[1]

This belief system and subsequent foreign policy led to the decimation of indigenous populations due to enslavement, mass killings, and disease. These policies ultimately became institutionalized in U.S. federal Indian case law, supporting the rights of the white, Christian elite to take ownership of land and natural resources across the country. The remaining "Indian problem" led to the creation of U.S. federal policies enacting the removal, assimilation, and extermination of Native peoples.

Decade after decade of violence against Native communities was not without consequences. Dr. Maria Yellow Horse Brave Heart defines historical trauma as "the cumulative emotional and psychological wounding over the lifespan and across generations, emanating from massive group trauma."[2] Brave Heart describes historical trauma response as a constellation of physical, psychological, and spiritual features, and has compared this response to the intergenerational transmission of trauma, grief, and the survivor's child complex among Jewish Holocaust survivors and their children.[3] The many challenges facing Native communities today are the traumatic legacy of the last five hundred years of federal policies. Acknowledging our national history, we must consider both the short- and long-term effects of domestic and foreign U. S. policies driven by the values of the marketplace and justified by religious ideology brought to bear on communities, families, and individuals. Acts of physical, structural, and cultural violence not only impact the present but have almost certainly a profound effect for generations to come.

Book Overview

In the first chapter, we examine the destructiveness of war and the extraordinary potential of modern technology to destroy. Following this, chapter 2 examines the human capacity to kill other humans. We review our capacity to withdraw empathy from others, enabling us to see them as less than human and making their destruction appear tolerable. Chapters 3 and 4 consider the violence the global economy inflicts upon people and their surrounding ecology. In an era of globalization, transnational corporations operate in ways that increase violence and employ dehumanizing rules and amoral calculations to fulfill their purpose of making money. Chapter 5 confronts a taboo topic: the concentration of power. Corporations do not act alone but as part of a network of wealthy and powerful people whose personal success within the system convinces them of its inherent value. This network has become the gatekeeper over resources, lives, and livelihoods. The settings in which the most influential people come together, sometimes in secret, to chart future plans is described. Typically, however, the understandings they share are sufficiently entrenched in the day-to-day work of corporate and government agencies and in the electoral process so that conspiratorial meetings are not generally needed. Chapter 6 describes the methods and tactics used by those at the centers of power to continue a violent path and the strategic planning that provides rationales and promotes the means to exploit and destroy. The sometimes clandestine means have ranged from persuasion to economic threats, to bribes, coups, assassinations, invasions, and torture. In chapter 7, we survey the ways in which media serve powerful interests and how information is controlled to shape our views and to permit violence to appear both normal and inevitable. Chapter 8 draws from what has been presented to construct a theory of how and why this pattern of violence continues. We describe the widely shared cultural beliefs that permit powerful elites to engage in massive violence. Chapter 9 shows how core beliefs, many of them grounded in religious ideology, encourage ordinary working people, whose needs are repeatedly neglected by the economic order, to find scapegoats, which greatly enhances the ability of the powerful beneficiaries to rule. It examines how the tapping of such beliefs encourages fear among common people and the dangers of fascism that such fear makes possible. These chapters describe what common underlying factors are causing the human family to engage in protracted and recurrent violence. In viewing the enormity of the problem and the patterns that underlie it, we become able to say, and to believe, "Enough—there has to be a better way." Against the weight of the challenge presented, one can examine the myriad social actions, large and small, that are working to change this societal addiction to violence. The conclusion points to what is being done and what can be done to bring peace with justice to the planet.

Looking at the deeper causes of violence can be painful. Who wants to be reminded of the extent of destruction and killing? Such an examination, however, may be our best hope for ending this dysfunctional system and replacing it with one that brings out the best in us. This book asks something of the reader. It asks that you commit yourself to do five things:

1. Face up to the disturbing facts about the forms of global violence. Remind yourself that the numbers reflect real human lives.

2. Refrain from demonizing those most central to the promotion of this violence.

3. The book names people and organizations, but the task is not to blame but to understand the system in which global violence has become a central part.

4. Retain the hope that deeper understanding will contribute to empowering each of us in what we do to create a world of peace.

5. Grapple with this book in doses that fit your needs and find antidotes for the violence in caring contact with people, in the renewing powers of meditation, reflection, exercise, music, art, food, laughter, and the beauty of the land. Then, if any of this restorative bounty is worth preserving, come back to grapple with the violence that threatens our world and your place in securing the future.

1—The Costs of Modern War

Wars throughout history have been waged for conquest and plunder. . . .
The working class who fight all the battles, the working class who make
the supreme sacrifices, the working class who freely shed their blood and
furnish their corpses have never yet had a voice in either declaring war or
making peace. It is the ruling class that invariably does both. They alone
declare war and they alone make peace. . . . They are continually talk-
ing about their patriotic duty. It is not their duty but your patriotic duty
that they are concerned about. There is a decided difference. Their patriotic
duty never takes them to the firing line or chucks them into the trenches.

—EUGENE V. DEBS

It is only those who have neither fired a shot nor heard the shrieks and
groans of the wounded who cry aloud for blood, more vengeance, more deso-
lation. War is hell.

—GEN. WILLIAM TECUMSEH SHERMAN

Mankind must put an end to war or war will put an end to mankind.

—JOHN F. KENNEDY, Speech to UN General Assembly

IF WE ARE EVER TO MOVE away from the realities of global violence we must
first face them. In this chapter we look at the practice of military violence, the
circumstances that include organized efforts to use lethal force to destroy and to
kill others who are defined as adversaries. We also look at the extent of military

violence and its consequences. There are three major problems in conveying the costs of military violence. First, the forms in which military encounters occur have changed dramatically. Wars may refer to one-sided and barely contested interventions or to engagements between the military forces of rival nations. They may be said to include individual acts of terror, like suicide bombing, or massive bombing by missiles and aircraft. They may involve declarations of war, though not always, and they may be considered legitimate responses to defend against being attacked. Some military conflicts, however, are clandestine, undeclared, and denied. Here we will try to cover the consequences of all forms including the possibility of war without end.

The second difficulty is that consequences of contemporary global violence have been of such magnitude as to be barely comprehensible. War has caused more than three times the number of casualties in the last ninety years than in the previous five hundred years. Upwards of 250 major wars have occurred just in the post–Second World War era, taking over 50 million lives and leaving tens of millions homeless.[1] How can that degree of suffering be acknowledged, admitted into awareness, and become a part of the process needed to change it?

The third problem, for the developed world and particularly for the United States, has been the prominent history of the United States in contemporary war. It is difficult to accept culpability for so great a human tragedy. To acknowledge a pattern attributable to one's own nation is to accept a painful responsibility for what has occurred and a moral responsibility to make amends. Between the Second World War and the end of the last century, the United States led eighty-five military interventions throughout the world, almost double the total from the preceding fifty-five-year period.[2] Including all reported acts by U.S. military or intelligence personnel in which casualties resulted, 390 overt military interventions occurred between the end of the Second World War and 2008, with at least 20 million killed.[3] The United States has military personnel in 130 nations and maintains 900 overseas bases.[4] In the decade ending in 2011, the United States spent $7.2 trillion on defense, including the Pentagon's annual base budget, the wars in Iraq and Afghanistan, and nuclear weapons–related activities of the Department of Energy.[5]

Military spending is sometimes difficult to clarify. Some expenditures related to nuclear weapons are in the budget of the Department of Energy, not Defense. The care of veterans represents another category of expense. A major portion of interest paid on the national debt is for the unpaid costs of prior military expenditures. The Bureau of Economic Analysis (BEA) sought an accurate account for total government spending on defense and non-defense. The Bureau recalculated the 2004 federal budget outlay and concluded that the government had understated its defense spending by hundreds of billions of dollars. In FY 2011, approximately 58 percent of the discretionary budget was allocated to national defense.[6] Discretionary spending on national defense has been on an upward trend since the late 1990s. From FY 2001 to FY 2010, while domestic discretionary expenditures increased by approximately 24 percent, discretionary spending on national defense increased by 71 percent, almost three times the rate of increase in domestic spending.[7] The wars in Iraq and Afghanistan contributed significantly to these costs, with expenditures for total outlays estimated at 3 trillion dollars and growing.[8] Later in this chapter we discuss the consequences of this spending for individuals, families, and communities both in the United States and around the world.

The Changing Character of War

The practice of armed conflict takes many forms. These forms trace back to early societies, including hunter-gatherers, herders, and pre-industrial farmers. Some of these tribes , but certainly not all, engaged in warfare. The emergence of kingdoms and of nation-states with defined borders marked a long period in which wars were a natural outgrowth of the expressed purposes of rulers, that is, to retain and expand their influence and the territories under their control. Royal leaders and their kin led the actual battles in which rival armies faced each other directly, often in preplanned encounters. The costs were carefully considered and a preoccupation with strategy helped to create a military caste of experienced warriors. In the Western world, wars of liberation against acknowledged rulers occurred in France and in the United States. Abstract concepts of "liberty" and "consent of the governed" appeared as justifications for armed revolt. These were followed by other abstract rationales of equality, manifest destiny, democracy, religious crusades, communism, and fascism. Each of these provided an ultimate purpose and a rationale for greater sacrifice on the battlefields. Meanwhile private armies of paid mercenaries were hired by wealthy interests to protect or expand their privileged status. As nation-states grew sufficiently productive to maintain large military establishments, they were able, through force, to colonize much of the still tribal and agrarian world. Resistance to such colonial empires led to armies of occupation and, in response, to guerilla armies seeking to oust colonial rulers or their puppet governments.

As technology of warfare improved, the costs in lives increased and the evolution to wars with massive civilian casualties emerged. Now over 90 percent of casualties are civilians. Dating back to the Second World War the allied firebombing of Dresden killed at least 25,000 civilians with some estimates many times higher.[9] It was carried out, according to some historians, as a demonstration of raw Allied air power for Russians moving toward Berlin. Wars generally have unintended consequences rarely confined to their original goals.[10] Along with the technological and economic progress of developed countries in the twentieth century, war tactics used by these countries descended to a level of barbarity that violated the rules of engagement set at the Hague and at Geneva, marking this period in human history as the one most devastated by war.[11] Limitations on the types and numbers of weapons available for deployment in war have been attempted, both to remove provocations and to protect non-combatants, but with only modest success.[12]

The gradual independence of colonial states following the Second World War was ironically accompanied by the continuation of economic colonialism in which large corporate interests retained control over the resources of countries that had won formal independence. In these countries, military bases of the former colonial powers remained to protect foreign economic interests, often with the support or acquiescence of puppet governments that were armed and made wealthy by such arrangements. Conflicts not between nations but between governments and large segments of their own population have produced reigns of terror. Increasingly, wars have asymmetrical opponents in which large and powerful armies with high-tech weapons are pitted against the poorest and most vulnerable people.

Particularly where societies were stripped of resources needed for their viability, tribal conflicts, sometimes divided on ethnic lines, emerged over control of resources and governments. The global traffic in weapons has made such conflicts capable of producing genocide. Where the most powerful nation-states have been in agreement, they have allowed the evolution of United Nations peacekeepers to take an active role in such conflicts.

The character of war is changing from the historical image of military conflicts between nations. One study found that fewer than 10 percent of contemporary warring conflicts are between nation-states.[13]

> The level of ethnically based internal conflict remains far higher than in the decades prior to the 1990s, in marked contrast to the dramatic decline in wars between nations in the same period. Indeed, over the past 50 years, the most frequent settings for violent conflict have not been wars between sovereign states, but rather internal strife tied to cultural, tribal, religious, or other ethnic animosities. Between 1989 and 2004, there were 118 military conflicts in the world. Of those, only seven were between nation-states and the remaining 111 occurred within a single state, a large portion of which involved ethnic conflict.[14]

In part, this reflects the transition from Cold War tensions and wars of colonial independence to the emergence of widespread internal conflict and international terrorism. One must ask, however, why internal conflict and international terrorism are more prevalent now. Clearly there are cases, as in Rwanda, in which colonial exploiters fanned ethnic resentments to perpetuate their own dominance. With equal clarity we find the most powerful nations, particularly the United States, providing military support for authoritarian rulers and committing acts of state terror against those who oppose the usurping of their communities. A swell of resentment and resistance sometimes finds expression in organized acts of terror by non-state actors, in turn providing an excuse for asymmetrical and unconventional forms of war without an apparent end.

In summary, in today's world war is a) not necessarily fought between nation-states, b) most likely fought over control of resources, c) more likely than before to kill civilians in large numbers and to involve widespread violations of human rights, d) more likely to involve the use of weapons that can irreversibly alter the opportunity for continued life on the planet, and e) weapons are more likely to be supplied by corporations that are international weapons specialists.

The contemporary players in violent military conflicts now often include groups of hungry and displaced refugees, revolutionary groups of peasants or workers who are losing their land and their means of livelihood, and militant bands of revenge seekers espousing the tactics of terror. Scarce resources often lead to violent ethnic conflicts. Typically, smaller armed groups are pitted against more powerful elite military units with high-tech weapons, paramilitary forces, and privatized military contractors.

The emerging form of conflict is often referred to as asymmetrical, based on the pronounced difference in organization, resources, and methods on the opposite sides of a conflict. In fact, asymmetrical warfare hardly takes place on a designated battlefield but instead erupts within the domain of ordinary social affairs. Massive military superiority is faced by the ingenuity of taking hostages, suicide attacks, car bombs, blowing up pipelines, attacking symbolic targets or by nonviolent opposition. Asymmetrical warfare is similar in purpose to colonial oppression but is also different in significant ways. At present, oppression is less easily concealed and oppressed people now have more access to information from other parts of the world suggesting that things can be different. Asymmetrical military styles and strategies are accompanied by the disintegration of a boundary that has traditionally removed violent warfare from the public landscape. This heightens public fear and insecurity, clearly a factor leading to extremism by all parties involved. The threats of biological warfare, terrorist attacks, and nuclear arms capabilities are gradually slipping beyond the control of national governments. This change in the destructive capacity of weapons, and in their distribution, has paved the way for dramatic increases in military preparedness, particularly in the United States.[15]

Where major powers have agreed, United Nations peacekeepers have played some role in limiting the scope of conflicts. Yet global corporations that provide weaponry and logistics are typically active players in armed conflict as are those global corporations that benefit from military protection of their assets and their expansion.

A categorically distinct form of "enemy" took the industrial world by surprise on September 11, 2001, and has led to extensive military violence by the United States and a domestic turn toward suppression of dissenters and restrictions on civil liberties. Such actions on the part of a world superpower provide inducements for the recruitment of terrorists.[16] Attacks against European and U.S. targets by groups from the Middle East share a connection with popular insurgencies in Latin America and in Africa; both attest to popular repudiation of domination by the United States and its allies.

The driving force behind much of contemporary warfare has been the expansion of the global economy, which is explored throughout the following chapters. Advances in transportation and communication have made possible the emergence of large multinational corporations with interests they expect to be protected by governments over which they exert great influence. Much of modern war reflects that corporate interest and the opposition it has aroused. Just as corporate interests have become global, so too have social movements grown to thwart corporate domination. Some, in fact most, are nonviolent, while others have taken on tactics of inflicting terror as a reaction to perceived injustices or inequities.

Given this evolving history of armed conflict it is impossible to be precise about how great is the toll upon the human community. By any measure it is enormous. With increasingly powerful weapons, the risks now extend beyond the combatants to large-scale killing of civilians and to the destruction of habitats needed to support life in any form.[17]

The ability to make war and the extent of destruction in warfare depend upon the availability of weapons. Global arms transfer agreements between governments of both developed and developing countries came to $85.3 billion in 2011. The United States was the dominant supplier, accounting for 78 percent of all weapons sales, according to a report from the Congressional Research Service. The sales were more than triple the amount the United States made from arms agreements in 2010.[18] Though patterns in arms transfers have shifted since the Cold War era, weapon sales and distribution remain concentrated on developing nations.[19] This extensive world market in weapons trade provides the means by which ethno-political wars are being fought.[20]

Destructive Capabilities of Weapons

The ways in which wars are conducted have been changing. Environmental activist and epidemiologist Dr. Rosalie Bertell observes a fundamental change in the nature of warfare through the exponential increase of the number of civilian deaths and the amounts of indirect damage to the health of communities and to the natural environment.[21] Technological changes include advances in chemical and biological weapons. The capacity to wage biological warfare is widespread, and clandestine forms of transmission can protect its users from detection.[22] Bertell describes the evolution of such costs of combat over the past century:

The use of toxic gas as a weapon (WW I), poisoning of waterways or air, and using chemicals in warfare broke the taboo against widespread and indiscriminative killing of non-combatants. This trend escalated during WWII through carpet bombings, the nuclear bombs and the V2 rockets. Then chemists, using the chlorine gas, separated for a WW I weapon, developed Agent Orange and an array of pesticides, herbicides and defoliants which attacked both people and the living earth itself. The military used these in the Vietnam War. Extensive use of landmines in Korea and elsewhere, prolonged wars beyond the truce, and now we have the firing of radioactive waste, depleted uranium, at an enemy prolonging the mutilation and killing for generations after the war is over.[23]

The aftereffects of the Vietnam War, in particular the effects of the chemical warfare waged, will outlast the soldiers who fought the war. The most common chemical used was Agent Orange, a mixture of plant hormones used to kill vegetation. Along with Agent Orange were chemicals dubbed Agent Blue, Agent White, and Malathion. From 1962 to 1971, the United States military sprayed nearly 20 million gallons of material containing chemical herbicides and defoliants mixed with jet fuel, mainly in Vietnam, but also in parts of Laos and Cambodia.[24] The chemicals contaminated soil, vegetation, and all human and animal life in the area. These chemicals are capable of staying in the soil for decades before breaking down and can be passed from generation to generation.

Information about Agent Orange was not initially available. Later studies indicated that diseases such as cancer and liver dysfunction as well as severe personality disorders and certain birth defects could be traced to Agent Orange. Not only were the persons contaminated with Agent Orange affected, but their offspring also suffered from enlarged livers, kidney abnormalities, cleft palates, or early death. The environment was also damaged by this chemical warfare. Large areas that were once jungle are now covered with scrub and wild grasses. It is estimated that it may take hundreds of years for the land to recover.

The use of biological and chemical weapons has been illegal since the Geneva Protocol of 1925. However, the polarized thinking that often accompanies war results in differing interpretations of both what has occurred and what is legal. Pentagon reports in November 2005 first denied that white phosphorus had been used against people in the battle of Fallujah in Iraq. Later, reports insisted that it was only used against enemy combatants and that it was not a chemical weapon and therefore legal to use. Earlier declassified Pentagon reports, however, had accused Saddam Hussein's government of engaging in chemical warfare by using phosphorous as a weapon.[25] This surely is a double standard. In a larger sense, it raises important questions concerning our moral justification and tolerance of the use of inhumane methods of combat.

It is hard to fix the damage done by these herbicides and chemicals simply with money. Lawsuits have been filed against companies that produced Agent Orange during the war. So far, producers have paid over $180 million in class-action lawsuits. But the anguish and suffering transmitted down the generations continue to victimize people.

Nuclear Weapons

In all wars, suffering is great. But until the advent of the atomic bomb, war did not have the capacity to end, for all time, the continuation of human beings as a species or to threaten the continuity of life itself. The atomic bombs dropped on Hiroshima and Nagasaki produced the greatest immediate mass death from individual weapons yet known. The threat of nuclear weapons, the most frightening violent force known, seems to grow with restraints wholly inadequate to the extent of the danger. This psychological reality was expressed by President Kennedy:

> Today, every inhabitant of this planet must contemplate the day when this planet may no longer be habitable. Every man, woman, and child lives under a nuclear sword of Damocles, hanging by the slenderest of threads, capable of being cut at any moment by accident or miscalculation or madness.[26]

At a meeting of the National Academy of Sciences, former Secretary of Defense William J. Perry said, "I have never been more fearful of a nuclear detonation than now—there is a greater than 50% probability of a nuclear strike on U.S. targets within a decade."[27] Apocalyptic dangers like this, which we know exist but still ignore, continue to have an effect upon us. They push us away from a long-term connection to the earth, pressing us to live for the moment as if each moment might be the last.[28]

With government prodding, current public attention has focused upon the possibility of a nuclear weapon attack by terrorists. The RAND Corporation carried out a broad-based scenario analysis to examine the impacts of a terrorist attack involving a ten-kiloton nuclear explosion in the Port of Long Beach, California.[29] A varied set of strategic forecasting tools were used to examine immediate and long-term results. It concluded that neither the local area nor the nation are at all prepared to deal with the potential threat of a nuclear device being brought into the United States aboard a container ship. Long Beach is the world's third busiest port, with almost 30 percent of all U.S. imports and exports moving through it. The report noted that a ground-blast nuclear weapon detonated in a shipping container at Long Beach would make several hundred square miles of the fallout area uninhabitable, and that such a blast would have unprecedented economic impacts throughout the country and the world. As one example, the report noted that several nearby oil refineries would be destroyed, in turn exhausting the supply of gasoline on the West Coast in a matter of days. This would leave city officials to deal with the immediate gas shortages and the strong likelihood of related civil unrest. Blast effects would be accompanied by intense firestorms, and by long-lasting radioactive fallout, all contributing to a collapse of local infrastructure. Impacts on the global economy could also be catastrophic for two reasons: first, the economic importance of the global shipping supply chain, which would be severely hampered by the attack, and second, the well-documented fragility of global financial systems.[30]

By current standards a ten-kiloton nuclear explosion represents a minuscule sample of the power of larger nuclear weapons now in the arsenals of a growing number of countries. It is difficult even to imagine what a larger nuclear strike would mean. Another former Defense Secretary, Robert McNamara, recalls his experience during the Cuban missile crisis when the world came close to an exchange of nuclear weapons launched by the United States and the Soviet Union against each other. In his sober warning many years later, McNamara cited a report by the International Physicians for the Prevention of Nuclear War, describing the effects of a single one-megaton weapon:

> At ground zero, the explosion creates a crater 300 feet deep and 1,200 feet in diameter. Within one second, the atmosphere itself ignites into a fireball more than a half-mile in diameter. The surface of the fireball radiates nearly

three times the light and heat of a comparable area of the surface of the sun, extinguishing in seconds all life below and radiating outward at the speed of light, causing instantaneous severe burns to people within one to three miles. A blast wave of compressed air reaches a distance of three miles in about 12 seconds, flattening factories and commercial buildings. Debris carried by winds of 250 mph inflicts lethal injuries throughout the area. At least 50 percent of people in the area die immediately, prior to any injuries from radiation or the developing firestorm.[31]

Had the attack on the Twin Towers involved a twenty-megaton nuclear bomb, blast waves would have carried through the entire underground subway system. Up to fifteen miles from ground zero, flying debris, propelled by displacement effects, would have multiplied the casualties. Approximately 200,000 separate fires would have produced a firestorm with temperatures up to 1,500 degrees. A nuclear bomb destroys the fabric of water supplies, food, and fuel for transportation, medical services, and electric power. And radiation damages that destroy and deform living things would continue for 240,000 years.[32]

There is no reason to believe that a nuclear attack would involve the use of only one such weapon. Moreover, the illustrations above are for a nuclear bomb much lower in destructive capacity than most bombs now available on ready-alert status. These larger weapons are capable of what U.S. diplomat George Kennan has considered to be of such magnitude of destruction as to defy rational understanding.[33] Such bombs, and others still more destructive, are contained in the warheads of missiles, many of them capable of delivering multiple warheads from a single launch.

Following the collapse of the Soviet Union, nuclear weapon stockpiles far in excess of what would be needed to destroy all of the world's population have been reduced. There are, however, still 31,000 nuclear weapons in the world—most of them are American or Russian, with fewer numbers held by the United Kingdom, France, China, India, Pakistan, and Israel. The failure to end the Cold War nuclear confrontation between Russia and the United States leaves the two nations with more than 2,000 strategic nuclear warheads on high-alert status. These can be launched in only a few minutes and their primary mission remains the destruction of the opposing side's nuclear forces, industrial infrastructure, and political/military leadership.[34] We now have the capacity to destroy for all time every person, every blade of grass, and every living thing that has evolved on this planet. But has our thinking evolved to enable us to prevent this from happening?

Nuclear weapons are proliferating. The number of nations now having or capable of developing nuclear weapons makes the risk of their use quite high.[35] Despite a public willingness to view the nuclear threat as past, failures to curtail the development and proliferation of nuclear weapons and to move toward nuclear disarmament leave humanity vulnerable to its own rapid extinction.[36]

In 2005, the London *Guardian* revealed a secret document prepared by MI5, the British Intelligence agency.[37] The document identified more than 360 private companies, university departments and government organizations in eight countries, including Iran, Pakistan, India, Israel, Syria, and Egypt, and warned authorities to be wary of front companies in the United Arab Emirates. All posed dangers in the procurement of goods or technology for potential use in programs for weapons of mass destruction. The central role of Pakistan's black market in selling what is needed to develop nuclear weapons to several other countries has been documented.[38] The length of the list suggests that the arms trade supermarket is bigger than has so far been publicly realized.

During the Cold War, Soviet and U.S. militaries played a dangerous game of making the threat to use nuclear weapons credible. In the 1950s fallout shelters were encouraged in the United States in order to convince USSR officials that we were prepared for an attack (or a counterattack). During a subsequent period the hardening of missile sites and the use of submarines as launching sites were intended to demonstrate the invulnerability of our weapons. Elaborate precautions were taken to keep missiles on hair-trigger alert and responsive to any minimal indicator of an impending attack. Even if the population were totally annihilated, weapons would still have launched. The policy of Mutual Assured Destruction (MAD) produced some very close calls, some by accidents in reading radar signals, others by playing the game of chicken as in the Cuban missile crisis. When the United States used depth charges that destroyed critical air-cooling apparatus in a Soviet submarine, U.S. authorities did not know that the submarine was armed to launch nuclear weapons, that its crew was sick and growing desperate, that it had lost communication with Soviet headquarters. Only a decision by one Soviet officer overrode decisions by others to launch the nuclear war that other commanders had already assumed was begun.[39] We were that close.

Yet MAD as a strategy was credited with preventing an all-out nuclear war. Civilian strategists, unhappy with the standoff in nuclear weapons, laid out plans for a gradual escalation of warfare, moving from small provocations to exchanges of nuclear weapons. Their goal was no longer to defend people but to prevail in the horrible game plan. The use of nuclear weapons against Vietnam was seriously considered by President Nixon and his Secretary of State, Henry Kissinger. Kissinger considered it immoral to ignore options to have smaller nuclear wars instead of relying upon a big one. Public opposition to nuclear weapons most likely prevented their use at that time.

In fiscal year 2013, authorized spending of $11.5 billion was allocated for nuclear weapons development and related programs at the DOE. An additional $6.4 billion was estimated for the inherently expensive disposal of nuclear waste.[40] More resources are now committed to the development and testing of nuclear weapons than were spent (using constant dollar comparisons) at the height of the Cold War.[41] The dangers of this activity are concealed by a culture of secrecy at the weapons laboratories.[42]

The U.S. national obsession with nuclear weapons (an expenditure of approximately $40 billion on them annually, and more than $7 trillion to date) is a significant drain on collective resources that might otherwise be put toward education and scientific research pertaining to medical, economic, or genuine security needs. There are many sites, but Los Alamos, a $2.2 billion sinkhole annually for nuclear weapons research, design, and production, represents the most obvious example of this obsession with military spending.

The Comprehensive Nuclear Test Ban Treaty was the result of endless hours of negotiation by leaders of nations with and without nuclear weapons to assure that nuclear weapons would be eliminated forever as tools of warfare. The Non-Proliferation Treaty (NPT) requires that nations without nuclear weapons refrain from developing them. It also insists that negotiations for elimination of nuclear weapons on the part of nuclear powers should be held in "good faith." By rejecting the treaty, the United States is holding open the door to resumed nuclear testing. This has greatly worried many non-nuclear weapons countries and has already led to charges that the United States is acting in bad faith.

The Natural Resources Defense Council (NRDC) analyzes plans for nuclear policy. According to the council's analysis, the George W. Bush team assumed that nuclear weapons would be part of U.S. military forces at least for the next fifty years; it planned an extensive and expensive series of programs to modernize the existing force. Plans included a new ICBM to be operational in 2020 and a new heavy bomber in 2040. In addition, the Bush administration ordered the Pentagon to draft contingency plans for the use of nuclear weapons against at least seven countries, naming not only the "axis of evil" (Iraq, Iran, and North Korea) but also Russia, China, Libya, and Syria. The Pentagon also launched programs for research and testing of a missile defense system. While technically dubious, the large program has been viewed with alarm by other nations as a signal that the United States was working toward being able to attack other countries with the security that it could intercept missiles sent in retaliation. Such planning has had the obvious consequence of provoking other nations to develop their own arsenals, a process already taking place. Russia and China have responded with plans for new or updated development for nuclear weapons. Without enforceable controls, nuclear weapons technology is spreading.[43]

The Nuclear Posture Review is a legislatively mandated report that determines U.S. nuclear policy, strategy, capabilities, and force posture for successive five- to ten-year periods. The most recent *NPR* was released in April 2010.[44] Its general recommendations for cutbacks were elaborated with specific details in a study by a consortium of groups. The study provides the road map for a large and swift reduction in the nation's nuclear weapons and the sprawling government complex that develops and produces them. It outlines the case for a tenfold reduction in the nation's active nuclear weapons stockpile, to 500 deployed nuclear warheads by 2015. The report calls for a complex reduced from the current eight sites in seven states to just three sites in two states, Texas and New Mexico.[45]

The information technologies so central to command and control of dangerous weapons are often penetrated by unauthorized sources.[46] The combined threat posed by the estimated 27,000 nuclear weapons in Russia, the United States, and the other nuclear-weapon states, merits worldwide concern. However, the view is common among the nuclear powers that nuclear weapons from the first wave of proliferation somehow are tolerable, while such weapons in the hands of additional states are dangerous. In this view, the second wave of proliferation, which added Israel, India, and Pakistan, was not welcome. Political instability in Pakistan was a special source of concern. However, efforts to induce these states to roll back their nuclear weapons programs—as South Africa did—

are now largely abandoned. Since none of them was a party to the NPT, they could not be charged with a violation of the treaty. The third wave of proliferation attempts, attributed to Iraq, Libya, North Korea, and possibly Iran, was considered a mortal danger and met with forceful reactions.[47]

The danger in rejecting plans for the reduction, monitoring and elimination of nuclear weapons is great. This is compounded by the contradictory roles of the International Atomic Energy Agency (IAEA) being at one and the same time the promoter and the policeman of nuclear energy. Promoting nuclear energy leads more states to develop technical capacities that then offer a temptation to use them for military ends. In Iraq, Libya, and North Korea, the IAEA has in fact not been successful in detecting military programs or in preventing their development. Furthermore, it appears to be helpless when faced with a U.S. administration that is determined to develop new types of nuclear weapons and with a willingness to consider using them in pre-emptive strikes. If the world is to avert nuclear war, the inspection powers of the IAEA will have to be reinforced and made applicable universally.[48] Forbidding some countries from developing nuclear weapons while others are allowed to develop secret arsenals is a policy risking disaster. Why the dangers of current policy are being ignored is the subject of chapter 6.

Human Consequences of War

The consequences of war occur during its preparations, in its actual military actions, and in its aftermath. These costs are to life, to property, and to security. They are experienced by soldiers and by their families, with scars remaining long after hostilities have ended. The costs are also borne by civilians who are injured, killed, forced to be child soldiers, and by refugees displaced by the destruction of their homes and cities. The costs are to societies that expend their resources and their ingenuity upon the development of ever-more destructive weapons and the training of people to use them. The costs include living with realistic fear that weapons capable of levels of destruction so great as to threaten the continuation of all life will be used and will produce a final and fiery end to everything we hold dear.

Numbers are inadequate to portray the human cost of war. With every death, dreams and hopes are lost and families are broken. Yet numbers are all we have to convey the magnitude of the problem. We begin with the soldiers and other victims of wars in Vietnam and Iraq. Among wars since the Second World War, the Vietnam War took the lives of more than 2.7 million Vietnamese (the majority of them civilians) and approximately 64,000 U.S. and allied soldiers. It began with a U.S. effort to maintain an unpopular pro-U.S. regime in South Vietnam and ended with a withdrawal of U.S. troops. The war was approved by Congress and was based upon attacks, on two separate dates, on two U.S. Navy destroyers (the USS *Maddox* and the USS *Turner Joy*) by North Vietnamese Navy torpedo boats. It was later revealed that the second attack on the *Turner Joy* did not occur, but this fact was withheld by the National Security Agency.[49] It would be difficult to say what worthwhile objective was accomplished or even whether something positive might have been claimed if the war's outcome had been different. It is also unclear what has been learned from the experience.

False claims were also used to initiate the Iraq war. By July of 2012, more than 4,487 U.S. soldiers had been killed in Iraq, and more than 32,223 had been seriously wounded.[50] By that date, an estimated 116,409 Iraqi civilians had been killed, and hundreds of thousands of lives devastated.[51] The reasons offered for this military action have changed several times. As with Vietnam, each setback has been met with a call for even greater military involvement.

The U.S. soldiers who fought in these wars were typically from poor or lower middle-class backgrounds, distinguishing them from the government officials who had decided to engage in the war. Soldiers had either been drafted into service or, since the end of the draft, attracted to join by recruiter promises of education and job training that they could not pay for otherwise. The highest recruitment rates (defined as the number of recruits per thousand of the 18- to 24-year-old population) were found in counties that were relatively poorer than the rest of the nation. The top twenty recruitment counties had median household incomes below the national average. Nineteen of these ranked below the median average in their own states. The schools providing the greatest number of recruits were those offering GED degrees. No part of their recruitment or training described for the recruits the likelihood of their own death, the consequences to their families, or the effects that the experience would have upon them for the remainder of their lives. In contrast, the upper classes who benefit most economically from war have been practically absent from military service.[52]

The Effects of War on Soldiers

Soldiers who return from war do not come home unscathed. In the Iraq war, more than half of the over 32,000 wounded sustained major injuries.[53] Johnny Dwyer's photo essay in the *New York Times Magazine* in March 2005 described what the word "casualty" actually denotes: "Deep flesh wounds, burst eardrums, shattered teeth, perforated organs, flash burns to the eyes, severed limbs."[54] The images have a powerful impact that is greater than our typical images of survivors. Though the injured soldiers may have survived, their dreams—of playing sports, going to college, walking on the beach—will not.

The actual number of injured military personnel over the course of an unneeded nine-years-long war in Iraq is in the hundreds of thousands—perhaps even more than half a million if we include all the men and women who returned from their deployments in Iraq with traumatic brain injuries, post-traumatic stress, depression, hearing loss, breathing disorders, diseases, and other long-term health problems. We don't have anything close to an exact number, however, because this isn't something that has been tracked. The Pentagon's Defense and Veterans Brain Injury Center reports having diagnosed 229,106 cases of mild to severe traumatic brain injury from 2000 to the third quarter of 2011, including both Iraq and Afghanistan vets. A 2008 study of Iraq and Afghanistan veterans by researchers at the RAND Corporation found that 14 percent screened positive for Post-Traumatic Stress Disorder (PTSD) and 14 percent for major depression, with 19 percent reporting a probable traumatic brain injury during deployment. Researchers found that major depression is highly associated with combat exposure and should be considered as being along the spectrum of post-deployment mental health consequences. Applying those proportions to the 1.5 million veterans of Iraq, an estimated 225,000 of them would be expected to suffer from PTSD or major depression, with 285,000 suspected of suffering a probable traumatic brain injury. Another study, published in 2008 in the *New England Journal of Medicine*, found that 15 percent of soldiers reported an injury during deployment that involved loss of consciousness or altered mental status, and 17 percent of soldiers reported other injuries. Using that ratio would suggest that 480,000 Iraq vets were injured one way or the other. More than 40 percent of soldiers who lost consciousness met the criteria for Post-Traumatic Stress Disorder. Altogether, the Iraq and Afghanistan Veterans of America group estimates that nearly one in three people deployed in those wars suffer from PTSD, depression, or traumatic brain injury.[55] "You live," says Lt. Col. Craig Silverton, an orthopedic surgeon, "but you have these devastating injuries." Col. Joseph Brennan, a head and neck surgeon, adds, "Somebody's got to pay the price, and these kids are paying the price."[56] Writer and former U.S. Marine Anthony Swofford notes:

> Approximately 18 veterans kill themselves each day. Thousands from the current wars have already done so. In fact, the number of U.S. soldiers who have died by their own hand is now estimated to be greater than the number who have died in combat in Afghanistan and Iraq. Eleven years of war in two operating theaters have taken a severe toll on America's military. An estimated 2.3 million Americans have served in Iraq or Afghanistan, and 800,000 of those service members have been deployed multiple times.[57]

Cited casualty rates do not typically include those caused by psychological trauma. During the Vietnam War, these psychological effects became so common that the mental health category of Post-Traumatic Stress Disorder was created. The symptoms include persistent anxiety or increased arousal that were not present before the trauma, a persistent reliving of the traumatic event, hyper-vigilance, sleep disturbance, nightmares, a numbing of emotions, loss of concentration, feelings of estrangement, an inability to experience intimacy, withdrawal from feelings of connection to the outside world, and an avoidance of frightening reminders. Symptoms sometimes involve heightened fearfulness, amnesia, irritability and outbursts of anger, feelings of guilt and, in some cases, major depression.[58]

The National Vietnam Veterans Readjustment Study (NVVRS) 1986–88 provided a report more than a decade after hostilities had ceased. Among American Vietnam theater veterans, 30.9 percent of the men and 26.9 percent of the women were found to have PTSD. This is more than six times the rate found in the general population for men and more than twice the amount found for women. An additional 22.5 percent of men and 21.2 percent of women reported having some symptoms of PTSD at some time in their lives. Although some reports are not quite as high, it is nonetheless clear that more than ten years after the war many veterans still had not left the war behind.[59]

The report revealed other problems. Family life suffered. Forty percent of Vietnam veteran men were divorced at least once (10 percent had two or more divorces), 14.1 percent reported high levels of marital problems, and 23.1 percent had significant problems with parenting.

Of the male Vietnam veterans who were presenting symptoms of PTSD at the time of the survey, almost half had been arrested or in jail at least once—34.2 percent more than once—and 11.5 percent had been convicted of a felony. This might be expected, given the fact that many returned bearing the weight of serious trauma but with training in how to use a gun. Among male veterans, 39.2 percent had experienced alcohol abuse or dependence and 11.2 percent were still reporting serious alcohol problems approximately fourteen years after hostilities had ended. Drug abuse or dependence among male veterans was also substantially higher than the national average, and treatment facilities have never been sufficient for the number of cases needing help.[60] A congressional report in 1984, concluded:

> The suicide rate among Vietnam veterans suffering from PTSD is high . . . not because of massive underlying neuroses, but as a result of the harsh treatment they received in Vietnam, and experiences upon returning to the U.S.[61]

Dr. Arnold, Chief of Psychiatry at the VA Medical Center in Phoenix, Arizona, and an acknowledged expert on PTSD, explained to the congressional committee that the VA's most recent statistics indicated that while Vietnam veterans made up only about 14 percent of all the veterans they treated, they constituted 30 percent of veteran suicides, thus overcontributing substantially to the total number of suicides of their patient population.[62]

Because the NVVRS sample size underrepresented members of certain ethnic minorities, the Matsunaga Vietnam Veterans Project undertook further research with Native American, Asian American, and Pacific Islander veterans. The project involved two studies. The American Indian Vietnam Veterans Project surveyed a sample of Vietnam veterans residing on or near two large tribal reservations, one in the Southwest and the other in the Northern Plains. These populations had sufficient numbers of Vietnam military veterans to draw scientifically and culturally sound conclusions about the war and readjustment experiences.[63]

The Hawaii Vietnam Veterans Project surveyed two samples, one of Native Hawaiians (the indigenous peoples of the Hawaiian Islands, who constituted about 22 percent of the permanent population in Hawaii) and another of Americans of Japanese Ancestry (the descendants of Japanese immigrants who made up about 24 percent of the permanent population in Hawaii).[64] Native Hawaiians and American Indians were more likely than any other survey group to receive combat service medals in recognition of their hazardous combat duty. The Matsunaga Study's[65] key finding is that exposure to war zone stress and other military danger places veterans at risk for PTSD up to several decades after military service. Native Hawaiian and American Indian Vietnam in-country veterans had relatively higher levels of exposure to war zone stress and high levels of PTSD.[66]

The Persian Gulf War was depicted in the press as an example of strategic military success with "smart" directed weapons and few casualties. But the weapons were less smart than described and the human consequences were tragic. America's newest veterans are filing for disability benefits at a historic rate, claiming to be the most medically and mentally troubled generation of former troops the nation has ever seen. A staggering 45 percent of the 1.6 million veterans from the wars in Iraq and Afghanistan are now seeking compensation for injuries they say are service-related. That is more than double the estimate of 21 percent who filed such claims after the Gulf War in the early 1990s:

> These new veterans are claiming eight to nine ailments on average, and the most recent ones over the last year are claiming 11 to 14. By comparison, Vietnam veterans are currently receiving compensation for fewer than four, on average, and those from World War II and Korea, just two.[67]

An unusual set of symptoms led the Centers for Disease Control to create a classification for "Gulf War illness." It consisted of three distinct symptom types: fatigue; mood and cognition problems (for example, feeling depressed, moody or anxious, having difficulty remembering or concentrating, having trouble finding words, having difficulty sleeping); and musculoskeletal problems (for example, joint pain or stiffness and muscle pain).[68] According to one congressionally mandated study, 175,000 to 210,000 Persian Gulf War veterans have developed a pattern of symptoms called Gulf War syndrome.[69] Many veterans feared that the military's use of biological agents was the cause of these symptoms. Some research has begun to identify chemical agents and other substances as possible explanations for the physical and psychological symptoms of Gulf War syndrome.[70]

Since then, one comprehensive study examined the mental health impact of the wars in Afghanistan and Iraq.[71] Soldiers reported their experiences in the war zones and their symptoms of psychological distress. The results indicated that the estimated risk for Post-Traumatic Stress Disorder from service in the Iraq war was 18 percent, and the estimated risk for PTSD from the Afghanistan mission was 11 percent.

Soldiers in Iraq were at risk of being killed or wounded, were likely to have witnessed the suffering of others, and may have participated in killing or wounding others as part of combat operations. All of these activities have a demonstrated association with the development of PTSD:

> 94% of soldiers in Iraq reported being targets of small-arms fire. In addition, 86% of soldiers in Iraq reported knowing someone who was seriously injured or killed, 68% reported seeing dead or seriously injured Americans, and 51% reported handling or uncovering human remains. The majority, 77%, of soldiers deployed to Iraq reported shooting or directing fire at the enemy, 48% reported being responsible for the death of an enemy combatant, and 28% reported being responsible for the death of a non-combatant.[72]

An additional set of unique stressors stem from the fact that much of the conflict in Iraq, particularly since the announced end of formal combat operations, involved guerilla warfare and terrorist actions from ambiguous and unknown civilian threats. In this context, there was no safe place and no safe role. Soldiers were obliged to maintain an intense degree of vigilance and to respond immediately to threats. There was genuine concern that soldiers could have mistakenly regarded civilians who meant them no harm as enemy combatants. Soldiers need to be careful about possibly causing collateral damage to civilians in urban environments. U.S. soldiers were clearly at grave risk in Iraq, and continue to suffer even after they have come home. Troops return to the United States suffering from Post-Traumatic Stress Disorder and have been turning up in homeless shelters in cities through the country. Military medical officials place a premium on teams of mental health experts to help deal with the effects of engaging in battle. Lt. Gen. Kevin Kiley claims that in the modern age, such mental health experts are "worth their weight in gold." Clinical scientists have now developed methods for documenting the psychological effects of engaging in battle. In the case of the war in Iraq, the army's surgeon general reports that 30 percent of troops had developed mental health problems three to four months after returning home.[73] Coleman's sensitive study followed the lives of widows, like herself, of returned veterans who had received inadequate treatment for their emotional scars and had committed suicide.[74] The long-term results for these veterans, their families, and their communities continue to be felt even across generations. Coleman also provides evidence of the government's failure to provide proper treatment resources to those so afflicted.[75] One review of Coleman's book (by an Israeli author) suggests the universality of the larger issue, that is, that governments, including her own, take little heed of the long-term psychological costs of war.

Participation in combat activities is not the exclusive source of danger and stress in a war zone. There is some evidence that the stress of war is associated with an increase in sexual assault and sexual harassment, with both male and female soldiers at risk for this type of victimization:

Women in the military are raped and sexually assaulted at significantly higher rates than in civilian society. A 2003 study of women seeking health care through the VA from the period of the Vietnam War through the first Gulf War found that nearly 1 in 3 women was raped while serving—almost twice the rate of rape in U.S. society—and that 8 in 10 women had been sexually harassed during their military service. Rates were consistent through all periods and wars studied. Of those who reported having been raped, 37 percent were raped at least twice and 14 percent were gang-raped.[76]

In addition, a variety of environmental factors specific to each mission may contribute to the risk of mental health problems in veterans. For example, factors like poor diet, severe weather, and deficient accommodations will affect soldiers' responses to war zone deployments. Extensive time away from family members and the disruption of occupational goals may serve as severe stressors, particularly for National Guard and reserve troops. In contrast, some soldiers may find meaning and gratification in their helper roles in Iraq and Afghanistan, which can potentially buffer the impact of some war zone stressor.

The Effects of War on Children

Soldiers might arguably be said to have agreed to take part in war. This cannot be said of children, who are the largely forgotten but deeply affected victims of armed conflict. The noise, the unpredictable outbursts of weapons, the loss of parents and siblings, and the destruction of familiar settings appear in the stories and the dreams of children who have been in war zones. A 1993 study of Croatian children following the war in Kosovo found that symptoms of depression were high among the children during the war and equally high among those living in refugee circumstances. Refugee children reported more sadness and fear than local children who had not moved from their homes. A subsequent study in 1998 examined forty-five adolescents (ages between 14 and 19 years) who were displaced in the Republic of Croatia as a result of the war. Their most frequently reported stressful events were the loss of their home (80 percent), the loss of personal belongings (66.7 percent), separation from family members (66.7 percent), damage to their property (48.9 percent), exposure to enemy attacks (46.7 percent), and death of a family member or friend (37.8 percent). The exposure to a greater number of stressful events was related to increased depression. More post-traumatic stress reactions were observed in females, in adolescents who were exiled for longer periods of time, and in the children whose parents were more anxious. Youngsters experiencing a higher number of stress reactions had poorer expectations for their future.[77]

In Angola, civil war raged for twenty years. It followed a history of colonial oppression and was fanned by rivalries between superpowers and the international traffic in small arms. In some regions, 88 percent of the population was displaced from their homes. An estimated 4.8 million children were affected, 1.5 million were displaced from their homes and more than half had lost one or both parents. Famine, disease, and massive social disorganization contributed in this case to high rates of PTSD. A study of survivors confirmed that their symptoms were even more severe than those of children from other war zones, reflecting the effects of sustained and repeated trauma.[78] It is important to note that PTSD is a category designed by, and for use of, mental health professionals in a Western culture. What it describes does not apply equally to all cases. Particularly, a lack of attention to cultural factors in how people think, feel, and respond to trauma merits a caution. The cross-cultural use of PTSD in diagnosis and treatment may be severely limited without attention to the specific cultural and historic experiences.[79]

The Use of Child Soldiers

A blurred line between soldiers and civilians has extremely dangerous consequences for children who are also made to fight:

> Of the estimated 250,000 child soldiers in the world today, 40% are girls. Rebel groups often use child soldiers to fight the government, but governments also use child soldiers in armed conflict. Not all children take part in active combat. Some are also used as porters, cooks and spies. Many of the girls are used as "wives" (i.e., sex slaves) of the male combatants. As part of their recruitment, children are sometimes forced to kill or maim a family member—thus breaking the bonds with their community and making it difficult for them to return home.[80]

The use of children as soldiers often reflects an explicit decision by those who recruit them. They are targeted because they are cheap and convenient.[81] They differ from adults who elect to join in a war. Even in the most voluntary of circumstances, can a young child really be considered a soldier? Does the decision of a ten-year-old represent the high moral ground that we so often attribute to military service? Many of these children have been born into and spend the bulk of their lives immersed in war zones, and may have become habituated to violence as a way of life. In these environments of extreme fear and powerlessness, the money, protection, food, medical care, and education afforded by military recruiters is irresistible. Subject to the deepest forms of oppression, children and young teens may also respond particularly favorably to the rhetoric of military groups attempting to overthrow unjust parties.[82]

The behavior of child soldiers is easily molded by the complete control of rewards and punishments. Where there are no alternative sources for understanding human relationships, violent behavior becomes easily hardened into the ideology of the military culture.[83]

Civilian Casualties: Collateral and Targeted

Specific targeting of civilians is outlawed but it occurs nonetheless, and in fact has increased over the course of the twentieth century. Civilians are not asked whether they want to participate in a violent conflict that might kill them. The ratio of civilian to service casualties climbed steadily over the course of the twentieth century, now reaching a startling ratio of nine to one.[84] In wars fought between the armed forces of competing nations, civilian casualties are looked upon as unintended *collateral* damage.[85] Collateral damage is typically explained as an accident rather than a war crime. It likely constitutes the majority of civilian deaths in international wars worldwide. The total number of collateral damage deaths is two times higher than at the turn of the last century. The ratio of collateral damage victims to war crimes victims has increased sharply since the end of the Cold War. Between 1823 and 1900, unintentional deaths constituted 17 percent of all deaths in war, eighty-four civilians per year on average. Since 1990, that number has risen to 59 percent, 1,688 per year, representing a twenty-fold increase.[86]

Satellite-guided air-to-surface munitions were created as smart bombs to select military targets and minimize civilian damage. Of the 29,199 bombs dropped during the Iraq war by the United States and United Kingdom, nearly two-thirds (19,040) were precision-guided munitions (PGMs). In the Persian Gulf conflict in 1991, 8 percent of all bombs dropped were PGMs; in Yugoslavia in 1999 approximately one-third were PGMs; in Afghanistan in 2002 approximately 65 percent were PGMs.[87] The intent was to target opposing leaders—Milosovich, bin Laden, and Saddam Hussein—without excessive harm to civilians. A report by Human Rights Watch reveals just how persistently they were used to try to kill individual Iraqi leaders—and how consistently they failed. The use of drone warfare (to be described in chapter 6) adds significantly to the toll of civilian casualties.

Over the course of the Iraq war, U.S. air forces mounted fifty so-called decapitation strikes.[88] The bombs accidentally killed dozens of civilians who happened to be near the explosions, but they killed *none* of the Iraqi leaders they were intended to strike, largely because of faulty intelligence.[89] Although both war and genocide usually result in the deaths of numerous innocent civilians, genocide is always considered a crime while war is often considered just.[90]

Displacement

Violent conflict forces people to leave their homes and countries. Family members are lost and means of subsistence are destroyed. As of 2011, the number of forcibly displaced people worldwide exceeded 42 million, a result of persistent and new conflicts in different parts of the world. By the end of 2011, the figure stood at 42.5 million. Of these, 15.2 million were refugees: 10.4 million under UNHCR's mandate and 4.8 million Palestinian refugees registered with UNRWA. The overall figure also included 895,000 asylum-seekers and 26.4 million internally displaced persons (IDPs).[91] Today, 25 million would-be refugees from conflict are found within their home countries. A new strategy of containment has emerged preventing many refugees from finding asylum in developed countries. The number of internally displaced people (IDPs) is estimated at 25 million displaced from fifty different countries affected by conflict. More than three million people were newly displaced in 2002 and were forced to leave their homes because of human rights violations or threats to their lives. In 2003, 12,800 unaccompanied and separated children applied for asylum in twenty-eight industrialized countries. The largest numbers came from war-ravaged areas in Angola and Afghanistan, both countries with a history of civil war with weapons supplied by the United States and the former USSR.[92]

Landmines

For all those killed by war there are many more who are seriously damaged by it. Antipersonnel landmines are a particularly insidious source of death and disability that continue long after actual combat has ended. After hostilities end soldiers are typically demobilized and turn in the weapons that have been issued to them, but landmines do not recognize a cease-fire. A landmine cannot be aimed. It lies dormant and concealed until a person or an animal triggers its detonating mechanism. Then landmines kill or injure civilians, soldiers, peacekeepers, and aid workers alike. Children are particularly susceptible. Mine deaths and injuries over the past decades total in the hundreds of thousands. An estimated 15,000 to 20,000 casualties are caused by landmines and unexploded ordnance each year. Some 1,500 new casualties are reported each month, at the rate of more than forty new casualties a day. The numbers are an underestimate since some countries with a landmine problem such as Myanmar (Burma), India, or Pakistan fail to provide public information about the extent of the problem.[93]

More than eighty countries are affected by landmines and/or unexploded ordnance. Some of the most contaminated places are Afghanistan, Angola, Burundi, Bosnia and Herzegovina, Cambodia, Chechnya, Colombia, Iraq, Nepal, and Sri Lanka. Most of the casualties are civilians and most live in countries that are now at peace. In Cambodia, for example, there were 57,000 civilian casualties—18,000 killed and almost 40,000 landmine survivors—recorded between 1979 and 2002.[94] The Land Mine Monitor website identified 3,956 casualties occurring in 2009 that were caused by mines, victim-activated improvised explosive devices (IEDs), cluster munitions remnants, and other explosive remnants of war (ERW) in sixty-four states and areas. At least 1,041 people were killed and 2,855 were injured. As in 2008, Afghanistan had the greatest number of casualties (859), followed by Colombia (674). The report found decreasing casualty figures, likely due in part to successful clearance and awareness-raising. Still, many thousands of people face the risk of injury from mines, ERW, and increasingly IEDs in the course of their daily activities. In 2009, civilians made up 70 percent of all casualties for which the civilian/military status was known (2,485 of 3,531).[95]

Once triggered a landmine blast causes injuries like blindness, burns, destroyed limbs, and shrapnel wounds. Sometimes the victim dies from loss of blood or because he or she does not get medical care in time. Survivors often require amputations, long hospital stays, and extensive rehabilitation. Landmine injuries are not accidents, since the devices are designed to maim rather than kill their victims. Survivors need care but Landmine Monitor has identified at least forty-eight mine-affected countries where one or more aspects of assistance are reportedly inadequate to meet the needs of mine survivors.[96]

Landmines deprive people in some of the poorest countries of land and destroy infrastructure. They hamper reconstruction and the delivery of aid and delay the repatriation of displaced people. The casualties deprive communities and families of breadwinners, and assistance to landmine survivors places an enormous strain on resources. Mines kill livestock and wild animals and wreak environmental havoc. They remove land from food production since the mere suspicion of their presence turns a patch of land into a human danger zone.[97]

Through unprecedented efforts by nongovernmental agencies and governments, and for which Jodie Williams obtained a Nobel Prize, the Mine Ban

Treaty was negotiated in September 1997 and entered into force in March 1999. It has established an international standard rejecting antipersonnel mines. Eighty percent of the world's nations are party to the treaty, but not China, Russia, or the United States. The most significant achievement of the treaty may be the degree to which any use of antipersonnel mines by anyone has been stigmatized. This has had a strong impact even on those that have not yet signed.[98] The situation, though improved in recent years, nevertheless constitutes a global crisis. Antipersonnel landmines are still being planted today, and minefields dating back decades continue to claim innocent victims. Vast stockpiles of landmines remain in warehouses around the world, and a handful of countries still produce the weapons.[99]

Terrorism: The Calculated Use of Violence

Terrorism has been defined as "the (calculated) use of violence for political goals."[100] It is a form of violence (or warfare) directed primarily against civilians, rather than the uniformed military, police forces, or economic assets. It is used both by governments, against their own people or other countries, and insurgents.[101] The suicide bombing of the World Trade Center on September 11, 2001, presented the first occurrence of a tragedy of this magnitude that was perpetrated by a small group of individuals. The event highlighted the concept of terrorism in the popular culture. Surely the bombs that exploded over Hiroshima and Nagasaki claimed many more civilian lives. But until September 11, one might have taken all the individual mass murderers and all of the serial killers the world has known and found their victims to number in the hundreds. Even with that event, the more dramatic numbers of victims of terror are killed by sources other than deranged or obsessed individuals or criminal bands. The real mass murderers, by contrast, produce victims by the thousands and tens of thousands, many times dwarfing in number the tragic losses from the attack on the World Trade Center. Bombing buildings, assassinating leaders, destroying access to food or water, or shooting people in warfare are not easily distinguished from the same acts used more sporadically by non-governmental groups. The big-time murderers and terrorists are on the loose. They are called governments.

State-Sanctioned Terror

Terrorism gained attention when the Jacobins' rule, following the French Revolution, introduced a reign of terror. In 1773, Robespierre noted that "terror is nothing but justice—prompt, severe, and inflexible."[102] In the months that followed, the severe and inflexible guillotine severed the heads of 1,200 people, including Robespierre's. Since then, the power of states to inflict a domestic reign of death and terror has been expanded. The Soviet Union under Stalin, Germany under Hitler, and the United States under many administrations in the slaying of Native Americans are among the most destructive examples. Large numbers of civilian deaths took place, in peacetime, during the period in which Mao Zedong led China, especially during the Great Leap Forward program of the late 1950s. The number of deaths is in dispute as are the reasons for them. Some scholars have put the number in the tens of millions, and charge that these were the results of conscious government policies. Others, however, have disputed this, arguing that though deaths can be attributed to what the government did, there were other reasons as well, including weather disasters that affected the supply of food.[103] The form that took clear shape in the second half of the twentieth century was described in the Terrorism and Human Rights progress report prepared by Ms. Kalliopi K. Koufa, Special Rapporteur of the United Nations, June 27, 2001:

> State terrorism in the form of "regime" or "government terror" is characterized by such actions as the kidnapping and assassination of political opponents of the government by the police or the secret service or security forces or the army; systems of imprisonment without trial; persecution and concentration camps; and, generally speaking, government by fear. . . . This type of bureaucratized terror intimidates, injures and abuses whole groups, sometimes whole nations, and it is the type of terrorism that historically and today produces the most harm. . . . A further point that deserves particular mention is the role of the law in the reification and legitimacy of "regime" or "government terror." In fact, "regime" or "government terror" is exercised according to the law that the public authorities have themselves created.[104]

The term *desaparecido* became part of the human rights vocabulary in 1966 in Guatemala to describe people who vanished after being taken into custody by government officials, or with the acquiescence of government officials, and for whom the authorities claimed no knowledge of their whereabouts. A second type of terrorist activity is the extrajudicial execution. These are unlawful killings performed at the behest of a government without an individual being found guilty of any crime. Such political killings are frequently performed by the government either directly or indirectly through paramilitary groups. The use of contract killers guarantees impunity for the instigator. The barbarity of practices reveals the underlying goal of intimidation of dissent. Trade unionists, human rights activists, community leaders, lawyers, and teachers are frequent targets. But often targets are bystanders, street children whose hunger and homelessness is bothersome, or people just being in the wrong place.[105] Over the past half-century, there have been numerous instances of state terrorism. Here we have selected examples from Guatemala, Colombia, and Cambodia. Together they illustrate the modern face of war.

Case Studies of State Terror: Guatemala

Following decades of colonial rule, the first free election in Guatemala produced a leftist reformer as president. This was followed by a CIA-assisted coup returning the country to military rule in 1954. After the invasion, the government systematically destroyed the country's former communist and social democratic leadership. Peasants, labor activists, and intellectuals by the hundreds were subjected to detention, torture, and sometimes death. Many were forced into exile or to withdrawal from political activity. Any sign of opposition was vilified and labeled "communist." The Guatemalan case was one of the best documented, through the collaboration of the International Center for Human Rights Investigations and the American Association for the Advancement of Science.[106]

The CIA assisted successive military leaders, Armas (1954), Fuentes (1958), and Peralta (1963) to gain power. Elections were promised again in 1966. Twenty-eight members of the labor party (PGT), lured out of hiding by hopes of a fair election, disappeared and their bodies were never found. When Mendez Montenegro, a university law professor, was elected president, he was forced to sign a decree granting the military the right to fight against its opponents without interference from civilian authorities. U.S. military advisors supervised the bombing of villages, and government forces were responsible for the killing or disappearance of many civilians. Estimates of civilian deaths between 1966 and 1968 varied from 2,800[107] to 8,000.[108] Under U.S. guidance, the army organized a powerful military force and a network of counterinsurgency surveillance that would continue for more than thirty years. It would be used both to battle guerrillas and to control, in brutal fashion, the civilian population. Paramilitary death squads carried out much of the activity. Some were security forces dressed in civilian clothes. Others were private thugs of the extreme right. The secret nature of these groups created terror, but also gave the police and the army an opportunity to deny responsibility.[109]

In 1970, the army candidate, Col. Carlos Arana, became president. He created a counterinsurgency plan to exterminate the guerrillas and their supporters and a state of siege was declared. Legal protests against a corrupt government contract with a Canadian nickel mining concern were met with mass arrests and with occupation of the University at San Carlos. Death squad attacks against law school professors and other leaders followed. Killings and disappearances exceeded those of the late 1960s. After the leadership of the outlawed labor group PGT were tortured and killed opposition subsided, but not before the formation of the National Front Against Violence. This group of university students, church groups, opposing political parties, and workers called for human rights and constitutional rule.[110] Arana's handpicked successor, Defense Minister Laugerud Garcia, trying to gain public acceptance after a fraudulent election, permitted a degree of labor and popular organizing. State violence declined for a brief time, and a group of K'che and Ixil Indians found the courage to come to Guatemala City in 1980 to protest the kidnapping and murder of nine peasants. They were joined by a student group but were not well received. Their legal advisor was assassinated outside police headquarters, and when they occupied the Spanish Embassy, the police attacked, trapped them inside and watched both protestors and hostages burn to death.[111] Guerrillas began to harass the army and then retreated to the mountains. Typically they had substantial civilian support, since the guerrillas had worked closely with the peasant population, as many had come from those communities. Increasingly, the military viewed unarmed villagers as participants in the insurgency. "Operation Ashes" clearly stated the government's program of mass killings and burning houses, crops, farm animals and the scorching of entire villages.[112] The mass killings included children, women, and the elderly in a strategy that General Rios Montt called "draining the sea that the fish swim in." During almost four years under President Lucas Garcia the government was responsible for more than 8,000 killings and disappearances in what Amnesty International labeled a "government program of political murder."[113] Ethnic factors were central since the majority Maya population were viewed as less than human and suffered casualties in even greater proportion than their number in the population. General Rios Montt took power in a military coup in 1982. The U.S. Congress, which had cut off military aid to Guatemala in 1977, switched to restore aid at President Reagan's request. The aid came with assurances that the general could fight the war as he saw fit, without concern for human rights and without fear of losing the funding. With extensive military support from the United States, the military effort escalated. In remote villages the policy was toward overkill, beheading victims or burning them alive, smashing heads of children on rocks, and commonly raping women, including those who were pregnant.[114]

In the fourteen months of Montt's rule, 10,000 documented killings or disappearances occurred, although press censorship reduced the reporting of these at the time.[115] The proportion of unnamed victims rose dramatically from the previous era. Nonetheless, President Reagan described Rios Montt in December 1982 as "a man of great personal integrity and commitment . . . who is totally dedicated to democracy."[116] The killings, torture, and kidnappings became fewer but more selective under the regimes that followed. The remarkable efforts of peasant women in Guatemala and of students have helped to bring some attention and efforts at accountability to an appalling case of state terrorism. In 2013, Rios Montt was convicted by a Guatemalan court for the mass killings. The ruling was contested but reaffirmed in January 2015. Its importance lies in setting a precedent to hold heads of state accountable for crimes committed while they were in office.

Case Studies of State Terror: Colombia

The term "democra-tatorship" is used to describe the current Colombian amalgamation of democratic forms and state terror. In a continent severely marred by human rights abuses, Colombia has compiled the worst record of the past twenty years.[117] Assistance in training and arming the Colombian military has come from Britain, Israel, and Germany, but particularly the United States. Father Javier Giraldo, director of the Commission of Justice and Peace, published a report documenting atrocities during the first part of 1988. These included 3,000 politically motivated killings, 273 of which occurred in "social cleansing campaigns." In Colombia's cities, "social cleanup operation" is the official term for a night in which police or their collaborators murder drug addicts, homosexuals, prostitutes, vagrants, street children, and the mentally ill. In the larger cities—Medellin, Cali, Barranquilla and Bogotá—the assailants often gun down victims from motorbikes or trucks. Other times groups are rounded up and forced into trucks, their often-mutilated bodies later found in rubbish containers or on the roadside. Accurate figures on such killings are difficult to determine. Many of the victims are unknown, and most deaths go unregistered and unreported. One human rights group recorded 298 murders by death squads in the eight months of their 1992 study.[118] Despite the fact that Colombian police use their arms to inflict terror, American aid has continued to support the Colombian government. War against the guerrillas and narco-trafficking operations is the official State Department explanation for U.S. involvement. These groups were blamed for all of the violence. In 1989, President George H. W. Bush (Bush I) announced the largest shipment of weapons ever authorized under the Emergency Provisions of the Foreign Assistance Act. From 1988 to 1995, 67,378 Colombians (an average of 23.4 per day) were assassinated. The number of victims of political violence in this Colombian "democracy" far exceeds the combined number of political killings in Uruguay, Argentina, Brazil, Bolivia, and Chile during their years under military dictatorship. The Truth and Reconciliation Commission in Chile registered 2,700 politically motivated murders during the seventeen years of its brutal military dictatorship. This horrible statistic is nonetheless far less than the number of cases reported annually in Colombia for each year between 1986 and 1995.[119] Kidnappings by the revolutionary armed forces of Colombia have continued, as have the massacres by right-wing paramilitary groups such as United Self-defense Forces of Colombia (AUC in Spanish), which continued to conduct massacres of villagers even after agreements to desist.[120]

Case Studies in State Terror: Cambodia

One of the worst cases of domestic military brutality came under a government opposed by the United States. After the massive U.S. bombing of Cambodia and U.S. assistance in the overthrow of the popular Prince Sihanouk, the United States supported the unpopular rule of Lon Nol. The Khmer Rouge overthrew Lon Nol and sought to eradicate the severe destitution by a cruel set of reforms. In a plan similar to one that had been used by the United States in Vietnam, suspect village leaders were deposed and replaced by Khmer loyalists. Angkar, or "organization on high," provided a justification to commandeer vehicles, to order people out of hospitals, and to kill. Purges and massacres were commonplace. At their center was the Tuol Sleng School in Phnom Penh, which was converted for purposes of interrogation, torture, and execution. Records found when the Khmer Rouge fled showed that many of its victims included Khmer supporters.[121] Of 14,499 people held there, only four survived. Norkobal, the secret police system, replicated the death machine in the provinces with a far greater number of executions. Sixty-six thousand bodies were found in three provinces in 1981. In 1982, 16,000 bodies were found in the Kampot province in 386 mass graves. But uncounted numbers were buried in the 1,400 mass graves in the provinces.[122]

Only a few illustrations of state terrorism are presented here. Others, including the prolonged occurrence in East Timor, will be referred to in later chapters. But the inhumanity of this form of military activity is clear. The numbers are hard to comprehend. Each victim was robbed of the right to life in a social system that orchestrated their destruction. The death and the destruction in war destroy for non-combatants and for soldiers the only lives that each of them will ever know.

Material and Human Costs of Preparedness

Preparedness for war has been costly. The United States spent $10.5 trillion on the military during the Cold War.[123] The nuclear powers of that time spent a combined estimated $8 trillion on their nuclear weapons.[124] If current annual U.S. expenditures for nuclear weapons were instead invested into global lifesaving measures the result could have covered *all* of the following: the elimination of starvation and malnutrition, basic shelter for every family, universal health care, the control of AIDS, relief for displaced refugees, and the removal of landmines.[125] Money that was spent to harden missile sites or to develop missiles that might someday shoot other missiles from the skies might have been spent to strengthen the levees along the Mississippi River, already known to be inadequate long before the Katrina hurricane.[126] Meanwhile, the wars in Iraq and Afghanistan have meant that precious resources were and are being channeled toward destruction instead of into programs that could save people's lives and meet their basic human needs. When Hurricane Katrina struck, 6,000 members of the Louisiana and Mississippi National Guard were watching the catastrophe unfold from 7,000 miles away. Forty percent of Mississippi's National Guard force, and 35 percent of Louisiana's, were in Iraq at the time.[127] If the National Guard troops and their equipment from Mississippi and Louisiana hadn't been in Iraq, they could have responded more quickly to the devastation wreaked by Hurricane Katrina and lives could have been saved. The United States was pouring more than a billion dollars a week into the Iraq war that could otherwise have been spent on healthcare, schools, and infrastructure at home.

As with actual military violence, the costs of preparing for war are not just monetary. The development of nuclear weapons, apart from their use, has been a source of violence deeply affecting public health. The costs have often been concealed or minimized by public officials. On July 12, 1990, newspapers carried an announcement by Secretary of Energy James Watkins confirming, one day in advance of official release, a report of an occurrence of dangerous exposure to radiation. The report noted that Richland, Washington, the area of the Hanford Nuclear Research Facility, had indeed been the site of a release of radioactive iodine serious enough to affect the health of people. Secretary Watkins noted that we may have placed a number of persons under health risks. An accurate estimate of how great the health consequences, and to how many, still awaits the findings of a study by the National Centers for Disease Control. Secretary Watkins's announcement, however, was careful to note that the particular radioactive emissions occurred during a period when hazards of radiation were poorly understood. "As years went along, we got a little smarter. I don't want you to relate it to what's going on today."[128] And surely he did not wish us to do so. What the secretary wished to assure us was that the occurrence of subjecting our own citizens to a serious risk was a singular unforeseeable incident from which current scientific knowledge and the advanced technologies of today now offer protection.

This proposition is cast into serious doubt by a long history of developing dangerous technologies with little regard for their consequences. Reviews of technological development suggest precisely the alternative to Secretary Watkins's thesis, that is, that the health consequences are not isolated instances of accidents caused by an early but now corrected ignorance. Rather, these human tragedies are the sometimes intended, frequently rationalized, denied or ignored, and sometimes unintended consequences of the technological society. These consequences, rather than affecting isolated victims are ubiquitous, and the technological hazards contribute to our collective health problems at an accelerating and alarming rate.[129] The report, released the day following Secretary Watkins's announcement, indicated that 13,700 residents, or 5 percent of a ten-county population surrounding the Hanford Nuclear Reservation in eastern Washington State, had absorbed a dosage of radioactive iodine 1,200 times the level of airborne contamination that the Department of Energy (DOE) now considers safe for civilians living around its nuclear weapons plants.

The amount of radioactive absorption far exceeded the amount absorbed by Ukrainian citizens at Chernobyl and was 26,000 times the absorption at Three Mile Island. Hundreds of thousands of residents in Washington, Oregon, and Idaho were, according to the report, continually and secretly exposed for a quarter of a century to large quantities of radiation from the air, from drinking water, and from food. Some 400,000 curies of radioactive iodine were released as a by-product when irradiated uranium fuel rods were dissolved in acid to extract plutonium, the key component of nuclear weapons. The nine reactors at the 560–square mile Hanford reserve were cooled by river water, which was then returned to the environment to contaminate major fish hatching areas and drinking water while airborne radiation descended upon farmlands, exposing cattle and returning radioactivity through their milk to children in the surrounding areas.[130] The report is as frightening in its implications about the government as in its conclusions about the victims.

A half-century after the Hanford facilities' work on plutonium for the nuclear weapons program had ended, the site remains on the EPA Superfund list as among the most serious toxic sites in need for cleanup. Bechtel Corporation has the contract to turn millions of gallons of radioactive waste into glasslike logs to be stored in 177 underground tanks. The project was shut down in the summer of 2005 because of seismic problems, rising costs, and delays. After it was resumed in September, 600 workers had to be sent home following the third safety problem in a week.[131]

Increases in radiation exposure beyond natural background levels have serious consequences for health. The research of Dr. John Goffman and others indicates that there is no safe dose of radiation.[132] Increases in rates of cancer and birth defects have occurred around each of the eighteen nuclear weapons facilities in the United States and around the sites in Nevada and the Marshall Islands where nuclear weapons have been tested. Radiation is but one example of the health hazards that derive from the testing and use of lethal substances. Toxic chemicals released into the environment have similar effects. Between 1973 and 1998 cancer in the U.S. increased by 22.4 percent. This occurred during a time of added public awareness of the value of diet, exercise, and skin protection. In the United States more than 80,000 chemicals are produced or imported, some in the agricultural, automotive and computer industries and some in military preparedness. Toxic chemicals, many known carcinogens and many not yet studied for their toxic effects, have found their way into our food, water, and atmosphere and then into our bodies. Increasing evidence shows that even small doses can have significant effects, sometimes causing increases in rates of sterility, stillbirths, genetic deformity, respiratory problems, and several types of cancer, particularly among children.[133] Other studies show that the risk increases directly as a result of the amount of exposure to radiation.[134]

Years after Hanford was preparing plutonium triggers for nuclear weapons, it became a cleanup project. Hanford is the most contaminated worksite in the Western world, and the Department of Energy has not performed its safety mission well. Twenty years after a major cleanup project began in 1989, the results have been far less effective and far more costly than the originally planned $30 billion.[135]

People who worked on this cleanup effort have been suffering serious health consequences and filing complaints that they had been misled. A report by the Government Accountability Project documents the Department of Energy's pattern of interference with Hanford workers' claims, its inability to effectively oversee Contract Claims Services Incorporated, and its ongoing failure to resolve concerns that workers have raised since 2000 when the compensation program became self-insured and DOE became responsible for reviewing workers' claims. Yet, when workers seek medical care and compensation for their workplace illnesses and injuries, DOE often challenges and obstructs their claims and fails to provide them access to objective assessment and medical treatment. One worker testified at the Department of Energy's June 2005 State of the Site meeting: "I've seen people sick and lied to. You say public safety? Do you think the public trusts in you guys? Your workers don't even trust you."[136] The casualties of war preparedness come even when weapons are not used and the casualties of work with dangerous weapons, like the casualties of war, get little attention.

The twentieth century was the bloodiest in all of human history. The astonishing scale and intensity of violence occurred at the same time that advances in science, technology and economics were making people, on average, better off than ever before—eating better and living longer. The world in 1900 offered a prospect of greater human opportunities. The major reason for the scourge of violence was likely economic boom and bust volatility, which tore apart communities and promoted racial and class conflicts. Technology made larger-scale violence possible. The century also was a stage for a struggle between decaying empires and aggressive new states. Some talk of the result as a triumph of the American century. But a stronger case can be made that the outcome is the decline of Western dominance.[137] Yet in the new century the United States remains a key player in global violence.

United States' Responsibility

The United States is both the largest beneficiary of global inequality and the world's premier specialist in weapons. Networks of key corporate and government officials perpetuate both the gross income disparities and dominance in weapons. U.S. policy has often been guided by an assumption that interests defined by the United States take precedence over international agreements. This has occurred first in matters that might constrain U.S. military activities.

For example, in August 2001, the United States withdrew from a major arms control accord, the 1972 Antiballistic Missile Treaty. In July 2001 U.S. representatives walked out of a conference to discuss adding on-site inspectors to strengthen the 1972 Biological and Toxic Weapons Convention, which was ratified by 144 nations including the United States.[138] Meanwhile, U.S. preparations to use chemical and biological weapons at Fort Dietrich and other sites have been extensive.[139] The United States was the only nation to oppose the UN Agreement to Curb the International Flow of Illicit Small Arms. The Landmine Treaty (banning mines) was signed in 1997 by 122 nations but the United States refused to sign, along with Russia, China, India, Pakistan, Iran, Iraq, Vietnam, Egypt, and Turkey. Clinton's promise that the United States would "eventually" comply in 2006 was disavowed by President George W. Bush. In February 2001 the United States refused to join 123 nations pledged to ban the use and production of anti-personnel bombs.[140]

U.S. policy also dismisses legal accountability for its international actions. The International Criminal Court Treaty was created in 2002 to try political and military leaders charged with war crimes against humanity. The ICC Treaty was approved by 120 countries with only seven, including the United States, opposed. In December 2001 the U.S. Senate amended a military appropriations bill to exclude U.S. military personnel from the jurisdiction of the ICC. The UN General Assembly passed resolutions calling for an end to the U.S. embargo on Cuba for ten years, the last by a vote of 167 to 3 (the United States, Israel, and the Marshall Islands in opposition).[141]

The powerful position of the United States has permitted its stand as the protector of corporate prerogatives in the face of economic or environmental threats and even concerns for human rights. In 2001, the United States refused to participate in the Organization for Economic Co-operation and Development talks on ways to remove offshore tax and money-laundering havens. The United States alone opposed the G8 group of industrial nations in a clean energy plan. Where human rights might have some consequence for military or corporate dominance, the U.S. record again stood out. In the UN Human Rights Commission, the United States stood virtually alone in opposing resolutions supporting low-cost access to HIV/AIDS drugs, acknowledging a basic human right to adequate food, and calling for a moratorium on the death penalty. The United States was not reelected to the Commission in 2001.[142]

The most cited estimate on the number of small arms currently in use and in stockpiles around the world comes from the "Small Arms Survey" research project. It places the number at almost 640 million.[143] There are over 639 million small arms and light weapons in the world today, approximately one gun for every ten people on the planet. They are used both in war and to perpetrate acts of murder, rape, and torture. These weapons often act as catalysts for cycles of conflict and poverty in many of the world's most impoverished areas. Strict control measures are needed, but weapons dealers have found an almost unlimited market. The UN General Assembly in 2006 approved a resolution for a global Arms Trade Treaty by a vote of 153–1 with 24 abstentions. The United States cast the only opposing vote.

Weapons sales by the United States tripled in 2011 to a record high, driven by major arms sales to Persian Gulf allies concerned about Iran's regional ambitions according to a new study for Congress. Overseas weapons sales by the United States totaled $66.3 billion or nearly 78 percent of the global arms market valued at $85.3 billion in 2011. Russia was a distant second, with $4.8 billion in deals. The American weapons sales total was an "extraordinary increase" over the $21.4 billion in deals for 2010, the study found, and was the largest single-year sales total in the history of U.S. arms exports. The previous high was in fiscal year 2009, when American weapons sales overseas totaled nearly $31 billion.[144] International Narcotics Control programs provide another channel for the United States to fund military equipment and training to overseas police and armies. Serious human rights abuses by units receiving this aid have intensified criticism of the program, requiring Congress to pass restrictions.[145] Any theory of contemporary global economic and military violence should address all of the issues raised by such data.

Wars are not accidents. They are products of a social order that plans for them and then accepts this planning as natural. The system that sustains war and other forms of global violence is the system that will have to change if we are to stop the massive killing involved both in war and in economic exploitation. A social order that humans have created must now be transformed if the world that sustains life and enriches our human experience is to survive. The study of violent conflict confronts us repeatedly with frightening facts. We gain power by considering our painful awareness as an important step in a process of change. If we choose to ignore these facts, the facts will return to haunt us.

2—Killing: War and the Minds of Men

The need today is for a gentler humankind, for the hand that wielded the axe against the ice and the saber-toothed tiger now cradles the machine gun equally as lovingly.

—KONRAD LORENZ

And when the drums of war have reached a fever pitch and the blood boils with hate and the mind has closed, the leader will have no need in seizing the rights of the citizenry. Rather, the citizenry, infused with fear and blinded by patriotism, will offer up all of their rights unto the leader and gladly so. How do I know? For this is what I have done. And I am Caesar.

—ANONYMOUS

CHAPTER 1 LOOKED AT THE DEVASTATING consequences of war. Unlike costs of natural disasters, these costs result from decisions by humans that inflict suffering and death upon others. Among all forms of destructiveness, war is unique in the manner in which it is justified. A declaration of war gives a state the recognized right to order people to conquer, to destroy, and to kill. Considering the consequences, why do we do it?

The gains from war are questionable. Historian Barbara Tuchman's *The March of Folly: From Troy to Vietnam* details a history of the human propensity to engage in violent wars.[1] This history of bloodshed includes numerous cases in which the potential gain for any of the participants was small compared with the costs. In large measure, the reason wars are fought is to be found in the institutions that humans have created. A detailed review of U.S. wars since the Second World War shows that most have produced unintended consequences detrimental to the United States.[2] The consequences will be examined in later chapters. For now, we focus upon one contributing factor: the human capacity for inflicting violence.

War and Human Nature

Examples can be found of societies that have been relatively free of violent warfare for long periods of time. These cases are few, and many lie outside of the dominant societies modernized in the Western image. The Fore of New Guinea, for instance, provides an example of a society with no history of warfare and very little expression of physical violence.[3] One study selected seven examples that met five criteria of a peaceful society: no war on its territory, no involvement in external war, no civil or internal war, no standing military, and little or no interpersonal violence. All of the societies were small, and all had some exchanges with outside groups. All also contained some changing memberships. None had a strong pattern of an elite ruling lineage. Although some were able to accumulate surpluses beyond their immediate needs, the surpluses were used for the benefit of the group as a whole.[4]

These exceptions from societies that engage in war may be few, but they are nevertheless important. They show that major violence in societies, although common, is surely not universal. This bears upon a question debated within the field of psychology: Does human nature make war inevitable? Cruel, selfish, and violent activities appear to be as fundamental a part of human nature as creative, caring, and cooperative actions.

Aggressive inclinations may contribute to war but do not mean that wars are inevitable. Still, human aggressiveness is important. This chapter deals with one psychological aspect of what makes war possible—the capacity and the motivation of humans to be aggressive and to kill other humans.

In the natural world, animals devour other animals. But killing other members of one's own species is uncommon, and attempts to destroy an entire rival colony are rare. Competition between different bands of lemurs or chimpanzees does occur, but most of the fighting is bluff, and battles never have the ferocity or carnage of human warfare.[5] People, it appears, are distinguished as a species by their capacity to kill large numbers of their own kind as well as by their symbolic representations of reality. These two characteristics may be related. The symbols define for us a reality in which killing others is sometimes seen as necessary. Symbols are not simply word representations of objects, what Suzanne Langer has called *discursive* symbols. They include also *presentational* symbols, or larger sequences of meaning only understandable within a broader framework. The more complex of these presentational symbols include songs, stories, musical compositions, healing ceremonies, and religious rituals. The most comprehensive of these larger *life* symbols are the prevailing myths about who we are as human beings and as members of larger groups. Myths provide a framework for our beliefs and lead to ritual practices that are observed with the force of religion.[6]

The exceptional cognitive capacities demonstrated by humans have come late in the evolutionary process. We often fail to recognize how the systems of beliefs, or presentational symbols that humans have evolved, reflect tribal origins of human societies. We evolved in small bands that were vital to our individual survival. We have only recently in our evolutionary history created formal representations of teams, corporations, social movements, and nations that sometimes replace the identifications and the loyalties to our own clan or tribe that once helped us to survive.

The Human Psyche as a Source of Killing

Humans, more so than other species, construct in memory extensive maps using symbols of whom and what they have experienced. The symbols are arranged, sometimes even distorted, to preserve congruity and a positive image of the self. Such cognitive maps provide a guide to living with safety and satisfaction of needs. From the time of infancy, the stored images are assigned to different categories, the most primitive being the distinction between what is nurturing, comforting, and good and what is stressful, distasteful, or painful.[7] As images of the world grow increasingly complex, there remains a common tendency, more pronounced in some people, to continue to divide all things about them into good or bad. This basic psychological mechanism is helpful in explaining preoccupations with good and evil as well as the need for enemies.[8]

The evolved tendency for us humans to use presentational symbols to categorize ourselves into nations, religions, and other symbolic groups serves both to fortify a positive self-image and to find purpose and meaning in existence. This process, however, leads to a strong identification of the individual with the symbolic group, a connection often stronger than the individual's identification with the species as a whole. Such group attachments lead, in turn, to a sense of separation and a value judgment as to the worth of the group, with some groups clearly assigned to categories of good and others bad. The tendency to identify with one group over another sets the stage for group comparisons and rivalries. Such identities often pit one group against another and are used to justify ultimate purposes in war. These highly evaluative ideations raise the question of whether we can create belief systems in which the deep moral attachments we seek can be to all of humanity, even to all of life.

Central to each person's store of images is a concept of the self. Human selves vary greatly in the qualities we believe that we have. But almost universal is the need to look upon the self as good, worthwhile, and deserving to live. That self can be deeply threatened, but we are prone to reinterpret information that is dissonant. We seek congruity or consistency among our stored images, and we engage in much reinterpretation of experience in order to keep our self-concept surrounded by images of good people and separated from images of bad ones. We have survival mechanisms that allow us to experience overwhelming psychological trauma, to repress such images from awareness, and then to move on.

Although hidden, the buried memories continue to affect the human psyche, exaggerating fears of potential reminders and affecting perceptions of what is dangerous. The buried traumas increase our propensities both to deny danger on the one hand and to picture ourselves as brave and invulnerable on the other.

Killing in Our Minds and Motives

Particularly when our self-concepts are deeply affected by trauma, and we are sitting atop repressed memories of our own violent or disdainful motives and behavior, we become impassioned defenders of our self-concepts and vindictive opponents of those we see as bad. One common way this occurs is through the mechanism of projection. Aspects of our own self, too ugly or reprehensible to be admitted to ourselves, can more easily be seen in the attributes of others. Meanness to scapegoats can be justified as doing away with evil while never admitting evil intentions of our own. For some, the accommodation needed to feel secure about oneself requires domination over other people. Certain conditions—the granting of permission from higher authorities, the routinization of violent practices, and the dehumanization of the targets—frequently permit this violence to occur without moral restraint.[9]

A degree of aggressive motivation appears in many species and among all cultures. Yet all cultures that have endured have fostered strongly internalized restrictions on killing other people. Sanctions against wrongdoers are universal, but most restraint from violent behavior occurs because of the sense that it is not right in one's own eyes or in the eyes of one's group. People undergo disappointments, frustrations, and betrayals. They experience rage, sometimes out of proportion to the degree of inconvenience or the strength of the transgression against them. Aggressive expressions such as cursing, bullying, blaming, and ridiculing are common among humans. But most people do not, on their own, typically inflict upon others the extreme physical violence associated with war.

Inhibitions against harming others do need to be learned, and this typically occurs in the immediate family environment.[10] A major aspect of such learning is the development of empathy, the ability to identify with the feelings of others almost as if they were one's own.[11] So also does the willingness to kill need to be learned. The learning process that encourages violence also occurs in families but continues in other institutions charged with molding human personalities and shaping behavior.

The antithesis to empathy is an internalized hatred of people different from oneself. Frequently found among self-trained militias are groups such as neo-Nazis or skinheads. These are typically men who have received military training, are fascinated with guns, have few options for more constructive work, and believe in a racial purification through violence.

The Contexts of Killing

There are individual differences in the willingness to inflict pain or to kill. Because we have learned that this is wrong, those who readily engage in such behavior often reflect a history that has blunted their capacities for empathy. Individuals who are more prone to violence find inducements to act violently in a culture that accentuates individual achievement and seeks retribution against evildoers. The designation of some people as evildoers who must be found, imprisoned, or killed is a major theme in the way behavior is interpreted. But this interpretation reflects what psychologists have long studied as attribution error, the tendency to ascribe behavior to the enduring characteristics of individuals while ignoring the circumstances that are often the more important factor. The Nazis, who committed brutal and genocidal killings of unprecedented magnitude, are viewed as pathological killers. Yet Hannah Arendt, in her study of Nazi stormtroopers, noted that the most remarkable thing about the Nazis was how like the rest of us they were.[12] Compelling evidence supports the view that the capacity to engage in evil or harmful behavior lies within all of us and that surrounding circumstances play the major role in releasing violent behavior.[13]

Even when viewing killing at the level of individual homicide, we find convicted killers do not all share the same personality type. Some fit the image of strong, mean, aggressive, impulse-driven males with little sign of sensitivity or compassion for others. But other first-time homicides are committed by people who are more androgynous or feminine, gentle, shy, and with no prior record of violence.[14] In a famous series of experiments, psychologist Stanley Milgram showed that ordinary American citizens could be induced into administering harmful electric shocks to strangers under circumstances in which the experimenter explained to them that this was what they should do.[15] Remarkably, administering even a potentially lethal shock could be induced among most subjects, males and females, across all ages and educational levels. Ninety percent of the subjects would deliver the shock if the experimenter said it was okay, if they saw their peers doing it, and if the victims were presented as being in some way inferior.[16] According to psychologist Philip Zimbardo, a contractual agreement, verbal or in writing, contributes to the willingness to justify immoral violence.[17] One critical factor is the cover story that what is being done is for a really good cause. The depictions of Panama's Manual Noriega as a brutal drug lord and of Iraq's Saddam Hussein as a dictator stockpiling concealed weapons of mass destruction are examples of cover stories that were false but nevertheless helped to legitimize violence. Another major factor is the promise that the cruel activity can be done anonymously and without individual identification. The cloak of the hangman and the uniforms of soldiers contribute to such anonymity. Societies that mutilate their victims in warfare typically provide masks to their warriors.[18]

The people behind the cloak appeared on Christmas Eve 1914 on a Great War battlefield in Flanders. As the British and French troops were settling in for the night, a young German soldier began to sing "Stille Nacht" (Silent Night). Others joined in. The British and French responded by singing other Christmas carols. Eventually, the men from both sides left their trenches and met in the no-man's-land between them. They shook hands, exchanged gifts, and shared pictures of their families. Informal soccer games began, and a joint service was held to bury the dead of both sides. The generals on both sides were displeased by what had happened. Men who have come to know each other's names and seen each other's families are less likely to want to kill each other. War often seems to require a nameless, faceless enemy.[19]

Killing: War and the Minds of Men

If we adhere to the view that severe violence is caused by evildoers or individuals predisposed to do bad things, then our responses are limited. We might choose to force the perpetrators of violence to conform to agreed-upon social norms. We might kill them in retribution or punish them as a threat, and as a warning to others, show what will happen if they continue the violent behavior. Or we may incarcerate them so that they cannot attack the rest of us. The view that violent behavior is explained by an inherent individual disposition of the perpetrator removes the option of rehabilitating the individual and allowing for a restoration for the harm committed. The view that violence is caused by personal predispositions serves a comforting function because it defines an impermeable line between good people (us) and bad ones (them). In all cases, if the individual is to blame, we take society off the hook.[20]

Dehumanization and Enemies

We humans retain long-term conceptions of others, some of whom are known personally, others known only by the images offered to us by secondary sources. An intriguing experiment by psychologist Albert Bandura[21] shows how easy it is to set up negative images of an unknown group. In this case it was just overhearing some derogatory comments. People acted upon this information by applying greater punishments (more intense shocks) to the negatively represented group than to others. To engage in killing other humans, or to sanction such killing, we make use of a capacity to withdraw a human connection to the target person or group.

Dehumanization is a composite psychological mechanism that permits people to regard others as unworthy of being considered human. On a conscious level it can be fostered by blinding hatred and by appeals to hate a particular evil adversary. Beneath the level of awareness, dehumanization permits us to resolve self-doubts by finding a scapegoat as the target for blame. Psychiatrist Robert Coles offers an insight into the psychological advantages to be obtained from dehumanizing a designated enemy: "We crave scapegoats; targets to absorb our self-doubts, our feelings of worthlessness and hopelessness."[22] For many, dehumanization invades our perceptions by a process of desensitization.

What is repulsive at first becomes barely noticeable after numerous repetitions. A distancing abstraction can also reduce the impact. Statistics may numb, but they do not bleed. The brutal destruction of a person may leave a disturbing image, but accounts of thousands killed can take on an abstract quality that is more easily put aside. Psychiatrist Robert Lifton developed the concept of psychic numbing to explain the detachment that occurs as people contemplate mass destruction in the genocidal extermination of people or in coping with the threat of nuclear war.[23] Dehumanization may also be fostered by the process of dissociative thinking. The symbolic worlds that we construct are not always within our own awareness. Competing images of reality sometimes coexist in the same individual. Certain states of mind provide a view of reality in which our fears, our anger, and our fantasies take the center stage of our thinking. Within such altered states we experience aspects of reality that transcend our typical thoughts and feelings. Such dissociative states can help people connect to the world in spiritual ways that promote healing at every level. Dissociative states also give people an opportunity to act out within a distorted reality in which moral inhibitions fade and killing another person becomes acceptable, even wonderful.

Dehumanization is central to Olek Netzer's "direct causation" approach to explain how wars can happen. He looks upon multi-causal theories that consider imperialistic ambitions, the deprivations of poverty and gross inequality, or historical rivalries as abstractions. In contrast, the direct and most concrete cause is that one human being pulls a trigger or gives an order that immediately destroys another. For this to occur, the target must be transformed from a complete human to a less-than-human enemy. This process of dehumanization is considered central. If all other contributing factors remained equal but people would just not conceive shooting, bombing, burning, and killing as an option to solve their problems with other people, there could be no war. Thus, by only describing events taking place in the nonverbal world, we arrive at an awareness that is very uncommon in our and other cultures: the real causes of wars are not abstract but living people.[24]

Dehumanization constitutes a justification system within one's beliefs that destroying an inherent evil is not the same as killing a human being. People whose ordinary reality contains sharp inhibitions against inflicting violence may switch into an alternative reality that permits killing and even genocide. And because people define their identities by their connection with larger entities, a group belief can turn this alternative reality, in which killing enemies is permissible, into one that seems normal and necessary. That is an essential aspect of military training. An absolute authority structures the soldier's boot-camp reality, and killing is turned into beating enemies with the technical commission of skilled tasks. Proving masculinity is considered to be critical to the self-concept and the measure of success.[25] One American soldier told a reporter how, from the top down, there was little regard for the Iraqis, who were routinely called "hajjis," the Iraq equivalent of "gook." "They basically jam into your head: 'This is hajji! This is hajji!' You totally take the human beings out of it and make them into a video game. If you start looking at them as humans, then how are you gonna kill them?"[26]

The dehumanization is not restricted to enemy soldiers. Following such atrocities as the My Lai massacre in Vietnam, a generation before, U.S. Marines in Haditha murdered twenty-four civilians, including children and infants. Examples of such barbarity are typically used to incite fear and anger against enemies. The theory that such acts are the work of a few "bad apples" is inconsistent with the circumstances that Milgram showed can release such actions from most of us. The soldiers were under heavy pressure from authorities to capture or kill insurgents. They felt pressure from peers to seem tough and to avenge the deaths of comrades. And they had been trained to dehumanize.[27]

Systematic inculcation of the righteousness of a cause and the dehumanization of a grotesque enemy are needed. Soldiers would not perform as effective killers if their training helped them to recognize that they are not killing the ogre but rather others like themselves who have been oppressed by the ruler the soldiers have been taught to despise. The process of dehumanizing the enemy, common to all training of soldiers, shares certain important elements with the training of young people to become suicide bombers. That program utilizes a variety of social-psychological and motivational principles to assist in turning collective, often frenzied, hatred into a dedicated, seriously calculated program of indoctrination and training for individuals to become youthful living martyrs.[28] Distance from the target enhances such detachment.

Ethologist Konrad Lorenz observed that perfectly good-natured men who would not raise a hand to punish a child could nonetheless drop incendiary bombs on sleeping cities, committing thousands of children to a death in flames.[29] Often the professional distancing of high-tech killing is contrasted to what are called barbaric practices of kidnapping people or decapitating them, implying that there are respectable and disrespectable ways to kill one's enemies.

The era of drone warfare accelerates movement toward a world in which killing can be done with little recognition that real human beings, many not instrumental in the conflict, are the victims. Even with the task of killing quite remote, adverse psychological consequences have been reported for the perpetrators.[30] But the goal of training soldiers to kill without suffering remorse continues.

The Dehumanization of the Culture

Netzer's point about the importance and immediacy of dehumanization at the moment of pulling the trigger is well taken. [31] The combat soldier is less guided by ideology than by loyalty to immediate comrades and the willingness to destroy an adversary with the necessary detachment to act quickly upon orders. However, abstract beliefs related to the self-concepts of individuals also become real sources of motivation, particularly for those who support a war from a distance. Nation-states, like religious and ethnic groups, are abstract concepts made somehow real, and even sacred, by people's identifications with them. We are reinvested in our love for such abstractions in times of war.

The display of flags jumped dramatically after the attack of September 11, 2001. The French, even french fries, were ridiculed when the French government did not support the invasion of Iraq. We are also, at such times, easily coaxed toward dehumanization of enemies. Many who do not lift a gun feel perfectly fine about calling for the blood of an enemy. Fear and hatred in the words of the larger society provide a cover for the heroic but deadly service of the actual combat soldier.

Terror management theory (TMT) is about how humans manage not imminent threats but the existential anxiety and terror inherent in the human condition. Life is precious yet fragile, and cultural worldviews tell us that our lives have meaning. Even with the prospect of danger, loss, and death, cultural frameworks remind us that our families, our work, our faith, our community, and our country may go on. Cultural worldviews, according to the theory, provide a death-denying function in the form of symbolic and literal immortality. [32] Even pathological cultures gain an appearance of normality by providing this shield against a threat from others with opposing conceptions of reality. Because the culture buffers existential anxiety and terror, those who challenge the status quo risk becoming the scapegoats upon which the pathologically "normal" heap their unacknowledged and unaddressed anxiety and terror.[33] One way psychological equanimity is restored is through participation in heroic efforts, such as war or acts of violence. One of terror management theory's key insights is that for ordinary citizens to support and participate in acts of violence against a perceived enemy, a sufficient amount of terror, hate, and rage must be generated first. In later chapters we will see how this is generated and by whom.

Beneath the surface recognition of courage and heroism, wars involve a form of ritual sacrifice. Joanna Bourke's[34] account of the justifications for such sacrifice during the First World War is titled *Dismembering the Male*. She supports a view about the male body in war, that it was intended to be mutilated. Although wars are looked upon as vehicles for defense, for conquest, and for legitimized violent action, their inevitable consequence is injury and death. The society, according to Bourke, encourages the soldier's delusion of masculine virility and calls him a hero in order to lure him into becoming a sacrificial victim.

Dehumanization constrains our world of experience. Macy and Brown attribute many of the ills of our culture to the blinding but compelling power of psychic numbing:

> Fragmentation and alienation, escapist pursuits, addiction, random violence, political passivity, blaming and scapegoating, suppression of vital information . . . a sense of powerlessness and burnout. These effects in turn create more to exclude from our consciousness.[35]

In times of war, dehumanization may become part of a larger social reality. The Dalai Lama's observations on warfare capture the basic concern:

The unfortunate truth is that we are conditioned to regard warfare as something exciting and even glamorous: the soldiers in smart uniforms (so attractive to children) with their military bands playing alongside them. We see murder as dreadful, but there is no association of war with criminality. On the contrary, it is seen as an opportunity for people to prove their competence and courage. We speak of the heroes it produces, almost as if the greater the number killed, the more heroic the individual. And we talk about this or that weapon as a marvelous piece of technology, forgetting that when it is used it will actually maim and murder living people—your friend, my friend, our mothers, our fathers, our sisters and brothers, you and me.[36]

Different Realities

Wartime and peacetime tend to involve two very different perceptions of reality. During peacetime, perceptions of reality are more likely to permit shades of gray. In wartime, reality is more likely to become one of black and white, good and evil, them and us. Psychologist Lawrence LeShan[37] names three different specific perceptions of reality: the sensory, the mythic, and the magical. The *sensory* perception deals with the ordinary experience of everyday living. In contrast, the *mythic* introduces a reality in which larger-than-life forces take center stage and command an absolute dedication to a given idea. There is also a *magical* reality in which supernatural forces are felt to play a key role in our destinies. Each of these is used at different times with different effects, and most people are experts at switching from one to the next or even existing in different worlds of reality simultaneously. We are such experts that the shift between one and the other takes place without our realizing it.[38]

War tends to invoke the mythic reality characterized by the presence of absolute good and evil. The two forces are pitted against each other in what is experienced as an ultimate battle, which we come to believe will result in either everlasting happiness or everlasting horror. Moreover, this reality tends to involve abundant optimism that good—generally "us"—will inevitably triumph over evil. Hitler's writing and speeches used metaphors to construct a culturally shared mythic reality in which the German nation was one body, a pure living organism that was being contaminated by a parasitic force within. The Jew was depicted as a germ, a threat to the existence of a pure and superior race, thereby making possible the death camps, gas chambers, and crematoria that followed.[39]

There are differences but also similarities between the fantasy presented as reality by the Nazis and current depictions of nationalism in the United States. The United States rides a history of manifest destiny. Shortly after the American Revolution a U.S. congressman, Giles of Maryland, declared, "We must march from ocean to ocean. . . . It is the destiny of the white race."[40] Such notions of superiority are echoed in the sentiments of the document the "New American Century" that came to guide U.S. policy at the turn of the twenty-first century.[41]

The document, prepared by men who rose to positions of great power during President George W. Bush's administration, set a course for U.S. policy undeterred by the needs and concerns of others (see chapter 6). Its message to the world is that we do not need to understand them; they need to understand us. We are the world's sole superpower.

Patriotism and loyalty can be consistent with healthy societies that do not encourage killing. Pride in the familiar landscapes and the idealistic heritage of a nation or group can be experiences that enrich life and provide for the common good. But much of current nationalism in the United States celebrates form over substance. On Independence Day flags, fireworks, and food are celebrated rather than the Bill of Rights or the heritage of the revolutionary idea that governments should derive their just power from the consent of the governed. "The troops" as an abstract entity are elevated to a mythic status while the realities of their work, their losses, and the long-term consequences they will bear are lost.[42]

Beyond the period of outright warfare, the mythic reality is maintained by a culture espousing militarism. (The economic and institutional complexities of militarism will be discussed in chapters 5 and 6.) One definition includes the ideological or value dimension: the term "militarism" describes a society in which war, or preparation for war, dominates politics and foreign policy. Soldiers and military-minded civilians become a governing elite dedicated to expanding the military establishment and inculcating martial values.[43]

From the perspective of cultural beliefs that facilitate the process of dehumanization among individuals, militarism can be likened to a disease. We see it in a narcissism that discounts the existence of others. Its cultural symptoms include addiction to war, a timid media willing to be the propaganda outlet for officials favoring war, and the worship of soldiers through pageantry. Sometimes both sides in a conflict invoke a magical reality, that God (or the gods) will intervene miraculously on one's side. Even without supernatural intervention war often overrides both the hassles of personal life and the disheartenment that comes with the tedious nagging problems of illness, job insecurity, a weak economy, natural disasters, and the perpetual reminders that success requires that we must have more than we already possess. When war is in the air, presidents assume the role of defenders. Sometimes the casualties and horrors of the war are reported. But in the largest media outlets, it is the excitement of cracking down upon an evil enemy that is conveyed.

LeShan explains how human beings tend to shift from one reality to another. When people run out of logical solutions to a problem that they feel must be solved, they unknowingly switch to another reality. A switch into a mythic mode can quickly resolve a crisis in conscience over killing. A key example is the use of strategic language by politicians to shift public opinion toward the mythical worldview where endless battle against an evil enemy makes perfect sense. The visceral reactions of needing to fight and to win in order to survive are enhanced by a mythic reality that is itself hidden. Outside the myth, the sensory reality might compel us to consider the human and financial costs that war will entail and the needs that will go unmet as a result.

The sensory modality might call upon us to speak directly with adversaries to find options to war. Most important, the sensory reality might raise the value of the human lives, each one precious in its own right, that will be destroyed by armed conflict. This might enable us to consider that the particular war being promoted would clearly be folly. The ease of moving to mythic reality, or even of using reasoning abilities selectively to justify a war mentality, is one factor that makes war so pervasive and so capable of destruction beyond its original intent.

Killing and dying may be viewed as sacrificial rituals by which absolute devotion to the state is reaffirmed.[44] The mythic reality permits a romantic version of war in which mindless euphoria pushes poorly prepared youngsters to a likely death. It permits a lust for violent bloodletting that relies upon calls for honor. It offers an opportunity for people to participate in a larger cause, and in so doing, the ordinary problems of the day seem to disappear. The attractions of this mythic reality arise in part because the alternative reality includes choice, decisions, and responsibility. Many fear the uncertainties that come with freedom.

Choice comes with responsibility, with a risk of failure and of blame. Reliance upon a strong authority figure provides a measure of escape and relief. War, like the stern father, provides an escape, a temporary source of certainty.[45] With such certainty, people follow the urging of leaders to indulge in massive slaughter, as was illustrated in the rise of Nazi Germany.

Three groups are relevant to the permission to kill in war: those who kill as soldiers; those in an elite sector of society who plan, prepare for, and decide upon military action; and those in the larger society who support such activity.

The Experience of Combat

The path to combat for soldiers begins with their enlistment. Varying motivations for enlisting include a desire to fight, a patriotic obligation to support a leader's call to defend one's country, and the best choice available to escape from a background offering neither affordable education nor hope for a meaningful life. In poor communities military recruiters offer young people employment, training, a sense of belonging, and an opportunity for disciplined sacrifice as an escape from racial intolerance and degrading low-wage employment.

The U.S. soldiers who fought in wars since the Korean War have typically been from poor or middle-class backgrounds, distinguishing them from the government officials who had decided to engage in the war. Soldiers had either been drafted into service or, since the end of the draft, attracted to join by recruiters' promises of education and job training that they could not pay for elsewhere. The highest recruitment rates (defined as the number of recruits per thousand of the eighteen- to twenty-four-year-old population) were found in counties that were relatively poorer than the rest of the nation.

The top twenty recruitment counties had median household incomes below the national average. Nineteen of these ranked below the median average in their own states. The counties that provided the greatest number of recruits were those that offered the most GEDs in lieu of high school completion.[46] No part of their recruitment or training described for the recruits the likelihood of their own death, the consequences to their families, or the effects that the experience would have upon them for the remainder of their lives. While service to country is sometimes mentioned, most soldiers enlist for security of a job and a place to live and the absence of alternative opportunities at home.

Once enlisted, soldiers face two realities: an emergence into the world beliefs about a hostile enemy and the systematic training to accept discipline and to kill as a professional under clear rules of engagement. Selective tests do not rule out any soldiers with a propensity for undisciplined killing who might come from any level of social class or education.

Selection criteria are intended to rule out those who might not make the grade. However, to meet recruitment needs for soldiers in the Iraq war, standards have been relaxed to include non-citizen immigrants who may be desperate for work. Twenty-five percent of enlistees were accepted despite recognized mental or emotional problems.[47] Also included are some who have not met the minimal mental standards that would be needed to understand rules of engagement. Such individuals may inflict great damage in unprofessional behavior as racist soldiers or undisciplined killers.

Private Green entered the military under a lowered standard of "moral waivers" that permits recruits with criminal records, emotional problems, and weak educational backgrounds to be taught how to use weapons. Many instances of rape go unreported, but Green was described in sworn testimony by U.S. soldiers as guilty of the planned rape of Abeer, a fourteen-year-old, in Iraq. He was one of a group of soldiers who stalked her after one or more of them expressed the intention to rape her. They changed into black civvies; burst into Abeer's home; killed her mother, father, and five-year-old sister with bullets to the forehead; and took turns raping her. Finally, they murdered her, drenched the bodies with kerosene, and lit them on fire to destroy the evidence. After repeated efforts to spin the details of the case, the military found one individual with a history of violent behavior as an effective scapegoat.

If such unfit soldiers do survive their experience in war, they will be called heroes—and released back into society. Upon their return, their military training increases their danger as potential copiers of another veteran, Timothy McVeigh, and the Oklahoma City bombing.[48] Soldiers originally unfit for duty and others made unfit by the trauma they experience may also return to work as prison guards, police officers, or as mercenaries for contractors hired by the government.

Not everyone is drawn into the mass fervor of war. Yet a large number of thoughtful and loving men can come to love war. For many, war is a state that gives us meaning.[49] Older veterans sometime reminisce about the sense of life-

and-death involvement, the facing of horrendous danger, the loss of comrades, the camaraderie of their unit, and the acts of heroism that occurred. Their memories recall a time of their lives in which every moment mattered, and their absolute dedication to a task, ordered for them by others, provided more that was meaningful—surely more that was exotic—than what they recall of the more mundane activities they experienced at other times. They recall the sharing of a fear and horror too great to be able to convey to others who were not there. They recall the intense moments of courage and of cowering. On a deeper level, war provides for some a value less easily talked about, an ultimate experience of the unity of beauty and destruction, of facing mortality, and of power over life and death.[50]

Sometimes the search for glory is commingled with elements of military careerism. Sergeant Camilo Mejia wrote the following from Iraq:

> I can say from personal experience in Iraq that our commanders often make soldiers carry out orders that have nothing to do with reconstruction efforts or peacekeeping. Their clear purpose is to instigate firefights so that officers can get their combat experience, medals, and the glory they need to climb the military ladder.[51]

The experiences of intense involvement also serve to cover up what might otherwise be a source of guilt for what they had done. An army staff sergeant, who was sentenced to a year in military prison in May 2004 for refusing to return to Iraq after being home on leave, talked openly about what he did there:

> What it all comes down to is redemption for what was done there. I was turning ambulances away from going to hospitals, I killed civilians, I tortured guys and I'm ashamed of that. Once you are there, it has nothing to do with politics. It has to do with you as an individual being there and killing people for no reason. There is no purpose, and now I'm sick at myself for doing these things. I kept telling myself I was there for my buddies. It was a weak reasoning because I still shut my mouth and did my job. . . . It wasn't until I came home that I felt it—how wrong it all was and that I was a coward for pushing my principles aside. I'm trying to buy my way back into heaven and it's not so much what I did, but what I didn't do to stop it when I was there. So now it's a way of trying to undo the evil that we

did over there. This is why I'm speaking out, and not going back. This is a painful process and we're going through it.[52]

A substantial number of combat veterans have returned bearing the full pain of their experience. By October 2004, the Department of Defense reported some 5,000 U.S. soldiers who were refusing to return to combat in Iraq. Their return to normality has given them a mission to educate others about the horror and the false justifications of war. At a July 4, 2004, memorial of placing crosses for killed soldiers in the sand at Santa Monica Beach, one Marine collapsed in grief. He had been the sole survivor of a mortar attack in Iraq and had lost sixteen of his comrades. He was so bereft that he couldn't write the names of the men. The volunteers helped him, and then he gingerly kissed all sixteen crosses and sat against the Santa Monica pier completely frozen until he could finally move again.[53]

Journalist Dahr Jamail interviewed participants at a Veterans for Peace Convention in Dallas, Texas. He asked what they would tell the president if they could speak to him. One corporal from an artillery unit replied:

> I don't think Bush will ever realize how many millions of lives he and his lackeys have ruined on their quest for money, greed and power. . . . To take the patriotism of the American people for granted—the fact that people [his administration] are willing to lie and make excuses for you while you continue to kill and maim the youth of America and ruin countless families and still manage to do so with a smile on your face. . . . You need to . . . take the billions of dollars you've made off the blood and sweat of U.S. service members, all the suffering you've caused us, and put those billions of dollars into the VA to take care of the men and women you sent to be slaughtered. Yet all those billions aren't enough to even try to compensate all the people who have been affected by this.[54]

Ron Kovic's memoir *Born on the Fourth of July* documents the transformation of this veteran who lost his legs in Vietnam. Among those soldiers whose experiences caused them to turn against the war, a number take a stand on ethical grounds while still in the service. One little-reported story from the Vietnam War is the extent of soldier rebellion. It occurred from the front lines to stateside bases. GIs produced more than 250 antiwar committees and underground news-papers to voice their discontent. Their efforts came not only from draftees but also from poor working-class soldiers who had joined voluntarily.[55]

Glory and the Sense of Purpose

Those who glorify their experience of war help to preserve its symbolic social meaning as service to one's country. War, however destructive, is always justified by its leaders and is typically honored. William James noted that the sentiments tapped by war are not all bad:

> Indeed they represent the more virtuous dimensions of human existence: conceptions of order and discipline, the tradition of service and devotion, of physical fitness, of unstinted exertion, and of universal responsibility.[56]

More recently, author Barbara Ehrenreich placed mystical experience at the core of her theory of war. Her claim is that war is a sacrament, a blood ritual that draws upon humankind's oldest and deepest impulses, typically buried in the realm of the unconscious.[57] Such a view might be misconstrued to make war appear as an inevitable outcome of human nature. However, in the Seville statement on war, a multidisciplinary group of distinguished scholars states clearly that war (and by implication the preparation to wage war) cannot be explained as a human instinct. Although militarism is not instinctual, the religious sentiment underlying it shows characteristics of primitive programmed reactions. History provides numerous instances of the religious passions of war. The Crusades and the Islamic jihad elicited spiritual strengths of self-sacrifice, courage, and honor.

During the twentieth century, nationalism provided an illustration of the same religious zeal. In Nazism, where religious rituals were specifically incorporated, but also in the Second World War generally, the absolute righteousness of the participants was paramount. Ehrenreich observes that "the passions of war are among the 'highest' and finest passions humans can know: courage, altruism, and the mystical sense of belonging to 'something larger than ourselves.'"[58]

The degree of immersion in the sacrament is surely different for those who are involved directly as soldiers or other victims of combat and for those who know it best in the movie version. The Dalai Lama observed:

In modern warfare the roles of those who instigate it are often far removed from the conflict on the ground. At the same time, its impact on noncombatants grows even greater. Those who suffer most in today's armed conflicts are the innocent—not only the families of those fighting but, in far greater numbers, civilians who often do not play a direct role. Even after the war is over, there continues to be enormous suffering due to landmines and poisoning from the use of chemical weapons.[59]

The Dalai Lama also noted the effects of the dispersion of destruction.

War brings a destruction of infrastructure, of roads, bridges, housing, farmlands, electricity, and medical facilities, as well as a general economic hardship. This means that with increasing frequency women, children, and the elderly are among its prime victims.

The history of sexual abuse of women in war is well documented.[60] Feminist scholars have frequently noted that the image of heroism in war has long been associated with proving manhood in patriarchal societies; the implicit message sent is that violence is erotic.[61] Rapes often occur in war and under military occupation. The reasons include a license to express power over a dehumanized enemy. It is also likely that the reality of imminent death drives the senses to capture the moment with sexual and romantic actions and fantasies. And rape, in many areas, has also been an explicit part of the humiliation intentionally encouraged as an instrument of war.[62]

Mozambican political leader and humanitarian Graça Machel's report to the United Nations on the effects of war on children documents the disastrous effects on young people.[63] These include the loss of young lives clearly not at fault, the mutilations, the separations from family, the forced child soldiers and child sex slaves, the fear, the trauma, and the unresolved anger that will later influence the survivor's own propensity to be a perpetrator or a victim of violence.[64]

The Dalai Lama also addresses the impersonality of destruction:

The reality of modern warfare is that the whole enterprise has become almost like a computer game. The ever-increasing sophistication of weaponry has outrun the imaginative capacity of the average layperson. Their destructive capacity is so astonishing that whatever arguments there may be in favor of war, they must be vastly inferior to those against. We could almost be forgiven for feeling nostalgia for the way in which battles were fought in ancient times. At least then people fought one another face-to-face. There was no denying the suffering involved. And in those days, it was usual for rulers to lead their troops in battle. If the ruler was killed, that was generally the end of the matter. But as technology improved, the generals began to stay farther behind. Today they can be thousands of miles away in their bunkers underground.[65]

The Decision Makers for War

The reality of being able to tap into, and to induce, a soldier's capacity to kill appears to be an insufficient explanation of the motives for war. Most of the decisions to use military force are not made by soldiers nor even influenced by their desires. Despite the frequent claim that wars must be fought, or expanded, in order to honor the sacrifices already paid by other soldiers, most of the decision makers have rarely seen a battlefield.

Political officials are influenced by high-ranking military officers, by intelligence sources, and civilian strategists whose work is to investigate potential enemies and prepare to confront them militarily. They are also influenced by close ties to powerful corporate officials seeking protection for their investments and to weapons scientists whose life work has been in developing weapons and planning for their use. Such defense-planning strategists define their goals as gaining competitive advantage for their own side and are often preoccupied with strategies that enable them to outsmart or coerce adversaries. The defense intellectuals, however, display behavior that suggests their work meets deep psychological needs. Among themselves they speak with a dry technocratic language that distances their reality from the cost in lives.

Military planners talk about missions, operations, securing an area, destroying a high-profile target, creating a strategic advantage, or a favorable cost-benefit ratio. The nuclear weapons laboratories develop the most lethal of all weapons. But human suffering is not part of their discussion. They exist in a culture in which every atom, every molecule, every weapon, every person, every agency, every toxic-waste product is a separate entity to be isolated, studied, mastered,

and exploited. It is a symbol of a culture in which bigger is better, in which rationality prevails over intuition and feelings, in which the culture of macho bravado
is provided a sophisticated form of expression and a beneficent rationale. It is
connected to, indeed a creation of, the federal government in its honorable pursuit of security. But closer studies of this elite group of men (they are almost all
male) reveal that the vocations also provide gratification for masculine identities
that play with a god-like power sufficient to destroy the planet. Such activities are
often pursued without conscious awareness of an underlying preoccupation with
the subjugation of the weak and the feminine.

Images of bullying and domination of women creep through the outward
rationality of their language.[66] Along with the emotionless technical language
of deterrence and counterforce capabilities are the words that assure a mastery
over the anxiety that might be caused by the images of radiated flesh, dying
Hiroshima victims, or of incinerated cities.[67] Instead we have "clean bombs"
or just "devices," "collateral damage," and "surgical strikes." But the images of
extraordinary male potency break through. The Harrier II missile is described
as having an "exceptional thrust-to-weight ratio . . . with vectored thrust capability that makes the unique rapid response possible. It is designed to maximize
runway cratering by optimizing penetration dynamics and utilizing the most
efficient warhead yet designed." Incidentally, the French used women's names
for each of the craters gouged into their test site at Mururoa Atoll. In case the
imagery is unclear, the Harrier II description adds "just the sort of 'big stick'
Teddy Roosevelt had in mind back in 1901." Frequently, the defense strategists ask, "Did you get to pat the missile?" Getting to pat the missile vicari-
ously appropriates all that phallic power as one's own.[68] One strategic observer
noted, after a test:

> Then just when it appeared as though the thing had settled down in a state
> of permanence, there came shooting out of the top, a giant mushroom that
> increased the size of the pillar to 45,000 feet. The mushroom top was even
> more alive than the pillar; seething and boiling into a white fury of creamy
> foam, sizzling upward, and then descending earthward, a thousand gey-
> sers rolled into one. It kept struggling in an elemental fury, like a creature
> in the act of breaking the bonds that held it down.[69]

The culture most difficult to see is one's own. The values of the nuclear weapons culture include the following assumptions: wars are inevitable; national interests justify the use of violent force; the views of scientists are correct; and the march of technology, despite its casualties, is inevitable. When we see that these views may also express deep psychological needs for masculine identity and power and may be reinforced by a clandestine organizational culture with cult-like attributes, we are able to understand better the addictive attachments that such beliefs may hold.[70]

The human needs fulfilled by war are but one factor contributing to global violence. But if war is to end as a human institution, the world may have to find ways to offer people the same sense of identity and belonging in the work of peace-building as they otherwise find in supporting or participating in war. Although the individual capacities that enhance human willingness to engage in war are important, they are not sufficient to explain it. The aggressive behaviors of nations may bear little resemblance to the aggressiveness of their people. Reinhold Niebuhr[71] has observed that a nation of submissive robots can be led to war more easily than a nation of aggressive individualists.

War and its preparedness are institutions of society. Even in the Second World War, which was fought with a righteous belief in the cause, soldiers still were mainly in service because they were drafted. Most served in combat duty only for as long as their assignments required. Studies show that they were fighting more for their loyalty to their immediate squadron than to their country.[72] Continuing to fight and bear the sacrifices had to be promoted, both for soldiers and for the nation. This war, like most, was sustained by propaganda, demonizing the enemy, and extolling the virtues of our effort.

The image of a hostile enemy is a precursor to war.[73] The period of the Cold War demonstrated the continuing power of a military and economic elite, on both sides, to create so awesome an enemy[74] that its containment could justify great sacrifices to freedom and to well-being at home. In the proxy wars fought in Angola, Korea, Vietnam, Panama, Afghanistan, El Salvador, and Iran, the public was typically treated to a televised vilification of an individual and a display of war that concealed its atrocities and its costs. Even then, extended war has been unpopular. This unpopularity reflects a brutality of the experience of mutilated people that cannot be overcome by flag-waving demonstrations.

For ordinary people, both in and out of uniform, for people whose information comes from a mass media relying mainly upon reports from the pressrooms of government agencies and large corporations, the myth fades and the reality of war is revealed as a horror. Even with the glorification of war, the hiding of casualties, and the media acceptance of terminology that transforms war into a tactical game devoid of pain, people grow weary of war.

The images of dedication, purpose, and belonging that it brings forth are often short-lived. The continuation of war requires organizational machinery to make it happen. That machinery is operated by a network of people for whom the gains of violent exploitation are greatest. Those who call for war are not necessarily evil. But they live in a world of information, rewards, and long-term practices that call forth a high level of violence and cause unspeakable harm to many.

Part of the social-psychological view of how to eliminate war has been to urge that we socialize our young people to grow up with a respect for life. The depth of the human commitment to the "Other" has been viewed as a factor critical to avoiding nuclear war.[75] Within humanistic psychology both Carl Rogers and Abraham Maslow recognized that society needed to be more inviting to the development of caring and concerned individuals. Yet both placed major emphasis upon the unfolding of the individual potential for caring engagement with the world beyond the ego.[76]

In partial contrast, existential psychologist Rollo May saw a darker side to human nature that made more difficult the unfolding of the human potential for replacing hatred with caring. He felt that movement toward freedom, toward participation and caring, was most realistic when it recognized the constraints of destiny. For May, these included a "daimonic" human quality that was the source of both creativity and destructiveness.[77] May's recognition of the destructive potential echoes a history of writing dating back to Sigmund Freud and his concept of the inner conflict between forces of life and love (Eros) and forces of death and destruction (Thanatos).[78]

This is a major contribution to the debate on what is needed to deal with the potential for violence and our hopes for peace. Indeed, it is this juxtaposition between the commitment to fulfillment of the human potential and the realization of the human capacity for violence that has led to one of the most important dialogues about human nature. If people cannot always be counted upon to restrict their own belligerent inclinations, then we may succumb to the situations that bring out violence in almost all of us. Hence peace will have to be accompanied by the creation of human institutions and cultural norms that hold us accountable when we might otherwise be drawn to war. Since institutions change, this is possible.

Humans have created laws to limit the law of the jungle. The invention of the Colt revolver led to an era in which one's sword could no longer define a safe space, and gentlemen gave up their swords. Now the power of nuclear weapons is such that no leaders can protect us while threatening others. Institutions like war that permit an exploitation of the earth's capacities to nurture life may destroy others first. But eventually they are likely to doom all of us. Most wars are fought because of perceived injustice. We focus next upon a set of non-military institutions and practices that are increasingly seen as unjust. They are a less visible source of violence, devastating in their own right, that increase the likelihood that we humans will continue to hate and to kill others of our human family and to diminish the life-sustaining ecology so needed for our survival.

3—The Hidden Structure of Violence

Human beings are like parts of a body, created from the same essence.
When one part is hurt and in pain, the others cannot remain in peace and
be quiet. If the misery of others leaves you indifferent and with no feelings
of sorrow, you should not be called a human being.

—SA'ADI, thirteenth-century Persian poet

ALTHOUGH INDIVIDUAL ACTS OF VIOLENCE are readily noticed, there is often a pattern underlying them that is less obvious. Violence is not adequately understood by the examination of occurrences of specific violent behavior. Rather, the view is that beneath these phenotypic events there lies a genotypic pattern, often hidden, that is a fundamental factor in its occurrence. The global economy consigns persons, communities, and habitats to roles that enhance the likelihood of violence in many forms. Pathways may be traced from the global corporate economy to violence against workers, consumers, indigenous communities, and life-sustaining habitats as well as to acts of personal violence, terrorism, human trafficking, and the spread of AIDS among poor women. Paradoxically, as we shall argue, globalism also offers opportunities to constrain the violent consequences of the global economy.

Author and activist Barbara Ehrenreich once questioned Ron Ziegler, who had been President Nixon's press secretary, about the propriety of $10,000-a-plate dinners for raising campaign funds. Ziegler's reply was that this was access and that they should have to pay for it. When asked how people who do not have that much money for a dinner might gain access to the White House, the reply was they would have to find other ways to get attention. Three days later the Los Angeles riots erupted. The underlying message had apparently been grasped by people unable to pay for access. The needs of poor and marginalized people are largely ignored by government, and they are often the recipients of brutality at the hands of law enforcement. One such case was evidenced by the beating of a black man, Rodney King, caught on camera in the 1992 Los Angeles riots. This pattern has been often repeated, recently through police shooting of an unarmed black man in Ferguson, Missouri. The case drew national attention to the militarization of police in local communities.

The plight of cities lies beneath such eruptions of violence. The last of the manufacturing jobs in south-central Los Angeles departed in the early 1980s for Mexico. The area lost 70,000 such jobs in the last three decades. One might argue that the street violence was not directed toward the appropriate causes as kids smashed windows and stole merchandise. But looting is a crude shopping spree in which people who are bombarded with messages to acquire more things find an opportunity to do so. The outbreak reflects an exploitative system that rewards the select few while pillaging and polluting the rest of the world. The kids would explain that "everyone was doing it," and perhaps they were right. The bankers were also looters, as were the defense contractors, the Wall Street inside traders, and the corporate mergers and takeovers.[1] An exploitative subculture of commandeering resources for competitive advantage, enacted and promoted by the elite, normalizes violence for the entire society.[2]

We define violence broadly as any affront to the life, well-being, or dignity of a person. Any activity that increases the suffering of others is violent. Johan Galtung, a founder of peace studies, defines violence as "avoidable insults to basic human needs, and more generally to *life*, lowering the real level of needs satisfaction below what is potentially possible."[3] Wherever unneeded suffering or death results from preventable human actions, violence has occurred. Galtung's concept of *structural* violence is helpful to understanding the impact of an exploitative system on its members. He sees culture—the normative beliefs and practices of a society—to be a source of violence by allowing a dehumanization of certain persons or groups. Cultural violence leads to structural violence when it is incorporated into the formalized legal and economic exchanges of the society. Although individual acts of violence have many causes, their occurrence is most frequently predicated upon a larger and often hidden structure that necessitates violence.

Structural Violence

According to Galtung, three different types of violence make up a "violence triangle"—cultural, structural, and direct violence—and they have different relationships to time. *Direct violence* is an event; *structural violence* is a process with ebbs and flows; and *cultural violence* is more invariant, remaining essentially the same for long periods and reflecting the slow transformation of a given society's basic culture.[4] In most cases of violence, Galtung claims, there is a causal flow. A persistent stream of cultural beliefs dehumanizing others leads to a structure justifying unequal or abusive practices and policies, which then erupts into acts of direct violence. Direct violence is used by both the underdogs and the top dogs of society, but the acts of violence by the two groups serve quite different purposes. Underdogs use violence as a way to get out of a structural iron cage of powerlessness and poverty or to get back at the society that put them there. The top dogs, on the other hand, use direct violence to gain or keep power; this use of direct violence maintains the status quo of persistent structural and cultural violence.

Structural violence is harder to identify than direct violence. Anyone can see that direct physical harm, such as rape or murder, is violent. Structural violence, however, looks normal on the surface. The harmful effects become apparent only after close inspection. Children may die of malnutrition. The conditions that displaced their family's farm by a mining corporation or an agricultural conglomerate are sometimes unnoticed. Therefore, structural violence, more often than not, is left unchanged, and the cycle of violence continues. The invisibility of the structure of violence is frequently a result of our inability—or refusal—to see below the surface. In the case of violence-generating corporate structures in the global economy, tools to uncover structural violence are in fact available. But the dissemination of information about these tools is seriously limited because the mass media (see chapter 7) are part of the global corporate machinery and are less inclined to display their own downside.

Psychological and Epidemiological Perspectives

The experience of police, emergency medics, mental health professionals, and war correspondents is with direct violence. Their tendency in ascertaining causal explanations has typically been to look within the person. When we see a case of family violence, the battering or torture of a defenseless victim, or the destruction or mutilation of an enemy combatant, the line of inquiry with which psychologists feel most at home is: How could the individual have done this? What motivation, what state of anger or emotional arousal, what genes, what horrific childhood or adult experience, what pathology of personality or thought pattern could help us to understand the case at hand?

Sometimes this look within leads us to posit hidden internal factors, such as repressed anger or raging hormones. Sometimes, however, this inquiry into the person takes us far into the search for identity, for meaning, and for spiritual connections beyond the particular person. The values and connections revealed by such inquiry also may illuminate a compelling structure of belief systems, a part of what Langer has called "life symbols."[5] These are perhaps better understood in cultures with a tradition of spiritual inquiry, wherein social structures are maintained by the psychological mechanisms of the individuals and the group to which they belong. The group's traditional worldviews may affirm broad values of caring or of killing. Psychoanalyst Carl Jung's work on Nazism and the phenomena of the collective inferiority complex and shadow projection of inner experience explores an extreme example of broad cultural values informing and justifying direct violence. A group's traditional worldviews and values need not be so extreme as Nazism and may still support direct violence.

The hidden structures to be found by observing and listening to individuals and by noting the symbols of their cultures, although essential to understanding violence, are not, however, the topic of this chapter. Rather, following the dictum of Kurt Lewin (founder of social psychology) that behavior is a function of both person and environment,[6] the hidden structures we will focus upon are part of the social order. Recall what Hannah Arendt noted: the most shocking fact about the genocidal brutality of the Nazis was the ordinariness of the perpetrators. They were remarkably like the rest of us. What was extraordinary was the social structure that enabled people to act in brutal ways and to ignore the brutality of their neighbors.[7]

Some forms of violence, such as genocide, are obvious examples of mass evil. In such situations, an understanding of one particular perpetrator or one particular victim is insufficient to understand where the responsibility really lies. One might need to discover the leaders of the effort and their powers over the individual perpetrators as well as the psychology of the bystanders.[8] Indeed, there are many forms of violence in which the actual event we witness may be better understood by locating forces many steps removed. Our thesis here is that the hidden force underlying increasingly frequent occurrences of contemporary violence is the global corporate economy.

Singular explanations for the roots of violence should be suspect. The goal here is not to find a scapegoat on whom to blame the preponderance of violence but rather to look at one particular contemporary structure that is an overriding, and too often hidden, cause. In the search for the roots of complex phenomena, it is frequently necessary to go beyond the careful clinical or laboratory examination of specific cases and move on to an examination of the conditions under which incidents occur. This epidemiological approach has been immensely effective in public health. In social epidemiology, the findings have presented an overwhelming case for three principal factors in the breakdown of both physical and psychological health: poverty, social marginality, and loss of control.

If we forget for the moment whether the particular pathology about which we are concerned is cancer, heart disease, AIDS, depression, substance abuse, child abuse, or homicide, and instead focus upon the circumstances surrounding all forms of breakdown, there are some remarkable similarities supporting the importance of these three factors. Those people who live in poverty are at a level of risk sufficiently greater than the rest of us, such that it becomes necessary to control statistically for economic level when explaining any other contributing factor.[9] Perhaps an even stronger, albeit related factor is social marginality. Socially marginalized individuals—that is, individuals not linked into a network of supportive care and reciprocal expectations—are also at risk for almost every form of pathology. Those of us who could not be considered marginal typically fall into the high-risk category when we suffer a loss or disruption in our supportive networks.[10] The third factor is a loss in control over circumstances that affect our lives.[11] Poverty, social marginality, and loss of control are often related. They are all factors that, in turn, are linked to certain economic arrangements that are inevitable outcomes of the global corporate economy. Hence illness, while experienced on a personal level, is often a symptom of structural violence.

Cases of Structural Violence by the Global Economy

Some illustrations of structural violence will be helpful. A death from stabbing in Toronto and a death from AIDS in southern Florida, apparently unrelated, share a common root. In Toronto, a Hispanic teenager was killed in a violent fight outside a bar. He had thrown a bottle at a man leaving the bar, accepted a challenge to fight, and was stabbed fatally with his own knife. We can speculate about the precipitating circumstances—the alcohol, the gangs, the taunts, and the lack of safe recreation facilities or youth employment for minorities—but this horrible tragedy really began ten years earlier in the Dominican Republic. Following the U.S. boycott of Cuban sugar, corporate agribusiness expanded its growth of cane sugar in the Dominican Republic. Corporate representatives of the sugar and shipping industries, closely connected to the Departments of State and Defense, engineered an intervention by U.S. Marines. This intervention prevented a restoration of the democratically elected Juan Bosch, who had been overthrown in a coup but was returning with popular support to Santo Domingo. The pro-corporate Balaguer government followed, and the Dominican Republic has since been a haven for international capital.[12]

Capital came to the Dominican Republic, as in most places of the less developed world, with a loss of indigenous local farming and crafts activity. The work of taking what is needed to nourish oneself and one's family from the local ecology meets the most basic human need. Agribusiness's hold on land for sugarcane forced many peasant farmers to the cities. For those who could find it, factory work came at the lowest of wages and with no security of employment. The Toronto youth's father lost his job, turned to alcohol, and was a dysfunctional parent; his impoverished mother avoided prostitution by finding work as a nanny in Toronto. Ten years later she had enough money to bring her son to live with her after his years of mistreatment back home, but migration away from the socioeconomic crisis introduced by agribusiness was not enough to keep him safe.

The woman who died in southern Florida had also emigrated from a village in the Dominican Republic. Flor Alvarez was among the many Dominican young women forced to move from a small, once sustainable town to the capital city.

She married a trader who made frequent trips to Puerto Rico. They lived in poverty. She never sought or received medical attention through three pregnancies until after the family emigrated to find better conditions, first to Puerto Rico and then to southern Florida. There she gave birth to a low-birth-weight baby girl, was diagnosed with tuberculosis, and later with candida. She was not notified about her positive testing for HIV because she had no telephone and could not be reached. She died of AIDS, leaving behind an HIV-infected infant. While the corporate hand was far removed from the hospital bed in southern Florida, as it was from the scene of the Toronto stabbing, it was surely a key contributor.

Shaped by corporate imperatives to eternally expand its pursuit of profit, the workplace in the global economy produces structural violence. Modern transportation and communication have removed the restrictions of giant corporations to any specific location. Free to move where environmental regulations are absent, taxes low, and labor cheap, all of the largest corporations have become multinational. The following are case examples of some of the ways in which structural violence is wielded through the activities of multinational corporations.

The Case of Nike in Indonesia

Details of the personal experiences of factory workers for the Nike operation in Indonesia offer a glimpse of the lived outcome of policies and practices that value increased revenues for corporations with little regard for the protection of human health, livelihoods, and well-being in the countries that host them. Cicih Sukaesih, a thirty-two-year-old woman, worked at the factory of Nike contractor P. T. Sung Hwa Dunia in West Java, Indonesia, from 1989 to January 1993. In September of 1992, almost all of the 6,500 workers went on strike over wages, benefits, and working conditions. The normal workday was 7:30 A.M. to 6:00 P.M., with one hour for lunch. Approximately three times a week, workers were forced to work as late as 9:00 P.M. The normal workweek was Monday through Saturday, but workers were sometimes required to work on Sundays. A worker who refused overtime received warnings. After the third warning, the worker was subject to firing. Additionally, the workers were financially coerced into putting in overtime hours. During the time Cicih worked at the factory, pay was about $2.10 a day in U.S. dollars. The overtime rate was double that. Only through working many hours of overtime could workers hope to cover their basic expenses.

Workers like Cicih labored under a pressured quota system and under oppressive factory conditions. They were so crowded together that the heat of their bodies, combined with the heat of the machines, made the temperature of the factory almost unbearable. Yet they were rationed only a limited amount of water to drink. Workers required a permission slip to use the bathroom. If a worker outstayed the time stipulated on the slip, guards would come to yell at her. Workers not feeling well were granted no exceptions. Should an accident occur, there was one doctor (present only two hours a day) for 6,500 workers.[13]

The factory workforce, typical of sweatshops, was largely composed of young women. A worker of twenty-eight was considered past her prime and could expect to be discarded. The women suffered sexual harassment. Workers were searched (manually, by guards touching their bodies) upon leaving work each day to verify that they were not stealing shoe components.[14]

Independent unions are forbidden in Indonesia; wildcat strikes frequently occur in Nike and other factories when the level of frustration reaches the boiling point. Typically, such actions are brief, massive walkouts—often successful with regard to specific grievances. However, after workers negotiate an agreement and return to work, management or the police or military will often interrogate workers suspected of leading the walkout. In the case of union leader Cicih, she and her twenty-three coworkers were summarily fired. Because of her opposition toward the Nike contractor, Cicih was likely blacklisted. In any case, at her age she had no prospects of finding further employment in a global sweatshop system, which spits out women at age twenty-eight as no longer of use. Cicih was obliged to leave her home to live with her sister.

Companies like Nike push for standards so low as to make a "no sweat" label meaningless. Nike uses its presence on a labor rights commission to depict itself as concerned and progressive. Transnational corporations like Nike benefit from U.S. promotion of the free market. China, Bangladesh, Pakistan, Honduras, and many others compete in a race to the bottom, each forcing workers to work fourteen-hour days, seven days a week.[15]

In 2011, Nike signed on to the Freedom of Association Protocol in Indonesia, along with other global sportswear companies such as Adidas and Puma. The Protocol aims to ensure that global brands and factories operating in Indonesia uphold the ability of workers to organize and negotiate for better working conditions. Facing continuous pressure from human rights organizations such as

Oxfam and Playfair, Nike is now being monitored by these organizations to see whether or not it is implementing the protocol. In spite of this pressure, Nike has refused to institute a living wage for its workers.[16] *Negotiating Freedom*, a documentary by filmmaker Sarah Rennie, follows the journey of five Indonesian union leaders working together to negotiate the Freedom of Association Protocol. The film also explores the broader challenges faced by factory workers who try to organize and claim their rights.[17] Corporate responses to factory workers agitating for better working conditions elsewhere in Southeast Asia illuminate some of these broader challenges.

McDonald's and Disney in Vietnam

Located in Da Nang City, the Keyhinge Toys factory produces the popular giveaway promotional toys based on characters from Disney films for McDonald's highly profitable "Happy Meals." Over the years, this Hong Kong–owned factory's various labor abuses have been exposed. The effects of fatigue from repetitive factory work are heightened by poor ventilation, and exposure to the chemical solvent acetone can cause dizziness, loss of consciousness, damage to the liver and kidneys, as well as chronic eye, nose, throat, and skin irritation. In one incident in 2000, a large number of women fell ill, twenty-five collapsed, and three were hospitalized. All appeals from local human and labor rights groups were rejected by Keyhinge managers, who refused to improve the ventilation in the factory or remedy other unsafe working conditions.

Along with demanding forced overtime, Keyhinge management did not make legally mandated payments for health insurance coverage for its employees, who receive no compensation for injury or sickness. Many of the workers making McDonald's Disney toys—most of them women between the age of seventeen and twenty—were paid well below subsistence levels. After working a seventy-hour week, some of the teenage women would take home a salary of only $4.20. A 1996 study found that they earned from six to eight cents an hour. Some earned just sixty cents after a ten-hour shift. The most basic meal in Vietnam—rice, vegetables, and tofu—cost seventy cents. Three meals would cost $2.10. Wages covered less than 20 percent of the daily food and travel costs for a single worker, let alone her family. By contrast, the CEO of Disney that same year earned $203 million.[18]

In 2005, Keyhinge Toys was in the news again, this time regarding striking workers. The two-day strike of 9,300 workers at Keyhinge highlighted workers' allegations of routine abuse and humiliation by supervisors, being forced to work twelve-hour days with no overtime, having wages cut if using the restroom more than twice a day, and no potable water in the factory.[19] The strike ended with the company agreeing to limit working hours to ten hours daily, with overtime, and a 10 percent pay increase—amounting to a wage still less than 20 cents an hour.

From the corporate point of view, the benefits of cheap production continue to outweigh the well-being of the factory workers required to produce. Disney ended its partnership with McDonald's in 2006. Yet despite more studies highlighting the growing epidemic of childhood obesity, McDonald's has continued to produce Happy Meals toys, now featuring other major motion picture and video game action figures marketing to children.

Wal-Mart

No multinational corporation has received more criticism for its domestic labor abuses than Wal-Mart. The rise of Wal-Mart and its policies and practices are explored more closely in chapter 8; here we focus on the company's role in dangerous working conditions for factory workers in Bangladesh.

Large companies like Wal-Mart have positioned regulating agencies, which are supposed to be monitoring their business practices, as buffers between the companies and their often unethical actions. In December 2012, more than one hundred people died in a garment factory fire in Bangladesh. The factory was owned by Tazreen, a subcontractor of many global brands, including Wal-Mart. This incident in Bangladesh could have been avoided if company officials had taken action in 2011, when garment factory owners, global retailers, government officials, and non-government organizations were brought together to discuss an agreement that would require retailers to pay Bangladeshi factories prices high enough to cover the of costs improving safety measures. The meeting was held in Dhaka, Bangladesh, where Wal-Mart was the first to say that paying the suppliers more to help them upgrade their facilities was too costly as it would involve a revenue loss equivalent to about 4,500 garment units.[20]

The April 2013 collapse of another factory in Bangladesh, which killed more than 1,000 factory workers, has brought increasing attention to the need for safety measures and other protections. While many major clothing manufacturers have signed on to pledges for increased worker protections and safety measures, Wal-Mart and The Gap have not. Public outcry to date has not proven to be effective motivation for the enactment of increased safety measures, and without action by governments or independent regulatory agencies to compel improvement, it is difficult to imagine a change to the status quo. After all, the pervasive inequality between labor and management is in no way unique to Wal-Mart—the violence with which corporate interests protect their profits is a common characteristic of labor relations throughout the less-developed world.

Foxconn and Electronics Manufacturing in China

In 2012, the Taiwanese-based manufacturing company Foxconn, China's largest private employer, came under scrutiny for the working conditions provided for the 1.2 million workers it employs. Foxconn is responsible for the manufacture of 40 percent of the world's electronics for companies including Dell, Amazon, Apple, and others.[21] Foxconn has been engaged in an intense dispute over the existing conditions for individuals working on the manufacturing of Apple's iPhone. According to China Labor Watch, thousands of workers have gone on strike or walked out of Foxconn's Zhengzhou factory. The walkout on the Zhengzhou factory happened just weeks after Foxconn was forced to close a plant in Taiyuan after a violent upheaval involving close to 2,000 employees left a number of them needing hospital treatment.[22]

The presence of violence, unrest, and strikes among the employees at Foxconn has increased dramatically after additional pressure was applied to meet manufacturing goals and production deadlines for the Apple iPhone 5. Apart from the strikes and forced closures of Foxconn production plants, several other instances of unethical labor practices have been found. Foxconn has come under criticism for forcing students to work on the production lines for Apple's iPhone 5. According to labor support groups, students had been forced by their teachers to assemble iPhones at factories around the country, requiring hundreds of students to work on assembly lines to help ease worker shortages in light of production deadlines.[23]

Investigations by news reporters as well as human rights groups have revealed crowded working conditions, underage workers, illegal amounts of overtime, improper disposal of hazardous waste, and industrial accidents; in one case, four people were killed and more than 100 injured. A rash of suicides among factory workers reported at Foxconn factories have brought added unwelcome scrutiny to the company. Despite increased public attention to Foxconn's labor abuses following this journalistic attention, consumer demand for Apple's iPhones has continued to grow. This expands opportunities for corporate violence against factory workers.

Violence against Consumers in the Global Marketplace

But the violence of the global economy does not only affect workers, leaving consumers untouched; consumers are also the victims of violence at the hands of corporate interests. Violence against consumers in the form of unsafe or untested products, foods, and pharmaceuticals are more commonly identified. The structural violence of corporate marketing practices is often most visible in new and emerging markets.

Avon in Brazil

Avon has an aggressive marketing campaign that brings expensive beauty products to the poor areas of Brazil. Avon's door-to-door sales model is uniquely suited for the company's strategy to capitalize on new and hard-to-reach consumer markets like Amazonia. Sales associates, often from local communities, are rewarded with lavish trips and cash prizes as incentives for increased product sales. The women then spend money needed to sustain their families on often-unhealthy products to pursue a Western image of beauty.

Women do everything to buy it. They stop buying other things like clothes and shoes. If they feel good about their skin they prefer to stop buying clothes and buy something that is on television. People think it is a real miracle.[24]

Channel One

Multinational corporations add to structural violence in the United States as well. An example of this is Channel One, an advertiser-sponsored school television program. Channel One is shown twelve minutes a day in 12,000 schools. In exchange for satellite dishes and video equipment, schools must show the pro-gram, which is filled with ads for sneakers, candy, and unhealthy fast food, to 90 percent of the children on at least 90 percent of the school days. The teachers are not allowed to turn off the program. Since Channel One is shown in school, children believed that the advertised products must be good for them.[25] In such situations, multinational corporations are using advertising to get poor people to spend beyond their means by telling them that they cannot get along without their products.

Corporate Sponsorship of Schools

In a similar fashion, starting in the 1990s, corporations such as Coca-Cola and Pepsi have served as "sponsors" to resource-challenged schools which receive funding for events and educational materials in exchange for exclusive agree-ments to sell or use products on school grounds and to feature increasingly prominent advertising that directly targets the schoolchildren. A study in 2005 showed nearly half of all public elementary schools and about 80 percent of pub-lic high schools had exclusive contracts with corporations.[26]

In exchange for its exclusive ten-year contract with Coca-Cola, the Rockford, Illinois, school district received $4 million in direct funding and an additional $350,000 to sell its products in schools, which has allowed the school to pay for field trips, gym uniforms, SMART programs, and other benefits beyond the scope of the school's annual budget.[27]

For students, one of the consequences of corporate sponsorship in the school system may be in the rise in childhood obesity. Twenty years after school corpo-rate sponsorship by such brands as Coca-Cola, Pepsi, Taco Bell, and other fast-food chains, new data have been gathered tracking the incidence of childhood obesity. Researchers have shown that children who live in states where the sale of junk food is not limited are much more likely to be obese than children who live in states that limit the in-school sales of such items.[28]

Systemic Violence against Women and Children

The incidence of sexual slavery and human trafficking among poor women and children represents yet another form of structural violence enhanced by the global economy. The United Nations estimates that there are currently 57 million female and child prostitutes. For ordinary families, destitution makes people vulnerable to prostitution and even to the sale of their children to traders who promise them jobs but instead sell them into slavery. The history and context of the Philippines provides one example of the establishment of the industry of sexual exploitation. [29]

Following fifteen years of a war with the Philippines that was justified by claims of racial inferiority and imperial expansion, the United States maintained the massive Subic and Clark military bases in the Philippines from 1903 to 1991. [30] The bases were served by a massive prostitution industry. After the Subic and Clark military bases closed, the industry was retained to serve soldiers on military training missions and increasingly to serve tourists and businessmen. Roughly 30,000 hospitality girls are registered in the Philippines, but the actual number is closer to 75,000—at a time when the Philippines is said to have prospered. [31] Its income growth is 4.5 percent per year, and a survey of the Asia-Pacific Economic Forum considered the Philippines one of the best places for investment among ten Asia-Pacific countries. [32] This reflects an early agreement to turn Subic Air Force Base into a free-trade zone, bringing in 150 large corporations. The benefits, however, have not reached the women. Their labor is underpaid causing extensive migration, and many who remain still sell their bodies. [33] In 2012, the Subic and Clark bases were reopened, ensuring that this issue will remain relevant for the foreseeable future.

Human Trafficking

In *Modern-Day Slavery*, Melissa Anderson-Hinn speaks to the presence of human trafficking in and around the San Francisco area:

> Trafficked thousands of miles from home, they arrive with great expectation for the opportunities of work and education they are promised. Beaten into submission and held in bondage, slaves work constantly for the profit and pleasure of their owners. Picked up before the sun rises and dropped off when the city is already asleep, they rarely see the light of day. They have no control. Even worse, they sign contracts in languages they cannot read, trusting the oppressors who promise them everything. [34]

The United Nations Office of Drugs and Crime (UNODC) report on human trafficking identifies sexual exploitation as by far the most common form of human trafficking, making up 79 percent of cases; it is also disproportionately composed of women, not only as victims, but also as traffickers. Female traffickers have a more prominent role in this form of present-day slavery than in most other forms of crime. The UNODC notes that this problem must also be addressed, particularly as many former victims become trafficking perpetrators.[35]

Other forms of exploitation, many of which are typically underreported, include forced or bonded labor, domestic servitude, forced marriage, and organ removal. As described in the example above, children are also exploited in the context of prostitution and pornography, domestic labor, and warfare.[36] More than 1.2 million children are trafficked across international borders each year.

The 2013 reauthorization of the Violence Against Women Act acknowledged the escalating problem of human trafficking, reauthorizing federal anti-trafficking programs and added new protections for victims of human trafficking, including provisions to strengthen safety and justice for American Indian women, provide assistance to domestic minor sex trafficking victims, and bolster protections for unaccompanied children in immigration detention sites.

The voices of human trafficking victims have been captured in Batstone's *Not for Sale,* which explores the return of the global slave trade and provides recommendations for how we can address it.[37]

AIDS as Structural Violence

The spread of AIDS is rampant where families can no longer stay together for the task of feeding and raising children.[38] Conservative thought sometimes favors a theory of AIDS prevention that hides the role of social structure. For example, cognitively based theories often assume that AIDS may be prevented if some new way can be found to teach that unsafe sex is really dangerous. This approach is seriously limited where the participants have few options. In the areas of Southeast Asia, the Philippines, Sub-Saharan Africa, Latin America, and central cities of the United States, the life and livelihood options open to poor women are increasingly restricted. Some find manufacturing or service-sector jobs that lack health benefits and pay too little to survive. Others turn to prostitution, relationships with drug traffickers and transients, and unsafe drug use practices such as sharing dirty needles and even the sale of children into the sex slave trade. Wherever the global economy expands into poor areas and replaces the means for local livelihood, we find the HIV epidemic to be spreading among women. The increase is usually combined with minimal access to treatment.

> As is the case internationally, the incidence of HIV infection [in the United States] is, like the incidence of addiction, heavily skewed by class . . . [and] HIV has disproportionally affected women of color. As early as 1987, AIDS was the leading cause of death among 15–45-year-old Black and Latina women living in NYC.[39]

The health behavior model, which tries to modify risky behaviors, falls short precisely where it fails to examine the behavior of those who are responsible for these conditions. Anthropologist Martha Ward observes:

> For poor women AIDS is just another problem they are blamed for and have to take responsibility for. . . . [Poor women's] sickness may be thought of as structural violence because it is neither nature nor pure individual will that is at fault, but rather historically given (and often economically driven) processes and forces that conspire to constrain individual agency. Structural violence is visited upon all those whose social status denies them access to the fruits of scientific and social advances.[40]

Poor women who are drug users are at increased risk for physical and sexual abuse. A New York City study of female intravenous drug users (IDUs) found that more than 60 percent had been physically abused at some point in their lives. Long periods of physical abuse, combined with drug use, leave many women feeling powerless about situations in their lives that involve drugs and sex.[41] Women have unequal access to clean needles. Female IDUs are more likely to borrow needles to avoid arrest for possession and more likely to lend needles as a form of life insurance in order to secure help in event of an overdose. This need for protection from male IDUs is why women are more likely to be in a sexual relationship with another IDU, again increasing their risk of infection. Connors observes, "The absence of a critical analysis of the role of poverty as a driving force in accelerating rates of HIV among women limits the development of programs to address the fundamental determinants of risk."[42]

The violence inflicted upon the mother is not confined to her. The parent with AIDS is typically indigent, with no prospect of employment. Families with seropositive mothers are in need of accessible and affordable healthcare, of welfare for living expenses, and of legal assistance to secure custody or guardian services. Between 7,000 and 10,000 American children are orphaned each year when their mothers die from AIDS.[43] Yet foster care and adoption assistance programs are among those least adequately funded in relation to the rise in cases. Globalization has meant legislation restricting taxes from corporations, thereby cutting the government safety net of entitlements that sustain these families. The *New York Times* reported that the Welfare Reform Bill of 1996 provided a combined total from block grants for child care, workfare, and cash assistance of less than $15 per underprivileged child per week in poor southern states such as Mississippi and Arkansas.[44]

Several trends lead to institutionalized poverty of women. These include cuts in Aid to Families with Dependent Children (AFDC), minimum-wage employment, and the incarceration of black men. Prison construction has become a highly lobbied growth industry. When men are sent to jail, it also hurts the women who have to take care of the family. Minimum-wage jobs do not make ends meet. Often, the only viable moneymaking options are to sell sex or drugs.

Crime increases for both men and women when better life options are restricted. So also do suicides. Following the economic crisis that has been facing the world since 2008, governments have introduced austerity programs to control levels of debt. One study estimates 10,000 additional suicides and up to a million extra cases of depression across Europe and the United States attributed to these measures since governments started introducing austerity programs in the aftermath of the economic crisis.[45]

The Human Effects of Free Trade

The North American Free Trade Agreement (NAFTA) and the neoliberal economic program that preceded it were presented in Mexico as the solution to sluggish growth rates experienced in the wake of the 1982 debt crisis. The United States, Canada, and Mexico entered into NAFTA on January 1, 1994. The agreement eliminates protective tariff and non-tariff barriers to trade and investment. NAFTA was promoted by pro-business interests as a measure that would raise living standards in all countries, increase democracy in Mexico, and create 200,000 U.S. jobs per year. Reality has not borne out this promise. Instead, the Mexican economy contracted and the country's productive capacity was seriously weakened. Mexico's trade deficit was filled by foreign investors who would then leave to find cheaper labor elsewhere and who would not renew short-term bonds, thereby creating a financial crisis. Free-trade agreements affect community well-being on both sides of the U.S.-Mexican border.

Mexico, like the United States, experienced the benefits of NAFTA, but these went mainly to the rich: a new group of multimillionaires was created while the rest of the country suffered. Mexican unemployment reached all-time highs. Massive Mexican military assistance was needed to buttress police efforts to clear out a protest that was massive enough to bring the largest city in the world to a close. The use of the military and a virtual press blackout were not surprising considering the corporate stakes on both sides of the border. The size of the protest should also not have been a surprise because real wages in Mexico had dropped by half since the General Agreement on Trade and Tariffs (GATT) was put into place. The extent of desperation has led to violence as the only perceived recourse.[46]

Mexico's first uprising in decades began on the day that NAFTA was signed. The rebellion in Chiapas pitted the indigenous rural poor against the Mexican government. Statements by Zapatista rebels indicated they were part of a larger movement for social and economic rights. On January 18, 1994, Zapatista leaders replied to the Mexican government's offer of conditional pardon:

> Who must ask for pardon and who can grant it? Why do we have to be pardoned? What are we going to be pardoned for? Of not dying of hunger? Of not being silent in our misery? Of not humbly accepting our historic role of being the despised and the outcast? Of having demonstrated to the rest of the country and the entire world that human dignity still lives, even among some of the world's poorest peoples?[47]

More than two decades have passed since the enactment of NAFTA. While trade and foreign direct investment have increased in Mexico, only 10 percent of the population has seen a higher standard of living. With millions of jobs made obsolete by cheap imports from the United States, Mexicans and Central Americans have increasingly sought work in the North. Since the 1994 passage of NAFTA, the number of Mexicans migrating to the North each year has more than doubled, although a bad job market in the United States, following the recession of 2008, has curtailed the number.[48]

At the time of President Clinton's 1997 visit to Mexico, there had been a 45 percent increase in the number of maquiladoras working just over the border. A "maquiladora" is a Mexican corporation operating under a "maquila" program approved by the Mexican Secretariat of Commerce and Industrial Development. A maquila program entitles the company to up to 100 percent foreign investment in the capital and in company management. Further, it entitles the company to special customs treatment allowing duty-free import on materials, and administrative equipment.

By 2010, the average earnings of maquiladora workers had dropped from $1 an hour to 70 cents. The leaders of their protests were in jail. The maquiladora sector at the northern border grew at the expense of manufacturing in other parts of Mexico. Still, China and India have surpassed Mexico's lead in textile and clothing manufacture, leading to the loss of Mexican jobs. For the United States, China has become the world's most powerful sweatshop provider. This status goes hand-in-hand with its abysmal working conditions, strict controls prohibiting worker organizing, lack of enforcement of labor laws, and a deliberate strategy by the Chinese government to convert a once-protected workforce employed in state-owned factories into a mobile and extremely vulnerable migrant labor force.[49] With economic decline and high unemployment in Mexico, immigration, both legal and illegal, has increased. Immigration has been blamed for the loss of jobs in the United States, and anti-immigrant groups have participated in violent vigilante activities against Mexicans coming over the border into Arizona.[50]

Domestic Terror

Mexicans, other immigrant groups, and racial minorities have been the target of serious racist scapegoating in the United States. Acts of direct violence such as church burnings reflect not only hatred but also the frustrations of those who perceive themselves to be the victims of foreign nationals taking away jobs or resources from them. Some of the violence—a form of domestic terrorism—is linked to the loss of personal control precipitated by the increasingly centralized control over local resources. The Unabomber, citing globalization, provided a more educated expression of this exclusion, but Timothy McVeigh, convicted of the Oklahoma City bombing, and the numerous militias are more typical. Their popular depiction as deranged individuals conceals some similarities in their ideologies and of the options that have been left to them by the global economy.

A splinter faction of one such group, members of which call themselves the Republic of Texas, held two hostages near Fort Davis, Texas, in 1997. Their claim was that Texas was never legally a part of the union, and they called for Texas to act like an independent nation. The group's weapons have made their beliefs more than bothersome misperceptions. The Republic of Texas hostage-taker Richard McLaren was criticized by his own group for having "gone completely off the deep end" and was impeached as its ambassador.[51] The evolution of the Republic of Texas is instructive: the group is an offshoot of the property-rights movement, which itself shades gradually from people who are disgruntled with a government they see as not serving them to others obsessed with guns, military maneuvers, "The Turner Diaries," race war, and blowing up government buildings. Their typical grievances are that wealthy Jewish bankers have control over the government and are taking away the rights and property of local citizens. They blame the government's affinity for racial minorities and immigrants who are getting the jobs deserved by "true" Americans for their ills.

It is too easy to dismiss members of the Republic of Texas as sociopaths or individuals unable to find a useful purpose in their own lives. The problem is that they cannot find a life with a useful purpose, and that is what accounts for the anger that winds up taking such bizarre turns.[52] Ironically, these "true Americans" are also the victims of the corporate economy and the political backbone that supports it. They have been led to believe in the "trickle-down theory" peddled by a ruling elite. Structural violence is pushed domestically on America's own citizens. These are people who have been misled by a corporate media and indoctrinated with fear by those in control.

Fear works as a tool to inculcate dependency, and paranoia helps to justify structural violence; terrorism reflects political and economic inequities. Half the working population of the United States has had falling or stagnant wages for thirty years. There is no future for young people who are not headed for college. The only time they are told that they are needed is as soldiers in meaningless wars, and they return with skills to shoot a gun but not to be part of the nation depicted for them on television. They hear in the media how well people are doing, how the economy is improving, how the good life can be bought on credit. But millions of people lack the education or skills to participate in a high-technology global economy. Few of them know how much of the land they see as rightfully theirs is actually owned by international corporate interests in mining and forestry with headquarters in South Africa, Japan, or an offshore island tax shelter.

The Doctrine of Global Corporate Growth

The theory of comparative advantage is an unquestioned assumption underlying one of the major tenets in trade theory. It contends that each country should enter the world market selling the products they produce best or have a comparative advantage in producing. In theory, comparative advantage will have everyone working efficiently; production and consumption will increase, which should provide more goods for all. In practice, this means that countries well endowed with raw materials and unskilled labor are to extract raw materials and provide labor for extracting raw materials and the menial tasks of assembly, while those well endowed with capital, technology, skilled labor, and scientists are to manage them. The doctrine serves as justification for a division of nations and communities according to what they bring to the production process.[53] This law traps countries in the place where their production profile has landed them, for historical or geographical reasons. It legitimizes an intolerable status quo and is itself a piece of structural violence.

The *National Security Strategy of the United States of America* turns such inequality into official policy. It notes, "History has judged the market economy as the single most effective economic system and the greatest antidote to poverty." Therefore, "the United States promotes free and fair trade, open markets, a stable financial system, the integration of the global economy, and secure, clean energy development." In this view the United States justifies invading the economies of many developing countries, sometimes with money, sometimes with military force, in order to preserve the global economic order shaped by the theory of comparative advantage.[54]

Proponents of the global economy argue that a rising tide raises all boats and that increased efficiency in productivity raises the standards of living for all nations and all peoples. It is likewise argued that international corporations bring in the jobs necessary in already impoverished areas and such jobs, even at low pay, provide a bridge for the country into the productive advancements of the industrially developed world. However, the nature of the jobs being produced should be examined. As in the case examples earlier in this chapter, people are making garments, shoes, toys, and electronic components. Young females have the needed dexterity and the lack of options for other work and are the most frequent employees. Like the farm workers who are exploited by agribusiness in California and Texas, these women are recruited by subcontractors. This removes responsibilities for their pay or working conditions from the corporations. Although they may work ten to twelve hours a day for long periods, they are treated as casual employees without benefits or job security. They work with informal agreements rather than contracts on highly fragmented tasks for which they can be easily replaced. In fact, displacement is what is occurring. Destitute women in the Philippines are losing these awful jobs as companies move to Vietnam or China, where the work can be done even more cheaply and where worker organization would be more difficult.[55] One problem in protecting human rights against oppression has been the mobility of capital. If a massive corporation can pick up and move when labor gets too uppity in one country, then labor has no leverage. Mexico's maquiladoras have seen this happen as corporations move to China.

Corporations have found other means to keep labor costs down while cutting the temporary costs of relocating their factories as well. The *mobile workforce* refers to a process by which a company may remain in one area while importing workers, through a contractor, from more destitute regions anywhere in the world. These migrants, who are poorer than the local population, are housed in cheap hovels, cut off from close familial ties, and entirely dependent upon the contractor. The structural violence of the global economy renders these dependent migrants extremely vulnerable to further exploitation beyond that enacted by their corporate employers.

The market is considered the primary source for economic entrepreneurship and technical innovation. However, markets do not instruct people with large incomes to consume no more than their rightful share of natural resources. They do not prevent retailers from selling guns to children. They do not require producers to recycle their waste. They give no priority for the allocation of scarce resources for basic needs to those who have little or no money before providing luxuries to those with great wealth. In fact, the market does just the opposite. Civil societies create governments precisely for citizens to establish and maintain rules that might restrict the forces of the market.

The shoe and apparel industries utilize low-capital investment (labor-intensive work) with little expenditure for technology that would improve the work environment. Such practice does not promote vigorous national industries. Nike claims credit for higher wages eventually won by workers in Taiwan and South Korea. Those wage increases were a product of popular movements for democratization. As repression lessened, workers were able to unionize and win better wages and working conditions for themselves. Large corporations are not generous. As conditions improve for workers, the company finds other locations and moves on.

The global economy rewards repression through investment and punishes freedom through disinvestment. The low-wage havens sought by corporations are also, not coincidentally, havens of repression. When South Korea and Taiwan began to democratize, Nike looked to Indonesia. Now China and Vietnam are the new magnets for investment. These corporations do not overtly support repression, but they most certainly profit from it. Multinational corporations conduct extensive research and can quickly move capital wherever the conditions of low wages, weak environmental laws, or assured profits can be found. Multinational corporations are currently engaged in a race to the bottom, where in order to be competitive they outsource their production facilities to the countries with the weakest environmental and labor laws.

The movement toward corporate globalism, although accelerated today, is surely not new. The earliest corporations, such as the Hudson's Bay Company, were created for the exploration and exploitation of new lands on behalf of imperial powers. What is new is the ability of the global economy to command the resources of almost every locality.[56]

Global corporations benefit from policies of the U.S. government and the World Bank, in which the United States has a controlling interest. Policies include supporting repression and loaning huge sums to swindlers who can deliver cheap labor. The result is that many countries are hopelessly in debt and at the mercy of the World Bank and International Monetary Fund, whose actions have proliferated low-wage, export-oriented economies. By the World Bank's own criteria,

37.5 percent of bank-funded projects in 1991 were failures at time of completion. An earlier study of four- to ten-year follow-up evaluations found that twelve of the twenty-five projects that were rated successful when completed eventually turned out to be failures. This means that less than a third of the projects provided an economic return sufficient to justify the original investment.[57] At least one country, Eritrea, has refused such loans and is slowly using its own resources to rebuild a railway that was destroyed by civil war. Its cost will be less than one-fifth of what international contractors would have charged.[58] Perhaps not by coincidence, the United States has supported Ethiopian military efforts to destabilize Eritrea.

Failure or not, the World Bank has no liability for its errors. The loans must be repaid by poor countries in scarce foreign exchange. This means absolute austerity in programs that might improve the lives of people. It is a great deal for corporate giants but a disaster for most of the world. Former World Bank economist William Easterly has documented the continuing, misguided approaches of the World Bank.[59] World Bank and International Monetary Fund policies have left the poorer countries in such debt that they have no choice but to allow international commerce to exploit their natural resources, pay their workers at poverty levels, and accept the toxic wastes of the developed world.[60] The global economy is creating populations with no measure of control over the local material and human resources they need to survive.[61]

Wealth Disparity

Former Labor Secretary Robert Reich acknowledged that Bill Clinton's "Putting People First" plan, which would have invested $50 billion a year in training people for skilled jobs that might support a purpose in life, is in the past. The political reality of bond traders during the budget surplus of the late 1990s called for balancing the budget, decreasing the debt, keeping interest rates at a level that satisfies Wall Street, reducing trade barriers, and cutting the safety net that prevents people from becoming victims of violence. These same policies reappeared during years of recession and high debt. They were neither nefarious schemes nor accidents of shortsighted policy, but were in fact direct consequences of corporate-dominated economic globalization. Agencies of government seriously concerned with job creation or living wages no longer have the ability to enact programs that could achieve these ends.

In the twenty-first century, the magnitude of public debt has been allowed to rise sharply. The borrowed money is not being used for education or for health-care. Schools, enrichment programs, and libraries are closing and medical facilities are understaffed. The beneficiaries of the debt turn out to be the wealthiest investors of global corporations whose taxes have been reduced markedly. Social movements the world over have turned against the domination of their lands by global corporations and the military forces that protect them. In response, the weapons development and production sector of global corporate activity has grown, as has the recruitment of soldiers. This contribution to debt provides one more path by which wealth is transferred to the largest corporations at the expense of poor and modest income people. Since the 1980s, the United States has witnessed a serious assault on the concept that government provides for the well-being of its people. A middle-class lifestyle providing education, freedom from hunger, safe and sanitary housing is often maintained by extensive debt and requires several incomes to sustain it. Many are just one job loss or one illness away from poverty.[62]

How bad a deal this is for poor people may be seen in the fact that poverty tends to increase regardless of whether the economy for investors is growing or shrinking. Debt bondage is the most common form of contemporary slavery in which families with nothing are forced to work merely to repay unjust debts to a landowner.[63] The debt of poor countries is being taken over by vulture fund companies. They buy the debt of poor countries, such as Zambia, at hugely discounted prices and then sue for the full amount plus interest and punitive damages. It is completely legal, but it dooms people in these countries to endless bondage. The vulture companies have no moral and legal obligations. Beyond debt forgiveness, a comprehensive debt-relief system would require companies to follow ethical and legal guidelines.

How great a deal is this economic structure for the global investors? There were 793 billionaires in 2005, up 15 percent from the previous year. Their combined net worth was $2.6 trillion with U.S. billionaires accounting for almost half of that amount.[64] The earnings of these billionaires are greater than the income of the poorer half of the world's population. During 2000, a typical year, there was an 11 percent increase in corporate growth, and CEOs from major corporations increased their incomes by 50 percent. The U.S. Congress, which cut 90 percent of funds for low-income housing, could not pass a law preventing corporations from deducting incomes in excess of $1 million as ordinary business expenses.[65] Corporate profits and executive salaries have continued this growth to the present time while tax loopholes have decreased the amount of revenues they pay in taxes.[66] Of the 100 largest economies in the world, fifty-one are now not nations, but corporations.[67] The 100 largest corporations are still the source of employment for just one-third of 1 percent of the world's population.

Risk and Responsibility

One basic rule of market economics is that the participants in transactions must bear the full costs of their decisions in addition to reaping the benefits. The best way to avoid losses, however, is to find another party that can be tagged with the responsibility for assuming risk from which you benefit.[68] Larger corporations go to considerable lengths to reap the benefits for themselves and to pass the costs on to others. They do not provide adequate health insurance for their employees. Wal-Mart is the world's largest and most profitable retailer and its largest employer. Early in 2013 the company ranked first on the Fortune 500 with sales of $466 billion and net profits of $17 billion.[69]

Yet Wal-Mart failed to provide company healthcare to half of its employees and instead offered advice on how their low wages could get them government coverage.

Taxpayers provide health care for hundreds of thousands of Wal-Mart Associates and their family members who qualify for publicly funded health insurance.[70] Indeed, according to data compiled by Good Jobs First, in twenty-one of twenty-three states that have disclosed information, Wal-mart has the largest number of employees forced to rely on the public rolls of any employer.[71]

The success of larger corporations over half a century has been based largely upon their ability to have the risks associated with their expansion underwritten by governments and, ultimately, by taxpayers. One example is the use of $20 billion in government funds to develop a satellite system that was subsequently transferred to AT&T. Nuclear energy, electronics, aeronautics, space communications, mineral exploitation, computer systems, agricultural technologies, and medical biogenetics are all areas of research subsidization.[72] The taxpayers whose incomes have funded development in these subsidized areas of research have not nearly benefited from it to the degree enjoyed by corporate recipients.

Costs of environmental damage are also transferred. The government not only fails to stop environmental damage but also contributes to it. There are over 20,000 radioactive and toxic chemical sites in U.S. military bases, contaminating air, water, and land. The Department of Energy has no safe way to dispose of radioactive waste, and it failed to stop the leakage of uranium into underground water supplies adjacent to several nuclear weapons facilities. The government has also let the military and the private sector dump radioactive nuclear waste into the ocean near fishing areas along the East and West Coasts.[73]

In *Democracy for the Few*, Michael Parenti states the essential problem:

Serious contradictions exist between our human needs and our economic system, a system whose primary goal is to maximize profits regardless of the waste, cost and hazards. We see that government is an insufficient bulwark against the baneful effects of giant corporate capitalism and often a willing handmaiden.[74]

Global poverty is tragic, but it is not an accident. A closer look, argues poverty researcher Maria Santos, suggests

a system-driven global impoverishment and poverty-creation, a process of high crime and grand fraud made all the more pernicious by its patent exploitativeness and extreme social injustice but also by its invisibility and concealment by the blinders of the market. It is thus a perfect crime, until of course it is exposed. But until then it is the world's best-kept secret.[75]

If one takes the perspective that violence is created by the blocking of human-needs fulfillment, the global economy presents some long-term problems. We are experiencing astounding economic expansion. But where do the resources come from that allow for exponential economic growth? Where will the wastes be stored? What will happen to the farmers who are displaced? How many roads will have to be built for how many cars, and how much of the earth's limited resources will be consumed? Where will we look for wisdom once global consumerism has produced a monoculture of the mind? How will we count the costs of the loss of wetlands and songbirds? When only growth and marketability are valued, how then will we cope with overcrowded cities with sporadic employment? How will we cope with inadequate care for children, elders, the disabled, poor single parents who raise their children, and other members of society whom we have labeled dependent? How will we cope with the stress of work sped up for the holders of temporary jobs? How much violence will be generated by this success of the global economy? When the key players are multinational corporations, then biogenetics, nanotechnology, weapons, and extractive industries may spread without ethical restraints, thus preventing economic growth from being a valid indicator of anything that we should care about.

Increasing trade is not something to be feared. Neither is technology the culprit. Globalization has potentials for creating a culture in which all humans are viewed as family. The problem is a process of integration into the global market carried out, at least since 1980, under circumstances of unsustainable finance. Wealth has flowed upward from the poor countries to the rich, and mainly to the upper financial levels of the richest countries.

> In the course of these events, progress toward tolerable levels of inequality and sustainable development virtually stopped. Neocolonial patterns of center-periphery dependence, and of debt peonage, were reestablished, but without the slightest assumption of responsibility by the rich countries for the fate of the poor.[76]

Thomas Piketty, in *Capital in the Twenty-First Century,* provides the strongest and best-documented critique of contemporary capital-driven economy.[77] Piketty argues that when the rate of return on capital rises faster than the rate of growth of output and income, then capitalism automatically generates arbitrary and unsustainable inequalities. These radically undermine the meritocratic values on which democratic societies are based. This is precisely what has been occurring through the nineteenth century until the present time. The wealth gap favoring an extremely small number of investors has already depleted the health and well-being of people and the promise of democracy. A major piece of evidence for the decline in human health and well-being is found in the work of two epidemiologists who show that it is inequality, rather than solely poverty, that predicts the highest rates of illness and health breakdown. The findings hold when comparing inequality levels across countries but even within parts of countries.[78] Without regard to ideology or to the question of finding better alternatives, the evidence is clear. Global capitalism necessitates rising inequality, which is bad news for human health.

The global economy is creating a borderless world shaped by capital efficiency and military and technological superiority.[79] It is a system that is flawed and as dangerous to spiritual meaning as it is to its viability for people and planet. The good news is that globalization has also contributed an amazingly powerful global movement to retake control over the basic resources needed for human well-being. Breakthroughs in communication have combined with the diminution of power and the malleability of boundaries of the nation-state. An international global network of NGOs and local grassroots groups is taking shape to challenge the reach and consequences of the global economy.

4—People, Farmland, Water, and Narcotics

Each generation has its own rendezvous with the land, for despite fee titles and claims of ownership, we are all brief tenants on this planet. By choice or default, we will carve out a land legacy for our heirs. . . . History tells us that earlier civilizations have declined because they did not learn to live in harmony with the land.

— STEWART LEE UDALL, *The Quiet Crisis*

This we know. The earth does not belong to man: man belongs to the earth. All things are connected. . . . Man did not weave the web of life; he is merely a strand in it. What he does to the web, he does to himself.

— ANONYMOUS

ECONOMIC GLOBALIZATION HAS BEEN SHOWN to create extremes of wealth among a few and serious poverty for many. This chapter examines an even greater impact of the same corporate economic forces upon the land, water, cultivation of food, and the precarious link between the ecological system and the continuation of life.

Ancient migrations were common as hunters and gatherers sought food and hospitable surroundings. Then, agriculture contributed to a sense of permanence and place that lasted across generations, sometimes even providing a surplus for trade and for more complex cultural development. People were once closer to the acre of land that fed them. The variety of products and the level of care that preserved the land for future use made these one-acre farms from 200 to 1,000 times more efficient than the corporate farms that have replaced them. Farmers nurtured the 2 billion microorganisms found in a spoonful of soil and saved the best seeds to improve their produce. The seeds, the values of attachment to the land, and the farmers themselves are being replaced.[1] Farmers whose families have been farming for up to six generations are forced to leave the land, but they cannot sell their farms for a price high enough to pay even the taxes on the land. A sense of failure has increased farm suicide rates in the United States and around the world. Farmers can no longer feed their families on what they produce.

The change in agriculture within the past 100 years, from small and medium size family farms to corporate, large-scale industrial agriculture, has devastated millions of family farmers. Modern agricultural firms such as Cargill, ADM, and ConAgra have bought up their smaller competitors and now constitute an agribusiness that maximizes profits with high pesticide and technology use and very low labor costs. They produce mono-crops for global distribution and are subsidized by acreage. They do not pay for the long-term costs of the devastation of the soil or of the communities they have transformed.[2] Large agricultural production facilities supply the needs of a few international food companies that control the processing and distribution of most food. Nestlé, the world's largest food corporation, has been involved with the marketing of infant formula to areas of the world where people have neither the money to continue using the formula once breast milk runs out nor clean water to mix it in.

Contemporary agriculture does produce a plentiful and sometimes inexpensive supply of food for supermarkets. However, with food supplies driven by criteria of profitability, much of the world's population (including many who used to be small farmers) is not getting this food.[3] Driven from once-viable farms to rocky hillsides, farmers in poor countries are forced to abandon the land and move into the money economy to support their families. Some find low-paying jobs in supermarkets and fast-food chains. Nearly half the world's population, 2.8 billion people, survive on less than $2 a day.[4] There is more food, more waste, and more hunger now than ever before. The psychological consequences have been devastating. Before colonial control over agriculture, men had meaningful jobs to do and more control over what they did. Colonial expansion routed men and women from more personally meaningful work to jobs defined by others, often leading to demoralization, discontent, and mental health problems.

Globalization of Food Production

Over 75 percent of the world's poorest people rely on farming as their way to earn a living. Paradoxically, many of them go hungry. The United Nations Food and Agriculture Organization estimates that nearly 870 million of the 7.1 billion people in the world, or one in eight, were suffering from chronic undernourishment between 2010 and 2012.[5] The human population is growing exponentially, with a quarter of a million people added daily; yet food production is only able to increase at a linear rate incommensurate with the demand, and the production of food for this increasing population is an overwhelming challenge.[6] However, people are not starving because there is too little food. Currently, there is enough food to feed everyone on the planet.

In the United States, more than one out of five children live in a household with food insecurity, which means they do not always know where they will find their next meal. According to the United States Department of Agriculture, in 2012 15.9 million children under eighteen in the United States lived in this condition—unable to consistently access nutritious and adequate amounts of food necessary for a healthy life.[7] The conditions of food insufficiency underlie movements for radical change in how the necessities of life are distributed.[8]

Economic Globalization

Globalization of the economy means "the spread of free-market capitalism to virtually every country in the World."[9] Its core assumption is that trade, unrestricted by national or local regulation, is good. International standards, determined by the World Trade Organization, aim to provide free rein to market forces. Globalization is the result of conscious political decisions that place international trade above other priorities.[10] Trade once reinforced nationalism. With globalization, trade undermines it.[11] Acquisitions, consolidations, and mergers, however, reduce free-market competition and concentrate power in the hands of a few.[12] A small number of large global corporations are now as powerful, if not more powerful, than many small- and medium-size nation-states.[13]

World Bank structural adjustment policies allow poor countries to address their development loan debt by extending terms of repayment. Restructuring is contingent upon the nation's acceptance of free-trade agreements and substantial restrictions in government spending. This has meant serious restrictions in education, aid to local farmers, and health care. Structural adjustment creates long-term debt that removes hopes for future solvency, leaving poor countries at the mercy of private corporations for meeting the basic needs of their citizens.[14]

One of the downsides of corporate globalization is the polarization of income. While the gross domestic product (GDP) in poorer countries may be growing, very little of this growth is expressed accurately in GDP per capita. Indeed, one of the biggest problems of economic development has been the uneven distribution of income profits and rising inequality. The poorer half of the world's population has a decreasing share, while the upper 5 percent has a markedly increasing share.[15]

Globalization has changed the entire food chain, including suppliers of fertilizers, pesticides, hybrid seed and tractors, as well as grain traders, transportation companies, processors and supermarkets.[16] ConAgra, the largest multinational food production corporation in the United States, is involved in every part of the food chain that begins with the seed and ends on the shelf of the supermarket. Six grain companies control the grain trade in the United States. Three meatpackers—JBS Swift, Tyson, Cargill—control nearly 90 percent of the beef industry.[17] Lacking economic power, farmers are being reduced by giant grain companies to a minimal role in the food system, whereas supranational corporations now rule world food production.[18]

In the United States, 50 percent of the farmland is owned by 4 percent of farm owners. Typically, farmers who own the land do not farm it but hire others. About 38 percent of the farm laborers hired to work the farms are paid either at or below the federal poverty level while working an average of forty-six hours per week.[19] Studies have long shown that towns with absentee ownership of the land have a lower quality of life on many dimensions—worse schools, fewer libraries, inferior community services, and shorter life expectancies.[20] Conditions are much worse for the landless in less-developed countries. The high profits from the multinational food production companies have done little for the workers.[21]

Most of the world's 183 nations depend upon imported food. Canada, France, Australia, Argentina, and the United States export 80 percent of cereal grain. With the U.S. population expected to double in seventy years, the cereal grain now exported to poor countries would be used to feed the addition of 540 million Americans. When American exports cease, countries in Africa and

Asia, now dependent upon imports, will be without food that is essential to their survival.[22]

Subsidies

During a visit to Haiti in 2013, three years after the 7.0 earthquake that devastated the country, former U.S. president Bill Clinton apologized to food aid leaders for the subsidies made to American rice farmers in the 1990s, which subsequently undercut rice production in Haiti. "It may have been good for some of my farmers in Arkansas, but it has not worked," he said. "I have to live every day with the consequences of the lost capacity to produce a rice crop in Haiti to feed those people, because of what I did."[23]

This remark was a reference to the U.S. free trade policies that forced Haiti and other countries to drop protective tariffs or taxes on imported food products, including U.S. subsidized rice. First implemented in 1933 by President Franklin D. Roosevelt in response to the Great Depression, the Agricultural Adjustment Act, or what came to be known as the Farm Bill, arranged for the federal government to pay farmers to stop the production of seven main crops. The intention was to decrease supply and increase demand. In 2012, U.S. taxpayers paid $14 billion in subsidies and crop insurance payouts.[24]

In the context of international trade and the development of large-scale, corporate agriculture, the subsidization of crops has had profound implications for international farmers and small domestic family farmers alike. While the United States produces around 2 percent of global output of rice production (half of it from the state of Arkansas), it is consistently among the top five exporters in the world.[25] With prices driven down, local markets were unable to compete with corporate interests. Villagers in Japan or Haiti purchase rice imported from the United States at a price lower than the rate of local farmers; Haiti imports roughly 80 percent of its rice from the United States.

Oxfam has described the subsidization of agriculture in the United States and Europe as "corporate welfare." In their briefing paper "Dumping on the World," Oxfam describes how sugar policies in the European Union are hampering global efforts to reduce poverty, with big farmers and corporate sugar refineries reaping the benefits of subsidy programs and dumping their surplus sugar on developing countries.[26]

Some policy analysts point out that while U.S. farm policy is highly discriminatory against small-scale agriculture, the focus on subsidies has obscured deeper forces underlying the long-term decline in global farm commodity prices, which are rooted in the market's lack of self-correcting mechanisms.[27] What is needed are price supports, for example, tariff controls on imported goods—which free trade agreements and structural adjustment requirements of the International Monetary Fund and World Bank have largely abolished—and supply management to support the needs of farmers.[28]

While receiving much criticism and calls for reform, the powerful farm lobby and its champions in Congress have prevented meaningful reforms. In 2013, the $1 trillion farm bill gutted funding for food stamp programs while increasing subsidies for rich farmers in a year of record crop prices.[29]

Biotechnology

Although scientific breakthroughs are often heralded as the answer to world hunger, several high-tech corporations are profiting from the global shortage of food. Alongside malnutrition and food insecurity, the biotechnology industry is booming. As of April 2005, the total value of publicly traded U.S. biotech companies was $311 billion.[30] Recently, Ernst & Young analysts estimated that global biotech industry profits for publicly owned companies increased from $80.6 billion in 2010 to $83.6 billion a year later.[31]

In agriculture, biotechnology is focused upon efficiency. This is driven by supranational corporations, such as Monsanto, that have entered the biotechnology industry with genetically modified seeds. The justification for adding fish genes to a tomato has nothing to do with its nutrition or taste but only with its shelf life. Shelf life is important only if we destroy local farms and replace them with transnational farm factories. Nearly $500 million a year is spent on media campaigns to tell us that this is good.[32]

With the introduction of genetically modified (GM) seeds, farmers are asked to sign licensing agreements to use the seeds. They must agree not to share the seeds with family or neighbors, and not to save any seeds for future harvests.[33] For additional protection for the multinationals, a researcher with the U.S. Department of Agriculture has developed a "terminator" gene, backed by Monsanto, to avoid seed piracy. The terminator prevents a seed from germinating. In essence the seed is sterilized and can only be used by the party signing the licensing agreement for that particular seed.[34] The farmer who once saved the best fruits for next year's seeds is then obliged to purchase seeds anew.

Biotechnology and Intellectual Property

Before 1930 the concept of intellectual property over living organisms did not exist. Plants were viewed as being part of the public domain, and their use could not be restricted. The passage of the Plant Variety Protection Act in 1970 in the United States established intellectual property rights for plants.[35] Intellectual property rights result when ownership is claimed for ideas and knowledge. Corporations have been accused of scientific poaching,[36] benefiting from the use of over 70 percent of the genetic pool of agricultural seed and livestock of developing countries without any compensation for the developing country.[37] Traditionally, one could gain a patent for an invented device, but the ideas on which the device was based were public. Watson and Crick did not patent their theory about the molecular structure of DNA. Gene splicing made this patentable because it is the application of the basic theory of the molecular structure of DNA. However, the distinction between public and private domain is becoming blurred:[38]

> The continuous squeezing of biotechnological inventions—particularly the patentability in Europe of inventions related to living matter—into the framework of patent law has obliged the introduction of rather strained legal concepts or blatant irregularities in the application of the law. Much of this tinkering has been prompted, of course, by transnational companies' needs to obtain cross-border protection.[39]

Rice is the single most important crop for feeding humans. Most rice has been grown through history in small paddy fields in China, India, and Indonesia. Now it is being genetically mapped by Syngenta, the world's largest agrochemical firm. It is also a major seller of seeds, just behind Monsanto and DuPont. The patent sought for rice could be applied to flowering plants in general, giving the firm a key foothold for control over agriculture. The firm's extensive lobbying budget and close connections with the Consultative Group on International Agricultural Research (CGIAR) and the UN Food and Agriculture Organization make it well placed to increase its fortunes through genetic modification and patents over seeds.[40]

Genetically modified seeds do not increase the farmer's yield. Monsanto has developed, licensed, and sold a GM soybean crop called Roundup Ready. It actually yields far less than other soybean seeds that are not genetically modified. But promotion by such companies as Asgrow, a Monsanto subsidiary of GM seeds, abounds in seed catalogues. This propaganda is also presented to farmers by major agribusiness through forums and propagated by researchers at the universities who receive government funds for agricultural research.[41] As a result, farmers are placed under great pressure to buy the GM seeds even if they yield less than seeds not genetically modified.

The green revolution of the 1960s and 1970s created designer hybrids of such basic crops as corn, soybeans, and wheat for higher yields and disease resistance. The resulting monoculture places the world's harvest at risk to unknown diseases. The greater the diversity of seeds and crops, the less likely is the system as a whole to be at risk.[42] When Hurricane Mitch hit Central America in 1998, traditional land management systems were found to be much more resilient to this natural disaster. Farms that used the monoculture method had 60 to 80 percent more crop damage, soil erosion, and water loss than those that used traditional farming techniques, such as water conservation, crop mixing, and biological pest control. A focus on this type of resilience from traditional farming methods protects the farmer's future livelihood just as diverse crops reduce the risk of agricultural blight.[43] Diverse crops reduce the risk of agricultural disasters just as diverse investment portfolios reduce risk of financial setbacks.

Seeds are the basis of life but are no longer viewed as part of the public domain. Once patented, no one can use the seeds without paying a royalty. This is true for organic seeds, such as those for colored cotton from Latin America,[44] as well as for genetically engineered seeds for corn, cotton, soybean, and canola owned by Monsanto.[45] Biotechnology has proven to be another tool for the domination of food production by corporate agriculture. As such, it has contributed to the erosion both of the soil and of people's capacity to provide food for their families. Unable to farm their traditional crops in a sustainable manner, they are either driven from the land or forced to produce for the drug trade.

The Privatization of Water

Beyond the sales of patented seeds, corporations have found other ways to make a profit from nature. Consumption of water, worldwide, is doubling every twenty years, more than twice as fast as population growth. In many parts of the world, such as India, Pakistan, northern China, and the western United States, groundwater is utilized at a faster rate than its natural replenishment.[46]

According to the United Nations, more than 1 billion people already lack access to fresh drinking water. Fresh water is a finite resource that accounts for less than one-half of 1 percent of the world's total water stock. It is rapidly being diverted, depleted, and polluted, largely by corporate agriculture. Every fifteen seconds a child dies from a condition associated with unsafe water. By the year 2025, two-thirds of the world's population will be living with serious water deprivation. By that time, fresh water demand is expected to rise to 56 percent more than is currently available. Technologies exist to increase water efficiency, but the global economy does not assure that they will be affordable to farmers.[47]

Recognizing an emerging market for water, global multinationals, such as Monsanto and Bechtel, have sought control of world water systems and supplies. Monsanto, which owns the patent for a water purification process, set forth plans to earn revenues of $420 million during the first decade of the twenty-first century from its water business in India and Mexico. The company estimated correctly that water would become a multibillion-dollar market in the coming decades.[48] The World Bank has accommodated to this new market by a policy of water privatization and full-cost water pricing. Governments are signing away control over water supplies by participating in the North American Free Trade Agreement and in the World Trade Organization. These agreements give transnational corporations the unprecedented right to the water of signatory countries.[49]

Bechtel vs. Bolivia

In 1999, the Bolivian government granted a forty-year concession privatizing the water system of its third-largest city, Cochabamba. A consortium led by the Italian company Water Limited and the U.S. corporation Bechtel immediately raised water prices. With many Bolivians working at a minimum wage of $65 per month, water bills of $20 or more proved an extreme burden. Some could not even afford the permits required by the company for water collection. Thousands of citizens protested for weeks. The Bolivian army killed one, injured hundreds, and arrested coalition leaders. In April 2000, the Cochabamba citizen coalition known as *La Coordinadora* won its demands, and the consortium of corrupt government managers and transnational corporations was obliged to withdraw.[50]

Eighteen months after being forced to leave the country, Bechtel and its co-investor, Abengoa of Spain, filed a $50 million lawsuit against Bolivia to compensate for its investments (estimated at less than $1 million) and lost future profits. The lawsuit was brought before a closed-door trade court operated by the World Bank. The trade court, the International Center for Settlement of Investment Disputes (ICSID), operates in a highly secretive manner; the public and the media are not informed as to where or when the case tribunals meet, who testifies, or what they say. As a report by the Institute for Policy Studies and Food and Water Watch describes it, the World Bank/ICSID dispute resolution process "has given global companies unprecedented power to undermine governments' authority to protect human rights and natural resources and pursue national development strategies."[51] In May 2007, three Latin American countries—including Bolivia—announced that they were ending their participation with the ICSID.

International trade courts aside, it is not easy to win a lawsuit against Bechtel, which *Engineering News-Record* magazine ranks as the largest construction company in the United States. The company's projects have included the Alaska Pipeline, the Hoover Dam, and the San Francisco Bay Bridge. Its work on natural gas pipelines in Algeria has displaced large numbers of people and contributed to a history of violence, as have their refineries in Zambia. In the past century, Bechtel has worked on 19,000 contracts in 140 different countries. The company signs new contracts around the world on a daily basis. Environmental and social impacts of the company's construction activities, such as the Bolivian water project, are rarely reported. Hopes to contest Bechtel's suit against the cooperative water project in Bolivia centered on the company's desire to avoid bad publicity.[52]

On January 19, 2006, Bechtel and its co-investor, Abengoa of Spain, agreed to drop their case in the ICSID. Sources directly involved in the settlement negotiations cited continued international citizen pressure as the reason the companies decided to drop the case.[53] This was the first time that a major corporation has ever dropped a major international trade case as a direct result of global public pressure. The case illustrates the importance of information exchange that goes beyond mainstream media. Equally important, it shows that citizen groups sometimes provide local voices with an opportunity to be heard in the promotion of effective water conservation.

Agriculture and the Production of Narcotics

Factory farms, accompanied by the domination of seeds and water by transnational corporations, have made small farms unprofitable. Former farmers the world over have been transformed into farm laborers, refugees, and pawns in the growth of crops for illegal drugs. The pattern has historical roots.

The concept of war between nation-states is overshadowed in history by the conquest and colonization of most of the world by European nations, particularly Great Britain. In many instances the conquests came against tribal societies, sometimes bribed and often coerced into accepting colonial domination. One major mechanism for control over colonized people was through the distribution of narcotics. In India in the eighteenth century, small-scale farming was forcibly replaced by the British East India Company, with larger cotton plantations and with the massive cultivation of poppies. The extracted opium was shipped to the coastal cities of China, Canton, and Hangchou, where it was initially given away. By 1906, 27 percent of the Chinese male population were users. As production and distribution expanded to create a passive and servile underclass, a worldview created by royal elites espoused their divine right to rule over this depraved group and to justify their own extreme privilege.[54]

The War on Drugs

The war on drugs, the U.S. campaign for drug prohibition, military aid, and intervention, which began in the 1970s, has largely left big narcotics cartels untouched and has not stopped drug laundering through established financial institutions. It is instead a war on drug addicts. Nonviolent first offenders in drug cases are in jail longer, on average, than murderers and other violent criminals. Since the initiation of the federal program Operation Weed and Seed in 1991, there has been an influx of police officers, National Guardsmen, and other federal agents into several U.S. inner cities. By way of aerial and video surveillance, anti-gang and anti-drug sweeps, and identification policies, the government aims to weed out violence, drugs, and gang activity. The program has succeeded in increasing incarceration for drug offenses. With only 5 percent of the world's population, the United States has 25 percent of the world's prison population, making it the world's largest jailer.[55]

The drug war is supported by the pharmaceutical industry, which markets its own legal forms of barbiturates, painkillers, and mood-altering substances. The pharmaceutical lobby is a strong supporter of the war on drugs, which criminalizes drugs labeled illegal.[56] While seed money is distributed to community-based development and social service organizations, funding for the Operation Weed and Seed program had previously been allocated to human services, where it could have been dedicated to improving the infrastructure of the inner cities and to work on correcting the root causes of crime, rather than developing prison and law enforcement systems.[57]

Colombia: Militarizing a Social and Economic Problem

The case of Colombia illustrates what globalization has caused in the transition from local farming to reliance upon drug cartels. Corporate agriculture is dominated by single-crop farms that deplete the soil and require large concentrations of chemical fertilizers and pesticides. With freedom to pass on the costs of soil and water contamination, with economies of scale and with major governmental subsidies, these corporate giants can sell at a price so low that local farmers cannot compete and are displaced. Some are forced to grow one remaining marketable crop, coca.

Colombia has 46 million people, with a 37 percent poverty rate, and as many as 6 million inhabitants living on less than two dollars a day.[58] Putumayo, in the middle of a southern Colombia jungle, has 330,000 residents, mostly farmers. These farmers colonized the area after fleeing the economic poverty and violence in other areas of the country. They grow coca in huge quantities and sell the processed paste to middlemen who distribute it to the United States and Europe. The coca production is in large fields, alongside some legal crops and even cattle, which provide food for the community. The toxic spraying continues despite protests by the farmers that fumigation kills the legal crops along with the coca. Although there is arable land, the farmers are unable to grow legal crops, in part because they are undersold by imports but also because there are few roads to take the crops to market. Coca can be harvested four or five times a year, and once it is reduced to paste can be carried out on horseback. After expenses and taxes paid to the paramilitary or the guerillas, described below, that control the Colombian coca industry, the farmer nets less than $150 a month for growing coca.[59]

Colombia receives extensive aid from the United States, the majority of which is spent on buying military assistance for the government. Since 2000, the United States has supported the Colombian government and military in the form of the Plan Colombia aid package, intended to combat the cultivation and trafficking of drugs through military means. Big beneficiaries have included corporations such as Sikorsky, Lockheed Martin, Monsanto, and Occidental Petroleum, which views military action as a way to secure oil exploration. During the congressional testimony in 2000 for Plan Colombia, the first year Congress passed the aid package, Occidental International Corporation, the company's Washington-based lobbying firm, spent $8.6 million to lobby the U.S. Congress for military aid to Colombia, stating that Colombian oil was very important to the United States because it would reduce the oil imports from the Middle East, describing that region as an unstable area.[60] Occidental Vice President Lawrence Meriage stated that oil drilling could be an alternative to drugs in developing the economy of Colombia.[61] In 2003 and 2004, $98 million and $110 million, respectively, of Plan Colombia's funds were allocated specifically for the protection of the Cano-Limon pipeline with a brigade of U.S.-trained Colombian Special Forces.[62]

Plan Colombia's war on drugs interfaces with a civil war in Colombia that has been going on for half a century. The various groups consist of drug lords, right-wing paramilitary death squads known as AUC (United Self-Defense Groups of Colombia), insurgent left-wing guerillas known as FARC (Revolutionary Armed Forces of Colombia) and ELN (National Liberation Army), and a government army that aligns with the paramilitaries. The guerillas kidnap for ransom, bomb pipelines, recruit child soldiers, and murder security forces and civilians.[63] It is the farmers, including those of land-based indigenous communities, that are most impacted by the Plan Colombia's policies. While some support the guerillas' cause to redistribute the wealth of the Colombian oligarchy to the people of Colombia, farmers are caught in the middle of a war between the guerillas and paramilitary groups, which is financed by drug lords, large landowners, multinational oil firms, and through the taxes farmers pay them for protection.[64]

The AUC has also been financed by the American banana-producing corporation Chiquita. Between 1997 and 2004, Chiquita made almost monthly payments to the AUC, totaling at least $1.7 million. The company claims it had to make payments under the threat from the AUC in order to protect its employees and property. Colombian officials are investigating reports that Chiquita may have also supplied the AUC with arms. In 2001, a Chiquita-owned ship was used in Colombia to unload 3,000 Kalashnikov rifles and more than 2.5 million bullets.[65]

Although there have been movements to address the civil war in Colombia, efforts have largely failed to improve the lives of civilians. In the early 2000s, a paramilitary demobilization process was instituted, removing more than 30,000 individuals from paramilitary organizations. However, human rights advocates believe that this has simply led to the formation of new paramilitary groups. In 2012, Colombia passed the Legal Framework for Peace constitutional amendment, with FARC guerillas initiating peace talks. However, the framework largely grants immunity to guerilla, paramilitary, and government military members and gives the Colombian Congress the authority to exempt entire cases of serious abuses from criminal investigation. Colombia's congressional leaders have been investigated for ties to paramilitary operations. The Colombian army's extrajudicial killings of civilians have largely gone unpunished as they fall under the jurisdiction of military courts. The 2012 Victims and Restitution Law, which aims to return millions of acres of land to internally displaced Colombian people, has been slow to enact change, and many persons seeking restitution are intimidated by threats and attacked by paramilitary groups maintaining control.[66]

While paramilitary death squads invade villages under the pretense of looking for those who support the guerillas, their main targets are labor and community leaders, human rights workers, and teachers. In a continent severely marred by human rights abuses, Colombia has compiled one of the worst records of all South American nations. More than 4 million Colombians have been internally displaced, and more than 100,000 continue to be displaced each year, making it one of the world's largest populations of internally displaced people.[67]

The United Nations and humanitarian organizations such as Human Rights Watch and Amnesty International year after year have denounced Plan Colombia. Human Rights Watch has highlighted that the United States does not enforce human rights conditions, even though under the auspice of military aid they are required to do so.[68] Amnesty International describes Plan Colombia as "a failure in every respect," arguing that "human rights in Colombia will not improve until there is a fundamental shift in U.S. foreign policy."[69] At this writing, the U.S. Congress approved allocations to Plan Colombia in the fiscal 2014 congressional budget.

The pattern of leaving people with no options for local agriculture, forcing them to rely on drug trafficking, and suppressing them militarily is repeated in Afghanistan and Burma with the production of opium.

Afghanistan: Opium and Intervention

Afghanistan's inhospitable terrain has steep mountains and sweeping deserts, yet it remains a strategic gateway to the trade route between Europe and India. As a result, Afghanistan's history has always involved fighting off invaders, from Alexander the Great in 328 B.C. to the Huns, the Turks, the Arabs, and imperial Britain. In 1979, the Soviet Union invaded Afghanistan, responding to U.S. -sponsored efforts to foment violent protest among Muslims in the eastern Soviet Union. The Soviets were met by Afghani resistance fighters known as the mujahideen, who were supported by the United States, Britain, Pakistan, Saudi Arabia, and the United Arab Emirates. In 1989, the USSR withdrew, leaving the land in ruin and the warring factions in chaos. Civil war ensued in which tribes fought for control. By 1996, the fundamentalist Islamic Taliban movement ruled most of Afghanistan but was met with resistance from the Northern Alliance, supported by Russia, Tajikistan, and Uzbekistan.[70] The legacy of that war includes a country with a 64 percent illiteracy rate, a reported 48 percent of its children suffering from malnutrition, and a life expectancy of 46 years.[71]

Afghanistan is composed of a complex group of people, worldly through their contacts with traders and conquerors, yet isolated by their terrain and tribal structure. The existing tribal system emerged 250 years ago from the province of Iran. At that time, it was agreed that each tribe would be governed by its own leaders. This type of tribal federalism remains even as the U.S.-led coalition attempts to superimpose a central government.[72] Over the last 250 years, there has been an intermixing of many different groups. More than thirty distinct languages are native to Afghanistan, and there are ten major tribes.[73] Afghans have never moved from an agricultural tribal existence, and as a result have not acquired a sense of nationalism. Each Afghan is either a Pashtoon (about 40 percent of the population) or a member of a smaller tribe such as the Uzbek, Tajik, or Hazareh tribes. Lacking a national identity, Afghans do not refer to themselves as Afghans until they leave Afghanistan.[74]

Despite their difficulties, most Afghans continue to live as farmers and herders of sheep and goats, as they have for centuries. Many are nomads with no permanent homes, and they move with their herds. Their sparse existence is upon a land that has been destroyed by years of war. As a result of the ten-year war with the USSR, there are 10 million landmines that must be avoided by children and adults. Afghanistan continues to be one of the poorest countries in the world. Following a three-year drought starting in 2000, the worst in thirty years, only 12 percent of the people had safe drinking water.[75] This has been devastating to a country where 85 percent of the estimated 21 million people are dependent upon agriculture. As a result of successive droughts, rivers used for drinking water and irrigation are almost dry, livestock have perished, and rural economies have collapsed.[76] There are few economic options in Afghanistan beyond labor migration. Becoming a mercenary or cultivating opium are the two primary options.[77] The global trade in illegal drugs generates billions of dollars in profits for the refiners and distributors, but not for the growers. In early 2000, Afghanistan became the largest opium producer, commanding 75 percent of the world's market. The poppy plant is a much better crop than wheat because it is drought resistant and every part of the plant can be used. Its cultivation is also labor intensive so that jobs are provided, and it can be harvested several times a year.

In July 2000, the Taliban leader Mullah Mohammed Omar, for religious reasons, banned opium poppy cultivation in Afghanistan. His edict became the greatest drug moratorium in modern history.[78] The CIA estimated that drug production dropped from 4,042 tons to 81.6 tons. Many believe that substance abuse can only be addressed by providing treatment for addicts and offering meaning in life for young people. But to the extent that production of illicit drugs contributes to the problem, the change in Afghanistan might be acknowledged as one of the greatest accidental accomplishments of drug enforcement.[79]

The paradox of the militarily mandated solution may be seen in other outcomes of imposed poverty and degradation. One of these is the incitement to strike back violently. Six months before the suicide bombings of the World Trade Center, President G. W. Bush's administration provided assistance to the Taliban as part of its own crusade, the militarization of the war on drugs.[80]

With the Taliban's loss of power, farmers have returned to opium cultivation. A fifty-four-year-old farmer describes how with ten children and twenty-eight people in his household, there is no other way to survive. From his 2.5 acres of land, he can sell the opium base at $100 per pound. This is 100 times more than what wheat and vegetables will bring. Without opium, his entire family would starve. In the global market, the opium will be worth billions of dollars and will supply millions of addicts worldwide.[81]

The farmers agree that poppy cultivation violates Islamic beliefs, but they also point out there is no industry; they are hungry, impoverished, and without choices.[82] One poppy farmer said that his message to the world is to help establish industries in Afghanistan. He views the Afghani people as diligent workers who would welcome the chance to work in factories. But there are none.[83] What the poppy farmer may not realize is that sweatshop factories in Mexico, Indonesia, and Vietnam have increased the poverty in those countries for all but a few. In Afghanistan, unlike Iran, whose economy is bolstered by the production of oil, poverty will continue to be a strong incentive for the cultivation of opium.[84]

Hundreds of millions of dollars of U.S. and British taxpayers' money have been spent on the eradication of the drug trade, but without positive outcomes. As of this writing, opium cultivation has reached record levels.[85] Some scholars argue that the U.S. and UK program of eradication is ill-conceived and undermines its own objectives. Crop eradication hurts poor farmers (who use cash from opium futures contracts to feed their families over the winter) and makes drug traders richer. After the announcement of crop eradication, prices increased from $90 to $400 per kilo.[86] And because opiates—raw or refined—have a long shelf life, traders stockpile crops for resale at higher prices.

Researchers explain that if stabilizing the economy and democracy in Afghanistan are truly the goal, rural communities need alternatives to the credit, employment, and cash incomes that opium provides. In the world market, drugs are the only item that Afghanistan has to exchange. Afghanistan does have the location for a pipeline for oil to the Caspian Sea, but the short booms created by massive construction projects replace what viable resources people had before. Such projects do not support small farms, schools, or medical facilities. Instead they devastate the ecology, leaving people as impoverished as they were before.

Both the United States and Britain see the drug trade as a threat to Afghanistan's economy and to buttressing a centralized government in the model of Western democracies.[87] But a military occupation, insensitive to the history and culture of the region, has cast into doubt the idea that either democracy or legitimate economic development can be attained by military force. There has been no justice for thousands of Afghanistan's civilians killed in U.S. and NATO operations. The U.S. military justice system does not hold its soldiers accountable for the unlawful killing of civilians.[88]

Burma (Myanmar): Oppressive Governments and Opium

Burma is a country rich in resources and fertile farmland. As a result of British rule, there has been bitter hatred between lowland Burmese and the highlanders, which has kept the country divided, isolated, and therefore prone to military takeovers.[89]

Between 1988 and 2011, Burma was ruled by a brutal military regime. The military government, the State Peace and Development Council (SPCD), changed the country's name from Burma to Myanmar.[90, 91] Although the Burmese people voted to oust the military through free elections in 1990, the regime refused to yield and continued to dominate by using forceful tactics, such as torture, slave labor, and the rape of ethnic minority women, to suppress dissent. Repeatedly condemned by the United States and the United Nations for its human rights violations, the country has one of the worst human rights records in the world.

Under the SPCD regime, all land in Burma was state-owned. Farmers' incapacity to own and mortgage land has had a severe impact on agricultural production. Land tenancy by the regime resulted in a reduced incentive for investment or improvement in the land, or incentive to produce.[92] For decades, United Nations, United States, and other aid programs have sought to support the cultivation of rubber, maize, and other crops, particularly in the Shan state, which is the seat of opium production. For Burmese families, growing poppies remains the best financial option; the United Nations Office of Drugs and Crime estimates that poppies provide typically half of a Shan family's annual income of $920.[93]

Burma's military and officials have long made money providing protection for growers and smugglers.[94] Researchers have argued that although the state's involvement in the drugs trade was driven by the need to co-opt insurgent groups, the state's involvement in the drugs trade has become a means through which state power has been developed and maintained.[95] As in the case of Afghanistan and Colombia, scholar Patrick Meehan highlights that policy must move beyond an emphasis on drug eradication in supply countries such as Burma and instead "actively engage in developing a better understanding of these emerging political complexes and a consideration of how they may become more development oriented."[96]

Since the country's movement toward democracy in 2010, drug production has increased. Burma continues to be the largest opium producer after Afghanistan. The former members of the military junta have been absorbed into new positions of leadership. While pro-democracy leader and Nobel Peace Prize–winner Aung San Suu Kyi was elected to the Burmese parliament after more than twenty years of living under house arrest, the popular leader is barred from the presidency due to continued opposition from the Burmese parliament.

The Obama administration eased financial and investment sanctions against Burma, restoring full diplomatic relations, and reestablishing a U.S. Agency for International Development mission in the country. In light of evidence of continuing human rights abuses, however, the House Foreign Affairs Committee created the Burma Human Rights and Democracy Act of 2014, HR 4377, to put forward actions to ensure that issues of military rule and abuses are addressed.

The Evolving Story of People and Land

If a timeline of how long human beings have been on earth is represented as twenty-four hours, then agriculture has been on earth for five minutes. Prior to that, humans were hunters and gatherers, and each family related to others in an interdependent way for food, shelter, and clothing. With the advent of agriculture, human beings have increased 10,000-fold during the last five minutes, and most of the increase has occurred in the last ten seconds. However, in the last few seconds, food production has gone from a community partnership to global domination, partly through the use of biotechnology and patents.[97] Land, food, and water throughout history were considered the sacred gifts of nature that existed to support life. Rapidly and without reflection, we are allowing a small number of companies to assume control over them. The ways to restore viability to the world of food production are known, but there must be a will to take the steps.

When people are displaced from viable local enterprises, they seek such options as living-wage jobs that the global economy has not been willing to offer. To survive, many will try to emigrate; some may engage in drug production or other illegal enterprises, including prostitution; some will join violent revolutionary groups; and others will try to organize protests to obtain food and justice. A military response to any of these activities ignores the prime cause of displacement by the global economy and can only make matters worse.

Separating people from food is violence. There are millions of people in impoverished countries such as Colombia, Afghanistan, and Burma who are starving because they are unable to grow food or are too poor to buy food that is available. In order to survive, they are forced to use the land to grow opium or coca to supply the global markets. Colombia, Afghanistan, and Burma are the major suppliers of all the illegal opium and heroin in the world. To avoid hunger and death from starvation, the poor people of these impoverished countries must grow an illegal substance that will ultimately kill many people in all parts of the world.

Separating people from the land is costly. We can sustain such activity only by turning our heads away from the violence it is inflicting upon people. When we stop treating nature as precious and see it only as something to be exploited, then we are in danger of losing it. Separation threatens to reduce the spiritual renewal that the land and the waters have given us.

The issues of globalization do not have to do with the increasing interdependence of the global community, nor even with whether regulations that affect international trade are good or bad. Rather, the issue is who participates in the decisions and whether values that reflect the long-term sustainability of communities and of the planet are heard.[98] Taiwan and South Korea are sometimes looked upon as early successes of economic globalization, but both have paid a heavy price in environmental destruction, another common casualty of market-driven development.[99]

An Alternative: Agroecology and the Food Sovereignty Movement

Recent advances in ecological research suggest that purchasing pure protected tracts will not stem the tide of devastating fertile land. Work with rural social movements is likely more important than the major work of large conservation organizations to purchase protected areas. Solidarity with the small farmers around the world who are currently struggling to attain food sovereignty may prove the only path to prevent the increasing depletion of life forms, including our own.[100]

Food sovereignty arose in the early 1980s in Central America as a response to the structural adjustment programs and their requisite dissolution of state support for agriculture, and the influx of food imports from the United States. At that time, the movement aimed for national food security and the right of peasants to continue being producers.[101] As defined in 1996 by the national peasant movement Via Campesina that coined the term, food sovereignty is "the right of each nation to maintain and develop its own capacity to produce its basic foods respecting cultural and productive diversity."[102]

Utilizing agroecological methods that blend modern, systems-informed agricultural methods with traditional cultural approaches to raising food and caring for the land, food sovereignty empowers land-based communities to self-determine food production, distribution, and consumption using cultural practices that are ecologically and socially responsible—and strongly opposes corporate-driven agriculture and transnational companies that destroy people and nature. On the ground, such projects include the creation of seed banks to save and exchange native seeds and combine permaculture and traditional cultural methods to manage pests, increase nutrients in the soil, and maintain water. At the political level, however, communities fighting for food sovereignty organize efforts against corporate-driven agriculture, focusing on the issues of free trade, land grabbing, labor practices, and climate change, among others. In urban communities, practitioners of food sovereignty are addressing the lack of healthy food in poor urban communities and the historical structural inequities brought to bear on these communities.

A change is needed from the values of the market to the values of participation and caring. The task will require a strong sense of solidarity with our sisters and brothers, which can be difficult because some in the rich nations may want to continue to benefit from the super exploitation of those in the poor nations. In the United States and in other affluent countries, we will have to examine and reduce our own consumption of valuable and finite world resources so that they will be available for others and for future generations. Included in the task is a need to renew our love for the land and its fruits and to support local alternatives that honor the environment. Finally, it will require us to pressure or persuade those with great wealth and power that people, along with all the species who share our planet, deserve a viable habitat and a voice in how it is to be used.

5—Networks of Power

Behind the ostensible government sits enthroned an invisible government owing no allegiance and acknowledging no responsibility to the people. To destroy this invisible government, to befoul the unholy alliance between corrupt business and corrupt politics is the first task of the statesmanship of the day.

—THEODORE ROOSEVELT, April 19, 1906

THIS CHAPTER EXAMINES THE TOPIC of power. Power is a phenomenon that is invisible to the naked eye, and one that is more deeply surrounded by taboos than was the topic of sex in Victorian days. We focus on the movers and shakers, the concentrations of power, from which flow decisions that contribute greatly to global violence. The lens of power is not the only one that frames our reality. There is also a reality that is captured in the daily lives of people finding joy and meaning, often under circumstances of war, displacement, illness, and loss. There are larger cultural and spiritual realties that connect us to the shared symbols of religion, community, supernatural deities, chiefs, people who achieved iconic status, and to special places. There is also a marketed reality of goods, sales pressures, or demands for competitive success to fill the void of emptiness in people's lives, and concerted efforts to place the blame for this void on hapless outsiders or petty criminals. Each of these realities is important and visible on a daily basis. The reality of large corporate decisions that determine how much we earn, who gets to eat, what dangers to our health will be removed, what candidates and issues will be on the public agenda, who will benefit from the human and natural resources of our communities, whether and where we shall go to war—these are part of the reality of concentrated power that are mostly out of view. This chapter brings them into the open.

What Is Power?

Power is the capacity to exert the effort we need to attain our wishes and to meet our needs. There is a dearth of power among most of the displaced people of the world. Typically one's power is relative to the strength of others who may compete for the same objectives. Power is severely lacking among those who have no choice but to live in a highly toxic environment or in a war zone, or who have no chance to attend college without joining the military. We speak of empowering such people as a means to enhance their choices. Some who are well positioned have extreme power to make decisions that will affect the lives of many others, thereby seriously limiting the amount of power or choice that others will need merely to live with dignity. Power can be abused, and power can be corrupting both for those conferring it and for those seeking it. The creation of the modern nation-state with great autonomous powers of sovereignty brought with it a critical distinction in social classes in which some few had special access to authorities and others did not.

Networks of Power

One way to look at power is as an attribute of a person—big muscles, big weapons, a big bank account, or an unrelenting motivation to compete. Looking at power in that way conceals the fact that an individual can only express power in relation to others and that power is itself embedded in a set of relationships, often hidden relationships. Chapter 2 indicated that destructive behavior is not merely an attribute of individuals but rather a function of circumstances; similarly, power is better understood as something that resides within a network of connections rather than within individuals.

Sociologist G. William Domhoff argues that the critical players are organizations. Organizations are little more than a set of positions and rules. The rules are agreed-upon ways of doing things to achieve some specific purpose. Organizations may be informal, such as a family or a support group, or formal, such as a corporation or a government agency. In either case, they typically have identifiable boundaries and memberships.[1] But in actual practice we find family members sometimes relating to fictive kin, that is, to non-kin, as if they were members of their own family. And with agencies, we often find key transactions with representatives of other organizations sometimes proving more important than those within the agencies themselves. It is useful to study actual exchanges without making reference to a particular defined entity such as the family, the neighborhood, the workplace, or the church, club, or company to which an individual claims membership. The concept of networks can clue us in to the actual transactions that take place.

Network Analysis: Revealing Networks of Power

Borrowing from an abstract mathematical theory and from efforts by anthropologists to study the latent social groupings that Western biases might conceal, the theory of network analysis has been revived. The concepts are seductively simple. It will be helpful to ignore, for the moment, the qualities of individuals and instead to focus upon a web or network of exchanges between individuals. Pretend that each person is but a dot in a big matrix. Each dot has connections with some other dots. The lines that connect them represent actual exchanges, transactions, interactions, and even attachments from one to another. They might consist of information, or exchanges of money or goods, or of loving care, or any of the many forms of social support. The transactions may be symmetrical, or they may go in only one direction. Some of the links are used continually, some rarely, and some only indirectly through connections to a third or more distant party. Some are ongoing connections, others singular happenings. The exchanges might as easily be applied to diffusion of new ideas or to transfers of small arms, of cocaine, or of political favors. The links might be reciprocal or unidirectional, frequent or rare. Network maps can be drawn from the point of one individual, your grandma or the Secretary of State, or with a defined group such as your household or the Defense Department, as the point of origin. Most important, the framework places no restrictions on what links might arise. This web or network will help to uncover a latent structure to show who, whether formally or informally, is linked to whom. Modern society is marked by rapidly changing acquaintances, marriages, residential locations, and jobs. Mapping a network of actual interactions

can be an important tool in determining whether the old familiar sources of identity, caring, and support have been lost or are merely being replaced by newer and
more flexible arrangements. The potential to reveal the less obvious underlying
networks is particularly useful in the study of power.

For the purpose of this chapter, we examine networks of power in order to
see who is central to these as well as who is excluded. Whose special interests
are intrinsically protected by their network connections, and who gets left out
of the vital connections needed to thrive in today's world? To find out who is
central in a powerful network, one would start with an examination of the multiple positions held by the occupant of an important political office. Take former secretary of the navy Gordon England. Secretary England was appointed
the seventy-second secretary of the U.S. Navy in May 2001. In this position Mr.
England led America's Navy and Marine Corps and was responsible for more
than 800,000 military and civilian personnel and an annual budget of more than
$120 billion. He joined the Department of Homeland Security in January 2003.
Prior to joining the administration of President G. W. Bush, Mr. England was
executive vice president of General Dynamics Corporation (GD), where he was
responsible for two major corporate sectors: information systems and technology
and international contracting. Previously, he had served as executive vice president of the Combat Systems Group, president of General Dynamics Fort Worth
aircraft company (later Lockheed), president of General Dynamics Land Systems
Company, and as the principal of a mergers and acquisition consulting company.
Such corporate-government connections are common. But corporations are also
connected with one another. One can track the board memberships of England's
GD colleagues as well as the accounting and law firms that serve GD. Among the
GD board are retired generals and admirals, directors of major financial firms
(JP Morgan Chase, LLC investment banking), the food industry (Sara Lee), and
pharmaceuticals (Schering Plough).[2]

The web of interconnections extends even further. With high-level government and corporate officials, one finds multiple links to certain financial institutions, law firms, accounting firms, and trade organizations such as the Petroleum
Institute or PhRMA. The networks include links to managers of major media
corporations, to research centers, and to think tanks. People central in these powerful networks are important not for their knowledge, intelligence, or their ethics
but for their connections. They are sought after for boards of universities and

major medical centers, where they can help attract donors as well as play a part in assuring the supply of trained persons to run and to serve the greater society in accord with unstated rules not to question the unfairness of policies that preserve gross inequality.

The most comprehensive use of network analysis to identify the central core of interconnected transnational corporations (TNC) was done by a team from the Swiss Federal Institute of Technology in Zurich. Using Orbis 2007, a database listing 37 million companies and investors worldwide, the authors identified all 43,060 TNCs and the share ownerships linking them. They then constructed a model of which companies controlled others through shareholding networks. These data were coupled with each company's operating revenues to map the structure of economic power. When the team untangled the web of ownership, it tracked most holdings back to a "super-entity" of 147 tightly knit companies. All of their ownership was held by members of the super-entity that controlled 40 percent of the total wealth in the network. In effect, less than 1 percent of the companies were able to control 40 percent of the entire network. Most were financial institutions, with the top twenty including Barclays Bank, JPMorgan Chase, and Goldman Sachs.[3] While not united on every issue, the network of 147 TNCs has the power to control the political and military agenda sufficiently to protect its shared interests in a system that assures and justifies great inequality and structural violence (as described in chapters 3 and 4).

Network analysis provides an excellent tool for examination of the social exclusivity of the super-rich, who have used their connections to amass ever-greater portions of wealth. They conceal their power over policy by making governments dependent upon their economic decisions and candidates dependent upon their financial support. In one example, the U.S. Supreme Court decided that the identities of those who met secretly with U.S. Vice President Dick Cheney to draft an energy policy need not be revealed. The consequences of such collaboration are that governments find it perfectly legal to provide major tax loopholes for multinational corporations. The fact that local contractors who provide low-cost services and barter exchanges are not in attendance at such meetings explains why government agencies treat them less generously. Lacking a seat at the table, local contractors are frequently harassed for evading taxes or violating ordinances[4] even while the government subsidizes the efforts of the largest corporations and does little to curtail their environmental abuses or tax evasions. We shall return later to the issue of exclusive elite groups that exercise unaccountable power.

Creating Authority

Those who hold great power over others rely less frequently upon brute force than upon claims that their positions give them legitimate authority. They renew this authority by reiterating their ability to control the rewards and the punishments of others, but also by claims to their legitimacy in accordance with cultural beliefs. In a democracy the belief is that the rules and decisions made are accountable to the wishes of the people. The belief is at best an ideal, and often a myth fanned by those with power. It is a myth that enables the largest purveyors of power to pass unnoticed.

In the United States the myth has been fueled by three important Supreme Court decisions. The first, *Santa Clara v. Southern Pacific Railroad* (1886), was the original case extending to corporations the Fourteenth Amendment due process and equal-rights protections originally intended for former slaves. Two other decisions, *Buckley v. Valeo* and *Bellotti v. First National Bank of Boston*, in the 1970s established that money for use in political activities is a form of free speech protected by the first amendment of the Bill of Rights and therefore may not be restricted. Other cases based on these rulings affect campaign spending and make it impossible to elect persons to state and national office who are unable to attract massive funding. These Supreme Court decisions remove much of the power of people to have their governments protect them against abuses by corporations.[5] The decisions ultimately have allowed corporations to become powerful, autonomous entities.

Effects of Concentrated Corporate Growth and Expansion

A business in which a local owner in a small town must face customers and employees on a daily basis will want to combine entrepreneurial ingenuity with accountability to the community. Such businesses do not typically sell shares in the financial markets and, unless squeezed by low-cost chain stores, do not have to expand continuously for their survival. Large corporations, by contrast, are designed to require continued growth of profits. By accumulating capital they provide options for exploration, investment, technology, mass production, and exploitation on a level that created the industrialized world. During some periods of this expansion, corporations were obliged to share the rewards of their success. A balance between the power of the largest automakers and the unions supplying their workforce, for example, permitted a period of great profitability while assuring workers a doorway into a world of reasonably secure employment, a five-day workweek, paid vacation time, and health insurance. However, an increasingly global workforce and continued pressures to increase profitability, built directly into the corporate system, upset this balance and led predictably to the destructive use of resources and of people.

The need to expand required that all countries should be available as sources of needed raw materials and as markets for consumer products. Dating from the birth of post–First World War experiments in social welfare and extending to the present time of opposition to debt-driven austerity, pressures arose to challenge unbridled expansion, State-owned or socialist enterprises limited such growth and were viewed with great alarm. In contemporary market economies, the welfare state has, however, provided a measure of free or inexpensive education, housing, and public parks for the entire society. The welfare state served to limit the desperation of people who work for meager wages, but it was also viewed as a burden to corporate taxpayers. In the Depression of the 1930s, the declining power of individual companies and declining rates of profitability were accompanied by other corporate fears. In Great Britain the threat of nationalization and of worker participation in corporate governance seemed real. In the United States, government intervention to improve public welfare was viewed as an obstacle to corporate growth.

In the 1970s major officers of large corporations in the United States and Great Britain responded. They formed what Michael Useem calls the "Inner Circle," a semi-autonomous network designed to provide a centralized corporate force to mobilize the interests of corporate capitalism.[6] Since corporations are legally autonomous entities, this network helped to provide an institutionalized form of corporate capitalism. It clearly distinguished the interests of the large corporate investors as a class and provided a corporate logic for a centralized and concerted advocacy.

A select group of corporate officials were, according to Useem's evidence, able to take on a leading role in consultations with the highest levels of national governments. They worked in the support of political candidates and in the governance of foundations and universities. They created a highly visible public defense of the free-enterprise system. One major goal of this network was, and continues to be, the promotion of a better political climate for big business. It engages in image building through philanthropy, including generous support for cultural programs. It also works by issue advertising, not tied to selling products but to shaping public opinion in its favor. Finally, the inner network has taken on a major role in financing political campaigns. A main goal is to control the power of the media that, in the United States, they consider far too liberal. Paradoxically, these same elites own the larger media outlets and constrain the messages that define public reality (see chapter 7).

On the media front, the influence of corporate America is highly enhanced, directly through media mergers and indirectly through high corporate advertising budgets. The corporate resources for advertising, public relations, and sales have permitted their extensive involvement in the packaging and selling of legislation and of candidates. The interventions of this "Inner Circle" have been extremely successful. President Reagan and Prime Minister Thatcher were partly products of business mobilizations. They lowered taxation, reduced government (except military) spending, lifted controls on business, and installed cutbacks on unemployment benefits and welfare.

The influence upon legislation is disturbingly direct. The American Legislative Exchange Council (ALEC) is the largest, nonpartisan, individual public-private membership association of state legislators in the United States. It has more than 2,000 members. Its mission is to advance "free-market, limited government and federalism at the state level through a nonpartisan public-private partnership of America's state legislators, members of the private sector and the general public."[7] Its twenty-three-member board of directors is composed entirely of state legislators. But it also has a "private enterprise board" of corporate representatives, including GlaxoSmithKline, PhRMA, Pfizer, AT&T, Koch Companies Public Sector, Altria (formerly Philip Morris) Client Services, ExxonMobil, and State Farm Insurance. Legislators join for $50 per year; private sector members join for between $7,000 and $25,000.

ALEC uses its funds from tax-deductible contributions to host closed gatherings of corporate officials with legislators. In these meetings legislation is drafted and then presented by the legislators. The group, largely unknown to the public, gained publicity for its role in promoting "stand your ground" legislation sought by the gun industry and considered responsible for the killing in 2012 of an unarmed teenager by a self-appointed stalker. As a result, a few corporate sponsors withdrew. Following that, the *New York Times* noted a likely violation of the group's tax-exempt status: "The secret world of undisclosed political contributions is in desperate need of sunlight."[8] The Internal Revenue Service and New York State's attorney general investigated whether nonprofit groups took tax-deductible contributions and then used them for partisan political purposes. Complaints were brought against ALEC, the National Chamber Foundation of the U.S. Chamber of Commerce, and Crossroads GPS, founded by Republican Party fundraiser Karl Rove. All these groups were spending tax-deductible dollars backing corporation friendly policies and candidates, essentially acting as corporate-funded lobbying groups.[9] Full disclosure of such corporate political spending is the aim of many good-government groups, such as the Center for Public Integrity.

One consequence of large corporate links to legislation is seen in the permission of large, supposedly regulated service corporations in phone, Internet, television, credit cards, electric utilities, water services, banking, and health services to jack up prices to consumers by the addition of difficult-to-understand fees to their bills. One survey showed that at least 97 percent of Americans were unable to understand their phone bills. We are all cheated, but when low-income subscribers to essential services are driven into debt or bankruptcy, a measure of structural violence has occurred.[10]

The symbiotic relationship between corporations and legislative government is but one example of "overlapping and intersecting socio-spatial networks of power."[11] Mann's Four Networks Theory of Power defines ideological, economic, military, and political realms of power; in each case it is the organizational resources for action that make one realm or another dominant. However, as in the case of the relationship between corporations (economic) and government (political), when two organizational realms come together in a symbiotic relationship, it not only benefits but strengthens them both.[12] Such has been the case of the military and economic realms in modern times.

The Military-Industrial Complex

In his farewell address in 1961, after eight years in the White House, Dwight Eisenhower warned of the "grave implications" of the conjunction of the military establishment and the arms industry:

> In the councils of government, we must guard against the acquisition of unwarranted influence, whether sought or unsought, by the military-industrial complex. The potential for the disastrous rise of misplaced power exists and will persist.[13]

The danger of this centralized power is that it directs U.S. foreign policy in a way that assumes the legitimacy and the inevitability of armed conflict and the absolute requisite of military spending for preparedness—without taking into account either the full range of domestic consequences or the public will.

The Military-Industrial Link

In modern times the military-industrial linkages have emerged as major concentrations of power. Contracts and subcontracts for military supplies, equipment, and bases are extremely widespread. Local communities that need the jobs will fight against the reduction of military spending. The Defense Department contracts provide opportunity for risk-free investments. The federal government is the sole customer, and contracts cover cost overruns in which profits increase when the contractor spends, or wastes, more than the estimate of the original bid. Equipment that is defective, used, or destroyed needs to be replaced by extending contracts. The details of these transactions are typically out of public view. Corporate facilities are sometimes employed directly for covert military operations, and contractors have become mainstays of a privatized military force. Most important, there is a revolving door of individuals moving from high-level military positions and from military appropriation positions in government to corporate boards, and from corporate contractors to government.

Career military professionals and corporate contractors create a specialized lobby. They serve both as a provocateur for military actions and an opinion force for the assumption that military force is the essential ingredient for national security. The military-industrial centers support groups that are ideologically driven by justifications for violent defense of God and country. The language of evangelical leaders helps to sustain the essential image of a godless enemy, while veterans' organizations are used to glorify and provide justification for the sacrifices of soldiers. The military-industrial complex is perpetuated by a massive federal defense budget and driven by a private industry reaping huge profits from military activities. Opportunistic relationships between political leaders, military personnel, and defense contractors grease this well-oiled machine.

National Defense Budget

The conjunction of the military and industry was strong during the Second World War and expanded throughout the years of the Cold War. The financial connections increased greatly with the G. W. Bush administration. U.S. Department of Defense budgets are somewhat unreliable estimates of the costs of war. Costs of nuclear weapons development come under the budget of the Department of Energy; care for veterans is not in the DOD budget; nor have the defense budgets included spending for the Iraq and Afghan wars. As of the end of 2012, Congress had already granted over $1.4 trillion for operations in Iraq and Afghanistan.[14]

The U.S. national defense budget in 2012 came to $716 billion. Compared to other departments within the United States in 2012, the next largest budget requests were for education and health, $139 billion and $361 billion, respectively. Over half of all federal spending is allocated for the military.[15] Compared to military spending in other nations, this was more than was spent by the next thirty countries combined and more than six times the amount spent by China, the next largest spender.[16]

To put these extraordinary numbers in perspective, in 2005 the U.S. military budget (not including spending for Iraq and Afghan wars) exceeded the combined military budgets for China, Russia, and the six "rogue" states: Cuba, Iran, Libya, North Korea, Sudan, and Syria. Their expenditures came to only 30 percent of U.S. military spending in the same year.[17] Now Nobel Laureate economist Joseph Stiglitz and his co-author, Linda Bilmes, reevaluating costs of the Iraq war, including the costs for rehabilitating injured veterans and interest on debts accrued to fund the war, find their 2008 estimates to be low. Their updated estimates now exceed $3 trillion.[18] American taxpayers are paying these costs. The average American taxpayer, however, may not be outraged or even aware of this expense because such information is not clearly or accurately presented to them (see chapter 7). The name War Department was changed to Defense Department to accentuate its continuing role. Its actual activity might more accurately have earned the name "Department of Foreign Intervention."

The Industry of Defense

The defense industry is quick to point out that military research and development (R&D) programs have driven the rapid advancement of technology. These military R&D programs push development in the private sector, which leads to mass production and lower prices for such items as computer processors, cell phones, high-tech cars, and appliances. As the argument goes, technological advancement is valuable—not just profitable—because it makes the military more efficient and safe, presumably saving lives.

> It takes far fewer people to fight and direct wars today than it did even a decade ago. That's because the speed and power of the front-line soldier have been so greatly amplified by smart weapons and smart delivery systems, and because accurate information now moves so easily up the chain of command. . . . Our civilian sector gave our soldiers the tools they needed to bring this war to its mercifully quick conclusion.[19]

There was, however, no "mercifully quick conclusion" to the U.S.-led war in Iraq. One tragic irony is that the technological advances most basic to the protection of U.S. troops—body armor—had been denied to them.[20] In light of this evidence, it appears safety is not the primary motivation for the advancement of technology.

Another argument in favor of technological development and private industry is that outsourcing as many tasks as possible to private contractors allows the military to be more efficient by focusing on combat. From the design and maintenance of high-tech helicopters to laundry detail, recruiting, even combat itself, such tasks are now performed by private companies. In the late 1990s, KBR (Kellogg, Brown, and Root), a Halliburton subsidiary, provided nearly all the food, water, laundry, mail, and heavy equipment to the roughly 20,000 U.S. troops stationed in the Balkans. During the first Gulf War, there was approximately one contractor for every one hundred soldiers. A year into the Iraq war, there was approximately one contractor for every ten soldiers.[21]

Having so many civilians "in the field" has prompted complicated questions for which military officials have no definitive or consistent answers. For example, should information-technology consultants carry arms? If employees of private companies run from their posts, are they considered deserters? If taken prisoner, will they be considered POWs covered by the Geneva Convention? Or, if they detain prisoners, are they responsible to comply with the directives of the Geneva Convention?

Profit is a clear motivation in the rise of the defense industry. For its service in the Balkans in the late 1990s, KBR was paid $3 billion.[22] Between 2002 and July 2004, KBR was paid over $11 billion for their services in Afghanistan and Iraq.[23] More recently, KBR has come under scrutiny (and found guilty of criminal acts) pertaining to their seeming lack of concern for the health and safety of their employees and related military personnel. Although they have been ordered to pay damages of $85 million to several Oregon National Guardsmen,[24] they continue to receive million-dollar contracts from the Department of Defense, such as the $35,833,635 contract awarded to them by the U.S. Navy at the end of 2012.[25] Auditing for the Department of Defense is outsourced to private accounting firms; many of these accounting contracts have been awarded through no-bid deals as are most of the contracts they must audit. The amount of sheer unaccountable waste and giveaways is astounding.[26]

Over the six-year period between fiscal year 1998 and fiscal year 2003, the Center for Public Integrity examined more that 2.2 million defense contract actions totaling $900 billion in authorized expenditures.[27] The Center determined that half of the Defense Department's budget went to private contractors. Only 40 percent of Pentagon contracts were conducted under "full and open competition"; in other words, over half of them fall under the category of no-bid contracts. Out of tens of thousands of contractors, the biggest 737 collected nearly 80 percent of the contracting dollars; the top fifty contractors got more than half of all the money. Topping the list for this fiscal period were Lockheed Martin ($94 billion) and Boeing ($82 billion). By fiscal year 2003, 56 percent of the Defense Department's contracts paid for services rather than goods.[28]

Not surprisingly, many companies have been accused of overcharging.[29] When auditors discovered that KBR, the Halliburton subsidiary, was overpaid $208 million to transport oil in Iraq, they also discovered that government employees doing the same job (in this case, the Defense Energy Support Center) were much more efficient. A Columbia University economist described this phenomenon in one word: *incentive*.[30] A government worker's pay is the same no matter what he or she does. But for someone working on a cost-plus contract (a contract in which all services are reimbursed plus interest), efficiency may not be in his or her best interest. What is most troubling, however, is that even though the discrepancy was discovered, the U.S. Army paid nearly $204 million of the $208 million overcharge. Was this because the army recognized Halliburton as being in favor with then–Vice President Cheney, the former head of Halliburton, or were army personnel hoping to find work with the company after retiring from duty? The vice president's influence was also prominent in Halliburton's contracts with an oppressive government in oil-rich Nigeria.[31]

The best hope for knowing the full extent of fraudulent activities lies with protection of whistleblowers, inside employees who speak out against corrupt practices. The unwritten rule on Wall Street has always been that insiders do not talk about illegal or unethical activities with law enforcement or regulatory authorities. Now threats, legal harassment, and gag rules are used to silence truth tellers. For example, KBR, one of the nation's largest government contractors, requires employees seeking to report fraud to sign internal confidentiality agreements prohibiting them from reporting violations to law enforcement authorities.[32]

No stone commandeering federal funds is left unturned. Even laws intended for protection of Native Americans have been used by the Department of Homeland Security as a ruse for large, no-bid corporate contracts on surveillance equipment, for example, that provide no jobs or benefits for the intended populations.[33]

If private companies are overcharging and profiting from loopholes in state and federal laws, how does the military-industrial complex benefit government? There are multiple ways that private industry benefits government—or more specifically, benefits politicians who receive campaign and political party contributions, and investment and economic stimulus in their own home districts. Elected members of Congress spend much of their time meeting with wealthy donors who provide for their reelection expenses or may choose to run a candidate against them in a primary campaign. Ranking military personnel and former members of Congress are in line for high-paying corporate jobs. But those who benefit most of all by the marriage of military and industry are those who represent both sides—they are the military industrial-complex. We illustrate with three corporations from among many.

The Government as Contractor: Bechtel, Carlyle, and Halliburton

Former Congressman Ron Dellums once remarked that he had to come to Congress to understand the difference between welfare and subsidy. Subsidy is a big check that goes to a few people. The degree to which wealthy interests are subsidized has been documented.[34] Nowhere is this more pronounced than in the defense sector:

> In this charmed circle of American capitalism, Lockheed Martin-, Boeing-, and Raytheon-manufactured munitions destroy Iraq; George Shultz's Bechtel Corporation and Dick Cheney's Halliburton rebuild Iraq; and Iraqi oil pays for it all.[35]

Like Mr. England, who was introduced earlier, many U.S. military and political officers move between positions in government and the private sector. The transition from positions in governing bodies to the companies soliciting contracts creates enormous conflicts of interest. But it is the connections between the officers of government agencies and the defense industry that are most egregious. With their connections to the upper echelons of government, these companies have had a tremendous impact on foreign policy.

The Bechtel Group

The Bechtel Group is one of the world's largest engineering, construction, and project management companies, including nineteen joint-venture companies and numerous subsidiaries. Based in San Francisco since 1898, four generations of the Bechtel family have led their business through more than 22,000 projects in 140 nations on all seven continents. From the revival of the American railroad system, they have gone on to such projects as the Hoover Dam, the Bay Area

Transit (BART) in San Francisco, and presently the management and operation of Los Alamos National Laboratories.[36] The company plays a major role in the nuclear sector, with its early involvement in the Manhattan Project and its construction or design of over half the nuclear power plants in America.[37] It is also one of the premier water-privatization companies in the world, as we explored in chapter 4.

With a history in the Persian Gulf since the Second World War, Bechtel has built oil refineries and pipelines, as well as major infrastructure such as highways and airports. During the 1980s, a Saudi Arabian client of one Bechtel subsidiary invested $10 million in the Bin Laden construction company.

The U.S. government, however, is the biggest financer of Bechtel and its subsidiaries. From fiscal years 1990 to 2002, the company received more than $11.7 billion in U.S. government contracts. Between 2002 and July 2004 Bechtel received nearly $3 billion from the agency USAID;[38] their results for 2011 indicated total revenues of $3.29 billion, with new awards at $53 billion.[39]

Bechtel's ties to the U.S. government facilitate this process. It began when Stephen Bechtel partnered with John McCone, who later became head of the CIA under President Kennedy. In the 1970s Bechtel hired numerous government officials, including Secretary of Health, Education, and Welfare Casper Weinberger (who in 1980 left the company to become President Reagan's Defense Secretary), former Atomic Energy Commission chief executive Robert Hollingsworth, former Marine four-star general and NATO Commander Jack Sheehan, and Richard Helms, who consulted on Iranian and Middle Eastern projects in 1978 after serving as CIA director and ambassador to Iran. Helms is known for his involvement with the attempted assassination of Fidel Castro and the overthrow of Chilean leader Salvador Allende.[40] The exchange has been bidirectional, with government officials moving into Bechtel positions and Bechtel officers moving into government.

George Shultz, former Treasury Secretary to Nixon, bounced back and forth between an executive vice president position in Bechtel to Secretary of State under Reagan and back to Bechtel's board of directors. As Secretary of State, Shultz sent Donald Rumsfeld to meet with Saddam Hussein to advocate for construction of a pipeline from the oilfields of Iraq to the port of Aqaba in Jordan. Meanwhile, as chairman of International Council of JP Morgan Chase, Shultz loaned $500 million to Saddam Hussein to buy weapons; Bechtel was one of the companies that sold the weapons.[41] As chair of the Committee for the Liberation of Iraq, Shultz wrote a *Washington Post* article titled "Act Now: The Danger Is Immediate," advocating a preemptive strike on Iraq.

Carlyle Group

Unlike Lockheed Martin and General Dynamics (who manufacture weapons) or Bechtel and Halliburton (who design, build, and manage large enterprises), the Carlyle Group specializes in investing. Since its founding in 1987, this Washington, D.C.-based corporation has made billions on investments, mergers, and acquisitions with defense manufacturing companies. As the military began to increase outsourcing of manufacturing and services to private companies, a new niche market was created for private-equity firms. The Carlyle Group found its initial success as a "leveraged buyout" firm by purchasing underperforming defense companies with borrowed money, installing their own management team, encouraging investment, passing off its debt onto its acquisitions and then selling the companies at a large profit. With the 1997 sale of BDM International, Inc., the group made a 650 percent profit.[42] That level of profit makes Carlyle heavily dependent on connections to Wall Street financial institutions, which underwrite these loans but also keep Wall Street solvent. That was illustrated by the 2008 bailouts. It also means that those companies, including government contractors, have to be very profitable to pay off those debts and enrich their new owners.

Links between high-ranking government officers and Carlyle are profuse. Former Secretary of Defense Frank Carlucci, chairman of Carlyle at the time of the United Defense sale, was the college roommate of G. W. Bush's Secretary of Defense Donald Rumsfeld at Princeton. Other notable links include William Kennard, former Federal Communications Commission (FCC) chairman, who under Carlyle directs the business investments of the companies he once regulated. Former Secretary of State James Baker and his former boss, George H. Bush, have also worked for Carlyle. Bush commands over $500,000 for his speeches in support of the company. Bush and Baker have been particularly valuable to the company as emissaries to investors in the Middle East, most notably the Saudi Arabian Bin Laden Group. Other Carlyle affiliates included Arthur Levitt, Bill Clinton's chairman of the Securities and Exchange Commission, and Mack McLarty, Clinton's White House Chief of Staff. The bin Laden family was a major shareholder as well, until both parties concluded that the relationship with the al-Qaeda leader's family (and the source of his wealth) was "receiving more attention than it deserved."[43] Carlyle invests in both conventional and digital defense contractors. Members of the Carlyle Group's board also have board seats or other affiliations with corporations that include ExxonMobil, MCI Communications, Sprint Nextel, Duke Energy, Reuters, and Ford Motors. Bank affiliations among Carlyle's leaders include Morgan Stanley, Goldman Sachs, and Bank of America.[44]

The Security/Digital Complex

Senator Diane Feinstein chaired the Senate Select Committee on Intelligence. Established in 1975, it has oversight responsibility for the sixteen civilian and military agencies and departments that make up the U.S. Intelligence Community. She expressed outrage over the fact that the National Security Agency had been secretly spying on records of the very committee charged with its oversight. The revelations of secret surveillance not only of government officials but of all who use the Internet came to light through the efforts of whistleblowers, particularly Edward Snowden. Rather than commend Snowden for his effort to make her and the rest of us aware of secret violations of constitutional rights, Senator Feinstein chose to consider Snowden's disclosures as treason, a view consistent with Feinstein's major corporate defense and intelligence campaign supporters that include General Dynamics, General Atomic, BAE Systems, Northrop Grumman, and Bechtel.[45]

Snowden's past employer, Booz Allen Hamilton, earns more than 98 percent of its revenue from the government. The *New York Times* reported on the firm's close government ties.[46] As evidence of the company's close relationship with government, the Obama administration's chief intelligence official, James R. Clapper Jr., was a former Booz Allen executive. The official who held that post in the Bush administration, John M. McConnell, now works for Booz Allen. That is a pure case of the revolving door.

In February 2014, Booz Allen Hamilton announced two new contracts with Homeland Security, worth a total of $11 billion, for program management, engineering, technology, business and financial management, and audit support services. Booz Allen Hamilton is now a member of the Carlyle Group. Booz Allen has contributed to the personal wealth of a number of well-known public figures from administrations of both parties. They include former president George H. W. Bush; Bush's Secretary of State, James Baker, and Defense Secretary Frank Carlucci; Arthur Levitt, Bill Clinton's chairman of the Securities and Exchange Commission; and Mack McLarty, Clinton's White House Chief of Staff. The bin Laden family was also a major shareholder.[47]

Halliburton

Founded in 1919, Houston-based Halliburton is one of the world's largest providers of products and services to the oil and gas industries. This company has made billions of dollars in no-bid contracts with the U.S. government (particularly the Pentagon) to build and repair oil wells and pipelines and construct military bases. More recently, the company has become a "privatized" sector of the military, offering all sorts of services from laundry and mail to information technology and intelligence. Halliburton has gained special notoriety among government contractors for two reasons: (1) the company's ties to former Vice President Dick Cheney, and (2) its track record of overbilling.

Overbilling

In 1992, the Halliburton subsidiary KBR was awarded the U.S. Army's first Logistics Civil Augmentation Program (LOGCAP) contract. LOGCAP is a U.S. Army initiative for peacetime planning for the use of civilian contractors in wartime and other contingencies. Under the "cost plus award fee" provision, a contract was awarded to KBR to provide support in all of the Army's field operations, including combat and intelligence. The contract guarantees a fee ranging from 2 to 5 percent on top of the cost of service. KBR came under scrutiny by the General Accounting Office (GAO), which reported that the company had padded its estimated costs by 32 percent. The company boosted its bottom line by charging $84 for a $14 piece of plywood.[48] In another case, Halliburton spent $82,000 for a shipment of natural gas from Kuwait to Iraq, but charged the government $27.4 million.[49]

Since 9/11, Halliburton and KBR have received billions in no-bid contracts in Afghanistan and Iraq, the most dubious perhaps being the two year $7 billion contract to rebuild Iraq's oil infrastructure. This overpriced contract was for fighting oil fires and reconstructing oil fields after the U.S. invasion, even though only eight gas wells and pipelines caught fire, and all but one had been extinguished by the time the contract was made.[50] Incidentally, KBR wrote the Army's contingency plan for the Iraqi oil-well repair.

The Pentagon's own auditors accused Halliburton of overcharging by over $100 million on just one of their task orders in Iraq. Congressman Henry Waxman from California initiated a congressional investigation and made twelve separate requests for information that the Pentagon rejected.[51] Waxman suggested that Iraqi oil proceeds were used to pay (or overpay) Halliburton. Notably, relocation of company headquarters to Dubai in early 2007 would protect their top executives against any future indictments by U.S. law enforcement.

Halliburton's political clout serves its own economic agenda, and cannot be overestimated. In the 1970s the company was contracted by Saddam Hussein to build two enormous oil terminals in the Persian Gulf off the coast from Umm Qasr. For the next thirty years, Halliburton was called upon to repair these terminals and pipelines that were repeatedly bombed by Iranian and later by U.S. forces. Just weeks before Saddam Hussein invaded Kuwait (which led to the first U.S. Gulf War), the Iraqi government paid Halliburton $57 million for work on one of the country's terminals and for assistance with exploration technology; only weeks later, the Pentagon paid the company $3.9 million to put out oil fires, while KBR was contracted to construct the bombed-out buildings of Kuwait City.[52]

In 1992 as defense secretary under President George H. W. Bush, Cheney hired KBR to write the privatization report that initiated the Logistics Civil Augmentation Program (LOGCAP). Three years later, Cheney became CEO of the company and remained there until 2000, when he left to become vice president. Upon leaving his position as CEO, Cheney received $30 million in stock options and continues to be paid up to $1 million per year in deferred compensation. As CEO, Cheney doubled the size of the company through business mergers as well as deals with the Pentagon. During this time, he landed a $1.1 billion Pentagon contract for services in the Balkans, as well as billions in government loans. During Cheney's years as CEO, the company donated $1.2 million to political parties and Congress, and spent over half a million on lobbying.[53]

A vast military-industrial complex promotes excessive corporate profiteering from military activities. Militarism inevitably leads to the use of strategic deception to lie to the public about why we go to war and who benefits from it. For a powerful industrial elite to steer a policy process with self-serving deals of this magnitude, one needs more than the pressures of independent corporate lobbyists. One also needs three other elements: (1) groups such as think tanks and advisory boards that meet together in the role of architects for new policy; (2) groups with resources to influence and implement policies; and (3) elite clubs to assure camaraderie and loyalty to their class.

Elite Clubs: Building Networks of Power

For elite brokers of power to transact business, there is a need for an underlying appreciation of the unspoken rules. Under the guise of representing national interests, corporate transactions are hidden from the public and conducted in secret societies. These societies create face-to-face familiarity that eases the flow of favors and positions across the inner network and promises confidentiality.

The Order of Skull and Bones

The Order of Skull and Bones, formally known as the Brotherhood of Death, is a secret society dating back to 1832. The Ivy League has many societies and clubs, but this one at Yale University is especially notable not only for its gothic ritual and utmost secrecy, but because of its membership. Former Bonesmen have included many of the most powerful families in politics and business, including the families Rockefeller, Taft, Harriman, Bush, and Kerry. Bonesmen have filled the Senate, the Defense Department, the CIA, and the Council on Foreign Relations (CFR); they have owned and managed banks, investment firms, major newspapers, and communications companies.

One anonymous Bonesman, in an interview with Alex Robbins, a Yale graduate who investigated the underground society, described that networking: "The biggest benefit to Skull and Bones . . . is the networking. In the rest of the world you get to know people through accident or through choice. In Bones you meet people whom you otherwise wouldn't get to meet. It's a forced setup among a group of high achievers, even the legacies."[54]

For generations, the Bush family—two President Bushes, the younger Bush's grandfather, uncles, and cousins—has called on, and been called upon by, the

Brotherhood. Three of George H. W.'s fellow Bonesmen—George H. Pfau Jr., Jack Caulkins, and William Judkins Clark—raised significant funds for his presidential campaigns. As president, he named Pfau to be director of the Securities Investor Protection Corporation. Numerous Bonesmen were granted positions as speechwriters and department secretaries. Several Bonesmen were appointed as foreign emissaries: Richard Anthony Moore as ambassador to Ireland, Paul Lambert as ambassador to Ecuador (although he had no diplomatic experience), and Bonesmen classmates David Grimes and Thomas W. Moseley represented Bush in Bulgaria and Uruguay, respectively.[55]

George W. got into Yale despite a weak academic record and has utilized Skull and Bones member connections like his father and grandfather did before him. When he formed his first company, Arbusto Energy, Inc., he sought the financial assistance of Bonesman uncle Jonathan Bush and William H. Draper III (Bones 1950). Bonesman Stephan Adams spent $1 million on billboard ads for Bush's 2000 campaign. At least fifty-eight Bonesmen contributed at least $57,972 to Bush's campaign, while others donated money in their wives' names.[56]

Not unlike his father and grandfather, George W. also returned the favor to his clubmates. In November 2001 he appointed Edward McNally (Bones 1979) to the newly formed Office of Homeland Security. Robert D. McCallum Jr. (Bones 1968) was named assistant attorney general of the Civil Department. This position, notably, represents the federal government in cases such as fraud, international trade, patents, bankruptcies, and foreign litigation.

The Bilderberg Group

This elite, private club is especially noteworthy for two reasons: (1) members of the group (selected by invitation only) are among the most prominent leaders in the world in financing, business, academia, and politics; and (2) the group's complete secrecy. Not only are the meetings sheltered from the public and the press, but the entire event is managed by its own staff—taking over as hotel, catering, and security staff several days before the onset of each meeting.

The manner in which the initial Bilderberg group formed illustrates the network of corporate power. The first relationship between the founders and corporate invitees occurred when Joseph Retinger, a political advisor, befriended Paul Rijkens, at that time president of Unilever, one of the world's largest and most powerful multinational corporations. Rijkens was also at that time on the board of Rotterdam Bank. Based on that relationship, other board members of Rotterdam Bank, such as H. M. Hirschfield, K. P. Van der Mandel, and H. L. Wolterson, became part of a clique.

To garner interest for membership in the United States, Prince Bernard, cofounder with Retinger, enlisted the help of his close friend Walter Bedell Smith, director of the CIA. Smith then turned to Charles D. Jackson, special assistant for psychological warfare to the president, and president of the Committee for a Free Europe (anticommunist) organization. Jackson appointed John S. Coleman, president of the Burroughs Corporation and member of the Committee for a National Trade Policy, as U.S. chair of the Bilderberg group.[57] Retinger, Prince Bernard, and Rijkens selected the invitees (drawn from corporate and government officials in the European NATO countries plus Sweden) to the first Bilderberg conference.[58]

The original members on the American side include names and entities recognizable to American citizens: George Ball, head of Lehman Brothers, a former State Department official and future member of the Trilateral Commission; David Rockefeller, head of Chase Manhattan Bank, member of the Council on Foreign Relations, member of the Business Council, member of the U.S. Council of the International Chamber of Commerce, and future founder of the Trilateral Commission; and Dean Rusk, U.S. Secretary of State (1961–1969), former president of the Rockefeller Foundation.[59]

Even more recognizable to Americans are these former and current members of Bilderberg: Donald Rumsfeld, former U.S. secretary of defense; Paul Wolfowitz, former U.S. defense secretary and past president of the World Bank; Peter Sutherland, chairman of Goldman Sachs, International and British Petroleum and former commissioner of the European Union; and Steven Harper, right-wing prime minister of Canada.[60]

The Bohemian Club

The Bohemian Club began in San Francisco in 1872 as a small group of artists and writers who wished to celebrate arts and culture in the post–Gold Rush era of San Francisco. For financial purposes, the club opened its doors to wealthy members of the business elite, who dominated membership soon thereafter.

Prominent leaders of government became members as well; in fact, every U.S. Republican president since 1923 (as well as several Democratic presidents) has been a member. Members and member emeriti include former secretaries of state Henry Kissinger, George Shultz, and Colin Powell; Donald Rumsfeld; David Rockefeller Sr. and David Rockefeller Jr.; S. D. Bechtel Jr. (Bechtel Corporation); Thomas Watson Jr. (IBM); Phillip Hawley (Bank of America); Ralph Bailey (DuPont); and A. W. Clausen (World Bank).[61]

The lectures, called "lakeside chats," are off-the-record presentations on world issues such as military budgets or global free trade. One such chat, given by a University of California political science professor in 1994, warned club members of the dangers of multiculturalism, Afrocentrism, and the loss of family boundaries. "Elites based on merit and skill are important to society," he explained. The "unqualified" masses, he concluded, cannot be allowed to carry out policy—the elite must set values that can be translated into "standards of authority."[62]

Sociologist Peter Phillips, who wrote his doctoral dissertation on the Bohemian Club, defines the club as institutionalized race, gender, and class inequality. He describes how these clubs model themselves after the gentlemen's clubs of nineteenth-century England, which became popular as the nation was concentrating on building its global empire. The clubs represented a place where gentlemen could discuss their ideas of expansion and domination away from the distractions of meddling of women, the underclasses, and non-whites.

As Phillips describes Bohemian Grove, it is an atmosphere of social interaction and networking. Here, one can sit around a campfire with ex-presidents of the United States and CEOs of Bank of America or Pacific Gas and Electric. You can share a cognac or shoot skeet with secretaries of state and defense. You can enjoy the high jinks alongside the members of the Council on Foreign Relations. Certain known principles of group dynamics explain the efficacy of the group's community-building. Physical proximity is likely to lead to group solidarity. Greater direct interaction leads to friendships, trust, and mutual liking. The relaxed atmosphere increases group cohesion. Social cohesion, in turn, helps to reduce conflicts and reach agreement on big issues.[63] One example of this last point is the Manhattan Project, which produced the first atomic bombs. It was conceived and informally set into motion at the Grove in 1942.[64] This atmosphere serves the purpose of developing social ties and cohesion within the elite social class. These ties "manifest themselves in global trade meetings, party politics, campaign financing, and top-down democracy."[65]

In networks of power, such networks have few connections across the lines of social class. For G. William Domhoff, the Bohemian Club is "evidence for the class cohesiveness that is one prerequisite for class domination."[66] The club becomes an avenue by which the cohesiveness of the elite class is maintained.

Think Tanks, Advisory Boards, and Councils: Creating Policy and Consent

Government officials work primarily to balance the needs and pressures from constituents and primary funders. The system has little room for participatory involvement in redefining major directions of policy or larger shifts of direction. That function is served by other exclusive groups, in and out of government, that are designed specifically to come up with ideas to steer national and global policy.

Council on Foreign Relations and the Trilateral Commission

Since its inception in 1921, the Council on Foreign Relations (CFR) has represented the elite "who's who" in America, with a membership that constitutes U.S. presidents, ambassadors, secretaries of state, Wall Street investors, international bankers, foundation executives, think-tank executives, lobbyist lawyers, Pentagon officials, media owners, senators, university presidents, Supreme Court judges, and corporate entrepreneurs. In their own words, they are "the privileged and preeminent nongovernmental impresario of America's pageant to find its place in the world."[67]

The CFR vision for America's place in the world is market domination. Throughout its history, the CFR has played a major role in shaping foreign policy to benefit American markets. At the end of the Second World War, members of the CFR, including David Rockefeller, presented the idea for reconstruction of Europe that would become the Marshall Plan. It sought to benefit U.S. corporations directly.[68] Carroll Quigley, professor of history at Georgetown University, stated that the CFR "believes national boundaries should be obliterated and one-world rule established."[69]

On March 12, 2003, just one week before the U.S. invasion of Iraq, CFR's Independent Task Force, chaired by former Defense Secretary and Energy Secretary James Schlesinger and former UN ambassador Thomas Pickering, urged President Bush to "make clear to the Congress, to the American people, and to the people of Iraq that the United States will stay the course" after a war in Iraq.[70] "Stay the course" became the oft-repeated justification to continue the war.

With success in Iraq "so clearly tied to American staying power," the task force released another report in June 2003, stating that the "Bush administration should therefore reaffirm its commitment to sustain a large presence of U.S. military forces to ensure stability as long as necessary" and urging him to make a major foreign policy address to explain the importance of "seeing the task through."[71] The report also advised the Bush administration "to improve management and operations in the oil industry . . . and [to] prepare for the next peace stabilization and reconstruction challenge after Iraq."[72]

The CFR is limited to Americans. The Trilateral Commission began at the behest of David Rockefeller in 1973, whose proposal to include Japan in the annual Bilderberg meetings was rejected. With the assistance of then U.S. National Security Advisor Zbigniew Brzezinski, the Trilateral Commission sought to bring the rising economic power—Japan—into political and business cooperation with America and Europe. At the time of its inception in 1973, the Trilateral Commission responded to the oil crisis by extending loans to developing countries. David Rockefeller's Chase Manhattan Bank loaned nearly $52 billion, and the IMF further expanded their loan program to developing nations.[73] The Trilateral Commission comprises political leaders, corporate CEOs, labor leaders, academics, and foundation executives. Many of its American participants are members of the CFR and the Bilderberg Group as well.

Business Advocacy and Lobbying Groups

Although a multitude of advocacy and lobbying groups exist for all types of citizens' needs, not all are equally influential. The National Rifle Association has long been effective in preventing restrictions on gun sales. The American-Israeli Public Affairs Committee has been highly effective in preventing congressional criticism of Israel or of the extensive military assistance that the United States provides to Israel. But the most effective lobbying efforts come from corporations. The amount of money wielded by some groups creates an uneven playing field and assures a force protecting the interests of the corporate elite.

National Manufacturers Association

The National Manufacturers Association (NAM) is a powerful advocate of a pro-growth, pro-manufacturing agenda. Representing over 100,000 companies, it is the nation's largest industrial trade association. NAM's mission is to "enhance the competitiveness of manufacturers by shaping a legislative and regulatory environment."[74]

With over 300 member associations, NAM seeks to be engaged in every congressional district. The NAM "Key Manufacturing Vote" notice alerts lawmakers to votes critical in implementing the NAM agenda. Among the thousands of advocacy groups, *Fortune* magazine ranked NAM among the top ten most influential advocacy groups in the United States.[75] Lobbying supports legislative boosts to the bottom line. The largest corporations, like the largest insurance pension funds, are acquiring capital for investment, often in operations selected by money managers and remote from their own business activities. Hence bottom-line-driven CEOs may be rewarded for activities that drain from their own operations to support lucrative speculations.[76]

The Business Roundtable

Another powerful advocacy group is the Business Roundtable. What distinguishes this group from other U.S. business associations and advocacy groups is that its membership is composed exclusively of the CEOs of the over 200 companies represented. The group is "committed to advocating public policies that ensure vigorous economic growth, a dynamic global economy, and the well-trained and productive U.S. workforce essential for future competitiveness."[77] The combined annual revenues of the companies that make up the group is $4.5 trillion.[78]

Two major policy issues for which these groups advocate are energy security and trade liberalization. By their own account, the manufacturing industry consumes roughly one-third of the nation's total energy supply and is therefore "disproportionately" affected by energy availability. Although NAM supports the research and development of all sources of energy production (including renewable sources and the promotion of improved efficiency), its primary goal is to "increase [national] access to domestic sources of reliable energy."[79] In December

2006, NAM achieved a major victory when Congress passed the Gulf of Mexico Security Act, which opened 8.3 million acres in the Gulf to new oil and natural gas production. This is significant because it represented the first increase in domestic energy production in twenty-five years. NAM has also been lobbying for Congress to lift the present legislation protecting the Alaska National Wildlife Refuge (ANWR).

NAM opposes federal and state government climate-change mandates that have the potential to "adversely affect U.S. manufacturing competitiveness."[80] In 2004, NAM hosted a conference titled "Environmental Issues 2004: How to Get Results in an Election Year."[81] The focus of the conference was how to present pro-industry environmental messages to the public and influence the 2004 elections—or elect those policy makers who favor industry over the environment. The keynote speaker at the event was Mike Leavitt, administrator of the U.S. Environmental Protection Agency (EPA), who declared, "We need to do [environmental policy] in a better way that doesn't compromise our economic competitiveness."[82]

Trade liberalization is another major agenda for business advocacy groups. The Business Roundtable was the most instrumental organization in the promotion of the North American Free Trade Agreement (NAFTA).[83] Their strategy included frequent congressional testimonies, regular press releases, and hundreds of lobbying sessions involving CEOs of such influential companies as General Motors, AT&T, and Arthur Anderson & Co. Lobbyists for the closely affiliated National Foreign Trade Council and General Motors lobbied for the NAFTA vote nearly 150 times. U.S. NAFTA members of the Business Roundtable regularly met with President Clinton for briefings with White House officials and worked with the president to select Lee Iacocca, CEO of Chrysler, as the president's "NAFTA Czar."[84]

A close network exists linking lobbyists to nonprofit groups and government officials.[85] Sociologist Michael Dreiling argues that these frequent associations within prominent decision-making circles are the result of "the unique structural location afforded inner circle corporate leaders."[86] He describes this powerful vantage point:

> As Useem argued (1984), inner circle corporate actors receive, in addition to numerous other advantages, the political advantages offered by

"the stature and resources of the premier business associations" which facilitate not only cohesion, but heightened visibility and access to "government circles . . . and special hearings."[87]

Powerful groups maintain their own public relations units, but increasingly the lobbying efforts are contracted to another growth industry, professional lobbying firms. They specialize not only in framing the message, but more importantly in peddling influence with government officials. The number of registered lobbyists in Washington has more than doubled since 2000 to more than 34,750. The exorbitant starting salaries of corporate lobbyists lure close to half of retiring members of Congress.[88]

The Project for the New American Century

While some think tanks attempt to sculpt the public's views on the effects of smoking or the state of the environment, others focus on shaping foreign policy. The Project for the New American Century (PNAC) was formed in 1997 with the explicit purpose of promoting and planning the American domination of global affairs. In 1998, the group sent a letter to President Clinton advising him to remove Saddam Hussein from power, by reason that his stockpile of weapons of mass destruction posed a threat to the United States, its Middle East allies, and the region's oil resources. They argued that an Iraq war would be justified by Hussein's defiance of UN inspections.

In their September 2000 paper "Rebuilding America's Defenses: Strategy, Forces, and Resources for a New Century," PNAC clearly outlined what must be done (by force of arms) in order to create their desired position as sole global superpower. Major themes included a massive increase in the national defense budget, an enlarged and modernized armed forces equipped with the most advanced technologies, and the development and deployment of a global missile defense system. President Bush's budget plan in 2003 called for the same exact dollar amount to be spent on defense that was requested by PNAC in their 2000 paper.[89] In a chilling line often quoted by critics, authors of the 2000 paper propose the perceived need for advanced technologies in the face of a "catastrophic and catalyzing event—like a new Pearl Harbor."[90] Such an attack on American soil did occur with air attacks on New York's World Trade Center and the Pentagon, which was used to justify a war with Iraq. Controversaries abound regarding evidence of U.S. government involvement in the failure to prevent the 9/11 terrorist attack and some data relevant to the case have still not been made public. A scholarly background to controversies regarding clandestine activities in intelligence communities can be found in historian Peter Dale Scott's *The Road to 9/11: Wealth, Empire, and the Future of America*.[91]

PNAC is especially disconcerting not only because they appear to have prophesied 9/11 and the U.S. invasion of Iraq, but because of who they are—men who held the highest positions in the G. W. Bush administration (Vice President Dick Cheney, National Security Council Director Eliot Abrams, Secretary of Defense Donald Rumsfeld, Deputy Secretary of Defense Paul Wolfowitz, Defense Policy Board Chairman Richard Perle, and Undersecretary of Defense Douglas Feith—all with continuing ties to the defense industry). PNAC also included members with ties to the oil industry (Dick Cheney, Jeb Bush), members with ties to the media (Donald Kagan, William Kristol), and members in the defense industry (Bruce Jackson, Vin Weber).[92]

The new paradigm strategy rests on a reading of the Constitution that few legal scholars share—namely, that the president, as commander-in-chief, has the authority to disregard virtually all previously known legal boundaries if national security demands it. Under this interpretation, statutes prohibiting torture, secret detention, and warrantless surveillance have been set aside.[93]

The Defense Policy Board

Whereas some elite planning bodies focus their efforts on legislation that affects their domestic and international corporate interests, others such as the Defense Policy Advisory Committee, also referred to as the Defense Policy Board (DPB), focus on the foreign policy issues that may affect their economic or political interests.[94] Formed in 1985, the board began its function as a bipartisan advisory body. However, under the G. W. Bush administration, it became overtly involved with making policy decisions, a role it is not mandated to do.[95] Douglas Feith, undersecretary of defense and a former Reagan administration official, chose the thirty members of the DPB for the Bush administration—nine of them had significant ties to major defense industry contractors including Bechtel, Boeing, TRW, Northrop Grumman, Lockheed Martin, and Booz

Allen Hamilton.[96] Four members were registered lobbyists, one of them representing two of the largest military contractors in the country. Members of DPB disclose their business interests annually to the Pentagon, but the disclosures are not available to the public.

In 2003, a controversy ensued around chairman Richard Perle, a cofounder of PNAC and a vocal advocate for the Iraq war. Considering his numerous corporate dealings, it was apparent that he would profit greatly from the war. At the time, Perle worked for Goldman Sachs, advising clients on investment opportunities in postwar Iraq. He also directed and has major shares in the British Autonomy Corporation, a manufacturer of high-tech eavesdropping technologies, whose major customers are the Department of Homeland Security, the Secret Service, and the National Security Agency. On top of these, Perle's venture-capital company, Trireme, invested millions of dollars in defense products (over half from Boeing). Ironically, none of these positions appeared to pose an ethical conflict; Perle only stepped down from the chair of the DPB after the Pentagon and FBI opposed his attempts to sell his telecommunications company's subsidiaries to a Chinese consortium.[97]

International Groups that Plan and Implement Policy

The leaders of corporate power are part of an international as well as a domestic network. This network is represented by formal powers invested in continuing organizations, particularly the International Monetary Fund, World Bank, and World Trade Association.

International Monetary Fund

The International Monetary Fund (IMF) emerged from the Bretton Woods conference in 1944. The main focus of the conference was to develop a system that would foster and develop open markets for trade. Industrial nations were encouraged to lower trade barriers and invest capital and were deemed responsible for managing and governing this system; the IMF was created as that governing body, and regulated international exchanges of currency. Voting was proportional to the capital contributed, as historian Howard Zinn points out, so that American dominance would be assured.[98] The fixed exchange rate system, however, collapsed between 1971 and 1973. Since that time, the IMF has increasingly become more involved in the fiscal counseling of member countries and worked as an advocate for the privatization of state industries.

The IMF website describes its mission as "working to foster global monetary cooperation, secure financial stability, facilitate international trade, promote high employment and sustainable economic growth, and reduce poverty."[99] In reality, "structural adjustment programs," which must be agreed to in order to get IMF loans, have devastated many developing countries' economies. These loans are granted with strict conditions that enforce trade liberalization and encourage direct foreign investment, resource extraction, and the privatization of state entities. Considerable criticism has been raised against the IMF and its policies that undermine national sovereignties and endorse corporate globalization.

Such criticism comes not only from nations devastated by IMF programs (such as Jamaica, Argentina, Ethiopia, and Malawi) that have called for its abolition, but from 2001 Nobel Laureate economist Joseph Stiglitz, who concluded that institutions such as the IMF and World Bank do not operate in the interest of developing countries and that the neoliberal position held by these institutions is basically erroneous.[100]

World Bank

Like the IMF, the World Bank also came into being during the Bretton Woods conference in 1944. Its first loan was approved in 1946 in the amount of $250 million to France for postwar reconstruction. Composed of five international financial investment and monitoring agencies, the World Bank aims to provide capital and financial advice for the purposes of economic development and the elimination of poverty. The organization's activities focus primarily on financing the building of infrastructure, the development of agriculture and irrigation systems, and the improvement of human services in education and health in developing countries.

Each agency within the World Bank is owned by its member governments. Voting rights are proportional to shareholding; therefore, the organization is effectively controlled by wealthier, developed countries. As put forth at Bretton Woods, the World Bank president is always a U.S. citizen and is nominated by the U.S. government (while the IMF is traditionally headed by a European).

Like the IMF, the World Bank has been criticized by academics for imposing economic (free market) policies that support Western interests. Since its inception, the World Bank has loaned tremendous sums of money to poor countries in need of infrastructure. Frequently, the governments of these countries are corrupt, hoarding much of the money for themselves, with little left to invest in the proposed development projects. Meanwhile, recipient countries incur an enormous debt that falls on the shoulders of their people. Economist Jeffrey Sachs explains that although corrupt governments are often blamed for their country's debts, the failures of these programs often have more to do with a systematic disregard of the related causes or exacerbations of poverty, including poor health care systems and severely damaged natural environments.[101] The companies that provide the work (and are paid the money) are invariably large Western corporations (including Bechtel and Halliburton) that intend to make a profit. As a Western entity, the World Bank's philosophy of development is based on Western ideals and principles, which may not only affect the economic sovereignty of non-Western nations but also cultural sovereignty.

World Trade Organization

The stated goal of the World Trade Organization (WTO) is to increase trade by lowering international trade barriers and by opening trade to international negotiation. It is an international and multilateral organization that creates rules for a system of global trade, and resolves disputes between its member states. The Agreement on Agriculture (AOA) was one of the first WTO rulings to come into effect after the inception of the organization in 1995. The AOA effectively increased subsidies to industrial agriculture, which may be increased without limit. As described in chapter 4, the United States grants 70 percent of its subsidies to 10 percent of its producers. Subsequently, this allows major agribusinesses to flood global markets with cheap products, thereby undercutting producers in poor countries. The AOA also mandates market access, or the reduction of tariff barriers, between member states. This creates a problem for small farmers in developing countries—for whom tariff protections were often designed. As a result, small-scale indigenous farmers are forced to compete with subsidized, industrialized agribusinesses.

Apart from the structural violence that free-market policies wield toward less-developed countries, the WTO also favors industrialized nations by turning a blind eye to health, safety, and environmental issues. For example, through the production and processing methods rule, safety precautions stating where and how something is produced are impermissible. Based on this ruling, lumber from protected forests may be sold indiscriminately, and genetically modified (GM) food products need not be labeled, in spite of their potential danger to human health and the environment.

The Corporatization of Elections: Taking Power from the People

However removed ordinary people may be from the daily transactions among higher levels of power that control the resources they need, there is still one line of input assured to citizens. They may not have direct access to corporate CEOs or governing boards, but they can hold their elected officials accountable with their votes. That belief enables officials to present the United States as a democracy. For the most powerful, the presence of free elections is an important factor in legitimizing a society in which they happen to be at the top.

Democracies are often considered to have governments that are obligated to reflect the views of people who elect them. One important study in the United States looked at more than 1,700 government policies for over twenty years to find out how public opinion actually translates into policy. Princeton University's Martin Gilens and Northwestern University's Benjamin Page concluded that wherever the public views differed from the views of an economic elite, the public (and public interest groups) had an estimated zero impact upon policy change, while economic elites and organized groups representing business interests were shown to have a very large influence.[102] The results do not mean that there is no difference between the two dominant political parties. They do mean that the government is an oligarchy rather than the democracy of, by, and for the people, as it claims to be.

It is not, however, in the interest of the wealthy oligarchy that voices from the least powerful, which might challenge their hold on resources, be heard. Despite viral exchange over alternative media sources, one month after the study appeared, no cable networks had reported on it and only three newspapers had produced blog reports. The inner network of the corporate elite owns the major media (see chapter 7). But could people still use the vote to reclaim a platform? This hope would have to take into account that the wealthy elite also exercise considerable control over many aspects of the electoral process. They are involved from the backing of candidates, to the accessibility of voting, to the design of electronic voting machines.

The Funding of Candidates

This corporate control of the democratic process begins at the earliest stage: business elites often solicit candidates from their own ranks, or like-minded celebrities, on the basis of how amenable and how effective the candidate appears to the interests of private business. When candidates for national office are exploring the decision of whether to seek nomination for a major political party, they are mainly assessing how much support they can get from major donors who are, in turn, evaluating what the return will be for their support.

The process works to identify candidates with the greatest potential to bring in big money from wealthy individuals and business corporations. Hillman and Hitt explain, from a management perspective, the "substantial interdependence" between the business world's economic or competitive environment and government.[103] Examples of the impact of government regulation on business include taxation, trade practices, employment regulations, and environmental standards. The authors recall that by the late 1960s the government was conceived by some to be a competitive tool to create the environment most favorable to business interests. The communications company MCI utilized this political strategy to create a market opportunity by influencing government officials to deregulate the U.S. long-distance telephone market.

Corporate Sponsorship

Proactive approaches to the "corporate political action," described by business school professors Amy Hillman and Michael Hitt,[104] include Political Action Committees campaign contributions, lobbying, advocacy advertising, and grassroots mobilization. The ability of corporations to make financial contributions to political candidates is made possible by a series of federal court decisions that interpret the law to view corporations as persons, thus giving corporations many of the same rights that protect individuals.

The idea of corporations as persons began with various challenges to the Fourteenth Amendment to the U.S. Constitution, which grants citizenship to all persons born or naturalized in the United States. In California, in 1882, when big business was epitomized by the railroad industry, the Supreme Court ruled in favor of the Southern Pacific Railroad in *San Mateo v. Southern Pacific Railroad*. Corporate lawyers for the railroad giant argued that by taxing the railroad's property differently than the property of natural persons, the state had violated the corporation's rights as secured by the Equal Protection Clause of the Fourteenth Amendment.[105] By interpreting "citizens" to include corporate entities, the federal courts thereby granted them personhood under the Bill of Rights protections of the First, Fourth, and Fifth Amendments.

In the 1970s court decisions equated political spending with free speech and voided a Massachusetts law prohibiting corporate interference, including funding.[106] It is this precedent that has allowed corporations to finance those candidates and political parties that will perpetuate their interests—specifically, the increased wealth of their business.

Some corporations provide support for both of the major political parties, although typically not equally. One method of enhancing the donation is to invite employees to contribute to the party or candidate of their choice through a voluntary salary deduction. The company then bundles the amounts and dispenses the funds, thereby enhancing the indebtedness of candidates to the company. The Supreme Court's *Citizens United* ruling, released in January 2010, tossed out the corporate and union ban on making independent expenditures and financing electioneering communications. It gave corporations and unions the green light to spend unlimited sums on ads and other political tools, calling for the election or defeat of individual candidates. Super PACs act as shadow political parties. They accept unlimited donations from billionaires, corporations, and unions and use it to buy advertising, most of it negative.[107]Despite repeated polls showing public opinion disagreeing with this *Citizens United* ruling by 4 to 1, it is the current state of affairs and a major factor in the belief that government represents mainly the interests of the wealthy.[108]

Political Action Committees

Political Action Committees (PACs) are private groups that organize to work toward the election of a political candidate and to promote legislation that advances their specific interests. Some PACs work for a specific cause, such as a woman's right to choose whether to abort a pregnancy; some represent an industry as a whole, such as the National Association of Realtors; other PACs represent the specific financial interests of one corporation.

As Greg Coleridge, director of the Center for Responsive Politics explains, the most sizable contributions come directly from corporations or through corporate-backed PACs. Lobbying groups represent the interests of major industries and major single issues, and contribute substantially to PACs.[109] Between 1998 and 2005 the finance, insurance, and real estate sector spent over $2 billion lobbying for legislation to benefit their business interests.[110] The Chamber of Commerce leads all other groups in lobbying expenditures. Money provided through corporate Super PACs far exceeds expenditures by unions. In 2014, for example, the Laborers Union spent $1.4 million on lobbying; the Chamber of Commerce spent $1.2 million.[111]

Corporations and corporate PACs donate to individual campaigns as well as national, state, and local governmental political parties with careful deliberation and in expectation of "commensurate political returns."[112] Considering that many modern corporations are wealthier than most of the world's nations, it appears that the U.S. government has granted them commensurate returns on their political investments.

Campaign donations by corporations have increased dramatically over the last ten years. In 2003 the G. W. Bush campaign raised $577,000 a day, while Senator John Kerry brought in $64,000 a day.[113] In 1992, spending for the presidential and congressional elections was $1.8 billion, increasing to $2.2 billion in 1996, nearly $3 billion in 2000, and up to $4 billion in 2004.[114] In 2012, spending for the presidential and congressional elections was estimated at $6 billion.[115]

Some contend that living in a democracy offers an opportunity to have one's voice heard and one's interests addressed by elected officials. Yet the playing field is so uneven that many eligible voters choose not to participate. Rarely is concentration of power a matter that is raised in electoral politics. But on a daily basis, quite apart from elections, corporate spokespersons exert a tremendous influence upon government decisions. Three factors make this happen.

First, entry into national politics requires a large amount of money. Major corporations provide this money, and government officials are indebted to their donors. Second, the personnel in major cabinet positions come from, and return to, executive positions in these same corporate sectors, making for a rather limited ruling network. Third, although anyone is free to lobby for their cause, the largest corporate players and their industry societies maintain well-staffed lobbies. The reasons for inequitable attention to the needs of certain constituencies may be clarified by looking at where the money is.[116]

Although money may either stall or hasten the process, government action is a relatively formal process embedded in the U.S. Constitution and affirmed by a history of legislation and precedent derived from adjudication. The real practice of official decision making (as opposed to what is taught in civics classes) centers around lobbying and campaign contributions by the moneyed special interests that have been described. What becomes enacted are often policies for which some groups spend lavishly. By contrast, it is difficult for citizens lacking the resources for lobbying and campaign contributions to achieve enactment of strong policies that have broad, long-term value for most people. Measures dealing with the environment, poverty reduction, third world development, women's rights, human rights, health care for all—matters that make a difference for most people—typically occur in watered-down compromises and then only after the efforts of strong citizen protest. The same is true for local community services. Local groups may expend great amounts of time and energy to organize a yearly lobbying visit. By contrast, corporate lobbyists work full-time year round at their tasks. The focus here has been upon federal policy, but cities and towns face similar restrictions as their resources are siphoned through powerful corporate influences to compete in what has been termed a "growth machine."[117]

In 2002 legislation introduced by Senators McCain and Feingold was enacted to address campaign finance reform. Major provisions were the prohibition of unlimited soft money contributions to national, state, and local political parties. However, in 2010, in the case *Citizens United v. Federal Election Commission*, the Supreme Court ruled in favor of Citizens United based on the First Amendment and its protection of free speech, allowing corporations and organizations to use their treasury funds for direct advocacy to endorse or oppose specific candidates.

In his ninety-page dissent against the majority opinion, Justice Stevens argued that the Court's ruling "threatens to undermine the integrity of elected institutions across the Nation," warning that a "democracy cannot function effectively when its constituent members believe laws are being bought and sold."[118]

The *Citizens United* ruling amounted to dramatically increased campaign spending during the 2012 U.S. presidential elections. Independent groups, mostly in the form of Super PACs that can raise unlimited money from individuals, corporations, and labor unions, spent at least $524 million on television advertisements and other efforts asking voters to elect or defeat candidates.[119] As stated, the total spending for the 2012 presidential and congressional elections was estimated at an unprecedented $6 billion.[120]

Polling Places and Electronic Voting Machines

Whereas the corporate hand in elections begins with the backing of a political candidate who will serve its legislative purposes, it ends with the physical act of voting itself. The corporate touch is evident in the newly evolved corporate sponsorship programs, in which companies "adopt" one or more polling places. These sponsorships are presented to the public in the form of a fundraiser for a local charity. Coleridge describes one such program in Broward County, Florida, where corporations place signs near precinct voting sites while company employees (wearing the corporate logos of their employer) perform the duties of poll workers.

Another more prevalent example of the corporate hand in the voting process is the use of electronic voting machines. In the 2000 presidential election, problems surfaced when voters in Florida, Ohio, and other states touched the screen for one candidate, while their vote was cast for another candidate. According to a federal commission, more than one million ballots were ruined in 2004 by faulty voting equipment.[121]

Eager to avoid a scandal like Florida's 2000 election, the federal government passed the Help America Vote Act and granted the Diebold Corporation $3.9 billion to develop and install more than 40,000 electronic voting machines. In July 2003 a team of computer scientists published a review of the machines' software. The report identified hundreds of flaws, from lack of password protection on central databases to a glitch that would allow holders of a "smart card" to vote as many times as they wanted.[122] In 2006, shortly before the midterm elections, whistleblowers asserted that top Diebold corporation officials had ordered workers to install secret files to Georgia's electronic voting machines shortly before the 2002 elections.[123]

The integrity of electronic voting equipment faces two major challenges. The first is the lack of access to company software. When a company's software cannot be viewed by the public, there is no way to account for its accuracy. When one touches the screen for a candidate, there is no way for that person to verify the accuracy of their intended vote. Public access to company software, however, brings up the second issue: computer software systems are vulnerable to tampering and malfunction, as made evident in both the 2002 and 2004 elections. As votes come in from disparate precincts, they are totaled in aggregate databases— databases that may easily be altered.

New Barriers to Voting

Even the right to vote is made difficult for many people. The 2002 Help America Vote Act has not, on balance, helped voters: new voter registration requirements have made it much harder for new eligible voters to register. Other policies are making it harder for those already registered to vote. Mike Slater, Laura Kyser, and JoAnn Chasnow of the League of Women Voters argue that the new and more stringent requirements "disproportionately impact those citizens who have been traditionally marginalized in the political process: women, low-income people, members of ethnic and racial minorities, youth, people with disabilities and seniors."[124]

New restrictions on voter registration drives, including registration and training requirements, hamper the efforts of large paid and small volunteer programs alike. New registration requirements ask that every program be registered with the state and include the identity of every employee and volunteer in advance of registration activities. State-mandated training programs are infrequently and inconveniently offered. In Delaware, for example, training was offered once a month at one location. These new restrictions have led to a decline in public agency registration of new voters.

A number of states are proposing laws that a require photo ID to vote. Americans without a photo ID are disproportionately people without resources. For example, in Missouri, the state legislature initially passed a photo ID bill in 2011 that was later vetoed by the governor. Conservatives are still working to get the bill to stick in the state, where an estimated 200,000 people of voting age do not have state-issued photo IDs. In Georgia, where the legislature is determined to pass the photo ID bill, 300,000 people do not have driver's licenses.[125] The Supreme Court's 2013 decision in *Shelby v. Holder*, which struck down a key section of the Voting Rights Act of 1965, has increased the number of states that require a photo ID to vote. Since the 2013 ruling, forty-one states have introduced some form of restrictive voting registration, the most popular of which is requiring a photo ID, a hardship for poor people.[126]

In close races where turnout of minority voters may be critical, conservative poll watchers have been charged with taking down names and even taking photos. Despite any evidence of anyone trying to vote fraudulently, anti-fraud campaigns have become prevalent in minority neighborhoods. Gerry Hebert, executive director of the nonpartisan Campaign Legal Center: "Consequently, it's a concern when word gets out about people encountering difficulty at the polls—it makes it doubly hard to get voters out." He says that such anti-fraud campaigns could have a "chilling effect" on turnout.[127]

Many choose not to vote, believing that the process is already rigged to exclude their interests. Many accept the dismal display of thirty-second television ads and public relations guided presentations by candidates as the reality of what it is legitimate to care about. In 2012, climate change, poverty, surveillance and targeting of U.S. citizens, and campaign finance reform were matters raised only by smaller political parties lacking funds to be heard and invitations to participate in debates.

Judicial Injustice and Social Exclusion

Differences between the wealthy oligarchs and others, particularly the poor, go beyond whose interests are promoted in the legislative and executive branches of government. The United States leads the world in per capita incarcerations. Most who are jailed have never been convicted of a violent crime and never even tried before a jury but have, nevertheless, been pressured to plead guilty for a lesser offense than originally charged after being represented by an overworked, underresourced public defense attorney. Journalist Matt Taibbi raised the question, Who goes to jail? In his book *The Divide: American Injustice in the Age of the Wealth Gap,* Taibbi explores how a Depression-level income gap between the wealthy and the poor is mirrored by a "justice" gap in who is targeted for prosecution and imprisonment. Once in the system, an individual's options for rehabilitation makes return to the community very difficult. Recidivism is high. Taibbi shows examples of the black man arrested in the middle of the night in front of his own house, on an empty street for "blocking pedestrian traffic." Prosecutions are needed to help district attorneys get elected, to justify police funding, and to fund the prison-industrial complex and its provision of cheap prison labor. It is much more grotesque to consider the non-enforcement of white-collar criminals when you also consider how incredibly aggressive law enforcement is with regard to everybody else. Many people died when corporations knowingly dumped chemical wastes into waterways. More died when manufacturers continued to market cigarettes and to produce unsafe vehicles, or to protect against massive oil spills. Bankers guilty of illegal schemes that caused a loss of lifetime savings, of homes, of family farms that gave meaning to many and whose loss has been associated with a rise in suicides—such corporate offenders are defended by expensive legal firms. Their cases, if pursued at all, result in fines representing a small portion of their assets and their settlements include no admission of guilt and only minimal protections against future harmful criminal activities.

Marilyn Taylor examines our understanding of communities segregated by income.[128] Communities and family ties, she argues, continue to persist, and their networks provide the glue for trust and responsibility—they constitute the social capital needed to sustain critical activities in poor and disadvantaged communities. Yet changing economic, social, and political conditions have also seriously weakened the range of what these local ties can do for people. Their social exclusion is not merely within the threadbare fabric of their personal networks, but also in the exclusion of their communities from the opportunities and protections offered to their wealthier and more powerful counterparts. The best we can do in nurturing local ties may be to help people cope with gross deprivations, but not to overcome them. That task would require that people have some meaningful bridges to another type of social capital, the type that might offer opportunities to bring wealth and decision power back to local communities. Locally grown produce, local goods, uncontaminated air, and, particularly in poor countries, local sources of clean water, seeds, and topsoil have in large measure been replaced or commoditized. Ironically, Taylor points out, it is the very rich who have locked themselves in gated communities. What keeps the rest of us out of their elite closed enclaves and their secretive societies and meetings is a political process that limits what representative democracy can accomplish.

In chapter 7 we will examine the role of the media in shaping a reality suited to the needs of a centralized elite. Although the centralized network of power may have differences within itself, there is no countervailing power that can restrict policies and activities that maintain the domination of centralized power. Many of these activities employ violence and manipulation. These activities are the subject of chapter 6.

6—Realpolitik: Strategies and Tactics for Winning

The crimes of the United States have been systematic, constant, vicious, remorseless, but very few people have ever talked about them. You have to hand it to America. It has exercised quite a clinical manipulation of power worldwide while masquerading as a force for universal good. It is a brilliant, even witty, highly successful act of hypnosis.
— HAROLD PINTER, Nobel Peace Prize acceptance speech,
December 7, 2005

IN CHAPTER 5 WE LAID OUT the system of interconnected military and corporate elites whose power dominates decisions that affect the use and distribution of resources. They exercise great, although not absolute, power over decisions about what measures should be taken to protect their wealth and power. As one part of their effort, they have invested heavily in the work of a large number of professional strategists—military planners, economists, and system scientists—who work in and out of government to bring creative ideas to the preservation of the war system and for ways to increase the power, influence, and profits of this elite group. What keeps the powerful in power is the ability to control the flow of large amounts of money. Those who would lay claim to this wealth for other human needs are looked upon as enemies, and a primary goal has been to prevent such a challenge.

In this chapter, we argue that the actions and policies of government are more about the economic control over resources than about political ideologies. For example, we make the case that both anticommunism and a war on terror were broad strategies or policy directives contrived by powerful corporate interests, and they serve to fulfill two main purposes: the continuity and the expansion of powerful interests within the military-industrial complex. Communist bureaucracies produced a great deal of violence. Yet, upon closer examination, U.S. global policies such as anticommunism were generated less by the autocratic nature of communist governments following the Second World War than by concern over any governments that restrained the activities of corporate entrepreneurs. Similarly, the war on terror was aimed less at protecting the security of the United States against a poorly defined group of Muslim fundamentalists who planned violent activities than at protecting corporate interests in the Middle East. We pursue the argument that the war on terror was vastly overblown in comparison to other greater threats to security; yet the promotion of an exaggerated fear was not a mistake but rather a consequence of the way the most powerful networks promote their interests.[1]

Creating the Enemy

It is useful to examine the strategies and tactics used by these powerful networks to achieve their ends. The principal strategy has been to create a fearsome and overarching enemy in the public mind. Hence, powerful interests work to vilify an enemy, making it appear self-evident that the adversary is both evil and out to destroy us. This vilification reduces the adversary to a fanatic demon, thus precluding opportunities to see how alike its leaders may be to some of our own more militant leaders or how its people are humans so like ourselves. It makes those who seek peaceful reconciliation appear to be either naive or unpatriotic and the object of scorn and harassment.

In the Cold War, extreme anticommunism sentiments led to calls to start and "prevail" in a nuclear war with the Soviet Union and to harass and deport communist sympathizers. This view vied with the beliefs of moderate, more realistic, bipartisan cold warriors over the best approach to defeat communism. Defeating communism was the accepted consensus and provided a cover for the Korean War, which ended in a stalemate and has never been officially terminated.[2] Then as in many times since, excesses of the extremists helped to move the center away from any attempts toward reducing weapons or reducing tensions through direct negotiations.

With the war on terror, a neoconservative group has called for the destruction of Arabic weapons and culture. Israeli prime minister Netanyahu expressed the invocation to all-out war on CNN: "Iran is Germany, and it's 1938. Except that this Nazi regime that is in Iran . . . wants to dominate the world, annihilate the Jews, but also annihilate America."[3] The prime minister worked closely with members of the Project for a New American Century (PNAC) who pushed the U.S. attack on Iraq and by 2007 was pushing for a preemptive military attack on Iran. A more cautious coalition that nonetheless supported a war on terror was recommended by the James Baker–Lee Hamilton Iraq study group. The latter called for maintaining both control over Middle Eastern oil and retention of military bases there, but favored a withdrawal of troops from Iraq and greater diplomatic efforts. However, plans for a surge of added troops had been designed within the Heritage Foundation think tank. These replaced the Baker-Hamilton proposals.[4]

Violent and Coercive Tactics

In repeated military incursions, an atmosphere beset with fear from a demonic enemy has provided a cover for a host of violent and coercive tactics aimed at retaining governments friendly to the dominant power circles (see chapter 5). These dirty tactics increase the adversary's fears, their animosity, their commitment to armament, and the likelihood of their retaliation.

The list of documented tactics includes financial gifts, loans, bribes, trade agreements, threats, and sale of weapons. They include also the overthrow of governments, media manipulation, the manipulation of elections, covert measures against groups that dissent, legal harassment, destroying habitats, assassinations, campaigns of terror, bombing raids, and finally sending in the Marines. More recently, the arsenal of choices actually deployed has included the use of weapons of mass destruction, barbaric practices of interrogation and targeted assassinations with remote weapons.[5] Such an array of activities involves the efforts of many people. Individually they may be kind or cruel, strong believers in the rightness of what they are doing or just doing the jobs that are assigned to them.

Regardless of their beliefs in the morality or the necessity of coercive or manipulative methods, these people participate in actions the ultimate results of which are destructive to many people. (This has been noted in chapter 1, dealing with war, and in chapter 3, dealing with economic globalization.) The costs are borne even by those most closely involved in perpetrating these activities.[6]

The atrocities described above should not be used to demonize the United States or its NATO allies. To understand the psychology of a group or nation, one must examine its cultural history. There is a heritage in Western civilization that has cultivated the creative use of the intellect and the spirit of adventure. This tradition has created a set of collective values centered on individual freedom and success, and provided opportunities for many to overcome adversity. The vitality of striving for excellence, working for the greater good, and of personal freedom is part of our heritage. The positive bases for pride in the United States have surely affected the lives of many Americans and have had an impact upon dedicated public service in government at every level. These patriotic values, discussed in chapter 8, nevertheless have permitted a small network of power brokers to create the pain and injustices that have been described. The people directly responsible for the violent acts are not, for the most part, what most would call evil people. The horror of what they do is the product of a system that has failed them and the ideals they serve. To say that these are not accidents or mistakes but rather understandable consequences of a distorted process is not to indicate the workings of an omnipotent conspiracy. Yet, hidden from the eyes of the citizenry, is a high level of planning in a high-stakes game of attaining competitive advantage. Game theory helps us to understand the mindset of the planners.

The Mind-Set of Competitive Games

Game theory is a part of the larger umbrella of decision theory or the science of rational decision-making. These theoretical frameworks were developed in business and engineering and have been added to tools of the military planner. Corporations deciding the particular investment strategies to compete most effectively commonly use such tools in their calculations.

Game theory is a classification system, not of material things but rather of situations. In each situation the players are identified, and goals are established. Winning might mean increasing one's profits or destroying one's competition.

It might be defined as all-or-none victory versus doing better than one's adversaries. The potential range of permissible moves is spelled out: yes for checking the king in chess, no for overturning the board; yes for bombing raids, no for poisoning the water supply. Mathematics then helps to select the best move. In some games there is a single move that is a best choice regardless of the countermoves of an adversary. In other games one must assign probabilities about what an adversary is likely to do. These estimates are based upon the desirability of different outcomes. They are designed to make a best guess, one that would have the greatest likelihood, in the long run, of coming out ahead. Some conflicts have two parties, others many. Some are characterized by a win-lose definition in which whatever is good for one side is bad for the other to that same degree. Others allow for outcomes in which both parties may come out worse or both may gain.

Applied to war, game theory serves to abstract the particular strategic structure of a conflict. It would be completely irrelevant whether the particular structure is played out on a game board with wooden pieces, on a computer simulation, or on a battlefield strewn with bodies. The magnitude of the payoffs (or losses) is a fact to be considered, as in poker, but the content of the payoff is irrelevant. It is permissible within game theory to consider which country might be coerced into assuring a greater amount of oil for the United States. It would not be permissible within game theory to ask whether more oil is a desirable outcome.[7]

Legitimizing Global Violence

The actual mathematical tools of game theory are not always employed by governments or by corporations. In fact, honest application of the theory might illustrate to the parties that certain conflicts are just too costly and should not be played at all. But the mind-set in which the world and its inhabitants are all instruments in a game to gain competitive advantage is very much a part of the belief system that legitimizes global violence. The theory plays the board as if no particular human exists on the other side. Even on one's own side the sacrifices are not of people but of pawns that will provide gains for one's company or country. In a military occupation where torture is used to find, to punish, and to intimidate resistance, the game has been redefined as one in which the rules permit such abuse. The risk exists that being found out might be bad for the side engaging in the practice and might produce blowback or retaliation. But they become just one factor in calculating the likelihood of being caught and determining the ability of the opposition to benefit from exposing the practice.

Externalities: The Acceptability of Risk

Just as the risks of being caught using immoral modes of treating people can be calculated, so also can the loss of lives be entered into the selection of actions. Indeed, we find major corporate decisions taking into account what economists call externalities. Many activities with an intended purpose to profit from developments designed (or justified) to improve or to protect life come with unintended consequences. Dangerous materials used in manufacturing, seriously overcrowded highways, unsafe vehicles or pharmaceuticals, toxic chemical or radioactive waste dumps, and unhealthy fast foods all enter into the cost-benefit analyses. The goal is to produce as cheaply as possible something that will provide the "greatest good" while keeping certain harmful consequences within the acceptable range. The greatest good is, of course, dependent upon whose interests are considered most important. Likewise, the acceptability of risks depends upon who determines what is acceptable. The acceptability may look different for executives of a corporation that produces toxic chemical pesticides used to dust crops than to the parents of a child with leukemia. The model of thought requires that we consider everything—including material products, human lives, timber for construction, and the sound of songbirds—to have a monetary value. The market, like a giant game board, is left to determine what risks will be undertaken. The players with the greatest domination of chips control the directions of the market.

End Goals of Global Games: The Expansion of Markets

Throughout history empires have typically followed the aspirations and military strength of rulers. Trade and resources have long been closely associated with the use of military force.[8] For the U.S. empire, the expansion was primarily a commercial one, dedicated to selling products overseas and dominating foreign markets. Pioneering American firms such as Heinz, Singer, McCormick, Kodak, and Standard Oil shaped the direction of an imperial process by linking the purchase of U.S. consumer goods abroad with "civilization" and "progress." During the late nineteenth and early twentieth centuries, consumerism and commercialism were driving forces, marketing not only products but also racial and gender stereotypes. The messages were apparent in ads for sewing machines, processed food, and agricultural tools. The values of consumerism and commercialism have shaped, and continue to shape, the way the United States is seen. Military force and government action tended to follow rather than to lead the expansion of markets.[9]

Ideological Beliefs

The mind-set of those whose decisions govern the paths of empires is important to understand. Surely wealth and power have been acknowledged motivations. But often accompanying such motives is a belief that the particular empire has a virtuous goal of spreading its benefits, as understood by its rulers, to other parts of the world. Powerful elites, successful in their own worlds, encapsulate themselves among a network of others who also believe in the virtue and legitimacy of their intentions. Ancient Rome, Qing China, France under Napoleon, imperial Britain, and the United States in the Americas did not simply invade and occupy other people's lands out of economic greed. In each case, empire was also driven, at times, by the desire to spread improvement and to export cultural and political practices that were seen as better and more civilized.[10] The contemporary goal of the neoconservative game is often expressed idealistically as the desire to make the world a better place, one with democratic elections and free trade.[11] Such thinking is often used to call upon soldiers and their families for sacrifices, but rarely does it call upon sacrifices from those who profit most from the expanded markets. When such thinking is accompanied by coercive interventionism, it is often the prelude to the fall of the empire.[12] Military historian Caleb Carr notes that empires with strong military forces have almost always taken on the tactics of terrorism, that is, brutal punitive attacks upon civilians as part of the way they maintained influence. This occurred on the part of Rome, recurred through Middle Eastern and European dynasties, and included the United States in its Civil War and in the Second World War. Carr also notes that such brutality to civilians is rarely successful and leads to a decline in the empire.[13]

Sanctions for Force: The Opposition to Communism

The major interest of large corporations is continued growth and expansion. The major threats to that expansion are the aspirations of people and governments that would apply the same resources needed for corporate growth to other purposes. Ideologies of local control, of nationalism, or of communism, each in their own way, are impediments to corporate expansion. In this section we examine the post–Second World War unification of the European market, and the ensuing corporate origins of the Cold War.

A "Permanent War Economy"

At the end of the Second World War, 70 percent of the industrial infrastructure of Europe was destroyed, and the European economy had collapsed. The U.S. economy was booming due as much to a military-industrial complex that made millions for the corporations involved in the war effort as to a backlog in consumer demand. Corporate profits rose from $6.4 billion in 1940 to $10.8 billion in 1944.[14] Charles E. Wilson, the president of General Motors Corporation (and later Secretary of Defense), was so satisfied with wartime profits that he suggested a continuing alliance between business and the military for a "permanent war economy."[15] Eager to extend this boom in profits, the American business community, as represented by the U.S. Council on Foreign Relations, initiated an investment plan to rebuild Europe.

The Marshall Plan

In 1946 Charles Spofford and David Rockefeller presented a speech to the Council on Foreign Relations titled "Reconstruction in Western Europe."[16] In 1947 U.S. Secretary of State George Marshall introduced his plan for the economic reconstruction of Europe; Congress enacted the agreement, which came to be known as the Marshall Plan, giving $13 billion in aid to sixteen Western European states.[17]

While at the outset the Marshall Plan appeared to be an "unprecedented exercise of international generosity (dubbed by Churchill the 'most unsordid act in history')," the less-acknowledged purpose of the plan was to benefit directly the U.S. corporations that promoted it.[18] For example, William Clayton, the undersecretary for Economic Affairs (who helped prepare the plan), personally acquired $700,000 a year, and his company, Anderson, Clayton & Co., secured $10 million.[19]

The Marshall Plan officially moved American investment capital into Europe. When the plan began, President Truman's Secretary of State Dean Acheson noted: "These measures of relief and reconstruction have been only in part suggested by humanitarianism. Your Congress has authorized and your government is carrying out, a policy of relief and reconstruction today chiefly as a matter of national self-interest."[20]

The committee that drafted the Marshall Plan enlisted well-placed advocates of corporate expansion, including chairman Henry Stimson (former Secretary of State and War, Wall Street lawyer, and director of the Council on Foreign Relations); Executive Committee chairman Robert Patterson (former Secretary of War); Executive Committee member Dean Acheson (Undersecretary of State and corporate lawyer of Covington & Burling); Winthrop Aldrich (banker and uncle to the Rockefeller brothers); James Carey (CIO secretary-treasurer); Herbert Lehman (Lehman Bros. Investment); Philip Reed (General Electric executive); Herbert Bayard Swope (former editor and brother of a former GE president); and David Dubinsky (labor leader).

The efforts of these American industrial leaders were not in vain. By 1963 American firms in France controlled 40 percent of the petroleum market, 65 percent of films and photographic paper, 65 percent of farm machinery, 65 percent of telecommunications equipment, and 45 percent of synthetic rubber. By 1965 American-controlled investments in Germany were an estimated $2 billion, while the gross capital of all firms quoted on the German stock exchange was only $3.5 billion.[21]

Economic Aid as a Political Tool

To the business elite, Europe represented a vast untapped market for American exports and unlimited investment potential (fronted primarily by U.S. taxpayers); to the U.S. government, economic aid was a political tool. As Secretary of State Averell Harriman explained, "Economic assistance is one of the most effective weapons at our disposal to influence European political events in the direction we desire."[22] Indeed, under the terms of the Marshall Plan, the strong Communist parties of Italy and France were shut out of the cabinets of those countries. From 1952 on, American aid to Europe became increasingly focused on building up military power in non-communist countries. Over the course of the next ten years, of the $50 billion in aid to ninety countries worldwide, only $5 billion was for nonmilitary economic development.[23]

To U.S. officials, communism was threatening less for ideological reasons, such as violation of individual freedoms, than because communist governments were opposed to the corporate capitalist economic system. The fight against the spread of communism was, in contrast to the way it has typically been described, a fight against the loss of available markets and needed raw materials. The deep fear was that the socialist idea might spread in Europe and in formerly colonized nations, thereby limiting corporate growth.

Creating the Communist Enemy

The American public has been conditioned to react strongly to the term *communist*. It comes with images of the worst excesses of the Stalin era, with wholesale purges and Siberian slave-labor camps. These images evoke fear of a world revolution founded in classic Marxist-Leninist ideology. This revolution is allegedly the intention of all subsequent actions by Communist states.[24] This changes the game to "us" against "them." Political scientist Michael Parenti explains:

> "Them" can mean a peasant in the Philippines, a mural-painter in Nicaragua, a legally elected prime minister in British Guiana, or a European intellectual, a Cambodian neutralist, an African nationalist—all, somehow, part of the same monolithic conspiracy; each, in some way, a threat to the American Way of Life; no land too small, too poor, or too far away to pose such a threat, the "communist threat" . . . has been largely irrelevant whether the particular targets of intervention—be they individuals, political parties, movements or governments—called themselves "communist" or not. It has mattered little whether they were scholars of dialectical materialism or had never heard of Karl Marx; whether they were atheists or priests; whether a strong and influential Communist Party was in the picture or not; whether the government had come into

being through violent revolution or peaceful elections . . . all have been targets, all "communists."[25]

The particular institutional form of socialism in the USSR presented an image in which state ownership of production came to be associated with a totalitarian government and atheism. Marxism, in particular, has been viewed as a directly opposing force since the start of the Russian Revolution. In the summer of 1918, when the First World War was winding down, approximately 13,000 American troops joined British and other allies inside the newly born Union of Soviet Socialist Republics to support the counterrevolutionary white army of the tsar. A young Winston Churchill, then Britain's Minister of War, explained that the goal was to "strangle at its birth" the Bolshevik state.[26] After two years and heavy casualties, the allies withdrew. Later, as a historian, Churchill wrote:

> Were they the allies at war with Soviet Russia? Certainly not; but they shot Soviet Russians at sight. They stood as invaders on Russian soil. They armed the enemies of the Soviet Government. They blockaded its ports and sunk its battleships. They desired and schemed its downfall. But war—shocking! Interference—shame! It was, they repeated, a matter of indifference to them how Russians settled their own internal affairs.[27]

An anticommunist propaganda campaign had begun even before the military intervention. In 1918 expressions like "Red Peril," "the Bolshevik assault on civilization," and "menace to world by Reds is seen" appeared frequently in the *New York Times*.[28]

Although Russian forces provided the largest part of the Allies' win against Nazi Germany in the Second World War, anticommunist sentiment resurfaced in U.S. foreign policy.[29] Historian Howard Zinn describes the transition between the end of the Second World War and the Cold War:

> When, right after the war, the American public, war-weary, seemed to favor demobilization and disarmament, the Truman administration (Roosevelt had died in April 1945) worked to create an atmosphere of crisis and cold war. True, the rivalry with the Soviet Union was real—that country had come out of the war with its economy wrecked and 20 million people

dead, but was making an astounding comeback, rebuilding its industry, regaining its military strength. The Truman administration, however, presented the Soviet Union as not just a rival but an immediate threat.[30]

From 1947 to the mid-1960s, an objective of U.S. policy was to instigate the downfall of the Soviet government and other Eastern European regimes. Hundreds of Russian exiles were trained by the CIA and sneaked back into Russia to set up espionage rings, to stir armed political struggle, and to carry out such acts of sabotage as derailing trains, wrecking bridges, damaging arms factories and power plants, and assassinations.[31]

Daniele Ganser of the Center for Security Studies at the Federal Institute of Technology in Zurich offers substantial evidence for an application in postwar Europe of what has later been called the "Salvador Option." Ganser's book, *NATO's Secret Armies: Operation Gladio and Terrorism in Western Europe,* describes how during the Cold War, U.S. and British intelligence sources worked with European governments to conduct secret attacks in their own countries in order to manipulate the population to reject socialism and communism.[32] The evidence is seen in a document for which the CIA denies authenticity. One of the NATO field manuals sets forth a clear message that if terrorism by a Communist Party could not be found, the secret armies were prepared to create some.[33] According to Ganser, the secret army was behind waves of terrorist attacks in Italy in the 1970s; it worked with the Franco dictatorship, supporting an estimated 1,000 attacks upon left-wing opponents. In Germany, the secret army had standing plans to murder leaders of the Social Democrat Party in the event of a Soviet invasion, and carried out terrorist actions against President de Gaulle and the Algerian peace plan in France. NATO's "Prometheus" plan was prepared to prevent a communist or a socialist government from coming to power. The plan was used by a group of Greek military officers in a coup that replaced a popularly elected government with a cruel and murderous dictatorship. The United States continued support for this reign of the Greek colonels.[34]

Communism in Russia and Eastern Europe has ended. But NATO still provides the cover for five major permanent U.S. military communities: one in Vicenza, Italy, the other four in Germany (Kaiserlautern, Landstuhl/Ramstein, Vilseck/Grafenwoehr, and Ansbach). Germany remains the hub for U.S. military operations in Europe, the Middle East, and Africa. Per U. S. plans, all U.S. facilities in Europe are being enlarged. The United States has built "forward bases" in the "New Europe," investing funds in bases in Romania, Poland, Bulgaria, and other countries. The United States has proposed a so-called missile shield in Poland and the Czech Republic. While the shield is marketed as a purely defensive instrument, it is not. The technology, even in its most optimal forecasts, cannot prevent many of the nuclear missiles from penetrating in a large-scale attack. It might, however, destroy a small number of missiles still able to fire *after* a devastating first strike. Hence, missile defense is only needed by a nation preparing or threatening to strike first. Opposition to this proposal is building, particularly from Russia.[35]

The increasing integration of the European Union has fulfilled one objective of protecting European nations from engaging in war or even extensive competition with each other, but it has not emerged as a force for peace.[36]

Ideological Irony

Noam Chomsky highlights the great irony of the Truman administration's ideological problem with communism. Truman reportedly liked and admired Stalin; in a cabinet meeting Truman once remarked that he could "deal with" Stalin, as long as the United States got its way 85 percent of the time. What happened inside the USSR was not his concern. With all of the emphasis and apparent value for "freedom" professed by U.S. leaders, the fascist regime of Mussolini was looked upon with admiration. Roosevelt admired the "Italian gentleman" who had dissolved the country's parliamentary system, blocked the labor movement, and halted domestic socialists and communists.[37]

Preceding U.S. entrance into the Second World War, major American corporations, with the support of the U.S. government, not only poured money into fascist Italy but also into Nazi Germany; some American corporations reaped the benefits of the overturning of Jewish assets under Hitler's Aryanization program. Between 1929 and 1940, U.S. investment in Germany increased by 48.5 percent.

Tactics to Defeat Communism in the Third World

Anticommunism provided a rationale for a violent foreign policy in the developing world. The Vietnam War was triggered by a report of the sinking of a U.S. ship in the Gulf of Tonkin, a report later found to be false.[39] The larger rationale was to prevent Vietnam's unification, which its people had already approved. It was fought with a strategy that killed and mutilated civilians, and destroyed their villages and crops. The overt strategy was based on a "domino theory," a gaming-mentality reasoning that one communist country, however democratically elected, would lead to successive revolts in all of Southeast Asia. The costs included more than 2 million Vietnamese lives, the lives of 750,000 U.S. soldiers, and the long-term traumatic injuries and scars suffered by the soldiers who served. Also lost were the funds needed to carry out the policies of President Johnson's war on poverty.[40]

Secretary of State Henry Kissinger helped President Nixon undermine the Paris peace talks on Vietnam on the eve of the 1968 election. Upon Kissinger's advice, the promise for a new plan to end the unpopular war was translated into the bombing of Cambodia and Laos, which killed approximately one million civilians. Kissinger was also involved in the assassination of Chilean Chief of Staff General Rene Schneider, whose loyalty blocked the first planned coup against the elected president, Salvador Allende. Kissinger's approval and support for Indonesia's invasion of East Timor and the resulting genocide is described later in this chapter. In 1971 Kissinger and Nixon supported the Pakistan military government's genocide in Bangladesh, and then supported a bloody military coup in independent Bangladesh in 1975. In all cases, the actions were justified as efforts to curb the threat of communism.[41] The human costs and even the futility of the wars were known within the Department of Defense and the executive branch.[42] It is difficult to hold in mind the suffering and grief involved in each individual injury or death or to accept that higher-level officials orchestrated wanton civilian killings and covered up the evidence. Strategic thinking helps people to ignore any emotional pain or ethical responsibility.

Creating Governments with the Corporate Agenda

Policies actually undertaken reflect a planning process in which the needs of key players in the global market place are pursued as objectives of the game. Any understanding of the degree of planning that goes into the U.S. corporate and military domination of other nations owes much to the revelations of John Perkins. His clandestine position, first with the National Security Agency and then with a private company, was predicated upon an ability to make economic forecasts and sell loans to heads of state in undeveloped countries. He supervised a staff that included economists who provided complex models that could be used to exaggerate the benefits to gross national product (GNP) of massive loans. The loans were always for the development of infrastructure, oil drilling and pipelines, dams, electric power grids, and building complexes. The contracts would be awarded to such corporate giants as Bechtel, Halliburton, and Brown and Root. The inducements to foreign leaders included military and police aid and train- ing, lucrative financial benefits, recognition in U.S. diplomatic circles, and even the procurement of personal mistresses. The contracts would make a small group within the accepting country very wealthy.

On the negative side, they would make the particular nation a client state of the United States, dependent upon further loans and adjustments to repay the incurred debts, and unable, therefore, to use the country's resources for forms of development that might provide sustainable productivity for its farmers, educa- tion and health care for its children, and protections for its environment. Some populist leaders found the terms unacceptable. Many of the leaders who were more representative of the needs of their own people and who refused the loan terms were removed in coups, assassinations, or plane or helicopter "accidents."[43] If that did not produce a compliant government, the next steps were to foment a violent revolt and finally to send in the bombs and the marines.

Economic Intervention

The major ongoing interventions, occurring without the fanfare of war, are economic. The manipulation of local economies has been part of a worldwide effort to impose what has been labeled the "Washington Consensus." This has been forced on developing countries, via procedures of the U.S. government, the World Bank, the International Monetary Fund, and the World Trade Orga- nization. John Williamson, a well-known British economist, developed its basic tenets in reforms calling for economic deregulation, privatization, encouragement of foreign investment, unrestricted movement of capital, liberalization of trade policies, and reduction in public expenditures. This program of neoliberalism has been aggressively pushed as a primary U.S. foreign policy goal. The strategy is focused upon pressuring developing countries that are dependent on aid, from major international lending agencies and the United States, to implement structural adjustment programs that prescribe the required changes that a specific country must make in order to be considered creditworthy.[44]

Increasingly, official U.S. strategy has been to support governments subservient to U.S. corporate and military interests, to keep them in power through financial indebtedness and military control over their dissenters, and to fancy a highly fortified Green Zone with lush accommodations for visiting officials—as if that façade, rather than the people of the country, was the true U.S. ally. This makes sense if one recalls that it is an elite network of diplomatic, financial, and military ties that determine the paths of information and influence. The strategy reflects not only the gamester's mentality and the dehumanization of casualties, but also the great distance between those few with great power and the rest of us, who are seen as lesser players and whose views are considered irrelevant to the elite-created reality. The more reprehensible tactics may be concealed or, if exposed, may be denied. Where support is needed, from voters or from soldiers, it can be handled through persuasion, employment opportunities, and public relations.

Bypassing Legal Constraints

Pressure to create governments willing to play by the rules of neoliberalism has not always been through legal means. Difficult and risky efforts at espionage are the stock-in-trade of highly trained special forces, such as the Navy Seals. Other than when used for public relations value in publicizing successful rescue attempts, the work of the special forces is known only to high-level authorities and can act to assassinate individuals and to create mayhem outside of public view.[45] The CIA, in addition to its highly publicized role of gathering information, has also played a more clandestine role of subverting governments, destroying buildings and trains, and bribing both officials and crowds of people to gather their support.[46] Actions to undermine the host government by the U.S. ambassador to Nicaragua clearly violated the April 1961 Vienna Convention on Diplomatic Relations, which asserts that representatives or diplomats "have a duty not to interfere in the internal affairs of that state" to which they may be assigned. Despite international law, the United States has rarely felt constrained over intervening in the internal affairs of other countries. The United States has also been able to bypass the legal constraints upon such activity by exerting its influence through private organizations.

The National Endowment for Democracy (NED) was founded in 1983 as a private organization funded completely by government revenue. Its purpose is to influence the direction of elections and policies in foreign countries through its recipient organizations, the National Democratic Institute (NDI) and the International Republican Institute (IRI). Such activities by another government would be illegal in the United States. The NED injects soft money into the domestic elections of foreign countries in favor of one party or the other. In a relatively poor country, a few hundred thousand dollars of assistance can have a decisive influence. It is particularly Orwellian to call U.S. manipulation of foreign elections "promoting democracy."[47]

Overthrowing Governments

One strategy for the exercise of power is to overthrow governments unwilling to accept domination by American interests. The United States has used military force to overthrow a legitimate government on fourteen occasions, starting with Hawaii at the end of the nineteenth century.[48] Historian Greg Grandin writes of numerous coup efforts by the United States in Latin America and the continuity of such U.S. responses in the Middle East:

> After the Second World War, in the name of containing Communism, the United States, mostly through the actions of local allies, executed or encouraged coups in, among other places, Guatemala, Brazil, Chile, Uruguay, and Argentina and patronized a brutal mercenary war in Nicaragua.... For 150 years Nicaragua has borne the brunt of more interventions than almost any other country in this hemisphere. . . . Indeed, Reagan's Central American wars can best be understood as a dress rehearsal for what is going on now in the Middle East. It was in these wars where the coalition made up of neoconservatives, Christian evangelicals, free marketers, and nationalists that today stands behind George W. Bush's expansive foreign policy first came together.[49]

We have selected four classic cases of the U.S. exercise of illegitimate force: in Iran, Iraq, East Timor, and Guatemala. These cases illustrate intervention by bribery, coups, support for genocide, and direct military attack.

Iran: A Model Removal of a Popular Leader

Popular or democratically elected leaders of countries who have lost favor with the United States have been forcefully removed. This occurred with Mossadegh in Iran;[50] Bosch in the Dominican Republic;[51] Arbenz in Guatemala;[52] and Allende in Chile.[53] CIA agent Kermit Roosevelt was sent to overthrow the democratically elected Mossadegh in Iran. Mossadegh's crime had been an attempt to nationalize the Anglo-American Oil Company. The agent began by bribing members of Parliament to denounce him in Parliament. Then religious mullahs were bribed to denounce him as an atheist enemy of Islam.

Within weeks of bribing reporters and editors, Roosevelt had 80 percent of the Teheran press on his payroll. Roosevelt also bribed members of police units and low-ranking military officers to be ready with their units on the crucial day. In his culminating scheme, he hired the leaders of street gangs in Tehran to help create the impression that the rule of law had disintegrated in Iran. At one point, he hired a gang to run through the streets of Tehran beating up any pedestrian they found, breaking shop windows, firing guns into mosques, and yelling, "We love Mossadegh and communism." This was sufficient to turn decent citizens against him. Then Roosevelt hired a second mob to attack the first mob, to give people the impression that there was no police presence and order had completely disintegrated. Within a few weeks, this one agent operating with a large sum of cash and a network of contacts from various elements of society had taken a fairly stable country and thrown it into complete upheaval. The first attempt at a coup failed, but the agent, acting on his own, arranged to give a good day's pay to be part of a mob shouting slogans on the street. None of the participants ever knew the CIA was paying them. Roosevelt had been spending $11,000 a week to bribe members of the Iranian Parliament who then whipped up the crowds. The average annual income in Iran at that time was about $500. At crucial moments, police and military units joined the crowd and started gunfights in front of government buildings, killing about 100 people in front of Mossadegh's house. A military leader Roosevelt had bribed arrived with a column of tanks, and Mossadegh was no longer able to retain his position. A general, selected by the CIA, was installed as prime minister. Shah Pahlavi returned from exile in Rome to become a particularly feared monarch. He, in turn, was eventually overthrown by the religious mullahs, who have remained suspicious of U.S. intentions ever since. Roosevelt went on to become a vice president for Gulf Oil. The CIA director at that time was Allen Dulles, an associate of the law firm providing legal counsel for the Anglo-American Oil Company.[54] Dulles was impressed by this example of regime change in Iran. Ten months later it was attempted in Guatemala, also against a democratically elected leader. This second success led to other attempts, from Indonesia to Chile, to Cuba, to Vietnam, to the Congo.

The shah of Iran followed pro-Western policies, particularly restoring control of oil reserves to Anglo-American Oil but with a substantial cut to U.S. companies. The shah relied upon brutal police methods to maintain control. The anti-Western blowback from the religious leaders who overthrew the shah was not what U.S. officials had intended, and the capture of American hostages by Iran in 1979 helped bring the Reagan administration into power.

Iraq and the Middle East: Preemptive Military Action

Plans for the U.S.-initiated war in Iraq were reminiscent of plans for the Vietnam War in certain ways. The enemy in Vietnam was an assumedly unified communism, which had to be stopped lest all of Southeast Asia fall like dominos. The elite strategists continued to ignore the history of Vietnamese nationalism including years of fighting off Chinese, Japanese, and French occupations. Iraq's history of 100 years of petro-imperialism was likewise ignored. In 1897 England's government assumed a protectorate over Kuwait, which was carved out of Iraq. As oil was gaining importance, England and Germany warred over the Berlin-Baghdad railroad, with Britain invading the entire region of Turkish Mesopotania, eventually overcoming German-led Kurdish troops. The secret 1916 Sykes-Picot Agreement arranged for a French and British split over the oil-rich area, although the British later claimed the greatest share. Turkey, in 1922, fought to regain the area of Mosul but was defeated. Reneging on promises of self-determination, the British, from 1919 to 1958, relied on aerial bombing to crush Iraqi resistance. In 1941 Iraq was the battleground for war between England and Germany (with Italy and the puppet Vichy government of conquered France). The first half of the twentieth century was a story of France, Britain, Germany, and the United States repeatedly overthrowing governments in Iraq and Iran in a struggle for domination over oil.[55] In 1959 the United States attempted a coup against Iraq prime minister Abdul Qarim Qasim in response to his nationalist intentions regarding the profits from oil. The history casts doubt upon the public rationale provided for an invasion of Iraq in 2003.

Heavy-handed involvement by the United States appeared in 1973, when Secretary of Defense Schlesinger sought British support for a joint airborne attack. To address the threat of OPEC control, the plan promoted by Secretary of State Kissinger called for seizing Saudi oil fields and installations. In 1983 President Reagan initiated a diplomatic opening to Iraq. Iraq was in the third year of a war of attrition against neighboring Iran. By 1982 the tide had turned to favor the larger Iran. The Reagan administration sent Donald Rumsfeld as an emissary to Iraqi ruler Saddam Hussein. Rumsfeld helped to arrange support for the Iraqi strongman, even after learning that Iraq had begun to use chemical weapons against Iran, the first sustained use of poison gas since a 1925 treaty banning chemical weapons.

After the Rumsfeld mission, the United States offered Hussein financial credits, making Iraq the third-largest recipient of U.S. assistance. It normalized diplomatic relations and began providing Iraq with battlefield intelligence that was used to target Iranian troops. And when Iraq turned its chemical weapons on the Kurds in 1988, killing 5,000 in the town of Halabja, the Reagan administration sought to obscure responsibility.[56]

On August 25, 1988, five days after the Iran-Iraq War ended, Iraq attacked forty-eight Kurdish villages more than 100 miles from Iran. The next year, President George H. W. Bush's administration doubled U.S. financial credits for Iraq. A week before Hussein invaded Kuwait, the administration opposed legislation that would have conditioned U.S. assistance to Iraq on a commitment not to use chemical weapons and to stop the genocide against the Kurds. At the time, Dick Cheney was secretary of defense and a member of the National Security Council that reviewed and supported Iraq policy. By all accounts, he supported the administration's appeasement policy. The Iraqi misdeeds were ignored by the administration and by the mainstream press, that is, until the United States had determined that Iraq was to be demonized in preparation for a U.S. attack. That Rumsfeld, subsequently, as secretary of defense, and Cheney, subsequently, as vice president, should be among those citing Iraq's brutal use of chemical weapons as a reason for war seems paradoxical. Yet it shows the internalized worldview of the strategic gamester. Iraq was supported as a balance to the power of Iran and a possible helper in the Middle East peace process. Hussein seriously miscalculated by invading Kuwait in response to its role in lowering oil prices. But the individuals who appeased this cruel ruler were the same who later accused opponents of the Iraq war of appeasing a Hitler-like monster. Informed observers see the neoconservative planned invasion of Iraq to have been based upon an ideological belief that the United States is the dominant military power; that it can privatize its resources and its reconstruction to the benefit of corporate investors; that it can take over and change regimes in other countries without attempting to understand their history, their values, or their culture, and without paying serious attention to the human consequences on the ground.[57] The righteous cause outweighed the obstacles and the need to hear other voices. A former CIA agent, Stephen Pelletiere, cites major deception by U.S. officials leading to both the 1991 and the 2003 invasions of Iraq, comparing them to the "big lie" that Germany used to defend its launching of the Second World War.[58]

In 1990, George H. W. Bush gave Saudi King Fahd a written promise that he would remove U.S. troops after the Gulf War. However, U.S. troops, warplanes, and other military hardware remained in the Gulf Arab monarchies thereafter. The continued presence of U.S. troops in Saudi Arabia is claimed to have so enraged Osama bin Laden that he orchestrated the horrific 9/11 attack on the United States.[59] On January 20, 2002, Secretary of State Colin Powell stated that the U.S. military presence in Saudi Arabia would end when the world had turned into "the kind of place we dreamed of."[60] Powell explained that the American troops on Saudi Arabian soil serve a useful purpose there as a deterrent to Saddam Hussein, but beyond that, a symbol of American presence and influence. "We've always wanted to maintain a presence in that part of the world, for a variety of reasons."[61]

There are two related answers to the question of why this is true. First, Iraq's rich oil reserves were relatively untapped. The other answer is seen in the history of map making. In 1914 the *Petroleum Review* of London printed its map of Mesopotamian oil and asphalt fields and the route of the Berlin-Baghdad railroad. Since 1930, two types of maps have evolved. The first indicated the nations, mostly new, that have been created. The second type cut the entire region into squares, each one with the initials of the petroleum corporate giant laying claim to the area. Maps prepared for Vice President Cheney's National Energy Policy Group in 2001 and the National Security Council were later revealed under a federal court order. These detailed Iraq's oil fields, pipelines, and refineries as well as a list of "foreign suitors for Iraqi oilfield contracts." That list included sixty firms from thirty countries—including Russia, France, China, and India— all of whom were ready to negotiate contracts with Iraq, much to the dismay of U.S.-based oil companies. Fadel Gheit, a New York–based oil analyst wrote, "Think of Iraq as a military base with a very large oil reserve underneath.... You can't ask for better than that."[62]

Preemptive attack is military aggression. The preservation of beliefs and institutions that condone such activity requires a theory that includes identification of the inner network of military decision makers, of their ability to create enemies, and of the mechanisms that facilitate multinational corporate expansion. This case also illustrates the need for a theory that explains why violence is itself cyclical rather than a means to ending violence.

Iraq was considered first on the U.S. list of targets for a new national security doctrine of preemptive action against states considered hostile. The United States would become a law unto itself, creating new rules regarding international engagement without agreement by other nations. Investigative journalists Michael Hirsh and John Barry, in 2005, disclosed a Pentagon plan to use the "Salvador Option" in Iraq. This was modeled upon an American counterinsurgency program in the 1980s. The original plan funded nationalist death squads to hunt and kill insurgents. The new plan would deploy secret special forces in both friendly and unfriendly countries to spy, to target terrorists and their sympathizers, and to conduct "hits," all without congressional oversight. Whether adopted specifically or not, U.S. actions in Iraq did bypass congressional oversight in the extradition of prisoners to other countries where they would be tortured.[63]

The plan, as outlined in the National Security Strategy, made explicit the objective of a major expansion of U.S. military presence on a global basis (beyond troops already present in approximately 130 countries) for constabulary or policing functions. It discussed the development of the "robust nuclear earth penetrator" for combat use, the use of American power to remove by force foreign leaders seen as threats, and the reliance upon American political leadership rather than that of the United Nations.[64] However, the threat from Iraq was not specific, not clearly established, and not shown to be imminent. The invasion, therefore, went beyond provisions of international law for anticipatory self-defense. A unilateral attack on Iraq was outside the framework of global law that the United States initially helped create.[65] The display of military power, the securing of oil reserves, and the hope to assure a government friendly to U.S. corporate interests have been noted as other motives for a war against Iraq: Contrary to propaganda orchestrated from Washington and London, the coming attack has nothing to do with Saddam Hussein's "weapons of mass destruction," if these exist at all. The reason is that America wants a more compliant thug to run the world's greatest source of oil.[66]

Viewed from the angle of global oil prices, there is a striking symmetry underlying the two U.S.-led wars against Iraq. The first in 1990 was started by Saddam Hussein because he considered the price of oil too low; the second in 2003 by George W. Bush because he considered the price of oil too high. Writing in opposition to the 2003 Iraq war, eminent international relations scholars Stephen Walt and John Mearsheimer pointed out that Saddam's decision to invade Kuwait in 1990 was primarily an attempt to deal with Iraq's continued economic vulnerability following the Iran-Iraq War. Kuwait exacerbated Iraq's problems by refusing to loan Iraq $10 billion and to write off debts Iraq had incurred during the Iran-Iraq War. Kuwait overproduced the quotas set by OPEC, which drove down world oil prices and reduced Iraqi oil profits.[67]

Conversely, a key objective of the 2003 Iraq war can be inferred from an economic vision for postwar Iraq propounded by Ariel Cohen and Gerald O'Driscoll, Jr., writing for the Washington-based conservative Heritage think tank. They note:

> An unencumbered flow of Iraqi oil would be likely to provide a more constant supply of oil to the global market, which would dampen price fluctuations, ensuring stable oil prices in the world market in a price range lower than the current $25 to $30 a barrel. Eventually, this will be a win-win game: Iraq will emerge with a more viable oil industry, while the world will benefit from a more stable and abundant oil supply.[68]

The opposite turned out to be true. Iraq's oil industry was destroyed. Between $5 billion and $10 billion would be needed to return capacity to prewar levels, and an additional $15 billion to $25 billion to raise output to 5 million barrels per day, leaving it still short of the 7 to 8 million barrels per day eventually envisaged by Cohen and O'Driscoll.[69] Limited supply during this time led to U.S. oil companies enjoying record profits. Likewise, U.S. corporations enjoyed a tremendous windfall from mismanaged and unsuccessful reconstruction efforts. One hundred fifty corporations received up to $50 billion in contracts. Military planning for the invasion and its aftermath are now widely recognized as seriously bungled.[70]

Nonetheless, stunning successes of corporations in penetrating Iraq have been recorded. As Antonia Juhasz points out in her book *The Bush Agenda: Invading the World, One Economy at a Time,* the contracts were meticulously planned by the consulting company BearingPoint, Inc., which received a $250 million contract to rewrite the entire economy of Iraq.[71] This was part of an attempt to implement the neoliberal economic policies of the Washington Consensus. The BearingPoint website proclaims the company's ability to deliver "sustainable success. Not just a single event but a series of successful outcomes." The people of Iraq, many of whom were still lacking regular electricity, running water, and sewage services three years after the reconstruction began, might differ from BearingPoint on the definition of success. One clear conclusion is that the neoliberal economic agenda, and consulting firms like BearingPoint that help implement it, are an integral component of the machinery of modern warfare.

In January 2007, George W. Bush announced his plan to increase the number of U.S. troops in Iraq by 20,000. Over 3,000 American soldiers and more than 600,000 Iraqi citizens were dead by that time. It had already became public knowledge that the U.S. and U.K. governments were radically redrawing Iraq's oil industry and opening the doors to the third-largest oil reserves in the world, allowing the first large-scale operation of foreign oil companies in the country since the industry was nationalized in 1972.[72]

This legislation introduced production-sharing agreements between the Iraqi government and oil industry giants Exxon Mobil, Shell, and British Petroleum; in exchange for investing in and maintaining the infrastructure and operation of the wells, pipelines, and refineries. Western corporations were set up to receive up to 75 percent of Iraqi oil profits for the next thirty years.[73]

Barry Lando, a former investigative producer for *60 Minutes*, reminds us of the U.S. president's repeated citing of the threat to freedom in Iraq if the United States withdrew:

But that lofty cause was nothing but political window dressing. Indeed, allowing the people of Iraq a real choice in their future had always been a *threat* to the U.S. and other great powers, not a goal. What counted was which local leaders would gain control of the region and its resources and how amenable they would be to great power interests. Not if they were freely elected.[74]

Eleven years after the invasion of Iraq, U.S. officials were relating only to a heavily fortified Green Zone and to a government serving at the behest of the occupiers as if that represented Iraq. The terms offered to that government of surrendering the oil reserves, permitting permanent U.S. bases, and crushing or containing those who resist, were a bitter pill for Iraqi citizens augmenting their sustained opposition to bombing and military occupation and leaving a U.S.-supported Iraqi government unable to manage its population.[75]

East Timor: Decimating a Civilian Population

Like Iran, Indonesia is another oil-rich country in which U.S. military aid created an oppressive government and turned a blind eye to its abuses. CIA involvement since 1958 was critical in the overthrow of the Sukarno government in Indonesia. This permitted a military rule responsible for the deaths of close to one million people.[76] That military was later responsible for major abuses that occurred in the Indonesian rule over East Timor. Approximately 800,000 people live in East Timor, half of an island off the eastern end of the Indonesian archipelago. In 1975, after 400 years of colonial rule, the Revolutionary Front for an Independent East Timor declared independence from Portugal. Nine days later, Indonesia's President Suharto met with U.S. President Ford and Secretary of State Kissinger. In the meeting, Suharto described the problem in East Timor and his desire to take rapid action. Kissinger and Ford discussed the use of U.S. arms and the technical and legal problems involved. Within hours after their meeting, the United States authorized an invasion of East Timor by Indonesian troops.[77] The National Security Archive declassified a secret State Department telegram detailing the Suharto, Ford, and Kissinger meeting.[78] Kissinger, in a Department of State telegram, observed:

> It depends on how we construe it; whether it is in self-defense or is a foreign operation. It is important that whatever you do succeeds quickly. We

would be able to influence the reaction in America if whatever happens, happens after we return. This way there would be less chance of people talking in an unauthorized way. The President will be back on Monday at 2:00 p.m. Jakarta time. We understand your problem and the need to move quickly but I am only saying that it would be better if it were done after we returned.[79]

U.S. military and political support was essential for the invasion of East Timor. Over 200,000 East Timorese died from bombings, napalm, and famine. Years after the invasion, successive Democratic and Republican administrations funneled hundreds of millions of dollars of economic and military aid to Indonesia and protected it from serious political challenge to its illegal occupation of East Timor. Disregard for international law must be an element of a theory of violent conflict.

After twenty-four years of occupation, 80 percent of East Timorese adults voted in a UN-supervised referendum on August 30, 1999, for independence from Indonesia. Within hours of the election, pro-Indonesian militias hunted down supporters, massacred them, burned down villages, and raped the village women. It was not until one week after this rampage that President Clinton made the decision to end U.S. support for the Indonesian military. Stapleton Roy, Washington's ambassador to Jakarta, explained why it had taken a U.S. president so long to reach this decision: "The dilemma is that Indonesia matters and East Timor doesn't."[80] Roy went on to head Kissinger Associates, the consulting firm of the former secretary of state who was instrumental in condoning the invasion of East Timor in 1975.[81]

On May 20, 2002, East Timor became the first new nation of the twenty-first century. But the period of brutal devastation has left its effects. The nation has a mortality rate of 200 children per 1,000 under the age of five. Malaria and tuberculosis are endemic. Of the 2,400 villages, over 50 percent have no wells or piped water.[82] The nation does grow organic coffee, and Starbucks is a major buyer. But although coffee is the main export crop and the major source of employment, it is an open question how much of the $10 million in revenue generated by coffee production makes its way into the pockets of the Timorese.[83] However, the main economic prospect is oil. It is estimated that when recently discovered oil fields are fully productive commercially the industry will earn $3 million annually and up to $28 billion in revenue over the next forty years.[84]

East Timor laid claim to the entire Greater Sunrise gas field in the Timor Sea. Its prime minister, Mari Alkatir, who was obliged to resign, looked upon Australia's claim to 80 percent of this huge gas reserve as a clear violation of current international law.[85] If this dispute is resolved legally, there is a possibility that East Timor can become a sustainable nation. This will not be an easy task. In April 2002, Secretary of State Colin Powell wrote a warning to the incoming government to give a written promise not to prosecute any U.S. citizens for crimes against humanity under the procedures of the newly established International Criminal Court. Otherwise, the U.S. Congress would find it difficult to go on giving aid. East Timor quickly gave in. Its new leaders were aware that Washington has long been willing to sacrifice their population and their popular government to promote U.S. interests.[86]

The case of East Timor provides a basis for the skepticism with which U.S. policy is viewed in much of the world. It also gives reason to doubt America's professed opposition to the use of violence against civilians.[87]

Guatemala: Supporting Violent Military Rule

In 1954, a mercenary army organized by the CIA staged the "liberation" of Guatemala. In fact, this was a coup that overthrew the democratically elected President Jacobo Arbenz and returned Guatemala to military rule.[88] Arbenz was a nationalist and a socialist who had sought to transform oligarchic Guatemalan society through land reform and the development of government-owned enterprises that would compete with the American corporations, which dominated the railroad, electric, and fruit-trade industries. Of these American interests, the United Fruit Company was the most influential. For decades the company was the largest employer, landowner, and exporter in Guatemala. With nearly half of its land expropriated by Arbenz's land reform act, company executives and board members (one of whom was CIA director Allen Dulles) appealed to the American government. In addition, United Fruit appealed to the public relations industry, which then painted Arbenz's government and the popular movement that supported it as communist, and therefore a threat to the American people.[89]

To form a new government, the CIA approached Ydigoras Fuentes, who was living in exile in El Salvador. Ydigoras later reported his encounter with the CIA, confirming that they wanted him not only to assist in overthrowing Arbenz but also "to favor the United Fruit Company, to destroy the railroad workers union, and to establish a strong-arm government."[90] Under U.S. guidance, the army organized a powerful military force and a network of counterinsurgency surveillance that would continue for more than three decades.[91]

Historian Susanne Jonas makes three important points about the U.S. intervention in Guatemala. First, the United States was unable to tolerate the Arbenz nationalist revolution because it was a direct threat not only to the foreign business interests at the time, but also to future business interests and the lucrative arrangement that the United States had enjoyed for decades. Second, there was little protest from within the United States because of bipartisan support in the tense climate of McCarthyism and little protest from the Soviet Union, which recognized Central America as the domain of the United States. Third, U.S. intervention easily succeeded, she argues, because of Guatemala's history of economic dependence upon the United States, and because Guatemala's landed oligarchy collaborated with the United States to overthrow the Arbenz government.

Immediately after the coup, the United States helped secure Castillo Armas as transitional leader, who soon set about reversing the ten years of reforms brought about by Arbenz and his democratic predecessor, Juan José Arevalo. Arbenz's land reform law, Decree 900, was revoked and the expropriation process reversed. The two largest labor organizations were abolished. Armas's U.S.-sponsored plan for the Guatemalan economy was to return to the post-colonial reliance on coffee and banana cultivation, which enriched the small landed aristocracy and foreign interests like United Fruit, while doing little for the majority of the Guatemalan people. Over the next three years, Armas's government would receive some $80 million from the United States, not including military aid, nearly all of it in direct grants.[92] This is particularly notable because U.S. economic aid program for all of Latin America was $60 million a year at that time. This period marked the beginning of the thirty-six-year civil war in Guatemala, a period of successive military dictatorships supported by the United States and the oppression and genocide of the Mayan people. Over this thirty-six-year period, various U.S.-sponsored military regimes killed over 200,000 civilians and wiped out 440 Maya villages. The UN-sponsored Commission for Historical Clarification found that the Guatemalan army had committed nearly 95 percent of the total war crimes, and had carried out over 600 massacres. The commission determined that the Guatemalan army's counterinsurgency campaign, by legal definition, constituted genocide against the Maya people.[93]

In 1955, a year into Armas's presidency, Vice President Richard Nixon visited Guatemala and declared: "President Castillo Armas's objective, 'to do more for the people in two years than the Communists were able to do in ten years,' is important. This is the first instance in history where a Communist government has been replaced by a free one. The whole world is watching to see which does the better job."[94]

While the situation, in reality, deteriorated the United States continued with the underlying objective of using the airport, ports, and military bases for the staging of the Bay of Pigs invasion. This event characterizes the explicit reason for U.S. presence and support throughout the civil war period: Guatemala was a foothold in a region characterized by popular revolution and, as it was presented, a hotbed of Communist activity. In the years to follow, continued U.S. aid would be offered in return for staging and manpower to launch counterinsurgency campaigns in Nicaragua, El Salvador, Honduras, and Panama. Some Pentagon voices expressed the view that the need to make credible U.S. power required regular military incursions. Michael Ledeen, former Defense Department consultant and holder of the Freedom Chair at the American Enterprise Institute, advised: "Every ten years or so, the United States needs to pick up some small crappy little country and throw it against the wall, just to show the world we mean business."[95]

The Vulcans Expand the Agenda

World history reveals many cases of brutal imperial expansion. The United States has a long history of supporting corporate and military interests through the use of military force, particularly in what was considered the U.S. sphere of influence. But toward the end of the twentieth century, a new and more far-reaching agenda was introduced. Until this time the elite centers of power were balanced by several directives. Corporations wanted few constraints and little government protection for citizens harmed by their risky activities. But many corporate leaders also held a profound commitment to some of the ideals of freedom and of the constitutional guarantees that got their families to such privileged status. Powerful religious leaders sanctioned the interventions into other countries for their missionary goals, but some also pressured for humane treatment of the victimized people. Military elites competed for allocations and for weapon systems for their own branch and sometimes promoted conflict. Yet some within the upper military echelons felt a responsibility for the loss of their soldiers and were cautious about unnecessary wars. These centers of power long dominated political decision-making, and their success is found in the enduring gross inequality described earlier. But a more recent center of power—the Vulcans—has been redefining the options of the United States for military intervention and control.

The Vulcans is the name coined by George W. Bush's original foreign-policy team to refer to themselves, in honor of the Roman god of fire, the forge, and metalwork. James Mann's book *Rise of the Vulcans* focuses on six individuals—Dick Cheney, Donald Rumsfeld, Collin Powell, Richard Armitage, Paul Wolfowitz, and Condoleezza Rice. Although the team included a wide variety of worldviews, they were united by their belief in the primary importance of using American power proactively to shape the world. They were a military generation, their wellspring being the Pentagon.[96]

Powell and Armitage questioned the increasingly overt disdain for the international community shown by the group and gradually moved out of the inner circle. Others such as Richard Perle, Elliott Abrams, and Douglas Feith retained a powerful insider status. In historical context, the more hawkish of the Vulcans represented a new mix in U.S. policy circles. They combined dispassionate realism with an idealistic belief about America's role in the world. It was important not just that America *possess* vast power, but that it *used* it. They envisaged an "unchallengeable America, a United States whose military power was so awesome that it no longer needed to make compromises or accommodations (unless it chose to do so)."[97] Such a public stance by the United States contributes to the aspirations of other nations, particularly those threatened by an existing nuclear power such as the United States, to develop nuclear weapons of their own. With this comes the added threat of nongovernment groups attaining such weapons and using them.[98]

The Vulcans were so convinced of their infallibility that alternative voices were shunned. The belief that American know-how and power can forcefully impose control over people, without even the need to listen to their own culture, is not new. But the scale of this operation and the degree in which it was turned over to contractors, selected for allegiance to the administration, was remarkable. Shortly after the fall of Baghdad, General Jay Garner, who was prepared to return the reconstruction effort to Iraqis, was unexpectedly dismissed and replaced by Paul Bremer of Kissinger Associates. This led to a dramatic turnover in the leadership managing the war. Over the objections of the military and the CIA, Bremer dissolved the Iraqi government and its military. Bremer then closed state-run industries, leaving the country impossible to run. Known experts were replaced with Bush loyalists to plan for rebuilding. A White House advisor to the Pentagon vetted all appointees for loyalty. People were asked whether they voted for Bush, opposed abortion, and favored the death penalty. A twenty-four-year-old loyalist with no experience or relevant education decided that the Baghdad stock exchange needed to be automated (it had been using blackboards) and could be done in four months. An extremely qualified public health physician in charge of health care rehabilitation was replaced by a politically connected social worker without relevant experience who focused on an anti-smoking campaign, built 150 new community medical clinics, and updated Iraq's formulary. The actual needs were for providing clean water, hospital generators, properly equipping emergency rooms, and ending shortages of medicines (twenty-six of thirty-two drugs used for chronic diseases were unavailable, and 40 percent of 900 drugs deemed essential were out of stock in Iraq's hospitals).

Anything that could be outsourced was. Iraqi unemployment jumped to 40 percent while private guards, flown in, made more than $1,000 per day. Custer-Battles, a firm with few employees that lacked both experience and working capital, was given a large contract to provide security at Baghdad airport. Funds were used to provide working capital to front companies to fraudulently boost profits to 162 percent. One year after Bremer left, auditors had concluded that as much as $8.8 billion of $20 billion Iraqi oil funds could not be accounted for.

Those running the show lived in Baghdad's Green Zone, which has been called the "Emerald City," a walled-off enclave of towering plants, posh villas, and swimming pools, which kept them totally disconnected with the world outside. Everything they had was flown in from Kuwait—food, consumer goods, and bottled water. The world outside the wall meant nothing to idealists, political appointees, and those who selected numbers they could use to justify the contracts they sought.

During the period of the Cold War, the threat of nuclear attack provided an excuse for military buildup but also a source of caution, lest a particular military incursion escalate into a nuclear war. An anticommunist agenda, pursued with a fanatical fervor by Secretary of State John Foster Dulles, permitted a number of proxy wars and secretive interventions in poor countries of the undeveloped world. But with the possibility of smaller conflicts escalating into a nuclear war, critics were asking whether the use of war as a tactic for resolving disputes had become an oxymoron. Nuclear weapons and delivery systems were considered useful in most policy circles, but only as a deterrent.

This period of standoff had its critics. In contrast to the relatively circumspect, cautious policies of containment and détente practiced during the Cold War, and the emphasis on economic interdependence fostered during the Clinton era, in the post–Cold War era the Vulcans saw an opportunity to assert military power without constraints. Wolfowitz, who had been charged with drafting a new military strategy for the Pentagon after the collapse of the Soviet Union, remarked that "we've never done it right in the past."[99] He charged that America had demobilized too quickly after the previous world wars and now needed instead to consolidate and expand its power. Their goal was to usher in a new era in which the United States would use coercion as the primary tool of foreign policy, a forward strategy of confronting and preempting any attempt at challenge from rising powers, rogue states, or non-state actors below. It would "build up its military power to such an extent that it would be fruitless and financially crippling for any other country to hope to compete with it."[100] In such a world, the potential for the deployment of violence is virtually unlimited.

One of the more frightening manifestations of this may be seen in Joint Publication 3-12, "Doctrine for Joint Nuclear Operations," by the Joint Chiefs of Staff, regarding policy on the use of nuclear weapons. The report indicates that the United States shall reserve the right for first use of nuclear weapons against circumstances deliberately left ambiguous in order to keep adversaries wary of U.S. intentions. In the disembodied language common in military planning, which does not use the words "massive killing with nuclear bombs," the document refers to "cautions in use of nuclear weapons within a theater."[101] This requires that nuclear and conventional plans be integrated to the greatest extent possible and that careful consideration be given to the potential impact of nuclear effects on friendly forces. A follow-up document, JP 3-12.1, "Joint Tactics, Techniques, and Procedures for

Theater Nuclear Planning," was designed to provide theater planners the nuclear-weapons data necessary to determine troop safety information such as minimum safe distances, collateral damage distances, and least separation distances.[102]

The detached view of first use of nuclear weapons is particularly worrisome with ideological true believers at the helm. The power motivations of the Vulcans appear insatiable, and their grasp of history and of diverse cultures appears faulty. Their ultimate belief in force has generated a threat in which the end states are unending war to preserve absolute subservience. In such a plan, only the increased likelihood of nuclear war or a collapse of the environment would lead to an alternative outcome, and the prevention of these disasters was not part of the plan. The willingness of the Vulcans to launch a war on terror of such significant cost and consequence that its end may never occur is becoming an enduring image for the twenty-first century. If there is any positive outcome that can come from the bloodshed created by the Vulcans and their supporters, it may be that their actions have raised some public consciousness about the extensive power of non-elected officials to shape a nation's destiny for questionable reasons.

Concentrating Power in the Executive

Immediately following the attack of September 11, a guiding principle for the world's most powerful nation became the search for enemies at home and abroad. Ron Suskind's *The One Percent Doctrine* describes the secret playbook, designed largely by Dick Cheney, that has been the driving force for wars in Afghanistan and Iraq and for the global search for jihadists.[103] The book's title comes from a policy expressed by Dick Cheney that even if the evidence suggested only a 1 percent chance of a subsequent attack, the consequences could be so devastating that any such instance required comprehensive and unrestricted action. The result of this could be predicted. The government squandered lives, resources, and human rights chasing shadows and overreacting to what little terrorist activity it did detect.

Suskind's investigation distinguishes the notable persons who appeared to explain the "war on terror" to the public—including the president and vice president, George Tenet of the CIA, and then National Security Advisor Condoleeza Rice—from a group of less visible underlings, who were left with directives to produce results but with little supervision from above. Their work was to improvise plans to defeat this new kind of terrorist enemy.[104]

The FBI became a major part of NSA plans in the hunt for potential terrorists within the United States. Its large budget required that it arrest suspects. Most of the detained were Muslims who were identified, by paid informants, as having views critical of U.S. policies. The typical practice was for the hired criminal, con man, and liar to befriend the individual, push him to declare some plan to commit a violent act of terror, even provide access to weapons, and then arrest him; coercive interrogation, actually suggested by the informant, was then used to break him down. The number of such cases reported was large and used to justify continued budgetary support. Apart from the allegations of FBI provocateurs, the actual number of domestic organized groups with explicit plans and possible capabilities to launch acts of terror is likely close to zero.[105]

Liberal democracies have evolved elaborate checks and balances to ensure that while the executive is sufficiently empowered to move decisively in critical situations, it is also constrained from acting unaccountably and abusing power. Writing in the *Political Science Quarterly* in 2005, Montgomery observed that after 9/11:

> The Bush-Cheney White House moved with more alacrity than had perhaps any administration since World War II to orchestrate an even greater concentration of executive power in the White House and to expand the mantle of secrecy surrounding executive branch actions. . . . [These developments were] an unraveling of much of the post-Watergate legislation that Congress passed to curb the enormous abuse of power by the executive branch under former President Nixon. The full extent of this concentration of power . . . and its ramifications, however, remain to be seen.[106]

What has been seen to date, however, is alarming. Amid the largest active antiwar demonstrations in the United States and throughout the world, and in defiance of the United Nations and most of its NATO allies, the United States along with Great Britain went to war against Iraq. The practices used to sustain that ill-conceived war have included the use of torture, arrests, and detention without charge in a network of secret prisons as well as the privatization of military operations to avoid international standards of military conduct. These practices have involved challenges to anyone who leaks information about them, while at the same time U.S. officials leak classified information when it might be used to threaten those who have opposed their policies. Finally, they involve the manipulation of information.

Paradoxically, one key tactic to preserve the ability to make war has been to reduce the influence of professional military voices at the highest decision-making levels. Cheney, Wolfowitz, and Rumsfeld learned an important lesson from the first Gulf War, in which Powell was outspoken about his doubts as to whether military action to liberate Kuwait was in America's best interests.

When military leaders advocate more use of military might they find a large public platform, but in this case the voice of Powell as chair of the Joint Chiefs of Staff was muted by the domination of Defense Secretary Rumsfeld at the podium of press conferences. Members of the administration, including G. W. Bush, were publicly waving a book titled *Supreme Command*, which argued that in time of war civilian leaders should make the key decisions on military strategy and should not show too much deference to their generals.[107]

That this tactic permitted Rumsfeld to continue to hold his job despite widespread criticism for a series of catastrophic military blunders—and even to seriously contemplate striking Iran—is testimony to its effectiveness. The strategy served to circumvent the natural cautiousness of generals (who must deal directly with those being put in harm's way) and to empower a group of civilian officials, whose inclinations for a grand power game are less hampered by personal experience with wartime deaths.

Civilian control over military activity did not in this case include either the public, which would have to provide the funds and soldiers, or the Congress, from whom information was withheld. Legal scholars feared that Bush had abrogated to himself much of the lawmaking role intended for Congress, as well as the Constitution-interpreting role of the courts. Phillip Cooper, a Portland State University law professor, noted that the Bush administration has been involved in a carefully thought-out process of expanding presidential power at the expense of the other branches of government.

The Matter of Torture

When an authority has power to execute policies without need for accountability, then excessive means are likely to occur. The Abu Ghraib scandal exposed the sordid underbelly of the war on terrorism and modern warfare in general. The shocking revelation that grisly torture practices had long been widespread and routine within the U.S. military and intelligence agencies provided a nasty wake-up call to the publics of liberal democracies.[108] Ideally, such governments owe their legitimacy to their adherence to laws and treaties enacted by representatives of the people. Many citizens of professed democracies assumed their governments were above the medieval practices thought to be the exclusive domain of tyrants and dictators.

However, as Darius Rejali explains in his book *Torture and Democracy*, the demand for and practice of such covert violence is actually greater in democracies than dictatorships.[109] The greater openness of democratic societies forces the practitioners of torture to cover their tracks more effectively. While the political position of dictators bent on imposing a reign of terror is actually strengthened by leaving evidence of their gruesome practices in plain public view, democratic leaders who subscribe to the practice are driven underground. The result is increasingly sophisticated strategies of concealment, or, when that fails, legal strategies of justification.

An example of such concealment is the practice of *extraordinary rendition*, an American practice in which an American extrajudicial procedure involves sending suspects to countries other than the United States for imprisonment and interrogation. According to former CIA case officer Bob Baer, "If you want a serious interrogation, you send a prisoner to Jordan. If you want them to be tortured, you send them to Syria. If you want someone to disappear—never to see them again—you send them to Egypt."[110]

The purpose of torture is sometimes misconstrued as the extraction of accurate information to assist in future military operations. For example, in the case of a "ticking time bomb," it is argued that torture is justified to elicit vital information that could save the lives of millions. However, the rationale does not meet the test of credibility. Torture is widely known to be ineffective in such instances because the victims will say whatever their captors want to stop the pain.[111] This raises the question of whether the prolonged misery inflicted on detainees in Abu Ghraib and Guantánamo Bay is instead aimed at deterring recruitment of new militants by demonstrating that jihadists will be denied the benefits of martyrdom, or perhaps as an excuse for sadistic revenge against an enemy who has been demonized.

A more compelling explanation, however, can be seen in the need to justify the harsh treatments that accompany any unpopular military occupation. Walter

Schrepel reminds us of the following actions by the French military in Algiers. The French created a counterrevolutionary form of warfare designed to fight against colonial insurrections, modifying some of the traditional constraints that had applied to international wars; they imposed an alien Christian and European political order on a rebellious Islamic people; they protected the seizure and control of the limited arable land; they engaged in mass killings of civilians; and they allowed the major elite force, the *paras*, to be self- governing. Hence, the *paras* showed greater loyalty and camaraderie to their fellow officers than to the needs and policies of the French government. The *paras* reacted to acts of terror with extensive acts of terror themselves and acted without moral restraint. They conducted indiscriminate arrests, and justified torture in interrogation. The *paras* violated the laws of war and fundamental standards of morality, and then court-martialed the lone whistleblower among their ranks.[112]

Schrepel argued that the Algerian case showed a need to professionalize the training of military personnel to prevent military behavior that clearly violates ethical standards of warfare. But perhaps the problem is deeper. *Battle of Algiers* is Gillo Pontecorvo's famed 1965 film about the National Liberation Front's attempt to liberate Algeria from French colonial rule. In one of the film's key scenes, Colonel Mathieu, based on real-life French commander General Jacques Massus, is being grilled by journalists about allegations that French paratroopers are torturing Algerian prisoners. Mathieu neither denies the abuse nor claims that those responsible will be punished. Instead, he flips the tables on the scandalized reporters, most of whom work for newspapers that overwhelmingly supported France's continued occupation of Algeria. Torture "isn't the problem," he says calmly. "The problem is the FLN wants to throw us out of Algeria and we want to stay. It's my turn to ask a question. Should France stay in Algeria? If your answer is still yes, then you must accept all the consequences."[113]

Military occupations, like any governments, have two mechanisms to rule. One is by consensus, the other by coercion. Lacking consent, the U.S.-installed Iraqi regime has relied heavily on fear, including the most terrifying tactics of them all: disappearances, indefinite detention without charge, and torture.[114] Cruel and abusive treatment or torture has a longtime association with war and with the punishment of resisters. U.S. participation in such practices is extensive.[115]

According to Marjorie Cohn, after the terrorist attacks of September 11, 2001, the G. W. Bush administration quickly established a policy authorizing the use of *enhanced interrogation techniques*, that is, torture and abuse. Cofer Black, head of the CIA Counterterrorist Center, testified at a joint hearing of the House and Senate intelligence committees in September 2002: "This is a very highly classified area, but I have to say that all you need to know is: There was a before 9/11, and there was an after 9/11. After 9/11 the gloves come off." In his January 2003 State of the Union address, President Bush admitted that more than 3,000 suspected terrorists had been arrested in many countries. Waterboarding, sensory manipulation, hooding, beatings, electric shock to genitals, starving, sodomizing with foreign objects, threatening to harm family members, and violating religious symbols were practiced in other parts of the world and secretly by the United States since the 1950s. But the effort to justify such practices reflects a decline in the standards of what it means to be human.[116] In 2015, the Senate Intelligence Committee placed into the official record a detailed documentation of the types of torture, the extent of their use during the Iraq war, and government efforts to hide these actions.[117] Orders came from high in the command. But the perpetrators roam free. In addition to behaviors of military and intelligence community employees, we have seen increased reliance upon mercenaries.

Mercenaries: Privatizing the Military

The use of mercenaries has a long tradition in the history of warfare, dating back at least to the Peloponnesian War.[118] Debate has raged ever since that time over whether and how to regulate them.[119] Although tacitly accepted until the end of the nineteenth century, since then there has been growing international consensus against their use. This culminated in 2001 with the ratification by twenty-two countries, in October 2001, of the "International Convention against the Recruitment, Use, Financing and Training of Mercenaries."[120] A 2005 report by UN Special Rapporteur Enrique Bernales Ballesteros noted that mercenarism "affects the self-determination of peoples and serves foreign interests that pose a threat to life and to the natural resources, political stability and territorial integrity of the affected countries."[121] However, although countries such as Angola, Libya, Saudi Arabia, Democratic Republic of Congo, and Uzbekistan are signatories, the United States is not. Among Western democracies, only Italy and Germany have signed (though Germany has not ratified).

When the world's most powerful states routinely ignore, or in the case of the United States even specifically attack such conventions, their enforcement remains problematic.

Despite widespread international condemnation, the use of mercenaries has recently grown rather than diminished, owing to a transformation in image. Mercenarism is now presented in a more sanitized form under the auspices of publicly traded private military corporations.[122] This more respectable façade makes them increasingly difficult to target under international law. In effect, there is now a serious gap between the spirit of international law, which clearly disfavors mercenary activity, and the letter of the law, which is yet to be amended to cope with private security contractors. Further, to the extent existing law and conventions do constrain the United States, the United States appears to have made a "concerted effort . . . to extricate itself from its obligations."[123] It has attempted to argue that international customs and conventions it has signed "create no obligations of compliance."[124]

Private security firms constitute "a new means of disguised efforts by their home states to influence conflicts in which the home states are technically neutral."[125] There has been both an increase in the availability of individuals with military experience and expertise since the end of the Cold War and an expansion of the market for such security contractors. For example, in early 2004 the United States was employing roughly 20,000 private military contractors in Iraq, many of whom may be providing interrogation support. An example is Blackwater Security Consulting (renamed Xe after losing a number of lawsuits for dealings with the United States), which provides mobile security teams composed of former special-operations and intelligence personnel.[126]

In April of 2006, Kathryn Helvenston-Wettengel, the mother of a security worker hired by Blackwater Enterprises, filed a suit against the company for the death of her son, Scott Helvenston, in Iraq. The company was able to use its large contract with the Department of Defense to rehire former special forces soldiers at salaries significantly higher than those paid to actual U.S. soldiers. Four men were killed in an ambush prior to the U.S. attack on Fallujah. Mrs. Helventson-Wettengel's son had been told that his job would be the personal protection of U.S. envoy Paul Bremer. However, on this mission, the men were sent without time to prepare and in unarmored vehicles with smaller teams than were required for security from attack. Blackwater's skimping on safety resulted in enormous profits. The U.S. military carries no legal liability for its contractors, so account-ability was left to a nonexistent Iraqi judiciary system.[127]

New Directions for the Warfare State

A new model of U.S. influence is now being practiced in the form of numer-ous small U.S. military bases scattered across the globe. While the largest Cold War era U.S. military bases such as Ramstein Air Base in Germany are down-sizing, the global infrastructure of U.S. bases overseas has exploded in size and scope. These new mini-bases, referred to as "lily pads," are small, secretive, inac-cessible facilities that feature a smaller number of troops, limited amenities, and prepositioned weaponry and supplies.[128] It is estimated that since the turn of the century, the Pentagon has constructed more than fifty of these lily-pad bases in secluded and strategic locations around the globe. Even as the Pentagon draws down troops in Iraq and Afghanistan, the U.S. military easily maintains the larg-est collection of foreign bases in world history: more than 1,000 military instal-lations outside the fifty states and Washington, D.C. Journalist David Vine notes President Obama's announced "Asia pivot" identifies East Asia as the center of the explosion of these new mini-bases, and how military planners describe the need to isolate and contain the new power in the region, China. This new twenty-first-century model of influence is executed quietly by special forces operations, the militarization of intelligence, drone aircraft, and with increasingly militarized civilian government agencies.[129]

In *The Way of the Knife*, Pulitzer Prize–winning journalist Mark Mazzetti reveals an undercovered story of a shadow war in which the line between soldiers and spies has been blurred. America now pursues its enemies with drones that kill and with special operations troops. Private mercenaries are trained for assassina-tion missions and used to set up clandestine spying networks. The United States continues to buttress unstable dictators, even to kill on their behalf in exchange for accepting drone access. The new way includes proxy armies and relies upon untrustworthy foreign intelligence services. It is considered a low-cost, low-risk alternative to big wars. The strategy has compromised CIA intelligence gathering in favor of a paramilitary force killing off people considered enemies, particularly in Pakistan, Yemen, and North Africa, while the Pentagon has taken on a larger role of spying in search of enemies.[130]

Jeremy Scahill reported on the Tuesday "kill list" briefings in the Obama White House that decide who is to be targeted for summary executions. Where precise identities cannot be located, *signature strikes* are permitted to allow teen or adult males in an area with suspected terrorists to be killed as well. Hence, a cadre of specialists now operate daily across the globe and, inside the United States, with orders from the White House to do whatever is necessary to hunt down, capture, or kill individuals designated by the president as enemies of America.[131]

In the interest of trimming the U.S. deficit, overseas bases have received Senate scrutiny from both Republicans and Democrats. Increasing scrutiny includes advocacy of a less costly practice of drone warfare. Drones are unmanned aircraft that range from small surveillance cameras to large, weapons-deploying vehicles—and, currently in development, nuclear weapon capability. The leading producer of surveillance and bombing drones, General Atomics, sold more than 430 Predator and Reaper drones to the Department of Defense between 2004 and 2010. The drone campaign began under the G. W. Bush administration in 2004, and rapidly increased under the Obama administration. Though the White House has declined to release the number of casualties by drone strikes, the New America Foundation has estimated that by February 2013, more than 350 strikes have claimed between 1,944 and 3,263 lives. The vast majority of deaths were reported to be potential al-Qaeda militants; however, civilians, including women and children, are also among these victims.[132] According to a 2011 New America Foundation report, just one out of seven drone attacks in Pakistan kills a militant leader.

The drone campaign has received scrutiny from several top former military and intelligence officials, including retired general Stanley McChrystal who led the Joint Special Operations Command (JSOC), which has responsibility for the military's drone strikes, as well as former CIA director Michael V. Hayden. McChrystal and Hayden have pointed out that the drone wars in Pakistan and Yemen are increasingly targeting low-level militants who do not pose a direct threat to the United States. General McChrystal noted in an interview that drones could be useful but were "hated on a visceral level" in some of the places they were used and contributed to a "perception of American arrogance."[133] General David Petraeus described the JSOC's campaign as "an almost industrial-scale counterterrorism killing machine."[134]

Abroham Karem created the Predator drone for use in the 1973 Arab-Israeli war. In the 1980s, Karem moved from Israel to Southern California with funding from the U.S. Defense Advanced Research Projects Agency (DARPA) to improve the technology. His company, Leading Systems, produced a more effective model than other major DOD contractors but lacked the political network to gain attention. However, he joined forces with billionaire brothers Linden and James Blue who had purchased General Atomics from Chevron in 1986. The Blue brothers had extensive connections from previous work supporting the Somoza regime and investing in cocoa and banana plantations and vast ranchlands in Nicaragua, and in nuclear power in Australia. Their corporate accomplishments include enriching uranium, developing nuclear power in Australia, dumping radioactive waste on a Native American reservation, infiltrating and spying on environmental activists, operating plantations with one of South America's most brutal dictators (the Somoza clan in Nicaragua), and an attempt to turn Telluride, the historic Colorado ski town, into a tract home development.[135]

The Blue brothers emerged as major players in global military operations after buying General Atomics (GA) from Chevron in 1986 for a reported $60 million. At the time, General Atomics was primarily involved in building civilian nuclear reactors, and losing out to bigger nuclear corporations like Westinghouse. However, GA hired retired Rear Admiral Tom Cassidy, a powerful insider in weapons procurement, and developed a successful lobbying strategy for its streamlined unmanned aerial vehicles.[136]

According to the *Financial Times,* "Behind its success in winning government contracts has been a formidable and at times controversial lobbying effort."[137] Members of Congress, their families, and staffs traveled around the world, meeting foreign leaders seeking clearance to purchase their drones.[138]

The drone program receives congressional support from the twenty-one members of the drone caucus (representing border states) to control domestic terrorism and provide a cost-effective tool for ongoing civil, military, and law enforcement operations. Drone caucus members received millions in the 2010 and 2012 campaign cycles from drone manufacturers.[139] U.S. policy on behalf of drone sales followed. Clearly the new strategy is having domestic consequences in the turning of society into a game board in which people can be added to lists of suspects, spied upon, and killed without opportunity for the legal protections pioneered by the United States.[140]

Pointing the Cameras on Ourselves

The temptation to expand the use of new technologies is great and is typically supported by fantastic claims of how they will protect us from *bad guys*. Drones are widely sold to local police departments and paid for by grants from Homeland Security. The practice of tracking people and all of their communications, apart from its violations of privacy, produces an absolutely incomprehensible amount of information or metadata. In an intensive two-year investigation of national security for the *Washington Post,* Dana Priest and William Larkin identified 1,931 private companies working in "about 10,000 locations" around the country, with 854,000 of their employees holding top-secret clearances.[141] The authors observed the problem that the data is not sifted, refined, and evaluated by human beings with human judgment.

To assure its consolidation into comprehensible categories, its protection from the eyes of adversaries, and its sharing across various agencies, *fusion centers* of information are now maintained in many locations. Managing the data bubble has proven to be an object of fascination and of explosive growth for the world's largest corporations but also for the world of intelligence.

Dominators of the market like Goldman Sachs and JPMorgan Chase capture a large chunk of the trades in a given area (for example, the top five U.S. banks control well over 90 percent of all derivatives trades). That metadata gives them extraordinary economic power. Financial institutions are now data institutions— and the "too-big-to-fail" ones are grabbing the power that comes with the hoarding of information.[142]

Despite all that data available, these banks would have failed anyway if they were not powerful enough to have had taxpayers rescue them. Metadata, whether it is used for credit scores, algorithmic trading, or national security, is inherently subject to flaws. These flaws cannot be corrected when its centers are operated in secret or purely out of self-interest.

Booz Allen Hamilton is the primary example of a giant corporation whose operatives hold high-level security clearance and are funded by enormous government contracts. Booz illustrates why the privatization of data centers comes to be a tool of the power elite to survey behavior and communication in a never-ending search for enemies. Major universities are accepting contracts to augment the data mine to include studies of all activities, domestic or international, in which there may be any form of dissent or protest against military or corporate power. Once identified, one is permanently marked in the watch list. Booz Allen Hamilton's corporate slogan is "Delivering results that endure." The fusion centers can help to diminish the influence of pro-democracy groups, whether from Arab Spring or Occupy Wall Street.[143]

The technology is new but the struggle is an old one. Corporations like the Hudson's Bay Company, Dutch East Indies Company, and the British East India Company used the trade of goods to create a wave of global colonization. Corporations in the military-industrial complex profit from mass-produced weapons of iron, steel, and chemicals. Increasingly, the weapons of the twenty-first century are made of electrons, not metal. But the goals of the corporate elite have not changed. The security-digital complex saps our wealth and has the potential to invade and monitor virtually every aspect of our lives. It could become even more powerful than its predecessor. That is why it was developed in secrecy and why the courageous whistleblowers brought to public attention have been treated so harshly.[144]

Justifying the Expansion of Power and Influence

The strategy serving a moneyed elite has consistently been to justify the expansion of their power and influence. Within the grand design has been the need to create fear by finding overarching enemies such as communism or terrorism. Once the enemy is identified, the goal becomes to magnify the threats, combat defiant governments, bolster compliant ones, and identify these corporate and military interests as *national* interests. The clearly amoral and sometimes clandestine tactics, whether successful in their intended objectives or not, are the real news affecting our lives deeply and preventing any efforts to move toward equality or to slow the pace of the empire. As historian Edward Said has explained, "Every single empire, in its official discourse has said that it is not like all the others, that its circumstances are special, that it has a mission to enlighten, civilize, bring order and democracy and that it uses force only as a last resort."[145] Despite similar justifications with past empires, the contemporary American empire does have a number of unique characteristics. It is the first truly world empire. The global terrain it dominates is in a state of serious environmental degradation. It keeps military domination even while the other parts of its imperial hegemony such as moral or cultural leadership appear to be collapsing. This disparity makes the decline of the American empire especially dangerous to the world.

At this time in history there are a remarkable number of allegations charging government complicity in the deaths of Martin Luther King, Jr., in the high-level government involvement through the CIA in drug trafficking, and in the bombings that occurred on 9/11. Of these, the drug trafficking revealed in the Iran-contra scandal is perhaps the best documented. [146] A pattern of secret dealings between the CIA and leaders of drug cartels, corporate contractors, and military rulers in Afghanistan, Colombia, and elsewhere has been documented in the work of Peter Dale Scott. The degree of influence of this non-recognized shadow government has earned it the term "deep politics."[147]

But all of these have been dismissed or trivialized, and few have had the quality of official investigation needed to reveal the entire truth. At this time we do know a good bit about the dehumanized mind-set that goes into selection of tactics to win the game pursued by the centers of power. We should at least be wary of dismissals of the allegations from official sources. One may reasonably ask why the evidence of practices that offend human sensibilities and bypass law does not produce widespread public outrage. One answer lies in systematic efforts at disinformation, to be examined in the next chapter.

7 —DISINFORMATION

The majority of politicians, on the evidence available to us, are interested not in truth but in power and in the maintenance of that power. To maintain that power it is essential that people remain in ignorance, that they live in ignorance of the truth, even the truth of their own lives. What surrounds us therefore is a vast tapestry of lies, upon which we feed.
　　　—HAROLD PINTER, 2005 Nobel Lecture, "Art, Truth and Politics"

"Who controls the past," ran the Party slogan, "controls the future; who controls the present controls the past." It was quite simple. All that was needed was an unending series of victories over your own memory. "Reality control," they called it, in Newspeak, "doublethink."
　　　—GEORGE ORWELL, 1984

Governments constantly choose between telling lies and fighting wars, with the end result always being the same. One will always lead to the other.
　　　—THOMAS JEFFERSON

Those who can make you believe in absurdities can make you commit atrocities.

　　　—VOLTAIRE

THE PRECEDING CHAPTERS HAVE DESCRIBED structural violence within industry and agriculture. The chapters have documented a multibillion-dollar defense industry and past military conflicts and coups for corporate gain. They have described a system of power that serves the largest corporate players, much to the detriment of many of the world's people. Since there are relatively few beneficiaries and many casualties of this system, one might expect there would be major voices of dissent. But there is little information circulating about power and influence. Opposing voices are heard, but focused discontent is discouraged by a flow of information that makes the system difficult to penetrate.

One answer to why there is so little outrage is that the media obfuscate issues of power and perpetuate beliefs that protect the broad interests of a powerful elite. Few people are present to watch a major financial deal that sets up a no-bid government contract for military supplies or for a natural gas pipeline. Few people witness directly the corporate and government decision makers in agreements that assure the destruction of an essential rain forest, or that perpetuate the routine loss of life from inadequate food and water, or that cause us to go to war. For most people, our knowledge about events beyond our immediate experience comes from the media. What is presented molds our views of the world. In studying the media we observe that the power to dominate resources comes also with a power to dominate ideas through control over the public discussion of issues. There are two primary methods to stifle dissent: public relations and military force. Force was illustrated in chapter 6; here, the focus is cast upon the public relations that have come to replace meaningful remedial action. This chapter describes how information is molded to support certain policies and attitudes, minimize exposure of exploitative power, and prevent widespread circulation of divergent views.

The information we get is routinely selected and filtered. It is sometimes exaggerated, sometimes trivialized, often used to demonize, and consistently used to affirm underlying values that favor those with power. The media contribute to co-opting our attention with trivia and with the lives of celebrities while important things that affect our lives, such as corporate welfare, voter fraud, carcinogenic contaminants, infant mortality, government involvement in the sale of narcotics, and the contribution of transnational corporations to the despair of poverty are often hidden. The message of social protestors in the major media is reduced to sound bites.

Private companies, non-governmental organizations, and government agencies alike pay millions to public relations firms that specialize in, according to the website of one group, "achieving information superiority in order to impact public opinion and outcomes."[1] Image managers are most effective when their packaging of the message is not noticeable. One of the largest and most successful companies in the area of image management is the Edelman Company, but few in the general public are even aware of its existence.[2] Between fiscal years 2003 and 2005, the U.S. government paid an annual average of $78.8 million to private public relations firms.[3] In five years following September 11, 2001, the Pentagon alone paid a single private public relations firm more than $56 million.[4] Furthermore, through corporate mergers over the last few decades, the media are now controlled by five or six megacorporations.[5] Newspapers and television stations, amusement parks, jet engine manufacturers, and nuclear power plants may all be owned by the same parent company. As business enterprises, the corporate media are legally bound to put the interests of shareholders above everything else, including the public good.

Mainstream media may be viewed as a threat to a democratic system because they do not represent or promote the interests of all people but instead serve the interests of a small, very powerful minority. Media historian Robert McChesney maintains that the core problem with the media today is that people in power are dictating what information is legitimate and newsworthy.[6] In this chapter we outline the ways in which information is restricted and modified to advance the agenda of a network of powerful interests. We look at the ownership of media and the resultant selling of biased views that commit us to a false "reality." We demonstrate this by tracing the gradual decline of journalistic integrity from the use of political propaganda in the First World War to the corporate dominion over current U.S. domestic and foreign policy.

The First World War and Propaganda

Propaganda originated not in totalitarian regimes but rather in more democratic societies.[7] The very first coordinated propaganda effort was put forth by Britain's Ministry of Information, during the First World War, with the explicit goal of convincing American intellectuals of the need to go to war with Germany. Sir Gilbert Parker, in charge of a secret propaganda bureau within the United States, began by creating a mailing list of 200,000 opinion leaders whose names were drawn from *Who's Who in America*.[8] These intellectuals received countless pamphlets, speeches, interviews, and films illustrating German atrocities. The appeal to these selected individuals played on the elitist sentiment that it was the responsibility of the intellectual community to determine what was best for the general population.

Lord James Bryce prepared the most influential document: The Bryce Report compiled over a thousand depositions taken from Belgian refugees. The report did not convince all opinion leaders, however. Will Irwin, American muckraker and U.S. war correspondent, noted there was no cross-examination of witnesses and was suspicious of Bryce's heroic tone. But the document seemed to "sustain the Allied claim that theirs was a contest of good versus evil."[9] Notably, in the 1930s the document was discredited altogether, years after the war ended.

The business community, represented by the League to Enforce Peace, advocated for war and was soon followed by the progressive community, which promoted the idea that U.S. participation in the war was an opportunity to advance democracy on a worldwide scale. The American people, however, were not interested in going to war; in 1916 they elected Woodrow Wilson, on an antiwar platform with the slogan "Peace without Victory."[10] Wilson was soon convinced of the need for war by the intellectual and business communities. Faced with the task of changing public opinion in favor of war, he supported the formation of the first (and only) major state propaganda agency in U.S. history.

The Committee on Public Information

The Committee on Public Information, headed by journalist George Creel, had a monumental task. Creel had to convince the American people to enter a war that had been going on for three years and thousands of miles away, without any direct threat to U.S. lives. He sent out over 70 million copies of various pamphlets about American ideals and the purposes of war across the United States, and millions more abroad. He hired 75,000 speakers, called the "Four Minute Men," to perform concise but influential patriotic speeches, which reached over 400 million people. Speaking at movie houses, churches, and grange halls, the presentations covered conscription, the Red Cross, income tax, and food conservation. The committee's division of pictorial publicity created poster art. In the words of the division's director, these colorful posters, displayed everywhere, were designed to "appeal to the heart."[11] Images invoked fear, with accompanying text calling for the purchase of war bonds. Other images idealized U.S. soldiers. Hollywood did its part by creating a multitude of anti-German films, including *The Beast of Berlin* and *The Little American*. The National School Service Bulletin was provided to public schools; the National Board for Historic Service took over *History Teachers Magazine*. At Stanford University, lectures on foreign policy leading up to the war came to be titled "The German Ideal of World Domination."[12]

The committee's efforts were highly successful. At the end of the war, Creel proudly and openly described the entire operation in his book *How We Advertised America: The First Telling of the Amazing Story of the Committee on Public Information that Carried the Gospel of Americanism to Every Corner of the Globe*.[13] The committee was dissolved at the end of the war, considered unfit for service during peacetime.

Creel was not solely responsible for the success of the Committee on Public Information. Another influential figure, Edward Bernays, pioneer of the public relations industry, wrote a number of books including *Propaganda, Crystallizing Public Opinion*, and *Engineering Consent*.[14] The success of the committee, he explained, showed that it is possible to "regiment the public mind every bit as much as an army regiments their bodies."[15] This was an undertaking that could only be performed by the intelligent minority to influence an unsophisticated majority. Bernays described this intelligent minority as "the invisible government . . . concentrated in the hands of a few because of the expense of manipulating the social machinery which controls the opinions and habits of the masses."[16] After the war, Bernays went on to launch an advertising campaign marketing cigarettes to women. Playing on the burgeoning women's movement, he hired models to march in New York's Easter Parade in 1929 wearing banners reading "Torch of Liberty," while smoking Lucky Strike cigarettes. The company was an immediate success.[17]

A highly respected journalist, Walter Lippmann, was another member of the committee. He was a strong proponent of the war at its onset, believing it to be an opportunity to spread democracy around the globe. Lippmann was of the mindset that the intellectual classes had a responsibility to make such decisions for the less-astute classes, or masses, of society. With propaganda, a "revolution in the art of democracy," as he described it, the public could be made to believe and support choices made without their knowledge or participation. He called this the "manufacture of consent."[18]

Unlike Creel and Bernays, Lippmann later expressed misgivings and questioned whether the committee's means of molding public opinion were congruent with democratic ideals. As a serious journalist, he was troubled that the committee had not reported factual information but rather "news and argument which put America in the best possible light and sustained the fighting morale."[19] Based on the success of their information campaign, leaders now viewed public opinion as critical. Looking into the future, Lippmann saw that in the interest of democracy, the news (on which public opinion was formed) must be protected from propaganda. The word *propaganda*, it should be noted, only became a pejorative term after it became associated with Hitler in the Second World War, who developed his own nationalistic propaganda campaign inspired by the success of the Allied program. But the manipulation of information available to the public is testimony not only to an elite perception that the public cannot be trusted to make informed judgments but also to the need to conceal truths that might prove embarrassing to those with power.

For centuries most of the world was ruled by kings or emperors who were unseen by all but a few of their royal followers. Those whom they ruled granted them a mystical or divine status. Such divine status permitted rulers to tithe farmers, raise armies, and construct palaces or monuments with indentured labor. The concept that masses of ordinary people had either the right or the wisdom to partake in broader decisions had evolved only in smaller entities, such as the Iroquois tribes, oceans away from the empires of Europe and Asia. It was not until the beginning of roads and of village literacy that some messengers, called town criers, were able to transmit rudiments of information that helped in the decline of the monarchies. With the rise of a merchant class able both to travel and to read, issues of participation in decision-making came to the fore. If people's voices could make a difference, then the question of what information they had was a matter of power. An elitist belief held that most people were too dumb and too uninterested about larger issues to take a reasonable part in decisions. They had to be fed with information prepared for them. But some journalists spoke out against abusive power.

The Muckrakers and Big Business

In the 1930s, a fight ensued over journalism's integrity. That integrity was founded upon work of the muckrakers who exposed powerful institutions and their use of the media to inform public opinion. Before that, in 1905–1906, Ray

Stannard Baker published a series of articles on the railroad industry. What began as an exposé on excessive rates for shipping customers and secret rebates for those in power (such as Rockefeller), the series ended by zeroing in on the railroad corporations' practice of hiring press agents to inform public opinion. Baker discovered that the heads of all the major railroad lines had joined forces and hired a publicity firm to launch a campaign against railroad regulation. Recognizing the power of newspapers in forming opinion, publicity agents prepared news-style articles and forwarded them to newspaper editors. When these agents found editors to be disagreeable, they played upon business and industry leaders in that city to convince editors not to favor regulation. Railroad interests prevailed in court by hiring witnesses to provide testimony.

Will Irwin is credited with exposing the newspaper business. In a fifteen-part series that began in 1911, Irwin described how editorials had become less fashionable, and a plethora of new and cheaply produced papers depended on sensationalistic news to sell their papers. Irwin explained the power plays that occurred between journalist and editor, and between editor and contributor. The old system of direct subsidies to newspapers from political parties and businesses had dissolved, with the new advertising system in its place.[20] Irwin noted that editors were careful not to offend their advertisers. Still worse, editors and publishers who identified with the wealthy class assimilated their views. As one progressive editor concluded:

> The future of America is safe as long as the American people have the ballot and can obtain information and facts on which to base an intelligent opinion. When, however, the steel trust, the railroads, the packers, the coal barons and the industrial plutocrats can pervert public opinion to suit their purposes then we are treading on dangerous ground.[21]

I. F. Stone wrote a detailed report on labor relations in the agricultural industry. Migrant workers were trying to organize and obtain protection under new labor legislation of the 1930s. Stone's article explained how California farm organizations had come together to form the Associated Farmers group in an attempt to block the efforts of labor organizations. Stone documented countless contributions of major corporations to Associated Farmers and showed how the association's publication discounted labor organizing as subversive communist activity.

Playing on this pervasive fear, hundreds of farmers were deputized by local sheriffs, enabling them to wield more power over strikers and labor organizers. Stone recounted to the National Labor Relations Board evidence of Associated Farmers using violent means to discourage workers from organizing.[22]

The pervasive fear of and fervor against communism perhaps best exemplifies the collusion of interests between government and corporate power. Indeed, as shown in the previous chapter, economic interests in foreign countries were frequently behind the U.S. "defense" against the media-enhanced image of encroachment of communism all over the world. With the Cold War behind us, the rallying cry against communism shifted to a rallying cry for democracy and free markets, and against an amorphous force called terrorism. The media are essential to the task of making such goals appear both good and inevitable. The next section outlines how corporations use media to shape public opinion and advance their own interests.

Media Monopolies and the Effect on Journalism

Since 1995, the number of companies that own commercial television stations has declined by 40 percent. In 1983, fifty companies owned 90 percent of American media. The corporate mergers that took place throughout the 1980s and 1990s have resulted in today's handful of megacorporations. In 2011, that same 90 percent were controlled by six corporations: GE which owns NBC; Murdoch's News Corp which owns Fox Broadcasting, which in turn runs FoxNews Channel. News Corp also owns the *New York Post*, the publisher HarperCollins, and the film production company Twentieth-Century Fox; Disney, which owns ABC; Time Warner which merged with AOL; Viacom (originally affiliated with CBS but now considered a separate company); and CBS. Presently, 232 media executives control the information diet of 277 million. The merger of Time Warner and AOL in 2000 was for $350 billion. Until then the largest merger permitted was for $340 million. Total revenue for the six media megacorporations in 2010 was $275.9 billion.

The effect of mergers is not limited to U.S. audiences. Viacom owns stations in Canada; NBC owns Telemundo, the Spanish-language network; Murdoch's companies own the DirecTV sector in Central and South America, British Sky Broadcasting, and STAR TV in Asia.[23] News Corp owns the top newspaper on three continents. Global outreach was a likely factor in News Corp's ability to avoid $875 million in U.S. taxes. Bertelsmann of Germany, a dominant owner of publishing companies internationally, is also considered among the most powerful media corporations. [24]

Consolidation and size equates to power over both setting of regulations and their enforcement. In 1995 the FCC forbade media companies to own more than forty channels. However, Clear Channel owns 1,200 stations dominating 80 percent of radio station playlists in the United States.[25] The international outreach and the highly sophisticated use of media deception have extended through Europe, Africa, and Asia.[26]

These corporations also have vertical integration beyond their media enterprises, controlling production and distribution of media-related products. This means companies are able to cross-promote and sell products across market sectors. In 1994, Disney's animated film *The Lion King* generated $1 billion in profits and produced 186 items of merchandise, which Disney had manufactured and sold, in part, through Disney theme parks. This merchandising potentially translates to a fourfold increase in profit beyond the box office.[27] Public media are not free from the corporate interest, because underwriting permits an opportunity both for subtle oversight and for tax-deductible image promotion. For example, Archer Daniels Midland, one of the three largest agribusiness conglomerates, joined AT&T, the giant of telecommunications, and Chevron in underwriting *The PBS NewsHour*.

The power held by the giant media corporations results in a strong bias, imposed from the top, on what passes for news. Robert Greenwald's documentary film *Outfoxed* examines the impact on society when one person, Fox News founder Rupert Murdoch, controls a broad consolidation of media. The film provides an in-depth look at Fox News and the dangers of ever-enlarging corporations taking control of the public's right to know. The documentary presents evidence by former Fox News reporters, producers, bookers, and writers who describe what working for Fox News is like. Former Fox employees talk about how they were forced to push a "right-wing" point of view or risk their jobs. Some chose to remain anonymous for fear of losing their current livelihoods. One employee observed, "There's no sense of integrity as far as having a line that can't be crossed." In August 2006 Serene Sabbagh and Jomana Karadsheh, two producers working for Fox News in Amman, Jordan, resigned in protest. Their action speaks to the integrity and courage of journalists working under coercive pressure. Their resignation letter stated, "We can no longer work with a news organization that claims to be fair and balanced when you are so far from that. Not only are you an instrument of the Bush White House, and Israeli propaganda, you are warmongers with no sense of decency, nor professionalism."[28]

Robert McChesney's award-winning video *Rich Media, Poor Democracy* showed that a sharp decline in the enforcement of antitrust violations and the increase in patents on digital technology, proprietary systems, and massive indirect subsidies have made the Internet a place of numbing commercialism. A society drenched in commercial information is not a democratic one. In *Digital Disconnect*, McChesney examined the effects of the advances of the digital age. A small set of monopolies now dominate the political economy. Google garners a 97 percent share of the mobile search market. Microsoft's operating system is used by more than 90 percent of the world's computers. Capitalism's economic elite have colonized the Internet with some major consequences. One is the collapse of credible journalism as professional reporting has diminished. Whatever pathways have opened for groups of people to reach out to others, the Internet has been turned into an unparalleled apparatus for government and corporate surveillance and a disturbingly anti-democratic social force.[29]

Many of the same advertisers who support the major media also support a group of talk-show hosts, typically conservative, who daily demonstrate that bullying, humiliation, and the "big lie" are attractive to a large audience ready to accept scapegoats. The values tapped here are discussed in chapter 8.

Interlocking directorates further complicate the interests of media companies. An interlock occurs when the same individual sits on the board of directors of more than one corporation. In this case, a board member of a media corporation is also a board member of a bank, an investment company, an oil company, a pharmaceutical company, and a technology company. This is only illegal, however, if the corporations involved would form a complete monopoly if they merged. According to an article in the *Columbia Journalism Review*, in 2003 Murdoch's News Corp, Disney, Viacom, and Time Warner had forty-five interlocking directors.[30] Network analysis (described in chapter 5) can offer a tool for precise plotting of the interlocks among the media giants and between these megacorporations and other sectors of the corporate world and government agencies. Some of the financial ties suggest the power for a monopoly over information.

Although classic capitalist philosophy predicts that competition in the free market leads to greater diversity and better quality of products, the opposite has proven true when there are only a few big players. With too much at stake in an all-or-nothing rivalry, the five media conglomerates compete only on a superficial level. Instead, their interests are better served by joining with one another. This joining of forces is accomplished by shared investment of media products; the big five media conglomerates share over 100 joint business ventures.[31] Media corporations may appear to be competing in ratings. A closer look at content, however, undermines this argument. Highly duplicative content—the current myriad of reality television programs—allows for only fractional losses compared to consistent gain. In television, for example, a 30 percent profit is considered low, while a 60 percent profit margin is considered good and consistently reached by successful broadcasters.[32]

The big five media conglomerates have come together most openly in one of the nation's most powerful lobbying groups, the National Association of Broadcasters (NAB). In the year 2000 the NAB spent $5.7 million on lobbying for laws and regulations to increase corporate power.[33] This figure does not include campaign contributions for that same year, in which 64 percent of NAB contributions went to Republican campaigns. On their own, the parent companies of the big five spent nearly $27 million on lobbying firms in the year 2000 alone.[34] Since then, the growth in NAB lobbying has been part of a greater digital-era effort including Google, Comcast, NBC, Universal, T-Mobile, and Sprint Nextel. The lobbying total for communications/electronics in 2012 was $390,520,921 supporting 2,067 lobbyists.[35]

It is ironic that when politicians hail the urgent need to defend our democratic traditions, giant media corporations that are essentially authoritarian structures of power communicate their words. There is no pretense of democracy in a corporation. Power flow is strictly top-down, and there is little employee and no public input in decision-making. The CEOs determine what gets stressed and what does not get broadcast.

Media CEOs yield to pressure from government and corporate officials on whom they rely for news. Reporters wishing to dig for facts to do their job are treated punitively. Gary Webb first reported in the *San Jose Mercury News* on CIA involvement in the scandal in which narcotics were sold in Los Angeles to provide secret money to fund the Nicaraguan contras, in violation of a law passed by Congress.[36] He was attacked, lost his job and committed suicide. The *New York Times* refused to publish a news story by their award-winning foreign correspondent James Risen exposing mistruths by government officials when they denied involvement in the torture of prisoners. Only after Risen had written a book about this on his own did the *Times* print Risen's account. Risen has now been threatened with long jail terms for refusing to name his sources. In his new book he presents the case that the U.S.-led wars in the Middle East, whatever their original intent, have come to be sources of corrupt accumulation of profit and career paths for those who reap the benefits of a war machine.[37] The intimidation of whistleblowers under the guise of protecting national security leaves the public with no chance to hold their public officials accountable.

Lack of Government Regulation

Government bodies created to protect consumers from overt corporate domination have become, in Robert McChesney's words, "toothless organizations." The landmark Telecommunications Act in 1996 resulted in the massive deregulation of media corporations. According to the *Wall Street Journal*, "Gingrich-class" Republicans initiated this legislation in 1994 that "asked the industry what it wanted and almost literally gave them the law they asked for."[38] Proponents of this legislation, operating by the ideology of the free market, argue that competition will result in better products and prices for the consumer—and therefore, in effect, the market will regulate itself. But the Telecommunications Act legislation has resulted instead in the monolithic cartel of media megacorporations. In the words of Rupert Murdoch, "We can join forces now, or we can kill each other and then join forces."[39]

The media sector most dramatically transformed by this ruling has been radio broadcasting. Between 1996 and 1999, half of the nation's 11,000 radio stations changed hands, and there were over 1,000 mergers.[40] In each of forty-three different cities, a third of the radio stations are owned by a single company, despite an existing law stating that no company can own more than eight in any market. Clear Channel, the nation's largest radio broadcasting company, owns over 1,200 radio stations. In Mansfield, Ohio, Clear Channel owns eleven of the seventeen radio stations; in Corvallis, Oregon, seven out of thirteen.[41] Clear Channel, home of right-wing propagandist Rush Limbaugh, reaches an estimated 20 million listeners daily.[42]

Consolidation of ownership of radio stations in local areas has permitted Clear Channel to reduce local personnel and coverage of local events and replace them with broadcasts from a remote central location. Ownership of stations by minorities has declined, as has the ability to respond to local emergencies. When a train derailment in Minot, North Dakota, released tons of toxic chemicals into a residential area, the panicked residents who called for help were told to turn to radio and cable television, but no help was available. Centralized corporate ownership of local media outlets has transformed American cultural and political life into a world of empty television news stations, preprogrammed radio shows, and copycat newspapers.[43]

Perhaps the most worrisome concern with media concentration lies in its inducement of what Bill Moyers has called a plantation mentality.[44] People can live under horrendous conditions, even slavery, and believe that the system is unchangeable. If they hear only the voices selected by more powerful others, then their own voices are silenced. They lose the potential to engage in dialogues with others like themselves in which they may come to see that the reality they assume is a social construction prepared by others, that such social constructions can be remade, and that, collectively, ordinary people hold the potential power for change.[45]

The Federal Communications Commission (FCC), created in 1934, recognized that airwaves belong to the public and leases require some responsibility. The FCC was to ensure that radio broadcasters would continue public service programs in an environment increasingly controlled by advertising. However, regulatory protection of the airwaves has been minimal, and government organizations and enactments originally created to protect the public interest now protect the interests of big business. When Viacom merged with CBS, the resulting conglomerate was in clear violation of the rule that no company can control stations that reach more than 35 percent of the total audience. The FCC responded by offering the emergent corporation a temporary waiver.[46] Major media conglomerates have been able to influence the FCC. Local news entities produced by independently owned outlets provide Americans a valuable tool in the public debate of issues. While the FCC was fighting to relax rules that would prevent further media consolidation, the agency was charged with suppressing the release of two federally funded studies showing negative effects of consolidation, including the reduction of local news coverage. The information was eventually leaked to the office of Senator Barbara Boxer. The FCC, however, has not become a proponent of corporate interests on its own accord. McChesney describes the FCC as the classic "captive" regulatory agency. For example, in 1994 the FCC proposed an investigation into Rupert Murdoch's broadcast empire. After being threatened by Representative Jack Fields, on the House committee and a friend of Murdoch, they dropped the investigation.[47]

This media entanglement with politicians (supposedly its regulators) and corporate interests is bound together by lobbyists. In exchange for government deregulation, the corporate media return the favor to their friends in government with enormous sums of money, thereby essentially giving them a "cut" from their unrestricted profits. Lobbying expenditures rose significantly, 74 percent in the years between 1998 and 2003, while the FCC was considering additional relaxing of ownership regulations. In 2001 Clear Channel spent only $12,000 on lobbying, but in 2003—the year of the FCC vote—it spent $2.28 million, an increase of 19,000 percent in two years.[48] In an interview with *Fortune* magazine in 2003, Clear Channel CEO Lowry Mays described the philosophy of his company: "We're not in the business of providing news and information. We're not in the business of providing well-researched music. We're simply in the business of selling our customers products."[49]

The cable, telephone, and Internet industries use several tools to gain a competitive advantage in telecommunications reform legislation. Some of these lobbying tools are easy to spot—campaign contributions, television ads that run only inside the Beltway, and meetings with influential members of Congress. Other tactics are more deceptive.

Using Fake Groups and Fake News

Telecommunications companies are increasingly using one of the tactics popularized by the missile industry. Dubbed "Astroturf lobbying" by former U.S. Senator Lloyd Bentsen, the practice involves creating front groups that try to pass as grassroots citizen groups but that are actually corporate-sponsored efforts to put fake grassroots pressure on Congress. Astroturf campaigns generally claim to represent huge numbers of citizens, but in reality their public support is minimal or nonexistent.[50] Common Cause researchers found nine such telecommunications front groups and Astroturf organizations: Consumers for Cable Choice,

Freedom Works, Progress and Freedom Foundation, American Legislative Exchange Council, New Millennium Research Council, Frontiers of Freedom, Keep It Local NJ, Alliance, and MyWireless.org. Behind these innocuous names, the groups get their funding from the telecommunications industry giants, sometimes working directly from their offices, rarely indicating the sources of their funds, and never mentioning the financial windfalls to the media giants from consolidation following the deregulation they advocate. In addition to fake groups, we find fake news reports, a problem that is particularly important for television.[51]

In recent years the number of media formats and outlets for information has grown dramatically. However, television has remained the major news source in the United States. According to a January 2006 Harris Poll, more than three-quarters of U.S. adults rely on local television news, and more than 70 percent turned to network television or cable news on a near-daily basis. However, clear trends show that people, especially the young, are turning to the Internet for more and more of their news. According to a study by the Pew Research Center, television for news was down to 55 percent in 2012.[52] Still, the quality and integrity of television reporting has a significant impact on what the public learns about consumer products, health services, and, most important, government policies.

Public relations firms have a keen desire to reach this audience with the messages of their corporate and government clients and have a way to make the markedly biased messages of their clients appear as an impartial reporting of the news. To add an appearance of credibility to clients' messages, the public relations industry uses video news releases (VNRs). VNRs are prepackaged "news" segments and additional footage created by broadcast public relations firms, or by publicists within corporations or government agencies. The VNRs are provided free to television stations and are designed to fit seamlessly into newscasts. Although the stations know the source of this information, they do not identify it in the broadcast. In the absence of strong disclosure requirements, viewers have no way of knowing when the news segment they have just seen was bought and paid for by the very subjects of that "report."

The Center for Media and Democracy (CMD) conducted a ten-month study of selected VNRs and their use by television stations. They tracked thirty-six VNRs issued by three broadcast public relations firms. Their results show that the television newscasts on which most Americans rely—frequently air VNRs without disclosure to viewers, without conducting their own reporting, and even without checking the facts in claims made in the VNRs. VNRs are overwhelmingly produced for corporations. They are part of larger public-relations campaigns to sell products, to brighten corporate images, or to promote policies or actions beneficial to the corporation.[53]

The Effect on Journalism

Corporations are, by design, money-producing entities. They are legally bound to put the interest of their stockholders as their first priority, above the public good. The ramifications of their decisions are considered outside the realm of their responsibility. When corporations own media, news becomes a product to sell, and the public audience is the consumer.

Advertisers (often owned by the same parent company as the media outlet) and media board members (interlocked with other industries) decide what is newsworthy. They promote their products and present a favorable corporate image to the public. A survey by FAIR (Fairness and Accuracy in Reporting) found that 75 percent of investigative journalists and editors surveyed in television news admitted that advertisers had "tried to influence the content" of news stories; 59 percent felt pressure from within their own stations to produce news stories to please advertisers.[54] In this environment the actual activity of many dedicated professional journalists reflects a difficult road of access to government sources, resources for other source materials, knowledge of the acceptable range of what can be said, and cautions about crossing that line.[55] McChesney describes how unlike the current situation is from the days of the muckracker journalists, who exposed corporate greed to protect the public:

> The corporate media system has none of the inherent interest in politics or journalism. . . . Its commercialized news fare, if anything, tends to promote depoliticization, and all evidence suggests that its fundamental political positions, such as they are, are closely linked to political and business elites.[56]

Consider, for example, the influence that General Electric, the world's largest company by market share, has over its media company NBC. GE is one of the world's top-three producers of jet engines, supplying Boeing and Lockheed Martin. GE has also designed ninety-one nuclear power plants in eleven countries. Former GE director Sam Nunn was the senator of Georgia for twenty-seven years and sat on the board of Chevron-Texaco.[57] The power held by such giant media corporations results in a strong bias, imposed from the top, on what passes for news. Journalism ceases to exist in an environment where the news is becoming a public relations mouthpiece for the corporate and political interests. The media then become a tool to disseminate propaganda for the interests that control and finance them.

The Rise of Social Media

Since the rise of the Internet in the early 1990s, the world's networked population has grown from the low millions to the low billions. Over the same period, social media have become a fact of life for civil society worldwide, involving many actors—regular citizens, activists, non-governmental organizations, telecommunications firms, software providers, and governments.[58]

In part by using the social networking sites, activists organized and published the unprecedented protests that gave rise to the so-called Arab Spring, which has so far seen longtime governments in Egypt and Tunisia fall, regimes in Syria, Libya, Yemen, and Bahrain clash with opposition, and the leaders in Jordan, Saudi Arabia, and the UAE offer more benefits to their populace.[59] Ups and downs since the initial uprisings continue, but the hashtag dissenters have increased visibility of opposition.

Social media's rise and its new activist uses have played a critical role in mobilization, empowerment, shaping opinions, and influencing change. It is no surprise that with the rise of social media comes the potential of government and corporations to control IT communication and to use it to identify and intimidate opponents and whistleblowers. Before this time, control of government and markets had depended on personal relationships and face-to-face interactions; now control is established by means of bureaucratic organization, the new infrastructures of transportation and telecommunications, and system-wide communication via the new mass media.[60] However, sociopolitical events—the women's peace and justice movements, the election of Barack Obama, and the Iranian Revolution—have been made possible by the utilization of social media to organize people. These events demonstrate that technology could also be used as a tool to

fight against some of the more entrenched obstacles to injustice and marginaliza-
tion, and as a means toward building solidarity.[61]

Some have held out hope for the Internet and broadband as a way to decen-
tralize control over information. Journalist Jeff Chester warns that the country's
powerful communications companies have other plans that threaten freedom in
the new digital world.[62] Assisted by a host of hired political operatives and pro-
business policy makers, major cable, television, and Internet providers are using
their political connections to gain greater control over the Internet and other digital communication channels. Bill Moyers notes the promise of digital communications but also the dangers:

> The Internet, cell phones and digital cameras that can transmit images
> over the Internet makes possible a nation of storytellers, every citizen a
> Tom Paine. Let the man in the big house on Pennsylvania Avenue think
> that over, and the woman of the House on Capitol Hill. And the media
> moguls . . . no longer own the copyright to America's story. It's not a top-
> down story anymore. Other folks are going to write this story from the
> ground up. And the truth will be out that the media plantation, like the
> cotton plantation of old, is not divinely sanctioned. It's not the product
> of natural forces. The media system we have been living under for a long
> time now was created behind closed doors where the power brokers met
> to divvy up the spoils. [Consolidation has added the danger that] . . . we
> are being shadowed online by a slew of software digital gumshoes, work-
> ing for Madison Avenue. Our movements in cyberspace are closely tracked
> and analyzed, and interactive advertising infiltrates our consciousness to
> promote the brand washing of America. . . . Do we really want television
> sets that monitor what we watch? Or an Internet that knows what sites we
> visit and report back to advertising companies? Do we really want a media
> system designed mainly for Madison Avenue?[63]

Political and Economic Agendas: The Modern-Day Manufacture of Consent

Recall the philosophy of Edward Bernays that the "the very essence of the democratic process" was that intelligent minorities of society can—and should—direct
the population through the "engineering of consent."[64] Bernays and especially

Lippmann, who coined the phrase "manufacture of consent," identified themselves as progressive democratic intellectuals. The idea of a small elite controlling
and manipulating "the bewildered herd" (as Lippman referred to the general public) was not their original idea. That idea has been promoted throughout Western
history. Important here is the belief that the public cannot be trusted to think for
themselves. If they do, it will only cause trouble, so they must be herded. During
the Reagan presidency, a high level of concern emerged when it was revealed that
the CIA was bypassing congressional laws by supporting the contras to overthrow
the government of Nicaragua. A scam known as the Iran-contra affair allowed the
CIA to fund this operation by permitting the aerial dropping of cocaine into the
United States and returning with arms routed from Iran. Although this was eventually uncovered, the administration set up a public diplomacy office directed by
Otto Reich. Its task, like that of other government ministries before it, was perception management. Its job was to present information in ways that would preclude
knowledge of such activities from reaching the public (and in this case a Congress)
who could not be trusted to support policies being used.

The techniques for managing public images are straightforward. Linguist
Geoffrey Nunberg addresses a self-fulfilling practice of repeating ignorant slogans until they become part of the culture in his book *Talking Right: How Conservatives Turned Liberalism into a Tax-Raising, Latte-Drinking, Sushi-Eating,
Volvo-Driving, New York Times-Reading, Body-Piercing, Hollywood-Loving,
Left-Wing Freak Show.*[65] Another linguist, George Lakoff, has described in detail
the art of framing issues in ways that are palatable to people and substituting
stereotypical buzzwords for actual understanding. Lakoff also elaborates upon a
theme by Erich Fromm, arguing that large numbers of people who reflect family backgrounds of a strong authoritarian father are seeking a leader who offers
simple, all-or-none solutions.[66] The message is to be passive before authority.
Well-funded corporate campaigning has been successful to get people to vote
against their right to know when the food they eat has been genetically modified
and media have been successful in turning people against the whistleblowers who
expose outrageous government policies.

Propaganda plays on simple but powerful images and slogans. A concise
message is repeated over and over until it is accepted and integrated seamlessly
into our thinking (and may remain long after the message has been discredited).
Fear provides the leverage, the motivating force behind propaganda. When we

feel threatened, we are most likely to stand behind leaders who take on the role of protector.

Psychologists Anthony Pratkanis and Elliott Aronson suggest four strategies of successful propaganda: (1) Create an environment or climate in which the actual message will be believed ("pre-persuasion"); (2) Refer to a credible source, a public figure, or a likable and/or authoritative speaker; (3) Present a simple and clear message; (4) For this message to take hold, fear must be evoked and projected upon some target group.[67]

Keywords and phrases, repeated incessantly, act as word-encoded symbols that contain our national history and identity—peace, democracy, defending freedom, God bless America, growth, and prosperity. But the symbols often have a dark side that is not acknowledged. Consider, as Michael Parenti does, the real meaning behind the keywords we are exposed to every day:

> "Peace" means global U.S. military domination. . . . "Prosperity" means subsidizing the expansion of U.S. corporate interests abroad. . . . And "democracy" . . . means a system in which political decisions are made by the transnational and publicly unaccountable corporate interests and their government allies.[68]

In Parenti's view an absence of military violence, because those facing gross degradation are too frightened to fight back, could be described in the media as a time of peace and stability; increases in gross national product are used to signify prosperity, even if the actual number living in poverty is increasing and the true beneficiaries are subsidized transnational corporations; and democracies can be said to exist even when wealth determines who has access to be heard and death squads intimidate voters. Chapter 2 looked at the media role in promoting enemy images prior to military violence. This section highlights examples of the propaganda campaign put forth by the G. W. Bush administration's war on terror, with the assistance of corporate media who have their own economic agenda in mind.

The Defense Department's Media Contracts

Although the first organized propaganda campaign was designed to create American support against Germany in the First World War, it was the Vietnam War that prompted the U.S. government—or more accurately, the Pentagon—to attempt more direct control over the media. The United States had followed China, Japan, and France in efforts to dominate Vietnam. The war was swept by a crusade of anticommunism and an unwillingness to consider the possibility that the U.S. war in Vietnam was an ill-conceived effort to bury the forces of Vietnamese nationalism. Many military officials believed that reporting on the slaughter of Vietnamese women and children, the mental and physical breakdown of American soldiers, and the suspicion of the government's political policy were responsible for the American defeat. Images of Vietnamese children screaming, their skin burning with napalm, were seared into American consciousness. For many in power, the disaster of the Vietnam War was not the loss of life but rather the interference of the public in what leaders had determined to be a policy addressing U.S. interests. The perceived need to mobilize both domestic and global opinion in response to a threat of terrorism was later addressed by a report of the Defense Science Board Task Force on Strategic Communication.

The G. W. Bush administration led a comprehensive and sophisticated propaganda campaign, first by contracts with public relations firms and second by appointing marketing experts to its official staff. In February 2006 the nonpartisan Government Accounting Office (GAO) released a 160-page report on recent media contracts by seven federal departments. Diane Farsetta points out that the findings were based on the self-reporting of federal departments.[69] They do not include the public relations activities of government employees, and the products generated under such contracts (the "deliverables") are undefined. However, the report gives some indication of the amount of government spending on public relations and the sharp increases sustained over the last several years. For example, between fiscal years 2003 and 2005, the Bush administration's reported spending on private public relations firms averaged $78.8 million per year, a figure more than twice that of Clinton's second term (1997–2000) of $32 million per year.[70] The GAO reported that the Pentagon alone spent $1.1 billion in media contracts over thirty months from 2001 through 2004.[71] An Associated Press investigation discovered that over the five years ending in 2009, the amount the military spent on winning hearts and minds at home and abroad had grown by 63 percent, to at least $4.7 billion. A major rise in public affairs spending, which is directed domestically, prompted one congressman to say, "It's not up to the Pentagon to sell policy to the American people."[72]

Why was this money spent? It was needed to convince the world of the good intentions of U.S. policy. In the words of President Bush one month after the 9/11 attack:

> How do I respond when I see that in some Islamic countries there is vitriolic hatred for America? . . . I'll tell you how I respond: I'm amazed. I'm amazed that there's such misunderstanding of what our country is about that people would hate us. I am—like most Americans, I just can't believe it because I know how good we are.[73]

A more independent and informed media might have asked the president how he would feel about a government that had supported tyrants and undermined governments in this country, but, given the influence of media ownership, those able to reach the president were not inclined to do so. A tremendous effort was initiated by the Pentagon to use information warfare to convince those who might otherwise not recognize the goodness of the United States.

The Rendon Group

One of the largest recipients of Pentagon contracts is the Rendon Group. Headed by John Rendon, self-described "information warrior" and "perception manager," the Rendon Group has worked for clients in seventy-eight countries, including the Colombian Army, the government of Indonesia, and Monsanto Chemical Company.

Rendon's work with the U.S. government began in the 1970s as an election campaign consultant to Democratic Party politicians, including Jimmy Carter. Head of his own firm in 1989, Rendon was contracted by the CIA to campaign for the U.S.-installed government of Panama after the ousting of Manuel Noriega. Following his success there, Rendon orchestrated opposition to Saddam Hussein during the occupation of Kuwait. In broadcasts all over the world, hundreds of Kuwaitis were seen waving American flags just as U.S. troops rolled into town.[74]

Immediately thereafter, Rendon worked for the CIA to run a covert anti-Saddam campaign in Iraq, encouraging Iraqi army officers to defect. Rendon worked with the Iraqi National Congress (INC), even giving them their name. As evidenced by Pentagon documents, between 2000 and 2004, the Rendon

Group received thirty-five contracts with the Department of Defense, totaling $50–$100 million.[75]

In the task of creating the INC, Rendon helped the CIA install Ahmed Chalabi as head of the organization. Chalabi is reported to have received $350,000 a month, channeled from the CIA, through the Rendon Group. In December 2001, nearly ten years after the inception of the INC, Adnan Ihsan Saeed al-Haideri was brought forward by the INC as an eyewitness to Saddam Hussein's possession of weapons of mass destruction (WMDs). Judith Miller, journalist for the *New York Times*, was granted worldwide exclusive print rights for an interview with the defector. In a correspondence with her bureau chief in Baghdad, Miller described how, for a decade, Chalabi had been one of her key sources on stories of WMDs. Paul Moran was the other journalist chosen to interview al-Haideri and granted worldwide broadcast rights for the story. Moran had not only worked for the INC but also the Rendon Group for many years, even before the organization of the INC.[76] Although al-Haideri failed a lie detector test, Bush administration officials brought him back to Iraq to point out the location of the weapons. Even after none were found and al-Haideri was discredited, his testimony was still cited in President Bush's State of the Union address—as evidence of Iraq's WMDs.[77] Judith Miller's articles in the *New York Times* were cited repeatedly. In May 2004 the *New York Times* ran an editorial to apologize for five articles written between 2001 and 2003 that described accounts of biological, chemical, and nuclear weapons in Iraq. The editorial stated:

> In some cases, information that was controversial then, and seems questionable now, was insufficiently qualified or allowed to stand unchallenged. . . . Looking back, we wish we had been more aggressive in reexamining the claims as new evidence emerged—or failed to emerge.[78]

The Lincoln Group

Another major PR firm, The Lincoln Group, states that its "expertise lies in providing insight to our clients in the markets they wish to reach and the ability to influence their target audience."[79] In November 2005, the *Los Angeles Times* reported that the Lincoln Group had covertly helped the Pentagon place "dozens" of pro–United States stories, written by the U.S. military, in Iraqi news outlets. Designed to mask any connection with the U.S. military, the Lincoln Group assisted in the translation and placement of the stories, while its Iraqi staff, posing as freelance reporters or advertising executives, delivered stories to Baghdad media outlets. The effort was directed by the U.S. military's Information Operations Task Force in Baghdad, which had reportedly purchased an Iraqi newspaper and taken control of a radio station in order to "channel pro-American messages to the Iraqi public."[80]

Voice of America noted that although their own official communications principles state information will be "timely and accurate," they "do not include any prohibition against paying to place stories in the newspapers."[81] The Inspector General, the Pentagon's internal watchdog, did conduct a review of three Lincoln Group contracts. The DOD report revealed that the Pentagon could not account for millions paid to the Lincoln Group for their propaganda program and that basic contracting rules were not followed. Nevertheless, an unclassified summary of results of the Inspector General's probe concluded that the contracts "complied with applicable laws and regulations in their use of a contractor to conduct Psychological Operations and their use of newspapers as a way to disseminate information."[82] This casts doubt on whether the military and intelligence sectors can ever be trusted to monitor themselves.

Official Manipulation: The Office of Strategic Influence

In September of 2004 the Defense Science Board, an advisory committee to the Department of Defense, released its report "Strategic Communication."[83] The report states that policy must be determined not by public opinion but by "interests," although opinion and the need to influence it must be considered an important factor. The report assumed as self-evident that the United States is engaged in a war of ideas with Islamic terrorists and that, despite immense amounts of money spent to disseminate our message, we had grown complacent by the past successful ways of marketing brand-name products and political candidates. We were thus losing out to a tiny more agile and insurgent voice. Building an insurgent global strategic culture that borrows from the most effective private-sector marketing and political campaign techniques would be at the core of rebuilding and reinventing the way the United States listens, engages, and communicates with the world.

In *Weapons of Mass Deception: The Uses of Propaganda in Bush's War on Iraq*, Sheldon Rampton and John Stauber show us a shocking world where marketers, "information warriors," and "perception managers" can sell an entire war to consumers.[84] The principle behind the practice had been explained before in 1945. At the Nuremburg trials of Nazi war criminals, Hermann Goering, minister of information, was asked how the Nazis were able to convince so many of the German people to support the war they initiated. He replied:

> Why of course the people don't want war. . . . But after all it is the leaders of the country who determine the policy, and it is always a simple matter to drag the people along, whether it is a democracy, or a fascist dictatorship, or a parliament, or a communist dictatorship. . . . Voice or no voice, the people can always be brought to the bidding of the leaders. That is easy. All you have to do is to tell them they are being attacked, and denounce the pacifists for lack of patriotism and exposing the country to danger.[85]

Missing entirely from the Department of Defense report regarding the situation in Iraq was the matter of what the opposing voices had to say. There are eloquent and well-reasoned attempts by scholars of Islamic history to explain why the U.S. government is distrusted and disliked. Neither were the actual words of the adversary taken into consideration. The name bin Laden appears in the report, but the actual words of the demonized adversary Osama are dutifully concealed. What bin Laden had written is:

> The White House policy, which strove to open war fronts to give business to their various corporations—in armament, oil, and construction . . . also helped accomplish these astonishing achievements for Al Qaeda. It appeared to some analysts and diplomats that we and the White House play as one team to score a goal against the United States of America, even though our intentions differ.[86]

The Office of Strategic Influence (OSI) was established shortly after the September 11, 2001, terrorist attacks in response to concerns that the United States was losing public support overseas for its war on terror. The Pentagon's official announcement of the OSI declared its goal as "to provide news items, possibly even false ones, to foreign media organizations as part of a new effort to influence public sentiment and policy makers."[87] This statement led to an immediate outcry by both public and congressional leaders. Addressing the Defense Writers Group, Undersecretary of Defense for Policy Douglas Feith explained, "We're going to preserve our credibility and we're going to preserve the purity of the statements that defense officials make to the public. . . . We're also going to preserve our option to mislead the enemy about our operations. And those are not inconsistent."[88]

So locked into the assumptions of a conflict in which we, the good side, are opposed by them, the evil side, the administration could not comprehend why its massive propaganda campaign did not win friends for the United States. The image created by saturation bombing, invasion, occupation, destruction of homes, torture, depleted uranium, killing hundreds of thousands of people, and daily humiliation of civilians of all ages was visible to most Iraqis. Only within the fortified Green Zone in which U.S. officials and visitors could be protected and treated to comfort was it possible to ignore the extent of the military debacle. The inept contractors, who failed to include Iraqis in plans for rebuilding the destroyed electric power stations and health care system, added to a visible reality that could not be spun to indicate good intentions. For unlike those who have the luxury to be engaged by trivial pursuits and to accept official mythologies, the direct victims of oppressive actions are not so easily deceived.

Official Manipulation: The Office of Special Plans

Initiated by Paul Wolfowitz, deputy secretary of defense, and put into action shortly after September 11, 2001, the Office of Special Plans (OSP) produced intelligence reviews to shape public opinion and American policy toward Iraq. The members and supporters of OSP are many of the same founders of the conservative ideology expressed in the Project for a New American Century and its spin-off, Committee for the Liberation of Iraq.[89] With access to an enormous amount of raw intelligence from the CIA (much of it sifted through and discredited by the CIA directorate of operations), various pieces of information were picked up by the OSP.[90] Combined with intelligence from their own sources—

specifically, Chalabi and the INC—the OSP synthesized intelligence to support the ideas that Saddam had chemical, biological, and nuclear weapons and links to al-Qaeda.

Intelligence experts point out that most of the OSP staff were not trained in intelligence. Pushing for action against Afghanistan immediately after 9/11, with less than ten full-time staff and mountains of intelligence documents to sort through, the office hired over 100 temporary consultants. Most of these lawyers, congressional staffers, and various conservative think-tank ideologues, were off the books, thus allowing the department to hire individuals without specifying their job description.[91] As defense analyst John Pike described it, such contracts "are basically a way they could pack the room with their little friends."[92]

Intelligence experts have criticized the OSP's reliance on defectors as sources of intelligence. In 1991 Abram Shulsky (the only OSP member trained in intelligence) co-authored a textbook about intelligence and the use of defectors. Despite their importance, he wrote, "it is difficult to be certain they are genuine. . . . The conflicting information provided by several major Soviet defectors to the United States . . . has never been completely sorted out."[93]

One defector informant, Colonel Saddam Kamel, supplied information that Bush and Cheney used to convince the public of the failure of the UN inspections. Kamel, along with his brother General Hussein Kamel, the man in charge of Iraq's weapons program, defected to Jordan in 1995, bringing with them detailed information about Iraq's efforts to produce nuclear weapons. Based on Kamel's testimony, Bush described the dramatic picture of thousands of liters of anthrax and stockpiles of biological weapons. Cheney stated that Kamel's testimony proved that "we often learned more as the result of defections than we learned from the inspection regime itself."[94] What is most interesting about the Kamel interview is what was left out from the OSP accounts. In the full record of Kamel's interview with UN inspectors, he notes that Iraq's stockpile of chemical and biological weapons—made before the first Gulf War—had been destroyed.

The International Atomic Energy Commission officially informed the United States that the claims of Saddam Hussein possessing nuclear weapons were untrue. The National Security Council described OSP evidence of Iraq's chemical, biological, and nuclear weapons program and Iraq's link to al-Qaeda as "a classic case of rumit—rumor-intelligence plugged into various speeches and accepted as gospel."[95]

The Media's Failure to Examine Questions about the Events of 9/11

The harsh fact is that all of what actually took place on 9/11 and what U.S. officials knew prior to the event has not been made available to the public, to Congress, or to the media. A group called Scholars for 9/11 Truth has called for immediate release of the full Pentagon surveillance tape and for videotapes seized by FBI agents, minutes after the Pentagon was hit. They asked for release of the complete inventory of plane wreckage and debris from the four flights or any other aircraft that crashed or was destroyed on the day of the attack and for a catalog of photographs and videotapes taken of any items from the planes, as well as results of all tests and examinations conducted concerning any of these items. The request also mentioned 6,899 photographs and 6,977 segments of video footage held by the National Institute of Standards and Technology; tape recordings of interviews by air traffic controllers, at least some of which were deliberately destroyed while in the possession of representatives of the government; a complete accounting of "terror drills" that were being conducted that morning, which may have been used to mask the attack; the cockpit voice recorders and other black boxes, three of four of which are reported to have survived the Twin Towers' collapse. Professor James Fetzer, cofounder of the Scholars group, noted that the Securities and Exchange Commission possesses knowledge of "put options" on American and United Airlines, which are suggestive of advanced knowledge that the attacks would take place. Secretary of Transportation Norman Mineta gave important testimony to the 9/11 Commission, which it chose not to include in its report. In addition, the Secret Service conducted itself in a manner suggesting that it knew there was no serious threat to the president, even following the attacks in New York, while the commander-in-chief ignored the unfolding drama. Fetzer notes:

> We are inclined to believe that these events were orchestrated by the Bush administration in order to instill fear in the American people. The use of violence and threats of violence to manipulate a populace based on fear is the definition of terrorism.[96]

The concerns raised, whether fully substantiated or not, are serious enough to merit investigation. The major media did not do this.

Historical Examples of Media Manipulation and the Justification for War

Media manipulation is not new. William Mandell reports of efforts supported by Columbia University and the *New York Times* revoking a Pulitzer Prize awarded in 1932 and suppressing even mention of Professor Walter Duranty. Duranty had won the O. Henry Prize for Best Short Story of the year in 1928 and had earlier won the Pulitzer Prize for journalism for his coverage of the Soviet Union for the *New York Times* from 1920 to the mid-1940s. He was falsely charged with denying the starvation in the Ukraine, but his real offense was an opposition to the growing hysteria of the Cold War.[97]

The deception carried out by the media to justify an attack upon Iraq was not a new phenomenon. In 2001 Robert J. Hanyok, a historian with the National Security Agency (NSA), wrote an article for internal publication. Although it dealt with an event that occurred in 1964, the paper was classified "Top Secret" and released only following a freedom of information request by other historians. Hanyok's paper showed that the agency's intelligence officers "deliberately skewed" the evidence that was passed on to policy makers and the public. They falsely suggested that American destroyers had been attacked by North Vietnamese ships on August 4, 1964.[98] Following the report that an attack had occurred, President Johnson ordered air strikes on North Vietnam, and Congress passed a broad resolution authorizing military action. Ignoring the evidence that Vietnamese nationalists had been fighting against Chinese, Japanese, and French colonizers for half a century, the NSA pushed its domino theory upon the public and Congress. If the puppet governments of South Vietnam fell to the communists all of Southeast Asia would follow. With media an unquestioning partner, the purported attack began the major escalation of a war that killed more than 58,000 U.S. soldiers and at least 2 million Vietnamese.

Many stories dutifully carried in mainstream media lead to major consequences long before they have been found to be untrue. Sometimes the lure of capturing a news story makes journalists vulnerable to being set up. A CIA plan to overthrow the democratically elected President Arbenz in Guatemala in 1954 was preceded by a report of a Guatemalan security threat. The publisher of the *New York Times* was persuaded by a United Fruit agent to send a reporter to Guatemala who "dutifully wrote a series of alarming reports about 'Reds' in the country."[99] Starting in the 1950s and extending into the 1980s, a series of reports appeared of "missile gaps," showing calculations that supported missile superiority on the part of the Soviet Union. The reports were exposed as fraudulent, but with a time lag that permitted their use to justify large contracts for a responsive U.S. buildup.[100]

Often media are relied upon to carry the message that it is one's own side that is offering peace while the adversary's refusal necessitates an escalation of the war. In 1965 U.S. bombing of Vietnam was greatly increased. This led to widespread protests within the United States, and the Johnson administration responded with reports that it was offering pauses in the bombing to provide opportunity for unrestricted talks with the North Vietnamese. The *New York Times* reported this with a comment that the responsibility for the war was now entirely in the hands of the Hanoi government. The ploy, dubious at the time, was later discredited with evidence that the secret offer was actually one requiring complete surrender.[101]

The media again have taken the bait with offers to talk with Iran about its security without first suspending efforts at regime change. By the start of 2007 such efforts already included a series of aggressive moves designed to achieve that outcome, including subsidizing internal dissidents within Iran, encouraging cross-border attacks from Iraq by Iranian expatriate terrorists, collecting data on Iranian targets by spy drones and on-the-ground incursions, and threatening to attack. The United States rejected a European Union effort to negotiate a deal with Iran by refusing to agree to security guarantees to Iran. Yet media replayed the Iranian refusal to accept U.S. demands to give up its nuclear facilities before talks can begin. The U.S. proposal was apparently intended to fail and to push the argument for sanctions against Iran, a path followed previously against Iraq.

The media's role in movement toward war seems clear. The suggested threat from abroad must be accepted as the real purpose of the activity. Media must ignore the military provocations and transgressions from the U.S. side and must insist upon removing the target country's right to self-defense. Media must then demonize the enemy of the moment—Gadaffi, Castro, Noriega, Milosevic, Khomeini, or Hussein—and ignore U.S. violations of international treaties or UN resolutions. There are exceptions, but in the lead-up to war media serve less as a provider of factual information and more as the propaganda arm for officials seeking war.[102]

Strategic Media: Embedded Journalism

Coverage of the Iraq war introduced a new phenomenon of embedded report-ers. U.S. General Tommy Franks called the press, once referred to as the fourth estate, the "fourth front."[103] Franks pulled together a team of media and public relations specialists to put the fourth front into action in the field. Heading his team was public relations professional Victoria Clarke. Clarke, who became a Pentagon official, wrote up extensive contracts with major media networks and news organizations, securing the Department of Defense's control of media. Proudly describing her work at the Pentagon to an audience at the Radio and Television Museum, Clarke stated:

> We took the same kind of planning and training and discipline that you put into military operations and put it into this aspect of the military oper-ations. And Rumsfeld and Myers, being enlightened guys, had included people like me in the war plan from the very earliest stages.[104]

Clarke oversaw this Pentagon media program, which embedded journal-ists with U.S. troops in the field. Journalists remained with the same battalion throughout their assignments, thus getting to know the soldiers in a very personal way. They heard about their families and about their fears. They lived with the soldiers and were, in fact, dependent on the soldiers for their protection. The situation is antithetical to one of the standard rules of journalistic ethics, that jour-nalists should not accept anything of value from the sources they are covering. The Pentagon developed a training course for embedded journalists at the outset of their assignments. The course was presented as survival training in which jour-nalists were instructed about chemical warfare—enhancing the fraudulent idea that the Iraqis were engaging in chemical and biological warfare.

Strategic Media: The Pentagon's Doha Media Center

The multimillion-dollar press center at General Tommy Franks's Central Com-mand headquarters in Doha, Qatar, constructed by a Hollywood set designer, was erected months before the U.S. invasion of Iraq. Far from the front line, the environment of the media center was calm and comfortably air-conditioned.

Here at least 700 journalists were gathered and sequestered for daily news briefings provided by the Pentagon. *New York* magazine correspondent Michael Wolff described such briefings as "a TV-ready war update spoon-fed to hundreds of journalists by the U.S. military."[105] A typical press briefing begins by viewing Pentagon-produced videos, which show, for example, the efficacy of precision bombing, or show smiling Iraqi children greeting American soldiers. Next, Pentagon officials brief journalists on such things as "terrorist"—meaning Iraqi—activity. When one reporter noted that the term *terrorist* refers to individuals who use violence against civilians and not soldiers, Franks declined to comment.[106]

Journalist and media critic Robert Young Pelton characterized the Doha media center as the fire-hose phenomenon:

> If you can give the media more content than they can handle and, as far away from the battlefield as possible, they will focus their energies where the source of that fire-hose is. So, Doha is the center of the fire-hose. And the idea is, you simply have press conferences every day, and every once in awhile you throw a little tidbit—you hand out videotapes, free coffee, whatever. So that if you leave, you're gonna miss the story that everybody else is covering. . . . Fire-hose coverage and fire-hose delivery blocks out all the secondary sources.[107]

When the war in Iraq went badly, the administration began to offer less information to reporters, and the media helped remove attention from the tragedies of the Iraq war.[108]

Media Complicity: Spinning the War on Terror

In March 2003, then chairman of the FCC Michael Powell (son of Colin Powell) assessed the media's coverage of the U.S. invasion and occupation of Iraq. He described how it was "thrilling to see the power of the media."[109] Media analysts, however, recognize the Iraq war as the lowest point in American journalism. In their book *Tragedy and Farce: How the American Media Sell Wars, Spin Elections, and Destroy Democracy*, Nichols and McChesney describe how the decline of quality in journalism is not related to inept or corrupt journalists, but rather is due to the massive corporate ownership of the media. As noted earlier, under corporate ownership the media become a product and the audience becomes a consumer: What is newsworthy is what will increase market share or reflect favorably on objectives that favor corporate advertisers. But how do corporate values and political agendas affect the practice of journalism?

One way such values and agendas affect journalism is through selection of content. In 2003 the Council for Excellence in Government published a study that found, over the preceding twenty years, coverage of the federal government dropped by 31 percent on television news shows, 12 percent in national newspapers, and 39 percent in regional newspapers.[110] The amount of international coverage in U.S. newspapers and on television news devoted to foreign affairs dropped by 70 to 80 percent in the 1980s and 1990s.[111] Based on news coverage in 2005, Michael Jackson's trial, Martha Stewart's conviction terms, and Natalie Holloway's disappearance appeared more interesting to the American public than the coverage of United States engaging in torture. This is not because of an overwhelming demand for this type of news; as John Nichols and Robert McChesney explain, this kind of journalism is supply driven. Covering the mishaps and romantic escapades of celebrities is more conducive to the consumer environment. It is also much less expensive for media companies to produce. It is entertaining, politically insignificant, and offers the "illusion of controversy."[112]

Meanwhile, issues that may actually have a major impact on the public or may inform public opinion slip by uncovered and unnoticed. The Downing Street Memo, minutes of a July 2002 British security meeting, described how Bush wanted to forcibly remove Saddam and was fixing intelligence and facts in order to justify doing so. The memo barely made it into U.S. print. Mainstream U.S. media kept quiet on the leaked document, which first appeared in the London *Sunday Times* on May 1, 2005. But the *Times* article circulated widely on the Internet, with bloggers wondering why the article was not being covered in U.S. media. At the first Bush press conference after the memo was leaked, not one of the nearly twenty reporters called upon asked Bush to respond to the memo.[113]

After mounting pressure from various media watchdog groups (such as FAIR), a handful of major media outlets finally reported on the memo; it didn't make the front page of a major U.S. newspaper until it was picked up by the *Chicago Tribune* on May 17, more than two weeks after the story broke. In an article about the British electoral campaign on May 20, the *New York Times* finally commented on the memo in a one-column story that did not mention manipulation of intelligence until the eighth paragraph. In response to a deluge of letters and emails, the *New York Times* editor explained how his Washington bureau chief had characterized the memo simply as the interpretation of British intelligence and not proof that Bush and his administration were distorting intelligence to support their push for war.[114]

A *Washington Post* article by Dana Milbank (which ran on page 18) referred to media activists calling for attention to the story as "wing nuts"; *Los Angeles Times* editorial page editor Michael Kinsley characterized activists as "paranoid." In most U.S. articles, discussion of the content of the Downing Street Memo was downplayed as proving what was already known to be true—contributing to ample, already established evidence—or by dismissing it completely as old news. FAIR reporters Julie Hollar and Peter Hart describe how such arguments are revealing:

> By acknowledging the "ample evidence" that indicates a secret, publicly denied Bush administration decision to invade Iraq, but then dismissing it as old news, journalists manage to avoid saying that the Bush administration lied to the American public—something they are exceedingly reluctant to do.[115]

Media concealment is not restricted to military matters. A major study showing that public opinion had no effect on government policy if it differed from the position of economic elites went viral in social media, but has hardly shown up in the U. S. corporate press. A month after its release there have been no network news mentions, nor has it appeared in the most influential newspapers—the *New York Times*, *Washington Post*, and *Los Angeles Times*—except as short buried blogposts.

Eliminating Journalists

The images from the siege of Fallujah came almost exclusively from reporters embedded with U.S. troops. This is because Arab journalists who had covered April's siege from the civilian perspective had effectively been eliminated. Al-Jazeera had no cameras on the ground because it has been banned from reporting in Iraq indefinitely. Al-Arabiya did have an unembedded reporter, Abdel Kader Al-Saadi, in Fallujah, but U.S. forces arrested him and held him for the length of the siege. Al-Saadi's detention has been condemned by Reporters Without Borders and the International Federation of Journalists.

This was not the first time journalists in Iraq faced intimidation. When U.S. forces invaded Baghdad in April 2003, Central Command urged all unembedded journalists to leave the city. Some insisted on staying, and at least three paid with their lives. On April 8, a U.S. aircraft bombed Al-Jazeera's Baghdad offices, killing reporter Tareq Ayyoub. Al-Jazeera has documentation proving it gave the coordinates of its location to U.S. forces. On the same day, a U.S. tank fired on the Palestine Hotel, killing José Couso of the Spanish network Telecinco and Taras Protsiuk of Reuters. Three U.S. soldiers faced a criminal lawsuit from Couso's family, which alleged that U.S. forces were well aware that journalists were in the Palestine Hotel and that they committed a war crime.[116]

Discounting Civilian Deaths

A major document completely dismissed by major U. S. news media was the results of a scientific study published by *The Lancet*, the journal of the British Medical Society. This study investigated the number and causes of civilian Iraqi deaths as a result of the invasion of Iraq. Conducting door-to-door surveys in thirty-three Iraqi neighborhoods (amounting to 8,000 interviews), researchers found that, compared with the pre-invasion period, Iraqi civilian deaths increased by 95 percent as a result of the U.S. and U.K. invasion. By conservative estimates, they believe that 100,000 Iraqi civilians had died since March 2003.[117] The findings showed the humanitarian cost to be extraordinary. Violence accounted for most of the deaths, and most violent deaths were related to air strikes. More than half of the deaths caused by the occupying forces were of women and children. The illustration raises serious concern over how facts were handled.

In the United States, major media news ignored or buried the story, while the article made headlines around Europe. Many U.S. news articles took a dismissive tone, casting doubt on the quality of research, despite the fact that previous mortality statistics of conflicts published by Les Roberts, of Johns Hopkins University, have been utilized by the U.S. State Department and the United Nations.[118]

Attempting to discredit the study, the *Washington Post* printed an article that quoted Human Rights Watch senior military analyst Marc E. Garlasco as saying, "These numbers seem to be inflated." In a subsequent interview, however,

Garlasco stated that at the time of the *Post* interview, he had not even read the report, and had told the journalist he was therefore unqualified to comment on it.[119] David R. Meddings, a medical officer with the Department of Injuries and Violence Prevention at the World Health Organization, points out why the study was so important: "If you can put accurate information out [on civilian casualties], it shifts the burden of proof onto militaries to substantiate why what they're doing is worth this humanitarian cost."[120]

A subsequent study by a team of epidemiologists revealed a far greater number of civilian casualties resulting from the invasion of Iraq. The study, also published in *The Lancet*, was conducted between May and July 2006. It made use of a national cross-sectional cluster sample survey of mortality in Iraq. Information on deaths was obtained from forty households in each of fifty different randomly selected areas. By comparing deaths since the invasion with the forty-month period preceding it, the study estimated that, as of July 2006, there had been 654,965 excess Iraqi deaths as a consequence of the war, corresponding to 25 percent of the population in the study area. Of post-invasion deaths, 601,027 were due to violence, the most common cause being gunfire.[121] This study also received little attention.

General Tommy Franks was widely quoted in media as saying, "We don't do body counts." The Geneva Conventions have clear guidance about the responsibilities of occupying armies to the civilian population they control. In particular, Convention IV, Article 27, states that protected persons "shall be at all times humanely treated, and shall be protected especially against acts of violence." It is difficult to understand how a military force could monitor the extent to which civilians are protected against violence without systematically counting those killed or, at least, looking at the kinds of casualties they induced. Civility and enlightened self-interest demand a reevaluation of the consequences of weaponry used by coalition forces in populated areas.[122] War is savage. The Geneva Conventions limit their scope. Media neglect permits violations of the Accords.

Spinning the Story

Another way corporate values and political agendas affect the practice of journalism is by "spinning" the story, wherein the facts and dynamics in the story are twisted—even fabricated—to lead to a specific interpretation. The Jessica Lynch story illustrates spin by Pentagon media specialists. Two weeks into the war, after coverage of the war had taken a less enthusiastic turn—including Al-Jazeera's footage of dead American soldiers—the media found the story it needed. Private Jessica Lynch, a blond nineteen-year-old from West Virginia, had been captured in an Iraqi ambush and taken to Saddam Hospital in Nasiriya. From Central Command's Doha media center, reporters learned that in a daring middle-of-the-night operation, U.S. Army Special Forces had rescued Jessica from the Nasiriya hospital. As *Time* magazine described, the story "buoyed a nation wondering what had happened to the short, neat liberation of Iraq."[123]

In the days following her rescue, different versions of the story began to circulate regarding how she was captured and what happened during her capture. A front-page story in the *Washington Post* cited unnamed U.S. officials that described Lynch with gunshot and stab wounds. The official was quoted as saying, "She was fighting to the death. . . . She did not want to be taken alive."[124] Many similar reports focused on the fierce battle Lynch was engaged in with Iraqi soldiers, some claiming that she had been abused or denied basic care by the Iraqis that tended to her. Other reports described an Iraqi lawyer who risked his life to tell U.S. troops where Lynch was after witnessing her being interrogated and slapped in the Nasiriya hospital.

An eyewitness account published in the London *Times* reported a very different story. Lynch's rescue by U.S. Special Forces "was not the heroic Hollywood story told by the U.S. military, but a staged operation that terrified patients and victimized the doctors who had struggled to save her life."[125] Doctors told the British reporters that the Americans had met no resistance, as Iraqi forces had left the city the day before the operation, and Lynch herself denied any mistreatment.

Spin was clear in the presentation of who to blame in the Abu Ghraib prison scandal. As evidence of the abuse of Iraqi prisoners at Abu Ghraib was revealed, the U.S. government—including Defense Secretary Rumsfeld and President Bush—repeatedly attributed the blame to "a few bad apples," an isolated case of rogue soldiers not following the chain of command. As the graphic photographs depicting physical and sexual abuse and humiliation circulated around the globe, causing a worldwide public uproar, politically conservative media hammered the notion of "a few bad apples" into the minds of their audiences. At Fox News, right-wing political pundits (under contract to deliver opinions prepared for them) echoed this idea with little discussion. Even more extreme was the commentary by right-wing radio host Rush Limbaugh, with weekly broadcasts to 20 million listeners, who trivialized the actions of the abusers as "blowing off steam":

> This is no different than what happens at the Skull and Bones initiation. . . . And we're going to ruin people's lives over it and we're going to hamper our military effort, and then we are going to really hammer them because they had a good time. . . . I'm talking about people having a good time. These people, you ever heard of emotional release? You heard of the need to blow off some steam?[126]

In their characterization of "a few bad apples," or just "blowing off steam," such media interpretations and reiterations show a disrespect of humanity but also demonstrate a flagrant disregard for journalistic integrity. In this case, proper investigation into prisoner abuse would have led to the acknowledgment of the widespread, systematic, and orchestrated covert program of prisoner abuse put into action by the Bush administration in its war on terror.

Such an investigation was conducted by Pulitzer Prize–winning journalist Seymour Hersh, in a series of reports on Abu Ghraib for *The New Yorker*. Unlike Bush and Rumsfeld's dismissal of accounts of abuse as the responsibility of a few young soldiers, the fifty-three-page report by Major General Antonio Taguba, obtained by *The New Yorker*, revealed "the collective wrongdoing and failure of Army leadership at the highest levels."[127] From Taguba's comprehensive study as well as accounts from intelligence and Pentagon officials, Hersh uncovered the real story behind Abu Ghraib, which began just weeks after 9/11 with the Pentagon's formation of a covert, special-action program designed to generate intelligence on al-Qaeda. Known inside the intelligence community by such code words as "Copper Green," the operation encouraged physical coercion and sexual humiliation of Iraqi prisoners.[128] Working under these explicit guidelines, the interrogators at Abu Ghraib—consisting of civilian-clad military intelligence officers as well as "interrogation specialists" from private defense contractors—used military dogs to frighten and attack detainees, forced them to perform humiliating sexual acts, beat and sodomized detainees, and poured phosphoric chemicals onto their skin.[129]

Taguba's report of Abu Ghraib shows how Army regulations and the agreements of Geneva Convention were routinely violated, and how the day-to-day management of prisoners was put into the hands of Army military intelligence and civilian contract employees.

Furthermore, the majority of detainees at Abu Ghraib, amounting to several thousand people (including women and teens), were civilians who had been picked up in military sweeps and at highway checkpoints.[130] Like the prisoners at Guantánamo, many remained in custody month after month, without the right to appeal or have their cases reviewed. In its February 2004 report to Coalition forces, the International Committee of the Red Cross (ICRC) reported that military intelligence officers told the ICRC that 70 to 90 percent of those in custody in Iraq the previous year had been arrested by mistake.[131]

Human Rights Watch describes Abu Ghraib as "Guantánamo meets Afghanistan." Outlining the Bush administration's policy to evade international law, Human Rights Watch points to Rumsfeld's description of the first detainees to arrive at Guantánamo on January 11, 2002, as "unlawful combatants," thus precluding them from protection as prisoners of war under the Geneva Convention. Also during this time, the Justice Department, made evident in a series of legal memoranda, was supporting the circumvention of international law by arguing that the Geneva Convention did not apply to detainees from the Afghanistan war.[132] In a memo to President Bush, Attorney General Alberto Gonzales endorsed the Justice Department (and Rumsfeld's) interpretation and encouraged the president to declare the Taliban and al-Qaeda as outside the coverage of the Geneva Convention, thereby adding flexibility in the U.S. war against terrorism.[133]

After the first reports of stress-and-duress tactics against detainees began to circulate in late 2002, Human Rights Watch asked President Bush to investigate and condemn the allegations of torture and inhumane treatment. In response, Department of Defense General Counsel William Haynes stated, "United States policy condemns torture," but failed to acknowledge the legal obligation to refrain from cruel, inhumane, and degrading treatment.[134] Haynes later appointed a working group, headed by Air Force General Counsel Mary Walker, which included senior civilian and uniformed lawyers from each military branch and which consulted the Justice Department, the Joint Chiefs of Staff, the DIA, and other intelligence agencies. In a classified memo, the lawyers argued that the president was not bound by the laws banning torture—that the president had the authority as commander-in-chief of the armed forces to approve almost any physical or psychological actions during interrogation, including torture, in order to obtain "intelligence vital to the protection of untold thousands of American citizens."[135]

Journalism Matters: The Effect of Propaganda

A research study by the Program on International Policy Attitudes (PIPA) illustrates the influence of false information presented by news sources on public perception. The study, which examined the results of seven nationwide polls, conducted between January and September 2003, found that (1) misperceptions held about Iraq were related to support of the war, and that (2) the variance of misperception corresponded with news sources.[136]

In-depth analysis revealed that 48 percent incorrectly believed that evidence of links between Iraq and al-Qaeda had been demonstrated; 22 percent believed that WMDs had been found in Iraq; and 25 percent believed that world public opinion supported the U.S. invasion of Iraq.[137] Such misperceptions were to be found "highly related" to support for the war. Of respondents who held none of the three misconceptions, only 23 percent supported the war; but of those respondents who believed all three misperceptions, 86 percent were in favor of war.

Furthermore, the study found that the frequency of Americans' misperceptions varied widely according to their source of news. Respondents who watched Fox News held the most misperceptions, with 80 percent of viewers holding one or more misperceptions, followed by CBS, with 70 percent of viewers holding one or more misperceptions. ABC and NBC tied with 55 percent of viewers holding one or more of the three misperceptions. Respondents who follow print sources for their news held slightly fewer misperceptions, with 47 percent having one or more misconceptions. Of the NPR/PBS news audience, 23 percent held one or more misconceptions. Variations in misperceptions are not a result of demographics; the same variations were found when comparing within demographic subgroups of each audience.[138]

The authors of the PIPA study concluded the following:

> While it would seem that misperceptions are derived from a failure to pay attention to the news, in fact, overall, those who pay greater attention to the news are no less likely to have misperceptions. Among those who pri-

marily watch Fox, those who pay more attention are more likely to have misperceptions. Only those who mostly get their news from print media have fewer misperceptions, as they pay more attention.[139]

In other evidence of the effect of disinformation, a September 2003 *Washington Post* poll found that 69 percent of Americans thought it was at least "somewhat likely" that Saddam Hussein was personally involved in 9/11.[140] According to a CBS News poll in November of 2003, 46 percent of correspondents said that the war in Iraq is a major part of the "war on terrorism," while 14 percent called it a minor part, and 35 percent saw them as two separate matters.[141] Because the events are distant and their effect upon the viewer is not an immediate one, it is only necessary to create the illusion that the facts are complex, that the experts are divided, in order to sow a latent public belief in something that is not true. This was done on the harmful effects of tobacco, the inadequacy of government response to Hurricane Katrina, and the dangers of global warming.[142]

News on the Home Front: Domestic and Environmental Issues

It has been said that when the guns boom the truth dies. War provides an optimal climate for disinformation. But the major media also contribute to a bias in what passes for news on a number of issues that deal with corporate power, distribution of resources, and the promulgation of scapegoats. Many of these are, at least in part, domestic issues. The reporting of the inadequate response to effects of Hurricane Katrina shows media involvement in the search for scapegoats.

On August 29, 2005, Katrina, the sixth-strongest hurricane ever recorded, hit the Gulf Coast of the United States, leaving its mark over 100 miles from the center of the storm and causing $75 billion in damages. New Orleans incurred the most dramatic damage: 80 percent of the city was flooded due to the inadequate levee system; nearly 2,000 people were killed directly by the storm. The slow pace of official response left many reporters to see for themselves the information that they might otherwise have gotten in filtered releases from official sources. Many Americans were reportedly shocked by the abject poverty of the city's mostly black residents. Relief from government agencies such as the Federal Emergency Management Agency (FEMA) was poorly executed and coordinated; basic supplies did not reach those who needed them for, in some cases, several days.

Some questions and criticisms of government relief efforts were initially raised by the mainstream corporate media. But what soon became evident in corporate media coverage of the aftermath of the hurricane was a shift in blame to the victims themselves. For example, *New York Times* columnist David Brooks reasoned, "Most of the ambitious and organized people abandoned the inner-city areas of New Orleans long ago."[143] In the Ft. Lauderdale *Sun-Sentinel*, Fox News pundit Bill O'Reilly had these words of advice for those "suffering" in New Orleans: "Connect the dots and wise up. Educate yourself, work hard and be honest. . . . If you don't . . . the odds are that you will be desperately standing on a symbolic rooftop someday yourself. And trust me, help will not be quick in coming."[144]

O'Reilly followed up these comments with the notion that outside assistance should not be offered: "The white American taxpayers are saying, 'How much more do we have to give here?'"[145]

Most racial stereotypes involved wild descriptions of New Orleans as a city under siege of looters, murderers, and rapists. Although later investigations showed that there was no more violence after Katrina than in any typical week in New Orleans, media focused attention on the violence that was, apparently, hampering relief efforts. Wolf Blitzer on CNN had this report:

> People with guns are opening fire, including on ambulances leaving hospitals. . . . There are many, many people who are stranded, they can't get out of their homes, they can't walk anyplace, A, because it's too flooded; B, because it's disease-ridden, many of those waters; and C, because it's getting very ugly and violent in many parts of New Orleans.[146]

In his report for the *Cincinnati Post*, Allen Breed described a similar scene with "Naked babies wail for food as men get drunk on stolen liquor" and a crowd whose "almost feral intensity" prevented delivery of water to victims by helicopter.[147] The *Washington Post* equated looting with the damage from the flood itself: "The city grew more desperate as thousands fled on foot, hundreds of residents clambered onto rooftops to escape floodwaters, and looters plundered abandoned stores for food, liquor, and guns."[148]

Later reports revealed that follow-up reporting had discredited the most extreme reports of pedophilic rape, murder at the Superdome, and gang members wreaking havoc on the city.[149] A Knight-Ridder report put to rest the unverified reports of snipers shooting at ambulances and other emergency vehicles, reporting that "more than a month later, representatives from the Air Force, Coast Guard, Department of Homeland Security and Louisiana Air National Guard say they have yet to confirm a single incident of gunfire at helicopters."[150]

The media's portrayal of victims, after several days without clean water, food, dry clothes or shoes, was frequently associated with the color of their skin. Blacks who desperately attempted to procure food, water, and clothing were portrayed as "looters," while whites were "finding" provisions.[151] Most portrayals of blacks described them as selfish at best, if not antisocial and criminal; whites, on the other hand, were represented as grateful, generous, and enterprising. Kris Axtman in the *Christian Science Monitor* described the white communities of suburban New Orleans as having "no shortage of enthusiasm and heart," in spite of the example of one such community showing their compassion by sending those trying to flee the city away by bus and even firing warning shots.[152]

One of the major myths of global capitalism is that discipline and hard work pay off in wealth and security for anyone. People buy this myth when the poor are hidden from view and when their poverty can be blamed upon low intelligence, low motivation, poor education, or flaws in character. The evidence against this theory is extensive. Yet the corporate media help to perpetuate this as a major tenet of modern society. The myth conceals a more flagrant cause of poverty, the ability of wealthy corporations to polarize the distribution of income in the global economy.

Hiding Scientific Warnings of Danger

Media play a role in the exposure of scientific findings to the public. Some scientific findings have critical importance for our lives. We can respond to them only if they are well covered. The case of global warming is an important one. Truth is not always easy to assess. Certain orders of monks have committed themselves to a lifetime of mental discipline to remove the vestiges of self-interest from their inquiries into the meaning of life. In contemporary society we rely on science to provide objective tests of certain ideas. Because these ideas have great potential to affect our lives, people need access to what scientists have found without concern for whether the findings might offend people in power. The Union of Concerned Scientists conducted a survey of 460 scientists from the National Oceanic and

Atmospheric Administration (NOAA) that gave evidence of political pressure on scientists. Among the findings, 53 percent of the scientists who responded said they knew of cases in which "commercial interests have inappropriately induced the reversal or withdrawal of scientific conclusions or decisions through political intervention." And 58 percent knew of cases in which "high-level U.S. Department of Commerce administrators and appointees have inappropriately altered NOAA Fisheries' determinations."[153] Such findings were similar to those of an earlier survey of 1,400 biologists with the U.S. Fish and Wildlife Service.

In 2002 the Environmental Protection Agency removed the part on global warming from an annual report on pollution, after the White House had heavily edited the section. This fits a pattern of censorship. In March, Rick S. Piltz resigned his position as a senior associate at the U.S. Climate Change Science Program, citing pervasive politicization of science by the Bush administration. He sent a fourteen-page memo to officials who deal with climate change at ten government agencies in which he detailed how the White House was interfering with the scientific mission of the program. Piltz included a flagrant example of a national assessment study on potential effects of climate change, produced by more than 100 expert scientists, that was deleted before it could reach either Congress or the public. He wrote:

> I believe the overarching problem is that the administration . . . does not want and has acted to impede forthright communication of the state of climate science and its implications for society. . . . [The administration] . . . decided early on to essentially send the National Assessment into a black hole.[154]

New York Times reporter Andrew C. Revkin documented the charge by Piltz. The documents Revkin found showed that a White House official edited climate science reports to discount the human impact on warming. Philip A. Cooney, then chief of the White House Council on Environmental Quality and a former official with the American Petroleum Institute, made dozens of changes. For example, in a 2002 draft of a summary of government climate-change research called "Our Changing Planet," Cooney struck out a paragraph on shrinking glaciers and snowpack. In margin notes, he claimed the paragraph was "straying from research strategy into speculative findings/musings."[155]

Between 2006 and 2011, the American Petroleum Institute, the top lobbying firm for the oil and gas industry spent at least $30 million to influence the U.S. federal government. It recently announced the funneling of oil money to politicians. API's $200 million budget accounts for a key role in the industry's climate denial movement that includes funding pseudo-scientists and coordinating a public relations strategy to create doubt over climate change.[156]

In June 2005 Michael Mann, director of the Pennsylvania State University Earth System Science Center, one of the leading researchers on global warming, and two of his research colleagues received letters from Representative Joe Barton (R-Texas), chair of the House Energy and Commerce committee. The letter demanded computer data and funding sources for Mann's work. The congressional investigation was to focus upon the famous "hockey stick" graph that shows the twentieth century to be the warmest in 1,000 years. The probe was intended to investigate "methodological flaws" in Mann's work that were alleged by two non-scientists in the *Wall Street Journal*. The action by Barton was considered by several colleagues in his own Republican Party to be an intimidation of scientists who publish scientific findings that are distasteful politically. Such intimidation threatens the relationship between science and the public. Good scientists welcome responsible criticism of the validity of their findings. But government interference in their work on behalf of corporate clients can remove the value of objective information. Barton had received nearly $200,000 in campaign contributions from oil and gas companies in his most recent run for office.[157] On *Democracy Now!* of January 8, 2007, Amy Goodman interviewed a director of the environmental group Greenpeace. They had been audited after they and two other groups filed a lawsuit on the withholding of information on global warming. The audit of Greenpeace records found nothing. The audit was paid for by Exxon-Mobil, raising suspicions of a lapse between the lines of government and business in efforts to retaliate against those who opt for a free flow of information.

In living systems, from the one-celled organism to the nation-state, we understand that as conditions change survival depends upon a capacity to adapt. Systems that continue to go in a certain direction without the ability to use corrective feedback are highly vulnerable. Democracy is, ideally, an experiment in which some large social systems obtain feedback from their citizens on how their policies are addressing the needs of these citizens, thus permitting changes in direction. Similarly, science is a way in which understanding of how things are related can be put to a test of their validity. In a complex world such knowledge can be essential in decisions about the benefits and the risks of different technologies and of different choices of behavior. Science tells us the probable outcomes of certain choices. It does not tell us what questions to study or what studies to fund. It does not tell us to use the knowledge to promote life or to destroy it. It does not tell people what to do with vexing problems about their health or about environmental issues such as global warming. Nor does science provide ultimate answers, but only the best, necessarily imperfect, information available. Policy makers can and should consider this before making their decisions.

Elected officials who wish either to protect the energy industry from regulations to control emissions or to reduce oil dependence have the right to favor the free market over regulatory controls. On issues of policy the final call is with officials who have been elected. The biases reflected in judgments of elected officials that do not coincide with the needs of their constituents often reflect the inordinate strength of ties between these government officials and wealthy donors such as oil companies. But interference with the findings removes the ability of people to make informed choices and damages the capacity of the society to correct its course.

Stressing particular findings to suit one's own interests is a common problem in the fair use of scientific knowledge, and abusing science for political ends did not start with the G. W. Bush administration. The G.W. Bush White House and some of its supporters in Congress have, however, gone beyond their legitimate policy-making roles to interfere with the free exercise of scientific inquiry. They have censored scientific information and the scientists themselves for political reasons. Citizens whose taxes fund research have every right to hear what it has yielded. Then they can use an accurate picture of what science has found to help make up their minds. Media manipulation and censorship are marks of an elite that does not trust ordinary people to hear information that might prove inconvenient or embarrassing. For them, the prevention of people from taking radical action to address the ubiquity of poverty, the dangers of global warming, and the costs of war requires a great deal of disinformation. Media that do not challenge the excesses of power are a necessary part of a violent world.

The degree of danger from any government that considers itself beyond the need to answer to other voices was seen in 2002 when *Wall Street Journal* reporter Ron Suskind met with the White House to discuss a recent story he had written that was critical of the administration. What a senior White House aide told Suskind captures the essence of a frightening propaganda machine:

> The aide said that guys like me were "in what we call the reality-based community," which he defined as people who "believe that solutions emerge from your judicious study of discernible reality." I nodded and murmured something about enlightenment principles and empiricism. He cut me off. "That's not the way the world really works anymore," he continued. "We're an empire now, and when we act, we create our own reality. And while you're studying that reality—judiciously, as you will— we'll act again, creating other new realities, which you can study too, and that's how things will sort out. We're history's actors . . . and you, all of you, will be left to just study what we do."[158]

Beliefs such as were conveyed to Suskind reflect an arrogant denial of our human capacities to learn from others or to value the truth. Psychologists would refer to such beliefs as delusional megalomania. To have people who think that way in positions with the power to determine what information others will receive is alarming. When corporate-dominated and centralized media provide a megaphone for such beliefs rather than a forum for accurate information to challenge them, we are a society in grave danger.

8—Values and Habits that Maintain
a Violent System

We must rapidly begin the shift from a thing-oriented society to a person-oriented society. When machines and computers, profit motives and property rights, are considered more important than people, the giant triplets of racism, extreme materialism, and militarism are incapable of being conquered.

—MARTIN LUTHER KING, JR.

THE THESIS POSED SO FAR in this book is that military and economic violence in the global era is a reflection of the increasing concentration of wealth and power among a few dominant players to the exclusion of others.[1] These influential players live in a world of selective information that reduces legitimacy from any who would contest their power. In this chapter we examine the widely held beliefs among ordinary people that help to preserve the power elite and its increasing threat to freedom.

When a U.S. president or a secretary of state visits a university campus or public forum, major security precautions are taken. The sites are carefully screened not only for physical safety but also from the wrath of people who have objections to government policy. Their official route is often barricaded to bar any view of protestors. When they hold a news conference, they speak to journalists who are dependent upon their words to do their job and who are known to them on a first-name basis. When they visit another country, they meet selected leaders with protestors often removed from the areas. When they mention another country by name, they are referring to its ruling policy makers and not its people. Hence, they may speak of allies for their policies even among countries where most of the people would be deeply opposed to those same policies. Whether that country is mired in poverty, destroyed by an earthquake, or torn by war, the officials are accommodated lavishly in highly protected green zones. Their hosts are typically important figures in a global network of corporate and military elites. The host governments' sources of information and their sources of money derive from their close contacts with a centralized elite group.

The network of dominating corporate interests has become a smaller group of more tightly interlocked megacorporations and grown more distant from ordinary people. They nurture their connections with governments that set the rules by which they compete, with the militaries that enforce such rules, and with the media who help to make their activities appear inevitable and even laudable. Their normal activities permit people to struggle for small gains but also perpetuate the violence of war and of poverty. We can construct, from what has been described so far, a theory of what perpetuates a world of recurring violence.

An elite group of military and corporate officials has sufficient power to act without fear of any countervailing power.[2] A global economy pushes natural and human resources and the flow of capital away from local communities and toward multinational conglomerates.[3] People displaced from prior sources of livelihood experience destitution and humiliation and sometimes fight back with either violent or nonviolent activities.[4] Powerful strategists, serving the elite, are organized to respond to these challenges with propaganda and military action.[5] Enemies are created by the government with the help of the mainstream media.[6] Suppression of these "enemies" by force or disenfranchisement leads to a cycle of violence.[7] Still missing from this theory is a description of what beliefs and institutions condone the activities that we have described. Why do the beliefs of many support the interests of a few?

Selling the Image of Being for the People

However powerful the central institutions may be, they are obliged to retain a measure of support from ordinary people that is sufficient to keep them in power. To retain such support they strive to control the media and to minimize a vast gap between the aims of their own networks and the concerns of ordinary people. With the help of public relations experts, they often project an image of opposition to powerful interests and deep concern for the unrealized hopes of ordinary people who know successful elites only by their media images. Corporations are able to polish their image with well-publicized efforts to combat poverty, expand a middle class, fight disease, and support the arts. Noble and useful as these activities may be, the efforts also serve a diversionary purpose. Take for example the sponsorship of Breast Cancer Awareness Week designed to encourage mammograms and early detection. The actions advocated do not include advocacy of controls on the cancer-causing residues in toxic industrial wastes or in chemical pesticides. The sponsors gain publicity for their public concern with women's health. One sponsor has been General Electric, which makes mammography equipment. Another has been Astra Zanteca, the pharmaceutical company that makes Tamoxafin, the widely used treatment for breast cancer. The sponsors benefit by substantial tax reductions for their charitable giving. The Bill and Melinda Gates Foundation has given generously to the global treatment of AIDS and to its prevention. Approximately 5 percent of corporate profits support the Foundation, enough to reduce income taxes of the donors to zero. The other 95 percent is judiciously invested in corporations selected for their return on investment. Some of these are companies whose activities create massive poverty in third world countries. Some are in the pharmaceutical companies that have blocked cheap access to their AIDS treatment drugs.[8] But the net effect of polishing the corporate image is to convince people that large corporations are ordinary good citizens rather than the amoral growth machines that they have become.

Psychologists Joanna Macy and Molly Young Brown point out that the power elite who benefit most from the global economy also benefit by encouraging us to rely on "experts."[9] Experts are sought from two sources. First are experts who see no detrimental relationship between products of the industrial growth society, such as smoke, climate change, radiation, pesticides, and their impacts to human health and the environment. Second are experts who study the tragic outcomes of these occurrences. Among this latter group of experts are a few, like Indian scientist Vandana Shiva, who question why such distressing affronts occur so consistently; these experts are not compensated by industry, and their reports and analyses are often not heard. Because we may be unable to explain our feelings of distress, it is easier to let our subconscious repress them, while letting ourselves believe the "experts." And they provide a collective endorsement of the idea that the problems are theirs to resolve and not ours.

Electoral Games

Nowhere is the distorted image that the government and corporate elite work for the interests of ordinary people more clearly marketed than in election campaigns. Electioneering has been taken from the hands of the politicians and turned over to "experts," advertising people and "strategists." While some such firms lean to one party, most are professionals who sell their service to whoever pays. Their personal opinions do not count. Their business is to sell the product. The main goal of an advertising expert in planning a campaign is not to explain the program of the party but to attract voters. Israeli writer and peace activist Uri Avnery describes the process:

> Election propaganda is like a gown. It should emphasize the attractive features of its owner and hide the less attractive ones. The difference is that the advertising expert can invent limbs that do not exist and cut off limbs that do, according to the demands of the market. One of the major headaches of the propagandists is that their candidates may speak up (and) expose their real views, thus spoiling the show.[10]

Hence election propaganda says little about the real aims of the leaders and their parties. Much of the content of the broadcasts can be assumed to be fraudulent and irrelevant to the monetary deals that are paying for television spots and expecting a return. A company distributing such a mendacious prospectus on the stock exchange might well be indicted.

Although the message does not reflect the true positions of the candidates, it does reflect an aspect of public opinion. These are not the opinions that people might express if given the opportunity to consider the implications of major issues affecting their lives. It is the surface public opinion, as it appears to experts who conduct daily polls and listen to test groups. The candidates have already been selected by their ability to raise money from corporate interests. The views they project are a combination of what the strategists can sell to voters and the wishes of the donors. Despite differences, the hidden promise is not to reshuffle the centers of wealth and power. The prosperous few will remain so and others will remain in need.[11]

The advocacy in 2007 for personal tax savings and of a raise in the minimum wage to $7.25/hr (over two years) were hailed as signs of caring for people, while the continuing deals with corporate funders were and continue to be carefully hidden by PR specialists. The inability of service sector workers to afford food and housing has prompted some to protest, even amid fear of losing jobs, and some municipalities have responded with modest raises in the minimum wage. We are taught to expect the most modest gains as solutions to problems that will continue without changes in the corporation-friendly lifestyles that comfort us. Al Gore's excellent warning on global warming was followed by suggestions to use energy-efficient cars and light bulbs but not to address the radical changes in life that must be part of a solution. George Monbiot, author of *Heat: How to Stop the Planet from Burning*, wrote:

> We wish our governments to pretend to act. We get the moral satisfaction of saying what we know to be right, without the discomfort of doing it. My fear is that the political parties in most rich nations have already recognized this. They know that we want tough targets, but that we also want those targets to be missed. They know that we will grumble about their failure to curb climate change, but that we will not take to the streets. They know that nobody ever rioted for austerity.[12]

The election process provides legitimacy for an underlying belief system to be described in detail. Yet elections are grossly unfair because of their dependence upon wealthy contributors. Money is as important for determining who and what are placed upon the public agenda as for the outcomes on particular issues.[13]

The wealth represents the same interests that propel corporate globalization.[14] Institutional practices that sustain gross inequality are made legal by a legislative process unduly influenced by corporate lobbyists.[15] The centrality of corporate involvement introduces an undemocratic element in the policy process. The power of corporate management is, in the political sense, irresponsible power and so answerable ultimately only to itself.[16] The mainstream media, described in chapter 7, serve to manufacture sufficient consent to allow this inequality and to justify the means needed to control those who do not fit into this system.[17]

Among such controls we find the depiction of dissenters as violent or as insignificant, and increased imprisonment of those who fail.[18] Other controlling factors are the inducement to insatiable consumption,[19] leading to an accelerated pace of life that involves longer working hours and less time for civic participation.[20]

The Public's Role in Protecting Centralized Power

We all play a part in the acceptance of the corporate image. Spokespersons for concentrated interests are helped in their efforts by a set of widely shared values and beliefs that extend far beyond the holders of great power. They are psychological and cultural beliefs and values to which most of us subscribe.

Most cultures define a set of preferred beliefs and practices, commonly accepted as given. Some are images of the "ideal culture," those likely to be found in the myths and folklore that are taught to children and are readily identified images of the way things ought to be. Often these beliefs are not entirely explicit. The internalized assumptions and beliefs underlying our actual behavior constitute the "real culture." The assumptions are typically latent and unnoticed. All cultures appear to give a special value to those who are identified as participants among the collectivity of its believers and practitioners. Some languages refer to those within one's own cultural group by the same term that is used to designate "humans." This prejudicial favoring of one's own group is of only academic importance in cultural settings that have no aspirations to proselytize or to subjugate their neighbors. For cultural settings that have more hegemonic aspirations, the latent assumptions may determine whether outsiders are to be converted, conquered, enslaved, or annihilated. The outlook toward outsiders is therefore essential to the understanding of aggressive societal policies. Similarly, most cultural collectivities attach high value to the ecological settings considered their own, some making little distinction between self, community, and ecological niche.[21] Others may still have pride in a place they identify as their own and yet consider the natural world something for those within their own group or country to exploit.[22]

What are these latent beliefs that define the dominant paradigm of Western culture? Who holds them? Who benefits from them? And who ascribes to them simply as the givens of the world they know? Much has been written about the dominant paradigm, particularly as it deals with a non-sustainable or exploitative orientation to the natural world. Starting with beliefs about the self, the Western view can be culturally identified as maintaining an individual-centered worldview and holding a belief in dominance over nature. The Western worldview promotes progress and growth, and has a distinctly linear perspective on time devaluing history, tradition, and the long-term preservation of the natural world. Boundaries are fixed and rigid, with a clear distinction between subject and object. Interests are oriented around the needs of the individual. The Western worldview holds a functional belief in materialism; the moral code is oriented toward the idea of self-fulfillment.[23] These beliefs are deeply embedded in Western culture, not as a set of popular views, but as a set of assumptive propositions. They are deemed to be true by elite sectors that benefit most from them and are considered inevitable by others, mainly because of the powerful institutions that promote them. They are, by such criteria, the dominant Western worldview.[24]

This Western worldview is a constellation of specific beliefs and values that appear reasonable and natural to those who carry them. We identify fifteen assumptions of the dominant paradigm:

1. All people have the freedom to pursue and compete for success, typically defined as the expansion of wealth.
2. Private property is to be favored by law over either unowned nature or public property.
3. Freedom to speak includes the unlimited right to use wealth to influence both opinion and policy.
4. Problems can be met with technical solutions.[25]
5. Corporations shall have the protection by law afforded to citizens.
6. Corporate investors are the creators of wealth and of jobs.
7. Efficacy is more important than ethical principle in the attainment and protection of wealth.
8. Disparities in wealth of any magnitude are natural and acceptable.
9. Poverty is explained by deficiencies in the poor.
10. Military force is justified to protect corporate interests (often defined as national interests).
11. Limited parliamentary democracy (mandating elections while allowing wealth to be used for persuasion) is the much-preferred form of government.

12. The resources of the world exist for the use or exploitation by those best able to take advantage of its gifts.

13. Those who do not accept these views or the policies that flow from them pose a danger and must be either trivialized or eliminated.

14. Psychocultural values of power, masculine domination, acquisition, and development support a worldview with hegemonic intensity and little tolerance for alternatives.[26]

15. The above beliefs and values define the path to progress. They should be, and inevitably will be, universal.[27]

The belief in the moral rightness of competitive individualism works to the advantage of those who are deemed successful. Their success is attributed to their own personal attributes and efforts; the poverty of others viewed as their own fault. The core values listed blend seamlessly into a conservative agenda with a catchy message, expressed by conservative strategist Grover Norquist: "You can spend your money better than the government can." The agenda has three basic themes. The first theme is that people rely upon individual initiative (their own or the charity of others) for health, education, financial security, and a safe environment. Hence, governments have no role in their well-being other than guarding the borders, policing within the borders, and national defense. Second, people elect the government, particularly a president, with complete authority. The third theme is that free markets are the natural way to assure that needs are met.[28]

Some Americans profess liberal goals that depart from the stark and harsh reality that would be imposed upon ordinary people by the conservative agenda. This alternative agenda leaves some attention to the government role as a steward of the commons. It recognizes that health care is not available to everyone in a free market, that commercial media do not on their own serve the public's diverse needs, and that the environment is devastated to the danger point by unrestrained corporate initiatives. This rather timid alternative voice does see a broader role for government, particularly in areas where quick profits cannot be made. However, neither the core values of the dominant pattern nor the rights of megacorporations to continue exploiting, nor the assumption of a vast military to secure these advantages, are questioned in either view.

Why Are These Core Values Supported by Ordinary People?

Such core values clearly work toward the interests of powerful elites who promote them as dogma. Why then do so many of us accept this version of reality? In actual fact, the promise of success and the good life as the reward for hard work has been a mythology for large numbers of people. Many poor and middle-class people are convinced of the gospel of wealth but find the American Dream to be more symbol than reality.[29] Some particular discourses about the real world become all-powerful within societies. Such representations are adopted and perpetuated while others are discarded. The possibilities seem infinite but only some attain dominance.

What appears real is, in fact, socially constructed. However the accepted ideologies may be promoted, their success depends, in part, on the tapping of fantasies shared with other members of a society. Sharing permits people to project their fantasies and wishes into reality. The content of the beliefs, however, suggest a latent meaning. It is to be free, in the libertarian sense of having no restrictions, while at the same time believing that the marketplace of all such self-serving efforts is ordained to provide the ultimate good.

Theology professor Harvey Cox finds that the themes on the financial pages of the *Wall Street Journal* are remarkably similar to religious themes found in the Book of Genesis. The God in the business pages is the Market. Because it is the ultimate right path, it can tolerate no other economic arrangements and whatever suffering has occurred must be explained either as the failure of other attempts that deviated from the Market or as the bitter price that must be paid to enter the kingdom. Like other gods, the Market is assigned magical qualities of omnipotence. Cox says that omnipotence is "the capacity to define what is real . . . the power to make something out of nothing and nothing out of something." The Market is moving toward omnipotence.[30] It has the power to change all created things into commodities. In actual fact a number of markets—banks, automakers, airlines, the country of Argentina—have verged on collapse and required resuscitation by massive infusions of government dollars. But adversity, in these instances as in any orthodox religion, is interpreted to strengthen the case. Some economists note that the largest centers of corporate activities in oil, agribusiness, transportation, chemicals, and electronic equipment are not the examples of free trade they purport to be but rather are buoyed up by extensive subsidies.[31]

What was considered sacred is now transformed into what can be sold. This can be tribal homelands, ancient forests, homes of poor people in gentrifying cities, or even shrines, churches, and graveyards. Anything can be purchased if the price is right. The human body, once considered the sacred temple of the spirit, can be sold for parts. Kidneys, bone marrow, sperm, eggs, livers, and hearts are now available as commodities for purchase. When everything, including human beings, carries a price tag, then nothing has inherent value. The Market is ever-present and moving into personal areas of life. Dating, family life, marital relations, and care of older parents, all once considered beyond the reach of the Market, are increasingly dominated by monetary transactions. Even our innermost spiritual parts are commoditized. Where inner peace once required a strong sense of connection to the land and to the community, it is now for sale in trips to a pristine wilderness. Ecstasy, spiritual connection, and self-realization are all advertised to be attainable through a weekend workshop or a tropical resort.[32]

One distinguishing feature of the Market from major religions that have preceded it is the belief that there is never enough.[33] Each year, $30 billion is spent to urge Americans to consume greater amounts of unhealthy addictive foods, high in salt, sugar, and fat. Children are coveted targets.[34] A corporate CEO allowing concerns of health or the environment ahead of short-term profits may be acting illicitly in the eyes of stockholders. Corporations must expand, people must be insatiable as consumers, and those at the bottom must grasp at the work available to them.[35] These values reward the wealthy and powerful elites. They also speak to the most important need for change. In chapter 6 we discussed the framework of game theory. One of the greatest errors made by our centers of power is to play all games as if they were purely competitive contests in which one's own success and the success of the other players is not possible. The most important contests, however, call for an optimum calculation of what is good for the commons, or for all parties. To beat one's competitors by permitting global warming or contaminating the environment, or by creating desperate conditions for people who may go on to become terrorists, is to be playing the wrong game.

But the dominant paradigm is widely accepted and one must ask what value these beliefs have for the rest of the people who hold them. The symbolic order may have been pressed upon people by elite opinion molders, but they were not imposed upon blank slates. Why, we must ask, have we permitted the construction of such a world? Are there psychological origins that underlie the societies that human beings have constructed?

George Lakoff and Mark Johnson developed a theory of cognition that is a reflection of deeply embedded characteristics of the person. Metaphoric meanings are not merely abstract aspects of the rich language of poets but rather a form of deep, perhaps bodily, attachment to certain beliefs and images that guide much of our thought and action. Often they reflect early familial expectations about egalitarian or authoritarian sources for determining what is right. Words like *motherland, fatherland, homeland, obedience, safety,* and *body politic*, according to this theory, cannot be detached from the organism that produces them.[36] The importance of this is that in order to effect change in the world order we may need to change not only our conditioned beliefs about the inevitability of the existing order but also the patterns by which we raise children so that the latent metaphors they bring to understanding the world will have more space for compassion, caring, connection, and justice. That is a part of major cultural change.

Actual population surveys tend to show few adherents to the dominant paradigm,[37] but its presence as a latent force seems clear. The dominant worldview stands in some contradiction to opinion polls that have consistently and increasingly found people to favor the protection of their environment,[38] the elimination of nuclear weapons,[39] and the belief that corporations and government entities have too much power to determine policy decisions that should be in the hands of local citizens.[40] The power of the core beliefs, however, does not reside in their popularity as much as in the assumption that they describe a historically inevitable path while providing advantages over life in countries that live by different assumptions.[41]

For example, the decline in real wages in the United States since the 1970s, the decline in secure union jobs with benefits, and the current reductions in funds for education, hospitals, and health care, libraries, and parks are all viewed, if viewed at all, as an inexorable and necessary consequence of the need to be competitive in a global economy. Austerity is considered the natural consequence of repayment of debt to the wealthiest parts of the financial sector. Why should unskilled workers expect a living wage when their labor can be replaced more cheaply by workers from China or India? Why should those earning more than $6 million per year have their taxes reduced while increasing numbers of people lack funds for education or for adequate nutrition? The expectations of those not wealthy for a better life are transformed into the competitive message to work harder for the leftovers and to push ahead of others who will remain more destitute than oneself. If being poor is a personal failure despite one's efforts, then someone must be blamed and corporate media must provide scapegoats that remove the corporate market from responsibility. The occasional leaks of corporate scandals or political bribes vanish from the media when elections turn on efforts to find scapegoats—homosexuals, immigrants, street criminals, or terrorists. As elections pass without producing deep changes in the concentration of power, the inevitability of the dominant power of an unrestrained market gets reinforced. Hence voters most in need of change withdraw from the political process.

Interests Served by the Dominant Paradigm

The value placed upon open competition affects the way people view their own worth. But departures from this value are permitted when benefits accrue to the largest corporations. If all the airlines were engaged in unrestricted competition, they would have no choice but to engage in price wars. This sort of competition occurred in the nineteenth-century railroads. Bankruptcy became commonplace until J. P. Morgan began to organize railroads into large cartels to prevent competition. According to economist Michael Perelman, no really competitive industry today is very profitable. Profits are highest in industries protected by intellectual property rights or by the influence necessary to garner government contracts.[42] Nowhere is this clearer than in the defense industries. Among the ten top contractors are General Electric, General Dynamics, United Technologies, Newport News, Northrop Grumman, and the Carlyle Group, all of which attain most of their business through no-bid contracts. These corporations thrive on the presence of disasters such as floods, drought, and war. While large corporations under colonialism exploited the raw materials and the wealth of poor countries, the game has shifted to privatizing and pillaging of governments. The corporate domination of governments and monetary policies assure what Naomi Klein has called the rise of disaster capitalism.[43] They have moved the economy to a new stage in which ordinary services for health care, education, water, transportation, law enforcement, even for the military, are increasingly privatized. They create incentives for war and for turmoil while economic incentives for a world at peace have been constricted. Record oil company profits are only possible because oil companies escape the costs that are passed on to taxpayers of global warming, oil exploration, environmental destruction, and wars to guarantee the oil. In Iraq, a major task of the U.S. occupation was to hire private security to protect U.S. administrators as they handed off the oil reserves and the basic services to a group of well-connected contractors.[44]

The professed dominant values negate the reality of people in different classes with different interests. It was James Madison who observed, long before Karl Marx was born, that there exists an inevitable conflict in society between those who have property and those who do not. More than 100 years ago, historian Charles Beard wrote that the U.S. Constitution represented the interests of the slaveholders, the merchants, and the bondholders, not those of working people or of slaves.[45] The idea that the CEO of Halliburton, Lockheed-Martin, or Exxon-Mobil has the same interests as the workers of their companies, or of soldiers who fight the wars that enrich them, or even of their own household servants, is a myth. It is perpetuated by the repetition of such terms as "national interest" and "national security." We are continually reminded that we are one nation that has been blessed by God.

American Greatness and Exceptionalism

Americans are taught in school that ours is a special land of equal opportunity. Our way of life is considered morally superior to all others and we, therefore, are justified in spreading our form of democracy and enterprise to all parts of the world. This moral superiority is not based on our actions as a nation. To be honest, we must face our long history of ethnic cleansing, in which millions of American Indians were driven off their land by means of massacres and forced evacuations. We were built upon a history of slavery, segregation, and racism that is still with us. We were conquerors in the Caribbean and in the Pacific and initiators of shameful wars against small countries such as Vietnam, Grenada, Panama, Afghanistan, and Iraq. We used the most destructive weapons known against civilian populations in Hiroshima and Nagasaki.[46]

Neither can a sense of moral superiority be honestly based upon how well people in the United States live.[47] Despite having the most expensive health care system, the United States ranks last overall compared to six other industrialized countries—Australia, Canada, Germany, the Netherlands, New Zealand, and the United Kingdom—on measures of health system performance in five areas: quality, efficiency, access to care, equity, and the ability to lead long, healthy, productive lives.[48] Forty-nine countries, including Cuba, have better records on infant mortality.[49] And as a clear sign of social pathology, the United States leads the world in the number of people in prison—nearly 7 million.[50]

The September 7, 2005, United Nations Human Development Report accused the rich countries of having "an overdeveloped military strategy and an underdeveloped strategy for human security." Among the report's striking findings is that when it comes to inequality, poverty, and mortality rates, the United States has little to justify a perception of success. According to UNICEF, only Romania among Euro-American countries has a child poverty rate higher than the United States.[51]

> Nearly 16 million children in the United States—22% of all children— live in families with incomes below the federal poverty line—$23,021 a year for a family of four. Research shows that, on average, families need an income of about twice that level to cover basic expenses. Using this standard, 45% of children live in low-income families.[52]

Such facts are psychologically dissonant with the emotionally appealing myths of moral superiority. With corporate domination of the global economy, the domestic agenda in the United States is overtly favorable to business. One State Department official noted that it is too hard for politicians to deliver at home in health care, job, schools, or homelessness. It is easier to appear to be doing something in a war that no one sees directly.[53]

The historic vision of the American Dream is not really of equality or even care for all its members. Rather, it is that continuing economic growth and political stability can be achieved by supporting income growth and economic security of middle-class families, without restricting the ability of successful business executives to gain wealth. This perspective is now being superseded by the view that providing maximum financial rewards to the most successful is the way to maintain high economic growth. Not raised in the public dialogue is whether pursuit of unlimited wealth is something that might be replaced by assurances of security and dignity to everyone.[54]

Historian Howard Zinn helps explain why we are so ready to accept the mythical version of U.S. greatness.[55] We accept presidential decrees about foreign threats as true since we do not retain, in our cultural memory, the deceptions that have occurred in the past. President Polk, for example, lied about the reason for going to war with Mexico in 1846. He said it was because Mexico "shed American blood upon the American soil." In actual fact, Polk, and the slaveowning aristocracy, coveted half of Mexico in order to create more slave states to resist the abolition movement. In 1898, President McKinley justified invading Cuba to liberate the Cubans from Spanish rule. In fact, McKinley, whose presidency reflected the emerging corporate monopolies, wanted Spain out of Cuba so that the island could be open to United Fruit and other American corporations. McKinley also claimed that the reason for our war in the Philippines was only to "civilize" the Filipinos, while what was actually coveted was a military and corporate foothold in the Pacific, even at the cost of killing hundreds of thousands of Filipinos. President Woodrow Wilson, characterized in history books as an idealist, deceived the public about the reasons for entering the First World War, calling it a war to "make the world safe for democracy." In reality it was a war to make the world safe for the Western imperial powers. President Truman lied when he said the atomic bomb was dropped on Hiroshima because it was "a military target."

There are many more recent examples of such mistruths. Three presidents deceived the people about Vietnam—Kennedy about the extent of early U.S. involvement, Johnson about the Gulf of Tonkin incident used to obtain congressional support, and Nixon about the secret bombing of Cambodia. President Reagan deceived the public by claiming Grenada was invaded because it posed a threat to the United States and again by denying his support for the contras' attempt to overthrow the government of Nicaragua. The elder President Bush claimed that the invasion of Panama, leading to the death of thousands of ordinary citizens, was because of drug trafficking rather than as an excuse to prevent Panama from negotiating with other nations regarding work on the Canal Zone. It would be hard to believe that the first President Bush's concern over the autonomy of Kuwait was not a subterfuge for intentions to assert U.S. military power in the oil-rich Middle East. And George W. Bush falsely claimed that the Iraq war was because Saddam Hussein had developed weapons of mass destruction, despite evidence to the contrary. However, without a memory of past presidential misrepresentations to justify war, there is little likelihood that most Americans would distrust the claims used to justify any war.[56]

In addition, Zinn observes, thought processes are constrained by an inability to think outside the boundaries of nationalism. We are penned in by the arrogant idea that this country is the center of the universe, exceptionally virtuous, admirable, and superior. In Germany in the 1930s, the Nazis proclaimed the doctrine of "Deutschland über Alles." The professed Aryan superiority was reinforced by a glorification of the military in parades and by Leni Riefenstahl's propaganda films.

Some conditions in the United States today are markedly different, but we do rejoice in the July Fourth holiday with flags, food, and fireworks. We are rallied to the defense of the homeland and give "the troops" a nearly messianic status. The actual meaning of Independence Day (autonomy and the overthrow of colonial rule) is barely noted. Nor is the brilliant concept of a government responsible to the people and people's rights guaranteed by the Constitution. Rather it is a glorification of the state and its inherent superiority.[57] This view projected in the United States is one that makes the great diversity of the world's cultures appear irrelevant to the tasks of peace and sustainable development. That diverse cultural knowledge, however, is vital to changes needed to preserve the species. Yet these diverse cultures are being gutted by military and economic expansion. Today, this arrogant posture is expressed by the adage, "We don't need to understand them; they need to understand us. After all, we are the world's sole superpower!" It is rooted historically in a belief in Manifest Destiny for white Americans as they displaced and decimated the native peoples of North America. Earlier in our history a congressman noted, "We must march from ocean to ocean. . . . It is the destiny of the white race."[58]

It is not so much that those who live in the heartland of Western society believe that the ways their society works are entirely preferable. Rather, the dominant beliefs are sufficiently in the background as to remain typically unexamined. And for many, they are not necessarily right; they just are. But the significance of these beliefs and patterned behaviors is that they perpetuate not only a way of life but also a social structure. It is a structure that provides legitimacy for the great disparities found in access to resources deemed good and necessary for an acceptable quality of life. Since Western institutions are establishing themselves in all corners of the world, beliefs and actions that sustain the power of these institutions are a critical pillar upholding serious, transnational domination of people and disparagement of their cultural strengths. The corporate culture that has taken hold poses dangers particularly because its amoral form invites both domination and tolerance for totalitarian states that condone violence.

Jerry Mander argues that corporate forms and the laws governing corporations determine the behavior of people who work in corporations. The large corporation is like a machine that spreads around the world. It turns people into consumers and converts natural resources into wealth. The ideology of corporations includes styles of acceptable behavior, ways of organizing people to work on a project, and values that legitimize, but also conceal, the extent of corporate power. These have come to be identified with the American way of life. Such corporate culture has sanctioned a corporate invasion of most of the world:

> *Corporate culture* has become the virtual definition of American life, to be defended at all costs, even militarily. Now that global trade agreements have removed most obstacles to corporate invasion of all the countries of the world, and with the power of U.S. media globally dominant, U.S. corporate culture will soon be ubiquitous.[59]

In the next and final chapter, we will explore the shift toward a society of working, but powerless, poor serving wealthy corporations in an era of fewer protections for economic opportunity and citizen engagement.

9—The Evolution of Concentrated Corporate Power to Inflict Violence and Injustice: Dangers and Hopes

Countering prior physicalist views, the new principles of causality affirm that subjective human values are today the most strategically powerful driving force governing the course of events in the civilized world—and the key to our global predicament and its solution.

—ROGER SPERRY

SO FAR THE HIDDEN STRUCTURE OF violence that we have uncovered is one of concentrated military and corporate entities and the networks that connect and protect them while excluding others. Here we move on to what these structures have done to our minds and to our sense of what it means to be human in a human community. Ultimately any shift from a world of violence will require from each of us a heartfelt and compassionate dedication to justice.

Although there have been radical changes in the operation of large corporations from the early 1900s to the present time, some themes of the early opposition to the corporate takeover have a long history that may be important in understanding how it may be controlled. The opposition was not only from well-educated socialist and communitarian scholars, but from ordinary citizens organizing for their rights.

Anti-monopolist critiques of the new industrial economy had broadly supported rural and populist beginnings. Well into the nineteenth century, corporate charters remained a privilege rather than a right. The diffusion of ownership to shareholders and the limitations on liability these corporate charters guaranteed could only be granted to the degree that they served the public interest. The large size that mass production required, however, led to intensive organizations of capital and management and to the modern megacorporations. In the 1890s, the Supreme Court granted legal personhood to corporations. With this, expected return on investment became a new category of property for a new type of citizen with eternal life and, therefore, no inheritance taxes.

Opposition came in the form of strikes in industrial areas that were brutally suppressed and in waves of agrarian revolt in the South and West. Industrial giants were widely viewed as evil economic cabals relying upon adulterated money and shady dealing. The muckraking journalists described in chapter 7 helped to call forth congressional hearings. The capital-generating potential of the corporation ultimately proved sufficient to trump the efforts of indebted homesteaders, farm cooperatives, and unorganized workers. Print and broadcast media have contributed to a gradual decline in public concern over the protests by those who have been hurt by corporate expansion. Moreover, both the First and Second World Wars contributed to a surge of support for corporations as a necessary evil in production for war. Nevertheless, the populist opposition to remote, "greedy" capitalists, who would take away their property and their communities, has remained. It remains in part because people who put in a solid day's work can no longer afford to buy a house, send their children to college, or even get sick. Under the guise of "freeing the market," conservative and corporate forces have been waging a covert war against the middle class, dismantling policies like Social Security, Medicare, the minimum wage, and fair labor laws—the safeguards that encourage economic opportunity and citizen engagement. The result is an economic system designed to enrich the super-rich and diminish the influence of everyone else.

A look at Wal-Mart helps us to understand the shift toward a society of working, yet powerless, poor serving immensely wealthy corporations under horrendous conditions.

The Humble Origins of Wal-Mart

The period from 1914 until 1973 has been characterized as one of mass production and consumption of durable goods. The Ford-inspired revolution, including the regimentation of work and of time and the creation of consumer desires ushered in an age of modernity. In that time power-sharing occurred on the part of big business, big government, and big labor. The era included social conformity through bureaucratic institutions, nuclear families, and a homogenizing nationalism, all of which were challenged by the turbulent protests of the late 1960s. The period since 1973, however, has relied increasingly on production and consumption for "niche" consumers of more disposable items. This was accompanied by a retreat from the government regulation and social safety nets that had sought to protect people in the face of cycles of boom and recession. This shift emphasized flexible labor markets and work arrangements such as low-wage workers hired only for shifts they are needed; inadequate regulation led to a dramatic acceleration of credit and circulating capital among subcontractors serving the needs of more centralized megacorporations and protecting them from the financial disasters they have created. The changed social and cultural emphasis was based upon differences between two groups: individuals who could market themselves and local families, businesses, and communities being displaced and left without decent options for work, housing, or safety. Behind this shift we find a surprising history of some progressive forces with a willingness to write off conservative, yet populist, groups of small-town farmers, small businessmen, and churchgoers. Some focus primarily on the latter's educational backwardness and ideological prejudices, and miss altogether the tremendous losses suffered by rural and small-town America at the hands of big business. Reacting to the elitism of urban government, much of the countryside has supported a political agenda that rejects government regulations, inadvertently making corporate takeovers easier.

Wal-Mart was mentioned in chapter 2 in regard to dangerous working conditions in overseas plants that produce its goods. Its history helps us to appreciate how gaps in meaningful life opportunities may be molded to support a harmful agenda. Wal-Mart is the world's largest retailer with 2.2 million employees, 1.4 million in the United States, and total annual sales of $405 billion. As of July 2012, in the United States it ran 2,746 Super Centers (187,000 sq. ft.), 152 neighborhood markets (42,000 sq. ft.), and 579 warehouse clubs. Wal-Mart

International operations include "more than 10,000 retail units under 69 banners in 27 countries."[1] Its sales on a single day reportedly topped the GDPs of thirty-six nations. If Wal-Mart were an independent country it would rank as China's sixth-largest export market, and its economy would rank thirtieth in the world (following Saudi Arabia). Its origin in the small north Arkansas town of Bentonville seems odd, and its story helps to explain the values of the American heartland. Bentonville is a town, like many in rural America, that in the 1930s fought against the intrusion of chain stores. The anti-chain store movement was something far greater than a call for protectionism by local merchants.

The Ozarks, including northern Arkansas, were ethnically homogenous, made up of 95 percent white folk as recently as 1996, and often included old stock, Anglo-Saxons with traditional Republican values of thrift, sufficiency, and hard work. Hunting, fishing, and Country Western music were the main recreational activities. In some parts, a diversified farm economy of small farmers produced livestock, fruit, and grain. With limited capital they could still make ends meet, and the area avoided the pattern of massive plantations of the South and the massive labor-exploiting commodity farms made possible in other areas by a flow of migrant workers, subsidies, and technology. The viability of this economy relied upon unneeded adults moving away and on the acceptability of low consumption levels. They lagged in farm machinery, electricity, phones, cars, and running water. The Ozarks were at the economic bottom of the United States in the 1930s.[2]

In the 1870s, railroads began to penetrate the area, permitting outside capital for clear-cutting forest reserves that had previously supplemented diets through game hunting. Unrestrained lead mining further harmed the soil, and families on marginal farms became a source of inexpensive labor as they struggled to keep up their decreasingly viable farm identity. By the late 1940s, the small farm independence had ended. Chemical fertilizers, herbicides, automatic tomato pickers, domination of single-crop hybrids, and mechanization all made farming so capital-intensive that only farms of vastly increased acreage could last. Farm subsidies to protect farmers were awarded by acreage permitting the mega-farms to displace their smaller competitors.

There was, until fairly recently with Tyson's massive poultry farms, little foreign immigration into the Ozarks. But the rural image, widely marketed, did attract younger whites, office workers from the Midwest drawn by the promoted image of outdoor living. Many of them later lost everything in unsuccessful efforts to plant fruit orchards. But the lure of the independent farm community was magnetic when the Great Depression revealed the vulnerability of depending upon bureaucratic enterprises. These hopefuls sought the image of a past in which Anglo-Saxon pioneers, rather than slaves or dark-skinned immigrant laborers, made good on the land. They knew little of the history in which Columbus and Cortès had helped lay claim for Spain to all of California and the Southwest, north to Kansas, and east to Georgia; indeed, they had little appreciation for indigenous people or those swept from eastern Europe into the melting pot. The white pioneer farmers were their image of Americans. Amid a sinking economy in the late 1970s, only the most ideologically or traditionally committed could hang on to their failing small-scale farms; they supplied many of Wal-Mart's early managers as well as hourly employees at very low wages.[3]

Through the early twentieth century, the wholesome image of nature and of farms provided an antidote to the image of crowded factories and cities. The image influenced federal funding to sustain farmers through the Homestead Act. Independent retailers in the big cities had no such glamour and gradually lost out to the larger and more efficient department stores. Small-town merchants, meanwhile, attempted to use the small farm allure to make their case against chain stores. The intrusion of catalogue stores was made successful by an extension of Parcel Post Service in 1912, shifting costs of the business to taxpayers. Still, at the time of the stock market crash, there were more than 400 local anti-chain organizations, supported by local radio and newspapers, the Farmers Alliance and even the Ku Klux Klan. The "chain store menace" drew most opposition in the Midwest and South, and many pieces of legislation came close to eliminating them. Progressive forces like *The Nation* magazine, however, came out in favor of the more efficient chain retailers' mandates to provide the modern route to consumer choice at lower costs. Two labor unions also helped to defend the chain stores. Their argument had a scientific ring. Big consolidated companies were seen as an evolutionary product of natural selection, which would favor laissez-faire capitalism.[4]

The competing fundamentalist position, which went on trial in the 1925 Scopes Trial, argued against teaching evolution and for a divine special status in humans and the preservation of their independent ways. Opposition was strongest in areas that had suffered most from the expansion of northern railroads,

eastern banks, and industrial monopolies that extracted the wealth of the countryside in a semi-colonial relationship. The Klan in Clarke County, Georgia,
called the chain owners a "Little Group of Kings in Wall Street" and warned that
Jewish and Catholic immigrants were using the chain to pauperize native-born
white Protestants.

The fundamentalist message was tied to the image of manhood in the pioneer
homesteader. Chain stores, in contrast, would be owned by distant stockholders
and managed "scientifically." The factory efficiency of Taylorism (work broken
down into repetitive segments) would standardize work creating "a nation of
clerks." Folks feared the dehumanizing northern factories that had swallowed the
immigrant populations. Working for the boss would turn boys into the "yes"-men
later characterized as "the man in the gray flannel suit." Wal-Mart came into being
in the heartland of fierce anti-monopoly capitalism. It had to overcome opposition to faceless and remote ownership and the threat to white rural masculinity.

Historically, rural Americans had personalized their hostility toward the corporate robber barons of the Northeast. The new tycoons of the Sun Belt were
able to put a human face on the boss as Everyman. Northwest Arkansas produced many examples, including Ozark chicken king John Tyson, whose son and
grandson dressed in the khaki uniforms of their employees. The multibillionaire
captains of such industries showed off their egalitarian and modest consumption
lives. The region's trucking empires were led by poorly educated men in over-
alls who did not take on trophy wives or yachts but instead turned their original
spouses into family business partners. Mrs. Helen Walton's family money, for
example, bankrolled the original discount stores, and her degree in economics
was a solid asset in the Waltons' enterprises. They stressed their entrepreneurial
family image. They kept family names and avoided "General" or "International."
Secrecy was presented as an aversion to sharing family discussions in public. By
insisting that they never forgot where they came from, they humanized the image
of some of the world's biggest corporate fortunes. Sam Walton was not actually
a rags-to-riches story since his grandfather and father had benefited from federal
handouts for homesteading after Native Americans had been driven out. The family made their money on land speculation and foreclosing mortgages on farmers
during the Depression rather than on actual farming. But a millionaire with a job
was itself impressive, and both major presidential candidates in 1992 honored
Sam Walton at his death. His paternalistic image included a wish to bring respect

to his employees using a family tradition rather than a managerial one. Managers were male and paid more than women who were clerks. A romanticized book and motion picture, *Where the Heart Is,* highlighted the personal touch of allowing a poor pregnant woman to hide in a Wal-Mart store where she kept track of all the goods she "borrowed." Sam Walton visits her and her newborn in the hospital, forgives her debt, and promises her a job. The image of honesty and low prices was carefully cultivated. Salespeople gave away nothing in fake inducements. At the headquarters, visitors and employees could help themselves to coffee with an honor system box into which they put 15 cents. Everything proclaimed the image of a sober, thrifty, church-going white patriarch; Walton's early store and pickup truck are preserved for visitors.

In its developing years Wal-Mart courted Wall Street investors like Warren Buffet with home-style barbeques and laid-back hunting and fishing excursions. The company's owners joyfully played up the contrast between hillbilly Arkansas and high-tech big business. Historian Bethany Moreton argues that founder Sam Walton was completely about planned innovation and that the folksy image is essentially part of Wal-Mart's sales plan.[5] The homey Sam Walton was an ad for Wal-Mart's local customers and useful in the financial markets as well.

Part-time hourly work permitted women to adjust to children's school needs and, in the early days, in-store baby showers and craft fairs provided an alternative to hard work in chicken processing or on their husbands' failing farms. Despite receiving less than minimum wage many women recalled work at Wal-Mart as a wonderful experience. Their attachment defies the business model assumptions of economics in which every person is an isolated, profit-maximizing, rights-demanding, and self-interested individual. The men who were paid more and moved around more as managers also derived non-material gains. They were real men, the bosses of a host of underlings as on the family farm, and they got to organize the flood of "guy" activities selling guns and fishing tackle with regular store displays of trophies. The family model helped in a critical transition to the service economy of the new capitalism. No longer did workers of successful corporations expect success in fighting to elevate their status.

The laborers of the *maquiladoras*, young women of Mexico, Honduras, or Guatemala, embroidering designs in sweatshops for the discount stores, are, like some of the current workers of Wal-Mart, expected to work off the clock, without affordable health care, subjected to age and sex discrimination and dismissed for talking about a union. Courageous opposition has emerged despite Wal-Mart's hiring of former CIA and FBI agents to spy upon and intimidate such activities.[6]

Wal-Mart strives to protect its image with monthly expenditures in the millions to public relations firms rather than to provide higher wages and affordable health care for its employees. Local businesses that once offered jobs and returned taxes to local communities have been forced out of existence by discount competitors. And Wal-Mart has gone beyond its country store image and moved into financial services and high-fashion merchandise as their high-tech management scouts the world for expansion and their political contributions oil their efforts to grow. In the 1980s, Wal-Mart boasted about its commitment to American-made products. In 2007, they were getting most of their products from suppliers in seventy different countries and paying lobbyists to oppose any requirement to label beef products for their country of origin.[7] But the structural violence inflicted by Wal-Mart and the big box retailers is only part of the story. The broader lesson is that corporate globalization not only picks our pockets for the benefit of a few but also persuades us to tolerate the use of scapegoats and thereby bury our compassion.

Divine Politics and Signs of Fascism

The rugged individual and family model values that propelled Wal-Mart reflect the larger phenomenon of a Christian fundamentalism that some see dangerously reminiscent of the Christian church and the Nazi Party in Germany of the 1930s.

One manifestation is seen in the debate over the use of the word *God* in the Pledge of Allegiance in schools. The apparently small issue is symbolic of a change in what the schools are becoming with regard to teaching citizenship. Some fundamentalists have viewed education of children as a way to shape their allegiance to the authorities of the state and the church. With the help of lobbyists in educational technology, they have pressed for disciplined schools with measurable outcomes in particular subjects as measured by standardized multiple-choice tests. Priorities are fixed upon obtaining marketable skills rather than upon problem solving, free expression, tolerance for diverse views, challenges to authority, and peaceful methods for resolving differences. A sympathetic former attorney general, John Ashcroft, suggested that criticism of the president at times of war should not be allowed. Others see such an agenda as training rather than education, training being more suitable to shaping the behavior of a laboratory rat or a follower of an authoritarian ruler. True democracy, they hold, requires a broad understanding of the humanities, of different cultural heritages and the value, in fact the imperative, of questioning authority.[8]

James Luther Adams, a professor of ethics at Harvard Divinity School who came to the United States after barely escaping the Nazi Gestapo, issued a warning letter. Adams recalled the fascist message in Germany of finding biblical support for labeling opponents—homosexuals, Jews, and non-Aryans—as satanic demons who had to be crushed. His analysis was that the great universities and the major media of the United States were, like those in Germany in the 1930s, self-absorbed and would be easily compromised by their close relationship with government and corporations. If they could be given a slice of the pie, research contracts, and access to higher circles, they would prove to be complacent and would not deal with the most fundamental moral questions that unrestrained government and corporate power would present. We would lack the spine to fight if the cost was to our prestige and comfort.[9]

A sign of this willingness to tolerate what happens to others is seen in the absence of challenge to planning for detention camps in the United States. Early in 2006, KBR, a Halliburton subsidiary, received a $385 million contract from the Department of Homeland Security to provide "temporary detention and processing capabilities." The contract was to prepare for "an emergency influx of immigrants, or to support the rapid development of new programs" in the event of other emergencies, such as "a natural disaster." The absence of details left the door open to cost overruns, such as have occurred with KBR in Iraq. A Homeland Security spokesperson has responded that this was a "contingency contract" and conceivably no centers would be built. Contracts are, however, already making the interdiction of immigrants a profitable industry.[10] So far, few U.S. citizens have expressed concern that detention centers could be used to detain American citizens, already listed as suspects via aerial surveillance records, if the president were to declare martial law.

Daniel Ellsberg, a former military analyst who in 1971 released the Pentagon Papers, the U.S. military's account of its activities in Vietnam, warns:

Almost certainly this is preparation for a roundup after the next 9/11 for Mid-Easterners, Muslims and possibly dissenters. They've already done this on a smaller scale, with the "special registration" detentions of immigrant men from Muslim countries, and with Guantanamo.[11]

The picture of scapegoating a group for coercive treatment is made easier by the Christian coalition's damnation of minorities and foreigners.[12] The wave of farmworkers and other immigrants, whose failed local economies have driven them to the United States to find work, fuels an industry of cruel detention and extradition of people.[13]

Since the enactment of NAFTA, billions of dollars have been spent militarizing the U.S. border. Missions called Operation Gatekeeper, Blockade, Safeguard, Hold-the-Line, Triple Strike, and Rio Grande have all failed to slow immigration, and the vigilantes have failed as well. The reason is that the policies are targeting immigration, which is the symptom and not the disease. The disease is a corporate, global economic system. It is the source of incredible misery, exploitation, and wealth disparity throughout the world and is forcing people to leave their home countries in search of work.[14]

A frequently raised fear of terrorists has allowed for legislation and enforcement of rules highly destructive to immigrant families. As U.S. companies unload cheap corn and wheat in Mexico and Guatemala, they destroy small farms and drive people to migrate north, many without legal permits, to find work. Their story reflects a long history of people forced to cross borders to find work in order to keep their families fed. Armed vigilante groups have appeared to assist their removal, and fences are being built to restrict their entry. In a program called Operation Return to Sender, the federal Immigration and Customs Enforcement (ICE) has arrested and detained thousands of immigrants in raids across the country.[15]

In a New Bedford factory in Massachusetts in 2007, ICE agents came with warrants for a few people, but they detained and arrested many more. Those arrested were mainly working mothers who were shipped without warning to a distant detention center in Georgia, separating them from their children. Dissatisfied white folk looking for scapegoats support the corporations that would do away with the system of family reunification, a system under which people get permanent residence visas to come to the United States to reunite their families. Legislation is being crafted to assure the flow of low-wage guest workers (but not their families) that agree to the terms of a company ready to hire them.

The media-enhanced public dialogue on immigration comes in the wake of widespread immigration from impoverished to wealthy countries. Current proposals would extend guest-worker programs to allow people to come to the United States only when they are offered a job or are being recruited by a big corporation. Such programs do away with the system of family reunification, under which people get permanent residence visas to reunite their families in the United States.

Beneath the media coverage lies the reality of the guest-worker program as a form of indentured servitude. The exploitation begins with unregulated private companies recruiting Mexicans, Central Americans, Thais, and Indonesians who borrow to pay high fees in order to be taken to a job in the United States. They arrive with great debt and with families to support. They are given temporary work, but not provided with housing, health care, or adequate sanitation. Their visas, passports, and Social Security cards are taken from them so they cannot leave when the hiring company wants them to remain. Complaints about wages or conditions result in being blacklisted so they cannot find work; moreover, threats of deportation and harm to their families back home are used against them.[16]

The seriousness of mistreatment of minority populations may be the prelude to broader oppression as seen in totalitarian regimes. Lawrence Britt's analysis of common themes in seven different fascist regimes—Nazi Germany, Fascist Italy, Franco's Spain, Salazar's Portugal, Papadopoulos's Greece, Pinochet's Chile, and Suharto's Indonesia—found fourteen common threads:

1. Powerful and continuing expressions of nationalism
2. Disdain for the importance of human rights
3. Identification of enemies/scapegoats as a unifying cause
4. The supremacy of the military/avid militarism
5. Rampant sexism
6. A controlled mass media
7. Obsession with national security
8. Religion and ruling elite tied together
9. Power of corporations protected
10. Power of labor suppressed or eliminated
11. Disdain and suppression of intellectuals and the arts

12. Obsession with crime and punishment
13. Rampant cronyism and corruption
14. Fraudulent elections[17]

Such indicators are important early warning signs for America. Anger in the public, fueled by support from wealthy corporate interests, can be a prelude to a fascist state. The Christian Coalition and the Tea Party are funded by corporate elites for their ability to deliver voters.[18] The wealthy Koch brothers have assisted the Tea Party as have foundations that the Koch brothers have funded. The power brokers of the Christian Coalition have moved closer to the centers of power.[19] They are inspired by a reconstructionist movement, which has amended the teachings that the Messiah would return, unaided, during the "Rapture" to escort the true believers to heaven. The more militant message is for a Christian society that is unforgiving and violent. Such crimes as adultery, witchcraft, blasphemy, and homosexuality should receive the death penalty. The world is to be subdued and ruled by a Christian United States. The new twist is that select preachers would lead the way to the development of a Christian country with dominion over the world. Dr. Tony Evans, minister of a Dallas church and the founder of Promise Keepers, has called on believers, often during emotional gatherings at football stadiums, to commit to Christ and exercise power as agents of Christ.[20]

Gary North, who founded the Institute for Christian Economics, wrote:

We must use the doctrine of religious liberty to gain independence for Christian schools until we train up a generation of people who know that there is no religious neutrality, no neutral law, no neutral education, and no neutral civil government. Then they will get busy in constructing a Bible-based social, political and religious order, which finally denies the religious liberty of the enemies of God.[21]

Portions of the Christian Bible, selected from the apostle Paul and the Gospel of John, divide the world into good and evil and provide an apocalyptic view with permission for violence. Secular humanists are considered the vilest targets. The message of peace, forgiveness, and embracing one's enemies is ignored. The march toward global war, even nuclear war, is not to be feared but welcomed as the harbinger of the Second Coming. The image of Christ as warrior is appealing to many within the radical Christian movement. The loss of manufacturing jobs, lack of affordable health care, negligible opportunities for education, and poor job security have left many millions of Americans locked out. This ideology is attractive because it offers them the hope of power and revenge. It sanctifies their rage. It stokes the paranoia about the outside world maintained through bizarre conspiracy theories, many contained in evangelist Pat Robertson's *The New World Order*.[22] The book is a xenophobic attack against the United Nations and many other international organizations. Blaming foreigners plays well to a working class that has felt abandoned by the larger society. The current war on immigrants is an example. A complex of military, prison groups, gun sellers. and construction contractors benefit from this misplaced anger of locals whose own serious needs have been neglected.[23] Their suffering has been crucial to the success of the Christian evangelical movement. The power of the Christian right can only be limited by reintegrating the working class into society through job creation, access to good education and health care, and, perhaps most important, an attention to their needs for community. Revolutionary movements may be led by scholars, priests, or generals but they are built on the support of an angry, disenfranchised laboring class. Neither the Christian fundamentalists nor the Islamic fundamentalists are exceptions.[24]

Powerful corporate elites have found ways to mobilize the leaders of evangelical groups. Whatever their politics or extreme beliefs, they have managed to organize working people around caring and nurturing church activities and a belief in some greater purpose than senseless competition and consumption. Among these working people are millions who have no use for ideological extremism and who devote parts of their life to making the world a better place. Laura Flanders reminds us not only of how extensive these activist efforts are but also of the fact that a political system, built upon protecting the interests of wealth, typically ignores local activists, contributing to a sense of fatalism.[25]

A Western Worldview—In Service to Whom?

Fundamentalist views exceed the dominant paradigm to which most of us give passive consent. Most Westerners would not identify with the core values of extremist ideologies as descriptions of their own values. But few would recognize the power that these assumptive beliefs have in framing the limits of what may change and what will remain the same. The paradigm to which most in the Western world tacitly acquiesce is the deeply held value system of a small elite network within its political, economic, and military sectors, a network that is the prime beneficiary of the institutions supported by these beliefs. They have found a way to partner with the dispossessed of Middle America. Writing in the *New York Times* in 1944, Vice President Henry Wallace described these power-aggrandizing corporatists:

> They claim to be super-patriots, but they would destroy every liberty guaranteed by the Constitution. They demand free enterprise, but are the spokesmen for monopoly and vested interest. Their final objective toward which all their deceit is directed is to capture political power so that, using the power of the state and the power of the market simultaneously, they may keep the common man in eternal subjection.[26]

As power develops and expands unchecked, it also desecrates the environment, generates poverty, and creates conflict and opposition. The dominant paradigm shelters institutions that have come to dominate people and environments the world over. Fortunately, courageous whistleblowers continue to expose the ways that powerful forces benefit from a violent system.

A Summary and Somewhat Hopeful Prognosis

The power structures described in this book are not invulnerable. The natural limits to growth and the resilience and creativity of humans are factors the power elite have not been able to control. Despite their efforts to shape beliefs, a massive public outcry ended official racial segregation in the United States and a costly war in Vietnam. A president who used illicit ways to retain power was obliged to resign. International protestors confronted the World Bank and the WTO wherever these bodies met, and some military intelligence agency voices joined the opposition to military expansion in the Middle East. The colonized South and Central America have thwarted complete U.S. domination by voting for leaders calling for an end to exploitation. The military outposts of the empire have grown unable to dominate even the "secure" zones of Iraq and Afghanistan. Plans for one-party domination of U.S. politics and imperial domination of the world have faced serious setbacks. The isolation of the Vulcans among the power elite, throughout the administration of the second President Bush, led to their assumptions of invulnerability and impunity. Yet they could not cover up all of the scandals and the greed that had become commonplace. The dream of an American empire appeared to fall victim to its cronyism and self-serving efforts to impose its own truth.[27] With all of the empire's power to manipulate, constrain, and often ignore the United Nations, its six major operating organs, and sixteen specialized agencies, five regional commissions, twenty research institutes, two universities, fifty worldwide information centers and transitional peacekeeping forces have continued year after year as a symbol of an interconnected world. The World Social Forum has emerged as a center for mapping new directions that speak more clearly to human needs. But the power base that Franklin Roosevelt's vice president, Henry Wallace, warned of, the networks described in this book, have not been shaken from their central hold on policy.[28]

This is sad for several reasons. The most cogent is that the institutions of governance, military force, and business, upheld by these core beliefs, lack the wisdom from other cultural settings that may be needed to address the most critical challenges of contemporary civilization. We have not found ways to live in harmony with our environs and are destroying what is needed to maintain life. We have not been able to convert our families, our neighborhoods, or our workplaces into mutually supportive communities.[29] We have not figured a role for the wisdom of elders in the fast-changing world that directs us more than we control it.

The cross-cultural psychologist and the anthropologist know many examples of cultures in which the ecology is treated as sacred and preserved. Like the natural surroundings, the tribe also becomes a source of one's belonging and identity. We know of cultures in which the wisdom gained in a lifetime is respected and not automatically deprecated by the know-how of the moment. We even know of societies that lived free of war. These are neither matters of nostalgia nor a belief in some romanticized image of the past, but rather an appeal to restructure those aspects of society that foster social injustice and exploitation.

The latent beliefs of one's own culture are often the most difficult to notice. Increasingly, the broad cultural force underlying what has been called Western Civilization has been vying for a degree of global hegemony that is unprecedented. Within the United States the clear message to diverse cultural enclaves

of successive waves of immigrants is that assimilation into the beliefs and practices, deemed as given, is essential to maintaining a satisfactory life and livelihood.
While advances in global communication create opportunities to see people in
cultural settings different from one's own, the appreciation of these differences
has focused largely upon their commercial value and the mainstream has tended
to look upon them as undeveloped both economically and psychologically, and
therefore exploitable.

The view of education to promote values of competition is highlighted in
President Obama's urging for "education that prepares our children to compete
effectively in the global marketplace." As Rabbi Michael Lerner points out, this
ethic means "learning how to advance oneself at the expense of everyone else
so that 'you can be number one and make America number one.'"[30] This message leaves many to see themselves as failures, needing a place to show mastery
over someone else. As we have shown, the values of the global marketplace are
enforced by direct, cultural, and structural violence against others who would be
our competitors. The mass shootings that have occurred in the United States—
including the shooting in Newtown, Connecticut, in which a gunman entered
Sandy Hook Elementary School and killed twenty-seven people, twenty of them
young children—may not simply be the result of a lack of gun control laws or an
underfunded mental health system. It may also be a consequence of the ethic
of violence and power over others. Surely the state of constant, justified warfare
against ubiquitous enemies adds to the mind-set invoking local violence.

The world is rapidly dividing itself into imperial powers, on the one hand,
and dissidents, the impoverished, and terrorists on the other. It behooves the
international social scientist to bring to our attention the blinders, the dangers,
and the arrogance of a cultural pattern that now contributes to the demise of
other cultures. If we are to continue the experiment of life on this planet, attention
to other cultures could provide an essential diversity of options for actions and
beliefs that have much to teach about caring for people and habitat. Conversely,
loyalty to a failing form of governance may be the most unpatriotic behavior imag-
inable. Mark Twain wrote:

> My kind of loyalty was loyalty to one's country, not to its institutions or
> its office-holders . . . institutions are extraneous, they are its mere cloth-
> ing, and clothing can wear out, become ragged, cease to be comfortable,

cease to protect the body from winter, disease, and death. To be loyal to rags, to worship rags, to die for rags—that is a loyalty of unreason . . . it belongs to monarchy, was invented by monarchy, let monarchy keep it. I was from Connecticut, whose constitution declares that "all political power is inherent in the people, and all free governments are founded on their authority and instituted for their benefit; and that they have at all times an undeniable and indefeasible right to alter their form of government in such a manner as they may think expedient." Under that gospel, the citizen who thinks he sees that the commonwealth's political clothes are worn out, and yet holds his peace and does not agitate for a new suit, is disloyal; he is a traitor.[31]

The challenge to contemporary patriots is to find the courage to guard our souls against pressures to accept a violent world and its promoters as inevitable. It is to take from the promises of a democratic heritage the task of hearing all voices, of reinventing loyalty to the entire human family and to the ecology that sustains it. The obstacles have been described. We can now move on to the question of whether wonderful projects, large and small, for peace, justice, and sustainability hold any hope for changing the colossus. There are reasons to believe this can happen and that the process has begun. The power of beneficiaries of violence is waning. Ralph Nader argues that conservative opponents of big government and liberal opponents to large corporations have begun to join forces on issues like affordable housing, minimum wage, and invasion of privacy in defiance of the dominant neoliberal consensus that leaves out their voices.[32] The world's only superpower is being challenged by the power of Asian nations and by the upsurge of progressive Latin American unity. The United Nations is accomplishing more than most people know. Blueprints for a peaceful and just world exist. Some major economies, like Germany, are breaking from reliance upon fossil fuels and nuclear power to renewable energy. They do this partly because it reduces their costs, but also because of the scope of disasters occurring with nuclear energy and with oil spills. The economic system is greening by popular demand. Amazing examples of involved communities developing their own projects, entrepreneurs, and links to other communities all around the world are occurring. More people than ever are parts of labor-owned workplaces, credit unions, and cooperatives that do not require the exploitative growth of corporations.[33] Most important, a surge in local grassroots involvement in projects large and small is creating a new type of social movement, not dependent upon adherence to some creed or following a leader but more like a groundswell of humanity toward creating a caring society and preserving a planet suitable for our long-term viability.[34] Pro-democracy groups in Burma, Iran, and Haiti have refused to be silenced. Voters in Greece have decided to reject the devastating effects of austerity and their perpetual indebtedness to the wealthy. Others are finding inspiration in their efforts. And across the United States the Occupy Movement has highlighted the disparity between the super-rich and their armies and the rest of the 99 percent. But these events are parts of a story being written by people outside of the main circles of power and with room for pages that each of us may add. That is the topic for another book.

Notes

INTRODUCTION

1. Newcomb, S. T. (2008). *Pagans in the Promised Land: Decoding the Doctrine of Christian Discovery.* Golden, CO: Fulcrum Publishing, xvii–xviii.
2. Brave Heart's website: *Takini Network Historical Trauma.* See http://www.historicaltrauma.com/.
3. M. Y. H. Brave Heart and L. M. DeBruyn (1998). "The American Indian Holocaust: Healing Historical Unresolved Grief," *American Indian and Alaska Native Mental Health Research*, 8/2, 60-82.

1. THE COSTS OF MODERN WAR

1. Peace Pledge Union (2005). *War and Peace.* Retrieved from http://www.ppu.org.uk/war/facts/.
2. Grossman, Z. (2010). *A History of U.S. Military Interventions, 1890–2010.* Retrieved from http://www.slideshare.net/mbralow/interventions-14275505.
3. Willson, S. B. (July 2012). *History US Military Overt and Covert Global Interventions.* Retrieved from http://www.brianwillson.com/history-us-military-overt-and-covert-global-interventions/.
4. Jacobson, L. (September 2011). "Ron Paul says U.S. has military personnel in 130 nations and 900 overseas bases." *Tampa Bay Times.* Retrieved from http://www.politifact.com/truth-o-meter/statements/2011/sep/14/ron-paul/ron-paul-says-us-has-military-personnel-130-nation/.
5. National Priorities Project (May 2011). "U.S. Security Spending Since 9-11." Retrieved from http://nationalpriorities.org/analysis/2011/us-security-spending-since-911/.
6. National Priorities Project (2012). *Fact Sheet: Military Spending.* Retrieved from http://nationalpriorities.org/en/analysis/2012/election-2012-voter-guide/fact-sheet-military-spending/
7. National Priorities Project (2010). *The Discretionary Budget: Military v. Non-Military.* Retrieved from http://costofwar.com/media/uploads/security_spending_primer/discretionary_budget_m_vs_nm.pdf.

8.   Stiglitz, J. E., and Bilmes, L. J. (2010). "The true cost of the Iraq war: $3 trillion and beyond." *Washington Post.* Retrieved from http://www.washingtonpost.com/wp-dyn/content/article/2010/09/03/AR2010090302200.html.

9.   Roovers, L. (July 2011). "The Literary Representation of Extreme History: Fact and Fiction, Memory and Trauma, Lies and Truths About the Bombardment of Dresden in the Writings of W.G. Sebald, Kurt Vonnegut and David Irving." (Master's thesis, University of Utrecht, Nederland). Retrieved from http://coolessay.org/docs/index-10013.html.

10. Hagen, K., and Beckerton, I. (2007). *The Unintended Consequences of War.* Chicago: University of Chicago Press.

11. Fergusen, N. (2006). *The War Of The Worlds: Twentieth-century Conflict and the Descent of the West.* New York: Penguin Books.

12. Pilisuk, M. (2007). "Disarmament and Survival." In C. Webel, and J. Galtung (Eds.), *Peace and Conflict Studies Handbook,* 94–105. London: Routledge

13. Cordesman, A. H. (2002). *Terrorism, asymmetric warfare, and weapons of mass destruction: Defending the U.S. homeland.* Westport, CT: Praeger; Grossman, Z. (2001). A century of U.S. military interventions: From Wounded Knee to Afghanistan (rev. 09/20/01). Retrieved from http://zmag.org/CrisesCurEvts/interventions.htm.

14. Handelman, H. (2008). "The Politics of Cultural Pluralism and Ethnic Conflict." In *The Challenge of Third World Development* (5th ed.). Pearson Higher Education.

15. Cordesman, A. H. (2002).

16. Klare, M. T. (2004). *Blood and Oil: The Dangers and Consequences of America's Growing Petroleum Dependency.* New York: Metropolitan Books/Henry Holt.

17. Schell, J. (2004). *The Unconquerable World: Power, Nonviolence, and the Will of the People.* New York: Henry Holt.

18. Hsu, T. (August 2012). "U.S. Responsible For 3/4 Of Global Weapons Sales, Government Says." *Los Angeles Times.* Retrieved from latimes.com/business/money/la-fi-mo-arms-weapons-sales- 20120827,0,3941461.story; Grimmett, R.F., and Kerr, P.K. (August 2012). "Conventional Arms Transfers to Developing Nations, 2004-2011." *Congressional Research Service.* Retrieved from http://www.crs.gov.

19. Shanker, T. (2005). "Weapons Sales Worldwide Rise to Highest Level Since 2000." *New York Times.* Retrieved from http://www.nytimes.com/2005/08/30/politics/30weapons.html.

20. Greider, W. (1998). *Fortress America: The American Military and the Consequences of Peace.* New York: Public Affairs; Renner, M. (1998). "Curbing the Proliferation of Small Arms." In Brown, L.R., Flavin, C., and French, H. (Eds.). *State of the World 1998,* 131–48). New York: W. W. Norton.

21. Bertell, R. (June 2004). "Health and environmental costs of militarism: Towards a world without violence, Barcelona." Retrieved from http://www.rosaliebertell.net/militarism.htm.

22. Barnaby, W. (1999) *The Plague Makers: The Secret World of Biological Warfare.* London: Vision; Wright, S. (2003). "Rethinking the Biological Warfare Problem." *GeneWatch* 16/2, February 2003.

23. Bertell (2004).

24. Pellow, D. N. (2007). "Ghosts of the Green Revolution." In *Resisting Global Toxics: Transnational Movements for Environmental Justice,* MIT Press, 159; Stellman, J. et al., "The Extent and Patterns of Usage of Agent Orange and other Herbicides in Vietnam." *Nature* 422: 681–687. Retrieved from httpwww.vn-agentorange.org/edmaterials/nature01537.pdf.

25. Reynolds, P. (2005). "White phosphorus: weapon on the edge." Retrieved from the *BBC News* website: http://news.bbc.co.uk/2/hi/americas/4442988.stm.

26. Kennedy, J. F. (September 1961). *Address to the UN General Assembly.* Miller Center, University of Virginia, Charlottesville. Retrieved from http://millercenter.org/president/speeches/detail/5741.

27. McNamara, R. S. (2005). "Apocalypse Soon." *Foreign Policy Magazine.* Retrieved from http://www.foreignpolicy.com/story/cms.php?story_id=2829.

28. Macy, J. R. (1983). *Despair and Personal Power in the Nuclear Age.* Philadelphia: New Society.

29. Meade, C., and Molander, R. (2005). *Analyzing the economic impacts of a catastrophic terrorist attack on the port of Long Beach.* RAND Corporation. W11.2 Retrieved from http://birenheide.com/sra/2005AM/program/singlesession.php3?sessid=W11; http://www.ci.olympia.wa.us/council/Corresp/NPTreportTJJohnsonMay2005.pdf.

30. Ibid.

31. McNamara (2005).

32. Scientists Committee for Radiation Information (1962). "The Effects of a Twenty-Megaton Bomb." *New University Thought* (Spring): 24–32.

33. Kennan, G. F. (1983). *Nuclear Delusion: Soviet American Relations in the Nuclear Age.* New York: Pantheon.

34. Starr, S. (2008). "High-Alert Nuclear Weapons: The Forgotten Danger." *SGR (Scientists for Global Responsibility) Newsletter,* No. 36. Retrieved from http://www.sgr.org.uk/publications/sgr-newsletter-no-36.

35. Renner, M. (1990). "Converting to a peaceful economy." In L. R. Brown (Ed.), *State of the World, 1990,* 154–72). New York: W.W. Norton.

36. Wessells, M. (1995). "Social-psychological determinants of nuclear proliferation: A dual process analysis." *Peace and Conflict: Journal of Peace Psychology* 1, 49-96.

37. Cobain, I., and MacAskill, E. (2005). "MI5 unmasks covert arms programmes." *The Guardian.* Retrieved from http://www.guardian.co.uk/nuclear/article/0,2763,1587752, 00.html; Cirincione, J. B., Wolfsthal, J. B.,, and Rajkumar, M. (2005). *Deadly arsenals: Nuclear, biological and chemical threats.* Rev. ed. Washington, DC: Carnegie Endowment for International Peace.

38. Langewiesche, W. (2007). *The Atomic Bazaar: The Rise of the Nuclear Poor.* New York: Farrar, Straus and Giroux.

39. Stone, O., and Kuznick, P. (2012) *The Untold History of the United States.* New York: Simon and Schuster.

40. Hellman, C., and Kramer, M. (2012). *The Nearly $1 Trillion National Security Budget.* TomDispatch.com. Retrieved from http://www.tomdispatch.com/post/175545/tomgram%3A_hellman_and_kramer%2C_how_much_does_washington_spend_on_%22defense%22/.

41. Schwartz, S .I. (Ed.). (1998). *Atomic Audit: The Costs And Consequences of U.S. Nuclear Weapons since 1940.* Washington DC: Brookings Institution Press.

42. Gusterson, H. (1991). *Rituals of Renewal among Nuclear Weapons Scientists.* Washington DC: American Association for the Advancement of Science.

43. Natural Resources Defense Council (June 2001). *The U.S. Nuclear War Plan: A Time for Change*; Roche, D. (2002). "Rethink the Unthinkable." *Globe and Mail,* March 12, 2002.

44. U.S. Department of Defense (April 2010). *Nuclear Posture Review Report.* Retrieved from http://www.defense.gov/npr/docs/2010.

45. Civiak, R .L. (2009). *Transforming the U.S. strategic posture and weapons complex for transition to a weapons-free world.* Nuclear Weapons Complex Consolidation Policy Network, Washington, DC. Retrieved from http://docs.nrdc.org/nuclear/.

46. Center for Defense Information (1996). "Nuclear leakage: A threat without a military solution." *Defense Monitor* 25/6: 1–7.

47. Weapons of Mass Destruction Commission (2006). *Weapons of Terror: Freeing the World of Nuclear, Biological and Chemical Arms* (p. 60). Retrieved from http://www.blixassociates. com/wp-content/uploads/2011/02/Weapons_of_Terror.pdf.

48. Cobain and MacAskill (2005).

49. Shane, S. (2005). "Vietnam War Intelligence 'Deliberately Skewed,' Secret Study Says." *New York Times*, December 2, 2005.

50. White, D. (January 2012). *Iraq war facts, results, and statistics.* Retrieved from http://usliberals.about.com/od/homelandsecurit1/a/IraqNumbers.htm.

51. Brookings Institute. (July 2012). "Tracking variables of reconstruction, and security in Iraq." Retrieved from http://www.brookings.edi/iraqiindex.

52. Roth-Douquet, K., and Schaeffer, F. (2006). *AWOL: The Unexcused Absence of America's Upper Classes from Military Service—And How It Hurts Our Country.* New York: HarperCollins; Ricks, T. E. (1997). *Making the Corps.* New York: Scribner; Bacevich, A. J. (2005). *The new American Militarism: How Americans Are Seduced by War.* New York: Oxford University Press.

53. White, D. (2012).

54. Robichaud, C. (2005, October). "Focusing on the Wrong Number." *The Century Foundation.* Retrieved from http://www.tcf.org/list.asp?type=NC&pubid=1125

55. Froomkin, D. (December 2011). "How Many U.S. Soldiers Were Wounded In Iraq? Guess Again. Beyond the Battlefield: Rebuilding Wounded Warriors." *The Huffington Post.* Retrieved from http://www.huffingtonpost.com/dan-froomkin/iraq-soldiers-wounded_b_1176276.html?view=print&comm_ref=false.

56. Robichaud (2005).

57. Swofford. A. (2012). "Anthony Swofford on the Epidemic of Military Suicides." *The Daily Beast.* Retrieved from http://www.thedailybeast.com/newsweek/2012/05/20/anthony-swofford-on- the-epidemic-of-military-suicides.html.

58. Grohols, J. (2005). "Facts About PTSD from National Center for PTSD, 26 Nov 2000." Retrieved from http://www.google.com/search?hl=en&q=National+Center+for+PTSD+&btnG; DSM-IV (1994). *Diagnostic and Statistical Manual of Mental Disorders* (4th ed.); Pilisuk, M. (1975). "The Legacy of the Vietnam Veteran." In D. Mantell, and M. Pilisuk (Eds.), "Soldiers in and after Vietnam." *Journal of Social Issues* 31/4 (1975): 312.

59. Cromie, W. J. (August 2006). "Mental Casualties of Vietnam War Persist: Lessons Learned Could Be Applied to Iraq." *Harvard University Gazette.* Retrieved from http://www.news. harvard.edu/gazette/2006/08.24/99-ptsd.html.

60. *National Center for Post-Traumatic Stress Disorder* (1991a). The Project National Center for Post-#C8191 Retrieved from http://www.ncptsd.va.gov/facts/veterans/fs_native_vets.html

61. House Report (1984). *Diversion of funds from Vietnam veterans readjustment counseling program: 67th report by the Committee on Government Operations.* Washington: G.P.O., House Report, 98-1167, Nov.1. Retrieved from http://catalogue.nla.gov.au/Record/3876029.

62. Teach Peace Foundation (2011, December). *Evidence supporting Vietnam suicides exceeds combat deaths.* Retrieved from http://www.teachpeace.com/vietnamsuicide.htm

63. National Center for Post-Traumatic Stress Disorder (1991b). *The Legacy of Psychological Trauma of the Vietnam War for Native Hawaiian and American of Japanese Ancestry Military Personnel: A National Center for PTSD Fact Sheet.*

64. Ibid.

65. National Center for Post-Traumatic Stress Disorder (1991a).

66. National Center for Post-Traumatic Stress Disorder (1991b).

67. Marchione, M. (2012, May). "Iraq, Afghanistan Veterans Filing for Disability Benefits at Historic Rate." *The Huffington Post.* Retrieved from. http://www.huffingtonpost.com/2012/05/27/iraq-afghanistan-veterans- disability-benefits_n_1549436.html.

68. Persian Gulf Veterans Coordinating Board (1995). "Unexplained illnesses among Desert Storm veterans: A search for causes, treatment, and cooperation." *Archives of Internal Medicine* 155, 262–68; Fukuda, K., Nisenbaum, R., Stewart, G., Thompson, W. W., Robin, L., and Washko, R. M. (1998). "Chronic multisymptom illness affecting Air Force veterans of the Gulf War." *JAMA* 280, 981–88.

69. Committee on Gulf War and Health (2008). *Gulf War and Health: Updated Literature Review of Depleted Uranium.* Washington DC: National Academies Press. Retrieved from http://www.nap.edu/openbook.php?record_id=12183&page=R1.

70. Price, J. L. (December 2004). *Effects of the Persian Gulf War on U.S. Veterans A National Center for PTSD Fact Sheet updated.* NCPTSD. Retrieved from http://www.ncptsd.va.gov/facts/veterans/fs_gulf_war_illness.html.

71. Hoge, C. W., Castro, C. A., Messer, S. C., McGurk, D. Cotting, D. I., and Koffman, R. L. (2004). "Combat duty in Iraq and Afghanistan, mental health problems, and barriers to care." *New England Journal of Medicine* 351,13–22.

72. Litz, B. T. (2005). *A Brief Primer on the Mental Health Impact of the Wars in Afghanistan and Iraq: A National Center for PTSD Fact Sheet,* updated April 7, 2005. Retrieved from http://www.ncptsd.va.gov/facts/veterans/fs_iraq_afghanistan_lay_audience.html.

73. Associated Press (2005). "More Troops Developing Latent Mental Disorders." Retrieved from http://www.msnbc.msn.com/id/8743574/

74. Coleman, P. (2006). *Flashback: Posttraumatic stress disorder, suicide, and the lessons of war.* UK: Beacon Press.

75. Ibid.

76. Hynes, H. P. (2012, January). "Military Sexual Abuse: A Greater Menace than Combat." *Truth-Out.org.* Retrieved from http://truth-out.org/index.php?option=com_k2&view=item&id=6299:military-sexual- abuse-a-greater-menace-than-combat.

77. Altawil, M. S. (2008). "The Effect of Chronic Traumatic Experience on Palestinian Children in the Gaza Strip." Theses collection, University of Hertfordshire, U.K. Retrieved from https://uhra.herts.ac.uk/dspace/handle/2299/2543.

78. McIntyre, T. M., and Ventura, M. (2003). "Children of War: Psychological sequelae of war trauma in Angolan adolescents." In Krippner, S., and McIntyre, T. M. (Eds.), *The Psychological Impact of War Trauma on Civilians,* 19–24. Westport, CT: Praeger.

79. Friedman, M., and Jarenson, J. (1994). "The applicability of the post-traumatic stress disorder concept to refugees." In Marsella, A. J., Bornemann, T., Ekblad, S., and Orley, J. (Eds.), *Amidst Peril and Pain,* 327–39. Washington, DC: American Psychological Association.

80. War Child International (May 2010). *War Child Annual Report 2009*. Retrieved from http://www.warchild.org.uk/about/publications/war-child-annual-report- 2009; Coalition to Stop the Use of Child Soldiers (2008). *Child Soldiers Global Report*. Retrieved *from* http://www.child-soldiers.org/publications_archive.php.

81. Wessells (1995).

82. Ibid.

83. Ibid.

84. Peace Pledge Union (2005).

85. Kimmel, P., and Stout, C. E. (Eds.)(2006). *Collateral damage: the psychological consequences of America's war on terror*. Westport, CT: Praeger.

86. Carpenter, C. (November 2009). *Tallying Collateral Damage*. Retrieved from http://duck-ofminerva.blogspot.com/2009/11/tallying, quoting Downes, A. B. (2008). *Targeting Civilians in War*. Ithaca, NY: Cornell University Press.

87. Human Rights Watch (2003b). "U.K. Military Practices Linked to Iraqi Civilian Casualties," Press Release, December 12, 2003. Retrieved from http:www.hrw.org/press/2003/12/uk-iraq-press.htm; Human Rights Watch (2003c). "Background on the Crisis in Iraq." Retrieved from http://www.hrw.org/reports/2003/usa1203/4.htm#_ftnref79, http://www.hrw.org/campaigns/iraq/ retrieved 3/10 /06.

88. Sadowski, D. (2013). *Drone warfare faces a barrage of moral questions*. Catholic San Francisco.org. Retrieved from http://www.catholic-sf.org/ns.php?newsid=1&id=61092.

89. Human Rights Watch (2003a). "Off Target: The Conduct of the War and Civilian Casualties in Iraq." Off target usa1203.pdf.

90. Barash, D. P., and Webel, C. P. (2002*). Peace and conflict studies*. London: Sage Publications.

91. United Nations High Commission on Refugees (UNHCR) (June 2012). *A Year of Crisis: UNHCR Global Trends 2011*. Geneva, Switzerland. Retrieved from http://www.unhcr.org/statistics.

92. United Nations High Commission on Refugees. *Trends in Unaccompanied and Separated Minors in Industrialized Countries (2001–2003)*. Retrieved from http //www.UNHCR.CH/Statistics.

93. International Campaign to Ban Landmines (2005a). Retrieved from http://www.icbl.org/treaty.

94. Land Mine Monitor Report *(*2003). *Toward a Mine-Free World*. Retrieved from http://www.icbl.org/lm/2003/.

95. Land Mine Monitor (October 2010). *Landmine and Cluster Munition Monitor: International Campaign to Ban Landmines*. Retrieved from http://www.the-monitor.org.

96. International Campaign to Ban Landmines (2005a), *International Campaign to Ban Landmines* (2005b). Retrieved from http://www.icbl.org/problem/what.

97. Ibid.

98. Land Mine Monitor (August 2003). *Toward a Mine-Free World*. Retrieved from http://www.icbl.org/lm/2003/.

99. International Campaign to Ban Landmines (2005b).

100. Kleff, R. (1993). "Terrorism: The Trinity Perspective." In H. H. Han (Ed.), *Terrorism and political violence: Limits, and Possibilities of Legal Control*. New York: Oceana Publications.

101. O'Neill, B. E. (1993). "The Strategic Context of Insurgent Terrorism." In Han (1993), *Terrorism and political violence*; Kleff (1993:15); O'Neill (1993:77).

102. Nunberg, G. (2001). "Terrorism: The history of a very frightening word." *San Francisco Chronicle*, October 28, 2001.

103. Chang, J., and Halliday, J. (2005), *Mao: The Unknown Story*. NewYork: Knopf. An interesting critique of Chang and Halliday is Carr, Joseph, "Did Mao Really Kill Millions in the Great Leap Forward?" http://monthlyreview.org/commentary/did-mao-really-kill-millions-in-the-great-leap-forward/.

104. Koufa, K. (2001). "Terrorism and Human Rights." *United Nations Economic and Social Council, Commission on Human Rights, Sub-Commission on the Promotion and Protection of Human Rights*. June 27, 45, 46.

105. Amnesty International (1993). *Getting Away with Murder: Political Killings and "Disappearances" in the 1990s*. New York: Amnesty International Publications.

106. Ball, P., Kobrack, P., and Spirer, H. F. (1999). *State Violence in Guatemala, 1960–1996: A Quantitative Reflection*. Washington, DC: American Association for the Advancement of Science.

107. Melville, T., and Melville, M. (1971). *Guatemala: The Politics of Land Ownership*. New York: Free Press.

108. Jonas, S. (1991). *The Battle for Guatemala: Rebels, Death Squads and U.S. Power*. Boulder, CO: Westview Press.

109. Black, G. (1984). *Garrison Guatemala*. New York: Monthly Review Press.

110. Aguilera Peralta, G., and Imery, J. R. (1981). *Dialectica del tierra in Guatemala*. San Jose, CA: EDUCA.

111. Blanck, E., and Castillo, R.M. (1998). "El palacio de las intrigas." *Cronica*; Centro Internacional para Investigaciones en Derechos Humanos (CIIDH) and Grupo de Apoyo Mutuo (GAM) (1999). *En Pie de Lucha: Organizacion y Represion en la Universidad de San Carlos, Guatemala 1944-1996*. Guatemala: CIIDH y GAM. From Ball, P., Kobrack, P., and Spirer, H.F., (1999). *State Violence in Guatemala, 1960–1996: A Quantitative Reflection*. Washington, DC: American Association for the Advancement of Science.

112. Americas Watch (1982). *Human Rights in Guatemala: No Neutrals Allowed*. New York: Americas Watch.

113. Amnesty International (1989). *Guatemala: Human Rights Violations under Civilian Governments*. London: Amnesty International.

114. Amnesty International (1982). *Guatemala: Massive Extrajudicial Executions in Rural Areas under the Government of General Efrain Rios Montt*. London: Amnesty International; Nairn, A. (1983), "Guatemala Bleeds," *The New Republic*, April 11; Falla, R. (1983), *Masacre de la Finca San Francisco, Huehuetenango, Guatemala*. Copenhagen: International Work Group for Indigenous Affairs.

115. Ball, Kobrack, and Spirer (1999).

116. Schirmer, J. (1998). *The Guatemalen Military Project: A Violence Called Democracy*, p. 33. Philadelphia: University of Pennsylvania Press.

117. Giraldo, J. (1996). *Colombia: The Genocidal Democracy*. Monroe, ME: Common Courage Press.

118. Amnesty International (1993).

119. Giraldo, J. (1996).

120. Wilson, S. (2001), "Paramilitary troops massacre villagers in Colombia," *Washington Post*, October 12, 2001.

121. Hawk, D. (1989). "The Photographic Record." In K.D. Jackson (Ed.), *Cambodia, 1975–1978: Rendezvous with Death.* Princeton: Princeton University Press; Quinn, K. M. (1989), "Explaining the Terror." In K. D. Jackson (Ed.) (1989), *Cambodia 1975-1978: Rendezvous with Death.* Princeton: Princeton University Press.

122. O'Kane, R. H. T. (1996). "Terror as government and its causes, Cambodia, April 1975–January 1979." *Terror, Force, and States: The Path From Modernity.* Cheltenham, UK: Edward Elgar.

123. Markusen, A., and Yukden, J. (1992). *Dismantling the War Economy.* New York: Basic Books.

124. Sivard, L. (1996). *World Military and Social Expenditures.* Washington, DC: World Priorities.

125. Gable, M. (1997). *What the World Wants and How to Pay for It.* What the World Wants Project, World Game Institute.

126. Fischetti, M. (October 2001). "Drowning New Orleans." *Scientific American.*

127. McQuaid, J. (2005). "The Drowning of New Orleans: Hurricane Devastation Was Predicted." *Democracy Now!.* Retrieved from. http://www.democracynow.org/search. pl?query=mcQuaid.

128. Boly, W. (1990). "Downwind." *In Health,* July/August, 58–69.

129. Glendinning, C. (1990). *When Technology Wounds: The Human Consequences of Progress.* New York: William Morrow; Gould, J. M., Sternglass, E. J., Mangano, J. J., and McDonald, W. M. (1996). *The Enemy Within: The High Cost of Living Near Nuclear Reactors: Breast Cancer, AIDS, Low Birthweights, and Other Radiation-induced Immune Deficiency Effects.* New York: Four Walls Eight Windows Press; Vyner, H. (1988*). Invisible trauma: The psychosocial effects of invisible environmental contaminants.* Lexington, MA: Heath and Co.

130. Boly, W. (1990**).**

131. Associated Press (2005). "Construction workers sent home early from Herald plant site." *Tri-City Herald.* September 23, 2005.

132. DeFrank, N. M., Gholke, J. M., Gribble E. A., Faustman E. M (2005). "Value of Information Approaches to Evaluate Models of Low Dose Radiation Effects on Neurons in the Developing Brain." Retrieved from http://birenheide.com/sra/2005AM/program/singlesession. php3?sessid=M4; Gofman, John W. (1996). *Preventing Breast Cancer: The Story of a Major, Proven, Preventable Cause of This Disease.* O'Connor, E. (Ed.). San Francisco: C.N.R. Book Division, Committee for Nuclear Responsibility, Inc.

133. Physicians for Social Responsibility (2004). *Cancer and the Environment.* Retrieved from Cancer_ and_the envir#11D668.pdf.

134. Fred Hutchinson Cancer Research Center (September 2009). "Radiation Research." Davis, S., et al. *An International Symposium Based on Radiation Research Partnership.* Retrieved from http://www.forumacil.com/cocuk-cizimleri-yazilar/94944-savasin-cocuklari.html.

135. Oregon Department of Energy (2009). Hanford Cleanup: The first 20 years." Retrieved from http://www.oregon.gov/energy/NUCSAF/docs/HanfordFirst20years.pdf.

136. Miller, R. D. (2006). *The Energy Employees Occupational Illness Compensation Program: Are we fulfilling the promise we made to these veterans of the Cold War when we created the program?* Testimony by Richard D. Miller, Government Accountability Project Committee on Judiciary US House of Representatives. Retrieved from http://commdocs.house.gov/ committees/judiciary/hju27335.000/hju27335_0.HTM.

137. Fergusen (2006).
138. Du Boff, R. (2001). *The US: Rogue Nation.* Center for Research on Globalization. Retrieved from http://www.globalresearch.ca/articles/DUB112B.html.
139. Barnaby, W. (1999). *The Plague Makers: The Secret World of Biological Warfare.* London: Vision.
140. DuBoff, R. (2001).
141. Ibid.
142. Ibid.
143. International Committee of the Red Cross (May 2006). "Unregulated arms availability, small arms, and light weapons, and the UN process." Small Arms Survey. Geneva, Switzerland. Retrieved from http://www.icrc.org/eng/resources/documents/misc/small-arms-paper-250506.htm.
144. Shanker (2005).
145. McSherry, J. P. (2005). *Predatory states: Operation Condor and Covert War in Latin America.* Lanham, MD: Rowman and Littlefield.

2. KILLING: WAR AND THE MINDS OF MEN

1. Tuchman, B. W. (1984). *The March of Folly: From Troy to Vietnam.* New York: Random House.
2. Hagen, K., and Beckerton, I. (2007). *The Unintended Consequences of War.* Chicago: University of Chicago Press.
3. Sorenson, R. E. (1978). "Cooperation and Freedom Among the Fore of New Guinea. In Montage, A. (Ed.), *Learning Non-Aggression.* New York: Oxford University Press.
4. Fabbro, D. (1990). "Equality in Peaceful Societies." In Cancian, F. M., and Gibson, J. W. (Eds.), *Making War/Making Peace: The Social Foundations of Violent Conflict*, pp. 127–42. Belmont, CA: Wadsworth Publishing.
5. Lorenz, K. (1966). *On Aggression* (p. 234). New York: Bantam; Lewontin, R. (1991). *Biology as Ideology: The Doctrine of DNA.* New York: HarperCollins; Goodall, J. (1986). *The Chimpanzees of Gombe: Patterns of Behavior.* Cambridge: Harvard University Press.
6. Langer S. (1942). *Philosophy in a New Key: A Study of The Symbolism of Reason Rite And Art.* Cambridge: Harvard University Press.
7. Kelly, G. A. (1963). *A Theory Of Personality: The Psychology of Personal Constructs.* New York: W. W. Norton.
8. Keen, S. (2004). *Faces of the Enemy: Reflections of the Hostile Imagination.* San Francisco: Harper & Row.
9. Kelman, H. (1973). "Violence without Moral Restraint." *Journal of Social Issues* 29/4: 25–61.
10. Ross, M. H. (1990). "Childrearing and War in Different Cultures." In Cancian, F. M., and Gibson, J. W. (Eds.), *Making War/Making Peace: The Social Foundations of Violent Conflict* (pp. 55–63). Belmont, CA: Wadsworth Publishing.
11. Bohart, A. C., Elliott, R., Greenberg, L., and Watson, J. C. (2002). "Empathy." In Norcross, J. R. et al. (Eds.), *Psychotherapy Relationships that Work.* New York: Oxford University Press.
12. Arendt, H. (2004). *The Origins Of Totalitarianism.* New York: Schocken Press.
13. Zimbardo, P. G. (2004). "A Situationist Perspective on the Psychology of Evil." In Miller, A. (Ed.), *The Social Psychology of Good and Evil: Understanding Our Capacity for Kindness and Cruelty.* New York: Guilford.

14. Lee, M., Zimbardo, P. G., and Berthof, M. (November 1977). "Shy Murderers." *Psychology Today* 11: 69ff.

15. Milgram, S. (1974). *Obedience to Authority.* New York: Harper & Row.

16. Bandura, A., Underwood, B., and Fromson, M. E. (1975). "Disinhibition of Aggression through Diffusion of Responsibility and Dehumanization of Victims." *Journal of Personality and Social Psychology* 9:253–69.

17. Zimbardo (2004).

18. Watson, J. R. I. (1973). "Investigation into De-individuation Using a Cross-Cultural Survey Technique." *Journal of Personality and Social Psychology* 25:342–45.

19. Wallis, J. (2006). "Christmas in the Trenches. *Sojourners*." Retrieved from http://www.belief-net.com/blogs/godspolitics/2006/12/jim-wallis-christmas-in-trenches.html.

20. Zimbardo (2004).

21. Bandura, A. (1988). "Mechanisms of Moral Disengagement." In Reich, W. (Ed), *Origins of Terrorism: Psychologies, Ideologies, Theologies, States of Mind* (pp. 161–91). New York: Cambridge University Press.

22. Coles, R. (1983). "The Needs for Scapegoats Causes War." In Bender, D.L., and Leone, B. (Eds.), *War and Human Nature* (p. 60). St. Paul, MN: Greenhaven Press.

23. Lifton, R. J. (1967). *Death in Life: Survivors of Hiroshima.* New York: Simon & Schuster.

24. Netzer, O. (2005). "The Real Causes of War Discovered." *Interactivist Info Exchange.* Retrieved from http://info.interactivist.net/article.pl?sid=05/08/13/2232239.

25. Eisenhart, R. W. (1975). "You Can't Hack It, Little Girl: A Discussion of the Covert Psychological Agenda of Modern Combat Training." *Journal of Social Issues* 31/4: 13–23.

26. Gilmore, I., and Smith, T. (2006). "If You Start Looking at Them as Humans, Then How Are You Gonna Kill Them?" *Guardian.* Retrieved from http://www.guardian.co.uk/Iraq/Story/0,,1741942,00.html.

27. Brooks, R. (2006). "Why Good People Kill: Iraq Murders Reveal the Warping Power of Conformity and Dehumanization." *Los Angeles Times,* June 9.

28. Merari, A. (1990). "The Readiness to Kill and Die: Suicidal Terrorism in the Middle East." In Reich, *Origins of Terrorism.*

29. Lorenz (1966).

30. Bumiller, E. (December 2011). "Air Force Drone Operators Report High Levels of Stress." *New York Times* Retrieved from. http://www.nytimes.com/2011/12/19/world/asia/air-force-drone-operators-show-high-levels-of-stress.html.

31. Netzer (2005).

32. Pyszczynski, T., Solomon, S., and Greenberg, J. (2003). *In the Wake of 9/11: The Psychology of Terror.* Washington, DC: American Psychological Association.

33. Becker, E. (1975). *Escape from Evil.* New York: Free Press. Fromm, E. (1955). *The Sane Society.* New York: Henry Holt.

34. Bourke, J. (1996). *Dismembering the Male: Men's Bodies, Britain and the Great War* (p. 336). Chicago: University of Chicago Press.

35. Macy, J. R., and Brown, M. Y. (1998). *Coming Back to Life: Practices to Reconnect Our Lives, Our World.* Gabriola Island, BC: New Society Publishers.

36. Bstan-'dzin-rgya-mtsho, Dalai Lama (1999). *Ethics for a New Millennium* (pp. 204–5). New York: Riverhead Trade.

37. LeShan, L. (2002). *The Psychology of War: Comprehending Its Mystique and Its Madness.* New York: Helios Press.

38. 43. LeShan (2002).

39. Koenigsberg, R. A. (2005). "The Soldier as Sacrificial Victim: Awakening from the Nightmare of History." http://www.libraryofsocialscience.com/essays/koenigsberg-the-soldier-as-sac.html.

40. Andreas, J. (2004). *Addicted to War: Why the U.S. Can't Kick Militarism.* Oakland, CA: AK Press.

41. Kagen, D., Schmidt, C., and Donelly, T. (2000). "Rebuilding America's Defenses: Strategy, Forces and Resources for a New Century." *Project for a New American Century.* Retrieved from http://www.newamericancentury.org/defensenationalsecurity.htm.

42. Peterson, E. A. III, (2005). Of Militarism, Fascism, War and National Consciousness. (NFPNZ essay). Retrieved from http://nuclearfree.lynx.co.nz/of.htm.

43. Ekirch A. A. Jr., (1999). *Militarism and Antimilitarism: The Oxford Companion To American Military History.* (pp. 2, 438). Oxford: Oxford University Press.

44. Koenigsberg (2005).

45. Fromm, E. (1964). *Escape from Freedom.* New York: Holt, Rinehart, and Winston.

46. United Press International. "Military Recruits Come from Poor Areas." November 3, 2005. Retrieved from http://www.military.com/NewsContent/0,13319,79770,00.html.

47. http://www.care2.com/causes/25-percent-of-army-soldiers-had-mental-health-problems-prior-to-enlistment.html.

48. Holthouse, D. (2006). *Extremism and the Military: A Timeline.* Southern Poverty Law Center. Retrieved from http://www.splcenter.org/intel/news/item.jsp?aid=66.

49. Hedges, C. (2003). *War Is a Force that Gives Us Meaning.* Woodston, Peterborough, UK: Anchor.

50. Broyles, W. Jr. (1990). "Why Men Love War: Socialization and Masculinity." In Cancian and Gibson, *Making War/Making Peace.*

51. Ensign, T. (2005). *The America's Military Today.* New York: New Press.

52. Jamail, D. (2005). Dahr Jamail's Iraq dispatchés. Retrieved from http://dahrjam.net

53. Fitzsimmons, A. (2004). "Mourning People on Santa Monica Beach: Arlington West." *Veterans for Peace.* Retrieved from http://www.veteransforpeace.org/.

54. Jamail (2005).

65. Cortwright, D. (1975). *Soldiers in Revolt: GI Resistance during the Vietnam War.* Chicago: Haymarket Books.

56. James, W. (1995/1910). "The Moral Equivalent of War." *Peace and Conflict: Journal of Peace Psychology* 1:17–26.

57. Ehrenreich, B. (1997). *Blood Rites: Origins and History of the Passions of War.* New York: Henry Holt.

58. Ibid., p. 238.

59. Bstan-'dzin-rgya-mtsho, Dalai Lama (1999).

60. Elshtain, J. B. (1987). *Women and War.* New York: Basic Books; Nikolic-Ristanovic, V. (1999). *Women, Violence, and War: Victimization of Refugees in the Balkans.* Budapest: Central European University Press; Brownmiller, S. (1975), *Against Our Will: Men, Women and Rape.* New York: Ballantine Books.

61. Morgan, R. (2001). *The Demon Lover: The Roots of Terrorism*. New York: Washington Square Press.

62. McKay, S. (1998). "The Effects of Armed Conflict on Girls and Women." *Peace and Conflict: Journal of Peace Psychology* 2:93–107; Morgan, R. (2006) "Rape, Murder, and the American GI." Women's Media Center.

63. Machel, G. (2001). *The Impact of War on Children*. Cape Town: David Philip.

64. Wessells, M. G. (1998). "Children, Armed Conflict and Peace." *Journal of Peace Research* 35:635–46.

65. Bstan-'dzin-rgya-mtsho, Dalai Lama (1999) (pp. 204–5).

66. Cohn, C. (1987). "Sex and Death in the Rational World of the Defense Intellectuals." *Journal of Women in Culture and Society* 12:687–718.

67. Frank, J. (1982). *Sanity and Survival in the Nuclear Age: Psychological Aspects of War and Peace*. New York: Random House.

68. Cohn (1987).

69. Ibid.

70. Gusterson, H. (1991). "Rituals of Renewal among Nuclear Weapons Scientists." Washington, DC: American Association for the Advancement of Science; Gusterson, H. (1998). *Nuclear Rites: A Weapons Laboratory at the End of the Cold War*. Berkeley: University of California Press; Cohn (1987); Pilisuk, M. (1999). "Addictive Rewards in Nuclear Weapons Development." *Peace Review: A Transnational Journal* 11/4: 597–602; Caldicott, H. (2002). *The New Nuclear Danger: George W. Bush's Military-Industrial Complex*. New York: New Press.

71. Niebuhr, R. (1952). *The Irony of American History* (p.84). New York: Scribners.

72. Stouffer, S. A. (1949). *Studies in Social Psychology in World War II: The American Soldier*. Princeton: Princeton University Press; Merton, K., and Lazersfeld, P. (1950). *The American Soldier*, vol. 2, Glencoe IL: Free Press.

73. Reiber, R. W., and Kelly, R. J. (1991). "Substance and Shadow: Images of the Enemy." In Reiber, R. W. (Ed.), *The Psychology of War and Peace: The Image of the Enemy* (pp. 3–39). New York: Plenum.

74. Bronfenbrenner, U. (1961). "The Mirror Image in Soviet-American Relations: A Social Psychologist's Report." *Journal of Social Issues* 17/3: 45–56.

75. Friedman, M. (1984). "The Nuclear Threat and the Hidden Human Image." *Journal of Humanistic Psychology* 24/3: 65–76.

76. Rogers, C. (1984). "Notes on Rollo May." In Greening, T. (Ed.), *American Politics and Humanistic Psychology* (pp. 11–12) San Francisco: Saybrook Publishing.

77. May, R. (1984). "The Problem of Evil: An Open Letter to Carl Rogers." In Greening, *American Politics and Humanistic Psychology*.

78. Freud, S. (1949). "Why War?" *Collected Papers*, vol 4. London: Hogarth Press.

3. THE HIDDEN STRUCTURE OF VIOLENCE

1. Wallis, J. (1992). "Violence, Poverty and Separation." *Public Welfare* 50/ 4 (Fall): 14–15.

2. Nooteboom, G (2015). *Forgotten People: Poverty Risk and Social Security in Indonesia*, Boston: Brill Press.

3. Galtung, J. (1996). *Peace by Peaceful Means: Peace and Conflict, Development and Civilization*. London: Sage Press; Christie, D. (1996). "Peacebuilding: The Human Needs Approach Locally and Globally." Presidential Address, 104th Annual Convention of the

American Psychological Association; Christie, D. (1997). "Reducing Direct and Structural Violence: The Human Needs Theory." *Peace and Conflict: Journal of Peace Psychology* 3: 315–32; Pilisuk, M. (2001). "Globalism and Structural Violence." In Christie, D., Wagner, R., and Winter, D. (Eds.) *Peace, Conflict, and Violence: Peace Psychology for the 21st Century 2001.* Englewood, NJ: Prentice Hall.

4.   Galtung (1996).
5.   Langer, S. (1942). *Philosophy in a new key: A study in the symbolism of reason, rite and art.* Cambridge: Harvard University Press.
6.   Marrow, A. J. (1977). *The Practical Theorist: The Life and Work of Kurt Lewin.* New York: Teachers College Press.
7.   Arendt, H. (2004). *The Origins of Totalitarianism.* New York: Schocken Books.
8.   Staub, E. (2001). "Genocide and Mass Killing: Their Roots and Prevention." In Christie, *Peace, Conflict, and Violence.*
9.   Syme, S. L., and Berkman, L. (1976). "Social Class, Susceptibility and Illness." *American Journal of Epidemiology* 104/1: 1–8; Browne, A., and Bassuk, S. S. (1997). "Intimate Violence in the Lives of Homeless and Poor Housed Women." *American Journal of Orthopsychiatry* 67/2: 261–75; Syme, S. L. (1989) "Control and Health: An Epidemiological Perspective." In Steptoe, A., and Appels, A. (Eds.), *Stress Personal Control and Health.* New York: Wiley and Sons; Pickett, K., and Wilkinson, R. (2011). *The Spirit Level: Why Greater Equality Makes Societies Stronger.* New York: Bloomsbury Press.
10. Berkman, L., and Syme, S. L. (1979). "Social Networks, Host Resistance and Mortality: A Nine-Year Follow-Up Study of Alameda County Residents." *American Journal of Epidemiology* 109/2: 186–204; House, J. S., Landis, K. R., and Umberson, D. (1988). "Social Relationships and Health." *Science* 241: 540–45; Pilisuk, M., and Parks, S. H. (1986). *The Healing Web: Social Networks and Human Survival.* Hanover, NH: University Press of New England.
11. Syme (1989).
12. Goff, F., and Locker, M. (1971). "The Violence of Domination: U.S. Power and the Dominican Republic." In Perrucci, R., and Pilisuk, M. (Eds.), *The Triple Revolution Emerging: Social Problems in Depth.* Boston: Little, Brown; Pilisuk, M. (1972). *International Conflict and Social Policy.* Englewod, NJ: Prentice Hall.
13. Bissel, T. (1997). "Campaign for Labor Rights," Nike Packet, parts 1–7, personal correspondence, April 24.
14. Ching Yoon Louie, M. (2001). *Sweatshop Warriors: Immigrant Women Workers Take On the Global Factory.* Boston: South End Press. Herbert, B. (1996). In "America: Trampled Dreams." *New York Times Archives* July 12, 1996; Herbert, B. (1997a), "Brutality in Vietnam." *New York Times Archives,* March 28, 1997,; Herbert, B. (1997b). "Nike's Boot Camps" *New York Times Archives,* March 31, 1997. (Based on Thuyen Nguyen's report upon return from an inspection tour of Nike's factories in Vietnam.)
15. Elich, G. (2006). *Strange Liberators: Militarism, Mayhem, and the Pursuit of Profit.* Valparaiso, IN: Lumina Press.
16. Rhodes, M. (1997). "Labor Protests Continue at Nike Factories." *The Campaign for Labor Rights Newsletter.* May 2, 1997. Retrieved from http://www.hartford-hwp.com/archives/54/index-ad.html; Shniad, D. (1997), "More Charges Against Nike." *International Confederation of Free Trade Unions. ICFTU,* http://www.hartford-hwp.com/archives/54/index-ad.html.

17. Rennie, S. (November 2012). "Negotiating Freedom." *Engage Media*. Retrieved from http://www.engagemedia.org/Members/labourrights/videos/negotiating-freedom.

18. Hacker, A. (1997). *Money: Who Has How Much and Why?* New York: Scribner; Rhodes, M. (1997b). Disney and McDonald's linked to $.06/hour sweatshop in Vietnam, personal correspondence, May 1, 16:48; Rhodes (1997c).

19. *Tapei Times* (May 2005). "Angry workers return to Happy Meal toy factory." Retrieved from http://www.taipeitimes.com/News/worldbiz/archives/2005/05/14/2003254672.

20. Bdnews24.com (December 2012). "Wal-Mart Vetoed Bid to Help RMG Units." Retrieved from http://bdnews24.com/details.php?id=237649andcid=4.

21. *New York Times* (September 2012). "Foxconn Technology." Retrieved from http://topics.nytimes.com/top/news/business/companies/foxconn_technology/index.html.

22. Ibid.

23. Barboza, D., and Duhigg, C. (September 2012). "China Contractor Again Faces Labor Issue On iPhones." Retrieved from http://www.nytimes.com/2012/09/11/technology/foxconn-said-to-use-forced-student-labor-to-make-iphones.html.

24. Moore, M. (1994). *TV Nation*, NBC, August 2.

25. Meadows, D. (1992). "Corporate-Run Schools Are a Threat to Our Way of Life." *Valley News,* October 3, 22.

26. Philpott, T. (2012). "80 Percent of Public Schools Have Contracts with Coke or Pepsi." *Mother Jones*. Retrieved from http://www.motherjones.com/tom-philpott/2012/08/schools-limit-campus-junk-food-have-lower-obesity-rates.

27. Bayer, C. (2010). "Schools' soda strategy trades wealth for health." *Rockford Register Star.* Retrieved from http://www.rrstar.com/news/x2096602077/Rockford-schools-soda-strategy-trades-wealth-for-health.

28. Taber, D. R., Chriqui, J. F., Perna, F. M., Powell, L. M., and Chaloupka, F. J. (2012). "Weight status among adolescents in states that govern competitive food nutrition content." *Pediatrics,* 130, 437–44.

29. Barry, K. (1995). *Prostitution of Sexuality*. New York: New York University Press; Rosenfeld, S. (1997). "Women Suffer Brutal Captivity." *San Francisco Examiner*, April 6.

30. Close the Base Campaign (2013). Retrieved from http://closethebase.org/us-military-bases/asia-pacific/; Ignacio, A., de la Cruz, E., Emmanuel, J., and Toribio, H. (2004), *The Forbidden Book: The Philippine-American War in Political Cartoons*. San Francisco: T'Boli Publishing.

31. Barry, K. (1995); Rosenfeld, S. (1997).

32. *World Bank* (2005). "Philippines Country Brief." Retrieved from http://www.worldbank.org.ph.

33. Augustine, E. (2007). "The Philippines, the World Bank and the Race to the Bottom." In Hiatt, S. (Ed.), *A Game as Old as Empire: The Secret World of Economic Hit Men and the Web of Global Corruption* (pp. 175–93). San Francisco: Berrett-Koehler; Erlbaum, M. (2005). "The Forbidden Book—A Book Review." *Socialism and Democracy Journal* 37/19 (Spring). Retrieved from http://www.sdonline.org/index2.htm.; International Solidarity Mission (ISM) (2005). *Report Back and Discussion on the Continuing Human Rights Violations in the Philippines*, UTLA Headquarters, Los Angeles, CA, Friday, October 21.

34. Anderson-Hinn, M. (2011). "Modern-Day Slavery." In M. Pilisuk and M. N. Nagler (Eds.), *Peace Movements Worldwide: History, Psychology, and Practices,* vol. 2, 248. Santa Barbara, CA: Praeger.

35. UNODC (2009). *Global Report on Trafficking in Persons. United Nations Office on Drugs and Crime.* Retrieved from http://www.unodc.org/unodc/en/human-trafficking/global-report-on-trafficking-in-persons.html.

36. Ibid.

37. Batstone, D. B. (2007). *Not for Sale: The Return of the Global Slave Trade—And How We Can Fight It.* New York: HarperOne.

38. Simmons, J., Farmer, P., and Schoepf, B. (1995). "A Global Perspective." In Farmer, P., Connors, M., and Simmons, J. (Eds.) *Women, Poverty and AIDS: Sex, Drugs and Structural Violence.* Monroe, ME: Common Courage Press.

39. Ibid., pp. 42–43.

40. Ibid., p. 23.

41. Connors, M., Daily, J., Farmer, P., Rhatigan, J., Katz, J., and Furin, J. (1995). "Women and HIV Infection—A Different Disease?." In Farmer, *Women, Poverty and AIDS.*

42. Ibid.

43. Gardner, W., and Preator, K. (1996). "Children of Seropositive Mothers in the U.S. AIDS Epidemic." *Journal of Social Issues* 52/3: 177–95.

44. Ellwood, D. (1996). "Welfare Reform in Name Only." *New York Times,* July 22.

45. Basu, S., and Stuckler, D. (2013). *The Body Economic: Why Austerity Kills: Recessions, Budget Battles, and the Politics Of Life And Death.* New York: Basic Books.

46. Mexican Action Network on Free Trade (Réseau Mexicain d'Action Sur le Libre-Échange), (n.d.). NAFTA and the Mexican Economy. Development GAP, fact sheet. Retrieved from http://www.developmentgap.org. This fact sheet is excerpted from Espejismo y realidad: el TLCAN tres años después, Análisis y propuesta desde la sociedad civil, by the Mexican Action Network on Free Trade (RMALC). The full report is available for US$10 from RMALC, tel/fax (525) 355-1177, email rmalc@laneta.apc.org. Translated by the Development GAP.

47. Farmer, P. (2005). *Pathologies of Power: Health, Human Rights, and the New War on the Poor.* Berkeley: University of California Press.

48. Witness for Peace (2010). "Fact Sheet: Unjust Trade and Forced Migration." Retrieved from http://www.witnessforpeace.org/downloads/Fact%20Sheet_Unjust%20Trade%20and%20Forced%20Migration_2010.pdf.

49. Maquila Solidarity Network (2005). "Asia-Latina Women's Exchange: Mapping the Impacts of the Quota Phase-Out on Workers' Lives." Retrieved from http://www.maquilasolidarity.org/resources/post_mfa/AWID%20exchange/index.htm.

50. Argetsinger, A. (2005). "Immigration Opponents to Patrol U.S. Border." *Washington Post,* March 31.

51. CNN (April 1997,). "Criminal Warrants Sought in Texas Standoff." Retrieved from http://www.cnn.com/US/9704/28/texas.militia.

52. Ivins, M. (1997). "So Much for Putting People First." *Houston Chronicle Interactive,* April 14.

53. Gomes, L. (2003). *The Economics and Ideology of Free Trade: An Historical Review.* Cheltenham, UK: Edward Elgar.

54. National Security Council (2006). *The National Security Strategy.* Retrieved from http://www.whitehouse.gov/nsc/nss/2006/.

55. Galtung (1996).

56. Korten, D. C. (2001). *When Corporations Rule the World.* West Hartford, CT: Kumerian Press and San Francisco: Berrett-Koehler Publishers.

57. Chatterjee, P. (1992). "World Bank Failures Soar to 37.5% of Completed Projects in 1991." *Third World Economics,* December 16–31, 2; Straus, S. (1997). "Eritrea a Do-It-Yourself Nation." *San Francisco Chronicle,* June 11.

58. Ibid.

59. Easterly, W. (2002). *The Elusive Quest for Growth: Economists' Adventures and Misadventures.* Cambridge: MIT Press.

60. Bello, W. (1994). *Dark Victory: The United States, Structural Adjustment, and Global Poverty.* London: Pluto.

61. Korten (2001); Pilisuk, M. (1998). "The Hidden Structure of Contemporary Violence." *Peace and Conflict: Journal of Peace Psychology* 4/3: 197–216.

62. Hartmann, T., and Miller, M. C. (2006). *Screwed: The Undeclared War Against the Middle Class—And What We Can Do about It.* San Francisco: Barret Koehler; Reich, R. (1997). *Locked in the Cabinet.* New York: Alfred A. Knopf.

63. "What Is Modern Slavery?" U.S. Department of State: http://www.state.gov/j/tip/what/index.htm, retrieved 4/8/2015.

64. BBC News (2006). "Forbes Reports Billionaire Boom." Retrieved from http://news.bbc.co.uk/2/hi/business/4791848.stm.

65. Korten (2001); Reich (1997).

66. Smith, Y. (2015), "How More and More U.S. Corporate Profits Escape the Corporate Income Tax." *Naked Capitalism.* January 29. Retrieved from http://www.nakedcapitalism.com/2015/01/u-s-corporate-profits-escape-corporate-income-tax.htm; Bivens, J. and Mishel, L. (2013). "The Pay of Corporate Executives and Financial Professionals as Evidence of Rents in Top 1 Percent Incomes." Economic Policy Institute, June 20, 2013, http://www.epi.org/publication/pay-corporate-executives-financial-professionals/.

67. Korten (2001); Reich (1997).

68. Leiss, W., and Chociolko, C. (1994). *Risk and Responsibility.* Buffalo, NY: McGill-Queens University Press; Leach, W. (1993). *Land of Desire: Merchants' Power and the Rise of the New American Culture* (p. xiii). New York: Pantheon.

69. CNN Money (2013). *Annual Ranking of American Corporations: Fortune 500.* Retrieved from http://money.cnn.com/magazines/fortune/fortune500/; Boesler M. (2013). "Wal-Mart Earnings Beat, Guidance Soft." *Business Insider,* February 21. Retrieved from http://www.businessinsider.com/wal-mart-q4-2012-earnings-2013-2.

70. Bucher, S. (2007). "Walmart: The $288 Billion Welfare Queen." *Tallahassee Democrat,* April 19. Retrieved from http://www.teamster.org/content/tallahassee-democrat-wal-mart-288-billion-welfare-queen.

71. Leonard, A. (2006, January). "How the World Works: Our Right to Know about Wal-Mart." *Salon.com.* Retrieved from http://www.salon.com/2006/01/23/georgia_13/.

72. Whalen, J. D. (1997)"Billion Dollar Technology: A Short Historical Overview of the Origins of Communication Satellite Technology, 1945–1965." In Andrew J. Butrica, A. (Ed.), *Beyond the Ionosphere: Fifty Years of Satellite Communication* Washington, DC: US Government, NASA Historical Series.

73. Parenti (1995); Renner, M. (1991). "Assessing the Military's War on the Environment." In Brown, L. R., et al. (Eds.), *State of the World* (p. 139). New York: W. W. Norton.

74. Renner (1991), p. 119.
75. Santos, R. A. M. (2003). *Crime of Empire: A Case against Globalization and Third World Poverty as a World System*. Los Angeles: Sidelakes Press.
76. Farmer (2005), p. 18.
77. Picketty, T. (2014). *Capital in the Twenty-first Century*. Cambridge MA: Harvard University Press.
78. Wilkenson, R. G., and Pickett, K. (2010). *The Spirit Level: Why More Equal Societies Almost Always Do Better*. New York: Bloomsbury Press.
79. Fisher, R. (1993). "Grassroots Organizing Worldwide." In Fisher, R, and Kling, J. (Eds.), *Mobilizing the Community: Local Politics in a Global Era*. Thousand Oaks, CA: Sage Publishers; Fisher, R. (1994). *Let the People Decide: Neighborhood Organizing in America* (rev. ed.). Boston: Twayne; Singer, P. (2002), *One World: The Ethics of Globalization*. New Haven: Yale University Press.

4. PEOPLE, FARMLAND, WATER, AND NARCOTICS

1. Institute for Food and Development Policy (2001). *The Global Banquet: Politics of Food*, film, Maryknoll Productions.
2. Goering, P., Norberg-Hodge, H., and Page, J. (1998). "Industrial Agriculture in Context." *IFG News*, 3: 4–5.
3. Corporate Accountability International (formerly Infact) (December 23, 2001). "Challenging Corporate Abuse, Building Grassroots Power Since 1997." Retrieved from http://www.infact.org.
4. See http://www.un.org/en/globalissues/briefingpapers/food/vitalstats.shtml.
5. See http://www.worldhunger.org/articles/Learn/world%20hunger%20facts%202002.htm.
6. Pimentel, D., and Pimentel, M. (1999). "Population Growth, Environmental Resources and the Global Availability of Food." *Social Research* 66: 417–28.
7. See http://feedingamerica.org/hunger-in-america/impact-of-hunger.aspx.
8. Lang, T., and Heasman, M. (2004). *Food Wars: The Global Battle for Mouths, Minds and Markets*. New York: Earthscan Publications.
9. Friedman, T. L. (1999). "A Manifesto for the Fast World." In Sjursen, K. (Ed.), *Globalization* (p. 5). New York: H. W. Wilson.
10. Murphy (2001) (p. 1).
11. Barber, B. R. (2000). "Challenge to the Common Good in the Age of Globalism." *Social Education* 64: 8–13.
12. Hayward, M. (1999). "Globalized Mergers and Acquisitions: The Dangers of a Monoculture." In *Competitiveness Review* 9: i–iv; Barnet, R. J., and Cavanaugh, J. (1994a), *Global Dreams: Imperial Corporations and the New World Order*. New York: Simon and Schuster.
13. Chang, S. J., and Ha, D. (2001). "Corporate Governance in the Twenty-First Century: New Managerial Concepts for Supranational Corporations." *American Business Review* 19: 32–44.
14. Bello, W. (1998). "The End of a 'Miracle': Speculation, Foreign Capital Dependence and the Collapse of the Southeast Asian Economics." *Multinational Monitor* 19: 10–16.
15. Korten, D. (1998). *Globalizing Civil Society: Reclaiming Our Right to Power*. New York: Seven Stories Press.
16. Murphy (2001) (p. 40).

17.   *National Family Farm Coalition (NFFC)* (2012). "Food, inc. and fresh: Facts and solutions needed to fix the food system!" Retrieved from http://www.nffc.net/index.html

18.   Murphy (2001).

19.   Nickerson, C., Morehart, M., Kuethe, T., Beckman, J., Ifft, J., and Williams, R. (February 2012). *Trends in U.S. Farmland Values and Ownership.* EIB-92. U.S. Dept. of Agriculture, Econ. Res. Serv.

20.   MacCannell, E. D., and White, J. (1984). "Social Costs of Large-Scale Agriculture: The Prospects of Land Reform in California." In Giesler, C. C., and Popper, F. J. (Eds.), *Land Reform American-Style* (pp. 35–54). Totowa, NJ: Rowman and Allenheld.

21.   Hayward (1999).

22.   Pimentel and Pimentel (1999).

23.   O'Connor, M. R. (Jan. 11, 2013). "Subsidizing Starvation: How American Tax Dollars Are Keeping Arkansas Rice Growers Fat while Starving Millions of Haitians." *Foreign Policy.* Retrieved from http://www.foreignpolicy.com/articles/2013/01/11/subsidizing_starvation.

24.   Lynch, D. J., and Bjerga, A. (Sept. 9, 2013). "Taxpayers turn U.S. farmers into fat cats with subsidies." Retrieved from http://www.bloomberg.com/news/2013-09-09/farmers-boost-revenue-sowing-subsidies-for-crop-insurance.html.

25.   Ibid.

26.   Oxfam International (n.d.). "Dumping on the World: How EU Sugar Policies Hurt Poor Countries." Policy Briefing Paper 61. Retrieved from http://www.oxfam.org/sites/www.oxfam.org/files/bp61_sugar_dumping_0.pdf.

27.   Beitel, K. (2005). "U.S. Farm Subsidies and the Farm Economy: Myths, Realities, Alternatives." *Backgrounder* 11 (3). Food First Institute for Food and Development Policy.

28.   Ibid.

29.   Stewart, J. B. (July 19, 2013). "Richer Farmers, Bigger Subsidies." *New York Times.* Retrieved from http://www.nytimes.com/2013/07/20/business/richer-farmers-bigger-subsidies.html.

30.   Biotechnology Industry Organization (2005). "Biotechnology Industry Facts." Retrieved from http://www.bio.org/speeches/pubs/er/statistics.asp.

31.   *Plunkett Research* (2012). "The State of the Biotechnology Industry Today." Retrieved from http://www.plunkettresearch.com/biotech-drugs-genetics-market-research/industry-and-business-data

32.   Kesan, J. P. (2000). "Intellectual Property Protection and Agricultural Biotechnology." *American Behavior Scientist* 44: 464–503.

33.   Murphy (2001).

34.   Kesan (2000).

35.   Brush, S. B. (1999). "Bioprospecting the Public Domain." *Cultural Anthropology* 14: 535–55.

36.   Kloppenburg, J. (1994). "Scientific Poaching and Global Biodiversity." *Elmwood Quarterly* 10/2–3): 7–11.

37.   Teitel, M. (1994a). "Ownership of the Seed of Life." *Elmwood Quarterly* 10/2–3: 2–6; Teitel, M. (1994b), "Selling Cells." *Elmwood Quarterly* 10/2–3: 12–14.

38.   Brush (1999).

39.   Padron, M. S., and Uranga, M. G. (2001). « Protection of Biotechnological Inventions: A Burden Too Heavy for the Patent System." *Journal of Economic Issues* 35: 315–22.

40.   Corporate Watch (2005).

41. Stumo, M. (2000). "Down on the Farm." *Multinational Monitor* 21: 17–22.
42. Hayward (1999) (p. 1).
43. Murphy (2001).
44. Teitel (1994b).
45. Stumo (2000).
46. Johnson, D. (2000). "Solving Water Scarcity." *Journal of Family and Consumer Sciences* 92: 17.
47. Barlow, M. (1999). "The Global Water Crisis and the Commodification of the World's Water Supply." Retrieved from http://www.ifg.org/bgsummary.html; Johnson (2000).
48. Shiva, V. (2000). "Monsanto's Expanding Monopolies." Retrieved from http://www.pure-food.org/Monsanto/waterfish.cfm.
49. Grusky, S. (2001). "Privatization Tidal Wave: IMF/World Bank Water Policies and the Price Paid by the Poor." *Multinational Monitor* 22: 14–19.
50. Goldman Environmental Prize (2001). Retrieved from http://www.goldmanprize.org/recipi-ents/recipients.html; Shultz, J. (2000a). "Bolivians Take to the Streets over the Price of Water." Retrieved from http://www.inthesetimes.com/issue/24/10/shultz2410.html; Shultz, J. (2000b). "Water Fallout: Bolivians Battle Globalization." Retrieved from http://www.inthe-setimes.com/issue/24/12/shultz2412.html; Shultz, J. (2005). "Launching the Final Battle in Bolivia's Water War." Retrieved from http://www.democracyctr.org/blog/2005_11_01_de-mocracyctr_archive.html.
51. Shultz, J. (2007). "Bolivia Pulls Out of World Bank Trade Court." Retrieved from http://www.democracyctr.org/blog/2007/05/bolivia-pulls-out-of-world-bank-trade.html.
52. Chaterjee, P. (2000). "The Earth Wrecker." Retrieved from http://www.sfbg.com/News/34/35/bech1.html.
53. Democracy Center (2006). "Bechtel vs. Bolivia." Retrieved from http://www.democracyctr.org/bechtel/bechtel-vs-bolivia.htm; Schultz, J. (2006). "Bechtel to Drop World Bank Trade Case over Water Revolt." Democracy Center, January 17. Retrieved from http://www.democ-racyctr.org/blog2006/01/bechtel-to-drop-world-bank-trade-case.html.
54. Richards, J. F. (1981). "The Indian Empire and Peasant Production of Opium in the Nine-teenth Century." *Modern Asian Studies* 15/1: 59–62.
55. American Civil Liberties Union (2013). "The Prison Crisis." Retrieved from https://www.aclu.org/safe-communities-fair-sentences/prison-crisis.
56. Adams, M. (April 2007). "The Secret History of Big Pharma's Role in Creating and Mar-keting Heroin, LSD, Meth, Ecstasy and Speed." *News Target*. Retrieved from http://www.newstarget.com/021768.html.
57. Parenti, M. (1995). *Democracy for the Few* (6th ed.). New York: St. Martin's Press.
58. *The Daily Herald* (March 2012). "Colombia Seeks Corporate Assistance to Battle Poverty." Retrieved from http://www.thedailyherald.com/international/4-international/26007-colom-bia-seeks-corporate-assistance-to-battle-poverty-.html.
59. Fratepietro, S. (2001). "Plan Colombia: The Hidden Front in the U.S. Drug War." *Human-ist,* 61: 18–21.
60. Ibid.
61. Cray, C. (2000). "The U-wa-Oxy Standoff." *Multinational Monitor* 21: 7–8.
62. Adams, P. (2005). "The Beginning of the End to a Coherent U.S. Drug Strategy." Council on Hemispheric Affairs. Retrieved from http://www.coha.org/NEW_PRESS_RELEAS-ES/_2005/05.82

63. Human Rights Watch (2014). *World Report, 2014.* Retrieved from http://www.hrw.org/world-report/2014/country-chapters/colombia.
64. Dudley (2000).
65. Goodman, A. (2007). "Chiquita's Slipping Appeal." *Truthdig.* Retrieved from http://www.truthdig.com/report/item/20070320_chiquitas_slipping_appeal/.
66. Human Rights Watch (2013). *World Report, 2013.* Retrieved from http://www.hrw.org/sites/default/files/wr2013_web.pdf.
67. Ibid.
68. Ibid.
69. Amnesty International (2014). "U.S. Policy in Colombia." Retrieved from http://www.amnestyusa.org/our-work/countries/americas/colombia/us-policy-in-colombia.
70. MSNBC (November 20, 2001). "Afghanistan: A History of Turbulence." Retrieved from http://www.msnbc.com/news/6555554146.asp.
71. World Bank (2001). *World Development Indicators.* CD-ROM. International Bank for Reconstruction and Development, available from University of California at Berkeley Library Network.
72. Makhmalbaf, M. (2001). "Limbs of No Body." *Iranian,* Opinion section, Retrieved from http://www.iranian.com/Opinion/2001/June/Afghan/index.html.
73. MacDonald, S. B. (1992). "Afghanistan's Drug Trade." *Society* 29: 61–66.
74. Makhmalbaf (2001).
75. Shen, F. (2001). "Hard Lives: People of Afghanistan Face War and Poverty." *Washington Post*, October 3.
76. Ford, N., and Davis, A. (2001). "Chaos in Afghanistan: Famine, Aid and Bombs." *The Lancet* 358: 1543–44.
77. Goodhand, J. (2005). "Frontiers and Wars: The Opium Economy in Afghanistan." *Journal of Agrarian Change* 5/2: 191–216.
78. Mendenhall, P. (2001). "Afghanistan's Cash Crop." MSNBC. Retrieved from http://www.msnbc.com/news/564809.asp.
79. Golden, T. (November 25, 2001). "A War on Terror Meets a War on Drugs." *New York Times*; Goodhand, J. (2000). "From Holy War to Opium War? A Case Study of the Opium Economy in Northeastern Afghanistan." *Central Asian Study* 19: 265–80.
80. Scheer, R. (2001). "Bush's Faustian Deal with the Taliban." *Los Angeles Times,* May 23.
81. Weiner, T. (2001). "With Taliban Gone, Opium Farmers Return to Their Cash Crop." *New York Times,* November 26.
82. LaVine, S., and Pearl, D. (2001). "As the Taliban Recede, Opium Blooms Again—Until Afghanistan Gets a New Government, Growers Are Planting." *Wall Street Journal.*
83. Weiner (2001).
84. LaVine and Pearl (2001).
85. Norland, R., and Ahmed, A. (Nov. 13, 2013). "Afghan Opium Cultivation and Production Seen Rising." *New York Times.*
86. Rubin, B. R., and Zakhilwal, O. (2005). "A War on Drugs, or a War on Farmers?" *Wall Street Journal* (Eastern Edition).
87. North (2005).
88. Amnesty International (2014). *Left in the Dark: Failures of Accountability for Civilian Casualties Caused by U.S. Military Operations in Afghanistan.*

89. Marlay, R., and Ulmer, B. (2001). "Report on Human Rights in Burma: Background and Current Status."*Journal of Third World Studies* 18: 113–28.

90. Coday, D. (2001). "Burma." *National Catholic Reporter* 37: 12.

91. McCarthy, S. (2000). "Ten Years of Chaos in Burma: Foreign Investment and Economic Liberalization Under the SLORC-SPCD, 1988 to 1998." *Pacific Affairs,* 73: 233–62.

92. Matthews, B. (2001). "Myanmar: Beyond the Reach of International Relief?." *Southeast Asian Affairs,* 229–48.

93. UNODC (2014). *World Drug Report, 2014.* Vienna: United Nations Office on Drugs and Crime.

94. *The Economist* (April 12, 2014). "Myanmar and Drugs: Getting Higher." Retrieved from http://www.economist.com/news/asia/21600748-opium-growing-rise-again-drug-consumption-getting-higher.

95. Meehan, P. (2011). "Drugs, Insurgency, and State-Building in Burma: Why the Drug Trade Is Central To Burma's Changing Political Order." *Journal of Southeast Asian Studies* 42; 376–404.

96. Ibid.

97. Teitel (1994a).

98. Makhijani, A. (1992). *From Global Capitalism to Economic Justice: an Inquiry into the Elimination of Systematic Poverty, Violence and Environmental Destruction in the World Economy.* Council of International and Public Affairs. New York: Apex Press.

99. Goldsmith, E. (1997). "Can the Environment Survive the Global Economy?" *Ecologist* 27/6: 47.

100. Perfecto, I.,Vandermeer, J., and Wright, A. (2009). *Nature's Matrix: Linking Agriculture, Conservation and Food Sovereignty.* London: Routledge.

101. Claeys, P. (n.d.). "From Food Sovereignty to Peasants' Rights: An Overview of Via Campesina's Struggle for New Human Rights." Retrieved from http://www.viacampesina.org/downloads/pdf/openbooks/EN-02.pdf.

102. Vía Campesina (1996). *Tlaxcala Declaration of the Vía Campesina.* Declaration of the Second International Conference of Vía Campesina, Tlaxcala, Mexico.

5. NETWORKS OF POWER

1. Domhoff, W. G. (2005). *The Four Networks Theory of Power: A Theoretical Home for Power Structure Research.* Retrieved from http://sociology.ucsc.edu/whorulesamerica/theory/four_networks.html.

2. Institute for Policy Studies (2012). "Profile of Gordon England." Retrieved from http://rightweb.irc-online.org/profile/England_Gordon; Mattera, P. (2012). "General Dynamics." *CorpWatch.* Retrieved from http://www.corpwatch.org/article.php?list=type&type=12.

3. Vitali, S., Glattfelder, J. B., and Battiston, S. (2011). "The Network of Global Corporate Control." Retrieved from http://www.plosone.org/article/info%3Adoi%2F10.1371%2Fjournal.pone.0025995.

4. Crenshaw, A. B. (2005) "Tax Abuse Rampant in Nonprofits, IRS Says."April 5.

5. Hartmann, T. (2004). *Unequal Protection: The Rise of Corporate Dominance and the Theft of Human Rights.* New York: St. Martin's Press.

6. Useem, M. (1984). *The Inner Circle: Large Corporations and the Rise of Business Political Activity in the U.S. and U.K.* New York: Oxford University Press.

7. American Legislative Exchange Council (ALEC) (2013) "About ALEC." Retrieved from http://www.alec.org/about-alec/.

8. *New York Times* (July 1, 2012). "A Window on Campaign Abuse." Retrieved from http://www.nytimes.com/2012/07/01/opinion/sunday/a-window-on-campaign-abuse.html.

9. Buzenberg, B. (2012). "ALEC Faces New Challenge to Tax-Exempt Status." *Weekly Watchdog*. Retrieved from http://ignoble-experiment.blogspot.com/2012/07/weekly-watchdog-alec-faces-new.html; Dunbar, J. (2012). "ALEC Faces New Challenge to Tax-Exempt Status: Legislative group benefits private, not public interest, complaint says." Center for Public Integrity. Retrieved from http://www.publicintegrity.org/2012/07/02/9246/alec-faces-new-challenge-tax-exempt-status.

10. Johnston, D. C. (2012). *The Fine Print: How Big Companies Use "Plain English" to Rob You Blind.* New York: Penguin.

11. Mann (1996) (p. 1).

12. Domhoff, W. G. (2005).

13. Eisenhower, D., as quoted in Kampfner, J., (2003). "The Pentagon Basks in Triumph." *New Statesman* 23 (April 28).

14. National Priorities Project (NPP) (2013). "Cost of War to the United States." Retrieved from http://costofwar.com/.

15. United States Office of Management and Budget (2012). *Fiscal Year 2013 Analytical Perspectives: Budget of the U.S. Government.* Table 32-1. Retrieved from http://www.gpo.gov/fdsys/search/pagedetails.action?packageId=BUDGET-2013-PER.

16. NPP (2012). "Total Spending FY2012." National Priorities Project: Democratizing the Federal Budget. Retrieved from http://nationalpriorities.org/; Huffington Post (2012). "Fact of the Day #8: U.S. Defense Spending Dwarfs Rest of the World." Retrieved from *http://*www.huffingtonpost.com/2012/08/06/defense-spending-fact-of-the-day_n_1746685.html.

17. Bilmes, L., and Stiglitz, J. (2006). "War's Stunning Price Tag." *Los Angeles Times.* Retrieved from http://www.latimes.com/news/opinion/commentary/la-oe-bilmes17jan17,0,7038018.story?coll=la-news-comment-opinions.

18. Stiglitz, J. E., and Bilmes, L. J. (Sept. 3, 2010). "The True Cost of the Iraq war: $3 Trillion and Beyond." *Washington Post.* Retrieved from http://www.washingtonpost.com/wp-dyn/content/article/2010/09/03/AR2010090302200.html.

19. Huber, P. (2003). "The Palm Pilot-JDAM Complex." *Forbes* 171/10): 88.

20. Moss, M. (2005). "Struggle for Iraq: Troop Shields; Pentagon Study Links Fatalities to Body Armor." *New York Times.*

21. Schwartz, A., and Watson, J. (2004). "The Law and Economics of Costly Contracting. *Journal of Law, Economics, and Organization* 20/1: 2–31.

22. Ibid.

23. Center for Public Integrity (2005). "Post-War Contractors Ranked by Total Contract Value in Iraq and Afghanistan from 2002 through July 1, 2004." Retrieved from http://www.publicintegrity.org/wow/resources.aspx?act=total.

24. NBC News (2012). "Iraq War contractor ordered to pay National Guardsmen $85M over toxic chemical exposure." Retrieved from http://usnews.nbcnews.com/_news/2012/11/03/14898987-iraq-war-contractor-ordered-to-pay-national-guardsmen-85m-over-toxic-chemical-exposure?lite/.

25. *Military Industrial Complex* (2012). "Kellogg Brown and Root, Incorporated Defense Contract for the NAVY given 12/06/2012." Retrieved from http://www.militaryindustrialcomplex.com/contract_detail.asp?contract_id=22134.

26. Cowles, D. (2005). "2 BR, 1.5 BATH, All the Defense Contracts You Can Handle." *The New Republic*, 8.

27. Makison, L. (2006). "Outsourcing the Pentagon: Who Benefits from the Politics and Economics of National Security?" Retrieved from http://usgovinfo.about.com/od/thepoliticalsystem/a/aboutpacs.htm.

28. Ibid.

29. Adler, M. (2006). "Sometimes, Government Is the Answer." *Los Angeles Times*. Retrieved from http://www.latimes.com/news/opinion/commentary/la-oe-adler4mar04,0,515451.story?coll=la-news-comment-opinions.

30. Ibid.

31. Ireland, D. (2004). "The Cheney Connection: Tracing the Halliburton Money Trail to Nigeria." *Los Angeles Times*. Retrieved from. http://www.laweekly.com/news/news/the-cheney-connection/1601/.

32. Thomas, J., and Devine, T. (2014). "Wall Street's New Enforcers Aim to Muzzle Whistle-Blowers." *New York Times,* July 21.

33. Jeff Heuners, as quoted in St. Clair, J. (2005). *Grand Theft Pentagon*. Monroe, ME: Common Courage Press; Roane, K. R. (2004). "All in the Family: Connecting the dots between an Alaska senator, his kin, and some fat U.S. contracts." *US News and World Report*. Retrieved from http://www.usnews.com/usnews/news/articles/041206/6stevens.htm.

34. Zepezauer, M., and Naiman, A. (1996). *Take the Rich Off Welfare*. Tucson: Odonian Press.

35. Caldicott, H. (2002/2004). *The New Nuclear Danger: George W. Bush's Military-Industrial Complex* (p. xxx). New York: New Press.

36. Bechtel (Dec. 12, 2006). Retrieved from http://en.wikipedia.org/wiki/Bechtel.

37. Caldicott (2002/2004).

38. Peterson, L. (2006). "The Windfalls of War: Bechtel Group, Inc." Center for Public Integrity. Retrieved from http://www.publicintegrity.org/wow/bio.aspx?act=pro&ddlC=6.

39. Bechtel (2012). *Bechtel Announces 2011 Results*. Retrieved from http://www.bechtel.com/2012-04-11.html.

40. Peterson (2006).

41. Caldicott (2002/2004).

42. Ismail, M. A. (2006). "Investing in War: The Carlyle Group Profits from Government and Conflict." Center for Public Integrity. Retrieved from http://www.publicintegrity.org/pns/report.aspx?aid=424.

43. Eichenwald, K. (Oct. 26, 2001). "Bin-Laden Family Liquidates Holdings with Carlyle Group." *New York Times*. http://www.nytimes.com/2001/10/26/business/bin-laden-family-liquidates-holdings-with-carlyle-group.html.

44. Eskow, R. (2013). "Big Money and the NSA Scandal . . . How Dangerous Is the Security/Digital Complex?" *Campaign for America's Future* 13: 17. http://ourfuture.org/20130610/big-data-big-money-big-defense-how-dangerous-is-the-securitydigital-complex?.

45. Ibid.

46 Appelbaum, B., and Lippton, E. (June 9, 2013). "Leaker's Employer Is Paid to Maintain Government Secrets." *New York Times*. Retrieved from http://www.nytimes.com/2013/06/10/us/booz-allen-grew-rich-on-government-contracts.html.

47. Eichenwald, K. (2001)

48. Caldicott (2002/2004).

49. Jeff Heuners, as quoted in St. Clair, *Grand Theft Pentagon.*
50. Caldicott (2002/2004).
51. St. Clair (2005).
52. Ibid.
53. Caldicott (2002/2004).
54. Anonymous Bonesman, as quoted in Robbins, A. (2002). *Secrets of the Tomb: Skull and Bones, The Ivy League, and the Hidden Paths of Power.* Boston: Little, Brown.
55. Robbins (2002).
56. Ibid.
57. Ibid.
58. Mendez, A. (n.d.). "An Uncommon View of the Birth of an Uncommon Market." Retrieved from http://www.bilderberg.org/bildhist.htm#Mendez.
59. Sourcewatch (2006e). "Council on Foreign Relations." Retrieved from http://www.sourcewatch.org/index.php?title=Council_on_Foreign_Relations.
60. Ross, R. G. Sr. (2004). *Who's Who of the Elite.* United States: RIE.
61. Pitt, W. (2003). "The Project for the New American Century." Retrieved from http://www.informationclearinghouse.info/article1665.htm.
62. Phillips, P. (1994). "A Relative Advantage: Sociology of the San Francisco Bohemian Club." PhD diss. Retrieved from http://libweb.sonoma.edu/regional/faculty/phillips/bohemianindex.html.
63. Ibid.
64. Cockburn, A. (2001). "Meet the Secret Rulers of the World: The Truth about the Bohemian Grove." *Counterpunch.* Retrieved from http://www.counterpunch.org/bohemian.html; William, G. (1974). *The Bohemian Grove and Other Retreats: A Study in Ruling-Class Cohesiveness.* New York: Harper, Colophon Books.
65. Phillips (1994).
66. Domhoff (2005c).
67. Council on Foreign Relations (2015). *History of CFR,* retrieved from http://www.cfr.org/about/history/.
68. Peters (2001).
69. Sourcewatch (2006e).
70. Council on Foreign Relations (2003a). "Iraq: The Day After." Retrieved from http://www.cfr.org/publication/5682/president_bush_should_stay_the_course_in_postwar_iraq_to_ensure_battlefield_victory_is_not_lost_says_council_task_force.html?breadcrumb=default.
71. Council on Foreign Relations (2003b). "Iraq: The Day After—(Chairs' Update)." Retrieved from http://www.cfr.org/publication/6075/iraq.html?breadcrumb=default.
72. Ibid.; Council on Foreign Relations (2003a).
73. Ross (2004).
74. NAM (2007a). "About Us." Retrieved from http://www.nam.org/s_nam/sec.asp?CID=4&DID=2.
75. NAM (2007b). "Bottom Line Policy Achievements for Manufacturers." Retrieved from http://www.nam.org/s_nam/doc1.asp?CID=24&DID=201889; NAM (2007c). "Official Policy Positions: Global Climate Change." Retrieved from http://www.nam.org/s_nam/sec.asp?TRACKID=&SID=1&VID=1&CID=43&DID=41&RTID=0&CIDQS=&Taxonomy=False&specialSearch=False; NAM (2007d). "Talking Points for Manufacturers: Energy

Security for American Competitiveness." Retrieved from http://www.nam.org/s_nam/doc1. asp?CID=202556&DID=238282.

76. Useem (1984).
77. Business Roundtable (2007). "About Business Roundtable." Retrieved from http://www. businessroundtable.org:80/aboutUs/index.aspx.
78. Ibid.
79. NAM (2007d).
80. NAM (2007c).
81. Griscom, A. (2004) "Industry Flacks Learn How to Snooker the Public with Their Not-So-Friendly Messages." *Grist*. Retrieved from http://www.grist.org/news/muck/2004/01/21/spin/index.html.
82. Leavitt, as quoted in Griscom (2004).
83. Dreiling, M. C. (2000). "The Class Embeddedness of Corporate Political Action: Leadership in Defense of the NAFTA." *Social Problems* 47/1: 21–48.
84. Ibid.
85. Domhoff, G. W. (2005b). "The Corporate Community, Nonprofit Organizations, and Federal Advisory Committees: A Study in Linkages." In *Who Rules America?* Retrieved from http://sociology.ucsc.edu/whorulesamerica/power.fac.html.
86. Dreiling (2000) (p. 39).
87. Ibid.
88. Birnbaum, J. H. (July 27, 2005). "Hill a Steppingstone to K Street for Some: More Ex-Lawmakers Who Join Private Sector Are Becoming Lobbyists, Study Says." *Washington Post*; Public Citizen-Congress Watch, (2005). "Congressional Revolving Doors: The Journey from Congress to K Street." Retrieved from http://www.lobbyinginfo.org/documents/RevolveDoor.pdf.
89. Pitt (2003).
90. Project for the New American Century (2000) (p. 51).
91. Scott, P. Dale (2007). *The Road to 9/11: Wealth, Empire, and the Future of America*. Berkeley: University of California Press.
92. Sourcewatch (2006b). "Project for the New American Century." Retrieved from http://www. sourcewatch.org/index.php?title=Project_for_the_New_American_Century#PNAC_Document; Caldicott (2002/2004); Pitt (2003).
93. Mayer, J. (2006). "The Hidden Power: The Legal Mind behind the White House's War on Terror." The *New Yorker*, July 3; Sourcewatch (2006b).
94. *Sourcewatch* (2006d). "Defense Policy Board Advisory Committee." Retrieved from http://www.sourcewatch.org/index.php?title=Defense_Policy_Board.
95. Caldicott (2002/2004).
96. *Sourcewatch* (2006d).
97. Caldicott (2002/2004).
98. Zinn, H. (1990). *A People's History of the United States*. New York: Harper Perennial.
99. *International Monetary Fund* (2007). Retrieved from http://www.imf.org.
100. Stiglitz, J. (2002). *Globalization and Its Discontents*. New York: W. W. Norton.
101. Sachs, J. (2005). *The End Of Poverty*. London: Penguin Books.
102. Gilens, M., and Page, B. I. (2014). "Testing Theories of American politics: Elites, interest groups, and average citizens." *Perspectives on Politics* 12/3: 564–81.

103. Hillman, A., and Hitt, M. (1999). "Corporate Political Strategy Formulation: A Model of Approach, Participation, and Strategy Decisions." *Academy of Management Review* 24/4: 825–42.
104. Ibid.
105. Grossman, Lindzey, and Brannen (n.d.). "Model Brief on Corporate Personhood. Program on Corporations, Law, and Democracy." Retrieved from http://www.poclad.org/ModelLegalBrief.cfm.
106. Zepernick, M. (2004). *The Impact of Corporations on the Commons.* Harvard Divinity School's Theological Opportunities Program. Retrieved from http://www.poclad.org/articles/zepernick02.html.
107. Dunbar, J. (2012). "The 'Citizens United' Decision and Why It Matters." Center For Public Integrity. Retrieved from http://www.publicintegrity.org/2012/10/18/11527/citizens-united-decision-and-why-it-matters?gclid=CN-84NOoprUCFeZ_QgodxQEAUQ.
108. Jarvis, B. (2011). "Citizens United? The need to get money out of politics may be the one thing Americans agree on." *Yes Magazine.* Retrieved from http://www.yesmagazine.org/blogs/brooke-jarvis/citizens-united.
109. Coleridge, G. (2004). "Closing the Circle: The Corporatization of Elections." *Free Press.* Retrieved from http://www.freepress.org/departments/display/19/2004/875.
110. Center for Responsive Politics (2005).
111. Center for Responsive Politics (2015). http://www.opensecrets.org/lobby/clientsum.php?id=D000000074 https://www.opensecrets.org/lobby/clientsum.php?id=D000019798.
112. Coleridge (2004).
113. Knott, A. (2004). "Who Gives the Most Money: Financial Corporations and Law Firms Dominate Career Patrons List." Center for Public Integrity. Retrieved from http://www.publicintegrity.org/bop2004/report.aspx?aid=168.
114. Center for Responsive Politics (2005).
115. OpenSecrets.org (2012). "2012 Election Spending Will Reach $6 Billion, Center for Responsive Politics Predicts." Retrieved from http://www.opensecrets.org/news/2012/10/2012-election-spending-will-reach-6.html.
116. OpenSecrets.org (2013). Retrieved from http://www.opensecrets.org/industries/indus.php?ind=E01.
117. Logan, J. R., and Molotch, H. (1987). *Urban Fortunes: The Political Economy of Place.* Berkeley: University of California Press; Molotch, H. (1999). "Growth Machine Links: Up, Down, and Across." In Jonas, A., and Wilson, D. (Eds.), *The Urban Growth Machine: Critical Perspectives, Two Decades Later* (pp. 247–65). Albany: State University of New York Press.
118. Justice Stevens, (2010). *Citizens United, Appellant v. Federal Elections Commission.* Supreme Court of the United States. Retrieved from the Cornell University Law School: http://www.law.cornell.edu/supct/html/08-205.ZX.html.
119. Quealy, K., and Willis, D. (2012). "Independent Spending Totals." *New York Times.* Retrieved from http://elections.nytimes.com/2012/campaign-finance/independent-expenditures/totals.
120. OpenSecrets.org (2012).
121. Coleridge (2004).
122. Berkman Center for Internet and Society (2004). *Diebold v. the Bloggers.* Berkman Briefings, Harvard Law School. Retrieved from http://cyber.law.harvard.edu/briefings/dvb.

123. Cardinale, M. (2006). "Diebold Added Secret Patch to Georgia e-Voting Systems in 2002, Whistleblowers Say." *Atlanta Progressive News*. Retrieved from http://www.atlantaprogressivenews.com/news/0091.html.

124. Slater, M., Kyser, L., and Chasnow, J. (2006). "New Barriers to Voting: Eroding the Right to Vote." *National Voter* 55/3: 7, http://findarticles.com/p/articles/mi_m0MLB/is_3_55/ai_n16689802.

125. Ibid.

126. Childress, S. (June 26, 2013). "With Voting Rights Act Out, States Push Voter ID Laws." *Frontline*. Retrieved from www.pbs.org/wgbh/pages/frontline/government-electios-politics/with-voting-rights-act-out-states-push-voter-id-laws/.

127. Khimm, S. (2010). "Barriers to voting." *Mother Jones*. Retrieved from http://www.naacpldf.org/news/mother-jones-block-vote.

128. Taylor, M. (2004). "Community Issues and Social Networks." In Phillipson, C., Allan, G., and Morgan, D. (Eds.). *Social Networks and Social Exclusion: Sociological and Policy Perspectives* (pp. 205–18). Hants, UK: Ashgate Publishers.

6. REALPOLITIK: STRATEGIES AND TACTICS FOR WINNING

1. Mueller, J. (2006). *Overblown: How Politicians and the Terrorism Industry Inflate National Security Threats, and Why We Believe Them*. New York: Free Press.

2. Stone, O., and Kuznick, P. (2012). *The Untold History of the United States*. New York: Simon & Schuster.

3. Netanyahu, B. (2006). Interview with Glenn Beck, *CNN Headline News*, November 17.

4. Unger, C. (2007). "From the Wonderful Folks Who Brought You Iraq." *Vanity Fair*, March 2007.

5. Scahill, J, (2013). *Dirty Wars: The World Is a Battlefield*. New York: Nation Books.

6. Bumiller, E. (Dec. 12, 2011). "Air Force Drone Operators Report High Levels of Stress." *New York Times*. Retrieved from http://www.nytimes.com/2011/12/19/world/asia/air-force-drone-operators-show-high-levels-of-stress.html,

7. Rapaport, A. (1964). *Strategy and Conscience*. New York: Harper and Row.

8. Gerace, M. P. (2004). *Military Power, Conflict, and Trade: Military Power, International Commerce and Great Power Rivalry*. London: Frank Cass.

9. Domosh, M. (2006). *American Commodities in an Age of Empire*. London: Routledge.

10. Colley, L. (2005). "The US Is Now Rediscovering the Pitfalls of Aspirational Imperialism." *Guardian*, December 17.

11. D'Souza, D. (2000). *The Virtue of Prosperity: Finding Values in an Age of Techno-Affluence*. New York: Touchstone.

12. Colley (2005).

13. Carr, C. (2002). *The Lessons of Terror: A History of Warfare against Civilians: Why It Has Always Failed and Why It Will Fail Again*. New York: Random House.

14. Zinn, H. (1980). *A People's History of the United States*. New York: HarperCollins.

15. Ibid.

16. Ibid.

17. Peters, M. (2001). "The Bilderberg Group and the Project of European Unification." Retrieved from http://www.xs4all.nl/~ac/global/achtergrond/bilderberg.htm.

18. Ibid.

19. Fleming, D. F. (1961). *The Cold War and Its Origins 1917–1960.* New York: Doubleday.

20. Peters (2001).

21. Zinn (1980).

22. Mendez, A. (2006). "An Uncommon View of the Birth of an Uncommon Market." Retrieved from http://www.bilderberg.org/bildhist.htm#Mendez.

23. Zinn (1980).

24. Ibid.

25. Parenti, M. (1969). *The Anti-Communist Impulse* (p. 35). New York: Random House.

26. Jardine, M. (2001). "Days of Infamy and Memory." *In These Times* 4/10.

27. Churchill, W. (1951). *The Second World War,* vol. 4: *The Hinge of Fate* (p. 428). London: Cassell & Co.

28. Churchill, W. (1929). *The World Crisis: The Aftermath.* New York: Scribners.

29. Stone and Kuznet, (2010).

30. Zinn (1980) (p. 417).

31. Blum, W. (2004). *Killing Hope: US Military and CIA Interventions since World War II.* Monroe, ME: Common Courage Press.

32. Ganser, D. (2005). *NATO's Secret Armies: Operation Gladio and Terrorism in Western Europe.* London: Frank Cass Verlog; Rajiva, L. (2005). "The Pentagon's 'NATO Option.'" *Common Dreams.* Retrieved from http://www.commondreams.org/views05/0210-22.htm.

33. Ganser (2005).

34. Ibid.

35. RIA Novosti (October 2012). "Russia Warns of 'Technical Response' to NATO Missile Plans." Retrieved from http://en.rian.ru/military_news/20121018/176719647.html.

36. Øberg, J. (2006). "Does the European Union Promote Peace?" Transnational Foundation for Peace and Future Research. Lund, Sweden, October 6.

37. Chomsky, N. (2003). *Hegemony of Survival: America's Quest For Global Dominance.* New York: Henry Holt.

38. Zinn (1980).

39. Scott, P. D., (2010). *The American War Machine: Deep Politics, the CIA's Global Drug Connection, and the Road to Afghanistan.* Washington, DC: Rowman & Littlefield.

40. Pilisuk, M., and Pilisuk, P. (1972). *How We Lost the War on Poverty.* Chicago, IL: Dutton.

41. Hitchens, C. (2001). *The Trial of Henry Kissinger.* London: Verso Press.

42. Blanton, T. (2001). *The Secret Briefs and the Secret Evidence.* National Security Archive Electronic Briefing Book Number 48. Blanton, T.S. (Ed.), Compiled by Prados, J., Meadows, E., Burr, W. & Evans, M. Retrieved from http://www.gwu.edu/~nsarchiv/NSAEBB/NSAEBB48/; Turse, N. (2008). "The Vietnam Exposé that Wasn't." *The Nation.* Retrieved from http://www.thenation.com/article/vietnam-exposeacute-wasnt.

43. Perkins, J. (2006). *Confessions of an Economic Hitman.* New York: Plume; Hiatt, S., (Ed.), (2007). *A Game as Old as Empire: The Secret World of Economic Hit Men and the Web of Global Corruption.* San Francisco: Berrett-Koehler.

44. COHA (Council on Hemispheric Affairs) (2006). "Report on Nicaragua: How the United States Continues to Manipulate Nicaragua's Economic and Political Future." Retrieved from http://www.coha.org/2006/06/22/how-the-united-states-continues-to-manipulate-nicaraguas-economic-and-political-future.

45. Robinson, L. (2004). *Masters of Chaos: The Secret History of Special Forces.* New York: Public Affairs Press.

46. Prados, J. (2006). *Safe for Democracy: The Secret Wars of the CIA.* Chicago: Ivan R. Dee.

47. Paul, R. (2003). "National Endowment for Democracy: Paying to Make Enemies of America." Retrieved from http://www.antiwar.com/paul/paul79.html.

48. Kinzer, S. (2006). *Overthrow: America's Century of Regime Change from Hawaii to Iraq.* New York: Times Books.

49. Grandin, G. (2006). *Empire's Workshop: Latin America, the United States, and the Rise of the New Imperialism.* New York: Metropolitan Books.

50. Tulley, A. (1962). *CIA: The Inside Story.* New York: William Morrow; Kinzer, S. (2003). *All the Shah's Men: An American Coup and the Roots of Middle East Terror.* Hoboken, NJ: Wiley & Sons.

51. Goff, F., and Locker, M. (1971). "The Violence of Domination: U.S. Power and the Dominican Republic." In Perrucci, R., and Pilisuk, M. (Eds.), *The Triple Revolution Emerging.* Boston: Little, Brown.

52. Pilisuk, M. (1972). *International Conflict and Social Policy.* Englewood Cliffs, NJ: Prentice Hall.

53. Leggett, J. (1978). *Allende, His Exit, and Our Times.* New Brunswick, NJ: Cooperative Press.

54. Wise, D., and Ross, T. (1964). *The Invisible Government.* New York: Random House.

55. Pelletiere, S. C. (2004). *Iraq and the International Oil System: Why America Went to War in the Gulf.* Washington, DC: Maisonneuve Press; Phillips, K. (2006). *American Theocracy: The Peril and Politics of Radical Religion, Oil, and Borrowed Money in the 21st Century.* New York: Penguin Books.

56. Galbraith, P. W. (2006a). *The End of Iraq: How American Incompetence Created a War without End.* New York: Simon and Schuster; Galbraith, P. W. (2006b). "The True Iraq Appeasers." *Boston Globe.* Retrieved from http://www.boston.com/news/globe/editorial_opinion/oped/articles/2006/08/31/the_true_iraq_appeasers/.

57. Galbraith (2006a); Ricks, T. E. (2006). *Fiasco: The American Military Adventure in Iraq.* New York: Penguin Press.

58. Pelletiere (2004).

59. Hiro, D. (2002). "Saudis: U.S. Go Home?" *Nation.* Retrieved from http://www.thenation.com/doc/20020311/hiro.

60. Knowlton, B. (2002). "Saudis Haven't Requested Pullout, U. S. Officials Say." *International Herald Tribune.* Retrieved from http://www.iht.com/articles/2002/01/21/diplo_ed3_php.

61. Ibid.

62. Roberts, P. (2004). *The End of Oil: On the Edge of a Perilous New World.* Boston: Houghton Mifflin; Phillips (2006).

63. Hirsh, M., and Barry, J. (2005). "The Salvador Option." *Newsweek,* January 14.

64. Bookman, J. (n.d.). "The President's Real Goal in Iraq." Retrieved from http://www.thirdworldtraveler.com/Iraq/Presidents_Real_Goal_Iraq.html.

65. Galston, W. A. (June 14, 2002). "Why a First Strike Will Surely Backfire." *Washington Post.* Retrieved from http://www.washingtonpost.com/ac2/wp-dyn/A54644-2002Jun14?language=printer.

66. Pilger, J. (July 14, 2002). "The Great Charade." *Observer.* Retrieved from http://observer.guardian.co.uk/worldview/story/0,,754972,00.html.

67. Mearsheimer, J. J., and Walt, S. M. (2003). "An Unnecessary War." *Foreign Policy*, January–February. Retrieved from http://www.foreignpolicy.com/users/login.php?story_id=169&URL=http://www.foreignpolicy.com/story/cms.php?story_id=169.

68. Cohen, A., and O'Driscoll, G. P. Jr., (2003). "Achieving Economic Reform and Growth in Iraq." Web Memo #236, Heritage Foundation. Retrieved from http://www.heritage.org/research/middleeast/wm236.cfm.

69. Barnes, J., and Meyers Jaffe, A. (2006). "The Persian Gulf and the Geopolitics of Oil." *Survival* 48/1: 152.

70. Diamond, L. J. (2005). *Squandered Victory: The American Occupation and the Bungled Effort To Bring Democracy to Iraq.* New York: Times Books.

71. Juhasz, A. (2006). *The Bush Agenda: Invading the World, One Economy at a Time.* New York: Regan Books, HarperCollins.

72. Floyd, C. (2007). "Claiming the Prize: Escalation Aimed at Securing Iraqi Oil." *Information Clearing House*, January 12. Retrieved from http://www.alternet.org/waroniraq/46602/.

73. Fortson, D. (2007). "Iraq Posed to End Drought for Thirsting Oil Giants." *Independent*, May 22. Retrieved from http://news.independent.co.uk/business/news/article2132467.ece.

74. Lando, B. (2007). *Web of Deceit: The History of Western Complicity in Iraq, from Churchill to Kennedy to George W. Bush* (p. 267). New York: Other Press.

75. Chandrasekaran, R. (2006). *Imperial Life in the Emerald City: Inside Iraq's Green Zone.* New York: Random House.

76. Wise, D., and Ross, T. R. (1964). *The Invisible Government.* New York: Random House.

77. Trowbridge, E. (2002). "Back Road Reckoning." *Dissent* 49: 101–13.

78. Hitchens, C. (2002). "Kissinger's Green Light to Suharto." *The Nation.* Retrieved from http://www.thenation.com/doc/20020218/hitchens.

79. Burr, W., and Evans, M. L. (Eds.) (2001). *National Security Archive Electronic Briefing*, Book No. 62. Retrieved from http://www.gwu.edu/~nsarchiv/NSAEBB/NSAEBB62.

80. Jardine (2001).

81. Ibid.

82. Da Silva, W. (2002). "Letter from East Timor." *The Nation*, July 22–24.

83. See http://dailycoffeenews.com/2013/10/25/organics-starbucks-and-east-timors-devastating-hunger-season/.

84. Trowbridge (2002).

85. Hill, H. (2006). "Why Do Australians Want Mari Alkatiri Out of the Prime Ministership of East Timor?" Retrieved from http://samanddaniel.blogspot.com/2006/05/why-do-australians-want-mari-alkatiri.html.

86. Steele, J. (May 23, 2002). "East Timor Is Independent So Long as It Does as It's Told." *Guardian.* Retrieved from http://www.guardian.co.uk/comment/story/0,,720552,00.html.

87. Robinson (2002).

88. Ibid.

89. Schlesinger, S., and Kinzer, S. (1999). *Bitter Fruit: The Story of the American Coup in Guatemala.* Cambridge, MA: Harvard University Press.

90. Wise and Ross (1964).

91. Amnesty International (1989). *Guatemala: Human Rights Violations under Civilian Governments.* London: Amnesty International.

92. Jonas, S. (1991). *The Battle for Guatemala: Rebels, Death Squads, and US Power*, vol. 5. Boulder, CO: Westview Press.

93. Guatemalan Commission for Historical Clarification (n.d.). *Guatemala: Memory of Silence*. Report of the Commission for Historical Clarification Conclusions and Recommendations. Retrieved from http://shr.aaas.org/guatemala/ceh/report/english/toc.html.

94. Schlesinger, S. C., Kinzer, S., and Coatsworth, J. H. (2005). *Bitter Fruit: The Story of the American Coup in Guatemala*, vol. 4. Cambridge, MA: Harvard University Press.

95. Ledeem, M. (2014), quoted in William Blum, *America's Deadliest Export: Democracy*, The Anti-Empire Report #129, June 6, 2014.

96. Mann, J. (2004). *Rise of the Vulcans: The History of Bush's War Cabinet* (p. xiii). New York: Viking.

97. Ibid.

98. Ibid.

99. Ibid., 198.

100. Ibid., 363.

101. Joint Chiefs of Staff (March 15, 2005). *Doctrine for Joint Nuclear Operations*. [Publication 3-12]. Washington, DC: Joint Chiefs of Staff.

102. Ibid.

103. Suskind, R., (2006). *The One Percent Doctrine* Parsipanny, NJ: Simon and Schuster.

104. Ibid.

105. Aaronson, T. (2013). *The Terror Factory: Inside the FBI's Manufactured War on Terror*. Brooklyn, NY: Ig Publishing.

106. Montgomery, B. (2005). "Congressional Oversight: Vice President Richard B. Cheney's Executive Branch Triumph." *Political Science Quarterly* 120: 615–16.

107. Mann (2004) (pp. 196–97).

108. McCoy, A. (2006). *A Question Of Torture: CIA Interrogation, from the Cold War to the War on Terror*. New York: Metropolitan Books, Henry Holt.

109. Rejali, D. (2009). *Torture and Democracy*. Princeton: Princeton University Press.

110. Rajiva, L. (2005). "The Torture-Go-Round." *Counterpunch*, December 5. Retrieved from http://www.counterpunch.org/rajiva12052005.html.

111. Department of the Army (1987). *Intelligence Interrogation*, Army Field Manual 34-52. Retrieved from http://www.globalsecurity.org/intell/library/policy/army/fm/fm34-52/.

112. Schrepel, W. (2005). "Paras and Centurions: Lessons Learned from the Battle of Algiers." *Peace and Conflict: Journal of Peace Psychology* 11/1: 71–90.

113. Klein, N. (2005). "Torture's Part of the Territory." *Los Angeles Times*, June 7.

114. Ibid.; Pilisuk, M. (2005). "Unprofessional Warriors: Lessons Small and Large." *Peace and Conflict: Journal of Peace Psychology* 11/1: 95–100.

115. McCoy (2006); Packer, G. (2005) *The Assassin's Gate: America in Iraq*. New York: Farrar, Straus and Giroux.

116. Cohn, M. (2011). *The United States and Torture: Interrogation, Incarceration, and Abuse*. New York: New York University Press.

117. Ackerman, S. (2014). "CIA's Brutal and Ineffective Use of Torture Revealed in Landmark Report." *The Guardian*, December 9.

118. Strassler, R. B. (Ed.), (1996). *The Landmark Thucydides: A Comprehensive Guide to the Peloponnesian War*. New York: Free Press.

119. Milliard, T. (2003). "Overcoming Post-Colonial Myopia: A Call to Recognize and Regulate Private Military Corporations." *Military Law Review* 176: 1–95.

120. Thomson, J. E. (1990). "State Practices, International Norms, and the Decline of Mercenarism." *International Studies Quarterly* 34/1: 23–47; Coleman, J. R. (2004), "Constraining Modern Mercenarism." *Hastings Law Journal* 55: 1493.

121. Coleman (2004).

122. Ibid.

123. Ibid., 1519.

124. Ibid., 1519.

125. Zarate, J. C. (1998). "The Emergence of a New Dog of War: Private International Security Companies, International Law, and the New World Disorder." *Stanford Journal of International Law* 75: 82.

126. Coleman (2004).

127. Scahill, J. (2007). *Blackwater: The Rise of the World's Most Powerful Mercenary Army.* New York: Nation Press.

128. Vine, D. (2012, July). "The Lily-Pad Strategy." Nation of Change.org. Retrieved from http://www.nationofchange.org/lily-pad-strategy-1342446318.

129. Turse (2008); Vine (2012).

130. Mazzetti, M. (2013a). *The Way of the Knife: The CIA, a Secret Army, and a War at the Ends of the Earth.* New York: Penguin; Mazetti, M. (2013b), "Rise of the Predators: A Secret Deal on Drones. Sealed in Blood." *New York Times.* Retrieved from http://www.nytimes.com/2013/04/07/world/asia/origins-of-cias-not-so-secret-drone-war-in-pakistan.html,

131. Scahill, J. (2013). *Dirty Wars: The World Is a Battlefield.* New York: Nation Books.

132. Sadowski, D. (2013). "Drone Warfare Faces Barrage of Moral Questions." Catholic San Francisco.org. Retrieved from http://www.catholic-sf.org/ns.php?newsid=1&id=61092.

133. Worth, R., Mazzetti, M., and Shane, S. (Feb. 6, 2013). "Drone Strikes' Risks to Get Rare Moment in the Public Eye." *New York Times.* Retrieved from http://www.nytimes.com/2013/02/06/world/middleeast/with-brennan-pick-a-light-on-drone-strikes-hazards.html.

134. Pilisuk, M. (2013). "The New Face of War." *The Peace Chronicle.*

135. Levine, Y. (2013). "The Strange Billionaire Brothers Behind America's Predator Drones—And Their Very Strange Past." *AlterNet.* Retrieved from http://www.alternet.org/investigations/strange-billionaire-brothers-behind-americas-predator-drones-and-their-very-strange?page=0%2C6&akid=10363.207032.TeeYX1&rd=1&src=newsletter830237&t=5.

136. Ibid.

137. Lerner, J. (June 15, 2009). "Profile: General Atomics." *Financial Times.*

138. Hennigan, W. J. (March 16, 2010). "Unmanned aircraft pioneer Thomas J. Cassidy Jr. retires." *Los Angeles Times.* Retrieved from http://articles.latimes.com/2010/mar/16/business/la-fi-general-atomics16-2010mar16; Benjamin, M. (2012), *Drone Warfare: Killing by Remote Control.* New York and London: OR Books.

139. Pilisuk, M. (2013).

140. Scahill, J. (2013)

141. Priest, D., and Larkin, W. "Top Secret America: *A Washington Post* Investigation." *Washington Post.* Retrieved from http://projects.washingtonpost.com/top-secret-america/.

142. Eskow, R. (2013). "Big Money and the NSA Scandal . . . How Dangerous Is the "Security/Digital Complex?" *Campaign for America's Future* 11/13: 17, http://ourfuture.

org/20130610/big-data-big-money-big-defense-how-dangerous-is-the-securitydigital-complex?utm_source=rss&utm_medium=rss&utm_campaign=big-data-big-money-big-defense-how-dangerous-is-the-securitydigital-complex.

143. Ibid.

144. Ibid.

145. Edward Said, quoted in Engdahl, W. (2004) *A Century of War: Anglo-American Oil Politics and the New World Order* (p. 270). London: Pluto Press.

146. Schou, N. (2006). *Kill the Messenger: How the CIA's Crack-Cocaine Controversy Destroyed Journalist Gary Webb*. New York: Nation Books; Scott, P. D., and Marshall, J. (1991), *Cocaine Politics: Drugs, Armies, and the CIA in Central America*. Berkeley: University of California Press; Webb, G. (2001), "The New Rules for the New Millennium." In Kick, R. (Ed.), *The Disinformation Guide to Media Distortion, Historical Whitewashes, and Cultural Myths* (pp. 38–39). New York: Disinformation Company.

147. Scott (2010).

7. DISINFORMATION

1. The Rendon Group (2005). Retrieved from http://www.therendongroup.com.

2. Sourcewatch (2007). "ALEC at 40: Turning Back the Clock on Prosperity and Progress." Daniel J. Edelman, Inc. Retrieved from http://www.sourcewatch.org/index.php?title=Edelman.

3. Farsetta, D. (2006). "The Devil Is in the Lack of Details: The Defense Department's Media Contracts." *PR Watch*. Retrieved from http://www.prwatch.org/node/4481.

4. McChesney, R. (2004). *The Problem of the Media: U. S. Communication Politics in the 21st Century*. New York: Monthly Review Press; Hedges, S. J. (Nov. 13, 2005), "Firm Helps U.S. Mold News Abroad." *Chicago Tribune*. Retrieved from http://articles.chicagotribune.com/2005-11-13/news/0511130330_1_rendon-group-pentagon-proponents-of-open-government/2.

5. Bagdikian, B. (2004). *The New Media Monopoly*. Boston: Beacon Press; Lutz, A. (June 2012), "These 6 Corporations Control 90% of the Media in America." *Business Insider*. Retrieved from http://www.businessinsider.com/these-6-corporations-control-90-of-the media-in-america-2012-6; (April 5, 2012). "The Big 6' Media Conglomerates: How Much Do They Really Control?" Retrieved from Colorado University, Boulder, Introduction to Sociology Course, http://introsociology.net/blog/2012/04/05/the-big-6-media-conglomerates-how-much-do-they-really-control/.

6. McChesney (2004).

7. Chomsky, N. (2002). *Media Control: The Spectacular Achievements of Propaganda* (2nd ed.). New York: Seven Stories Press.

8. Sproule, J. M. (1997). *Propaganda and Democracy: The American Experience of Media and Mass Persuasion*. Cambridge, MA: Harvard University Press.

9. Ibid., 8.

10. Chomsky (2002).

11. Sproule (1997) (p. 10).

12. Ibid. (p. 11).

13. Snow, N. (1998). *Propaganda, Inc.: Selling America's Culture to the World*. New York: Seven Stories Press.

14.   Bernays, E. (1928). *Propaganda.* New York: H. Liveright; Bernays, E. (1934). *Crystallizing Public Opinion.* New York: Liveright; Bernays, E. (1955). *The Engineering of Consent.* Norman: University of Oklahoma Press.

15.   Edward Bernays, as quoted in Chomsky, N. (2001), "What Makes the Mainstream Media Mainstream." In Kick, R. (Ed.), *The Disinformation Guide to Media Distortion, Historical Whitewashes, and Cultural Myths* (p. 24). New York: Disinformation Company.

16.   Edward Bernays, as quoted in Snow (1998) (p.18).

17.   Snow (1998).

18.   Chomsky (2001).

19.   Sproule (1997) (p. 18).

20.   Sproule (1997).

21.   William Evjue, as quoted in McChesney, R. (1999), *Rich Media, Poor Democracy: Communication Politics in Dubious Times.* Chicago: University of Illinois Press.

22.   Sproule (1997).

23.   Shah, A. (2006). "Media Manipulation." Retrieved from http://www.globalissues.org/HumanRights/Media/Manipulation.asp.

24.   Bagdikian (2004).

25.   Lutz, A. (2012); http://introsociology.net/blog/2012/04/05/the-big-6-media-conglomerates-how-much-do-they-really-control/ .

26.   Shah, A. (April 17, 2006). "Media Manipulation." *Global Issues.* Retrieved from http://www.globalissues.org/article/532/media-manipulation.

27.   McChesney (1999).

28.   *Democracy Now* (2006). "Fox News Producer Resigns over Middle East Coverage." Retrieved from http://www.democracynow.org/article.pl?sid=06/08/16/148232.

29.   McChesney, R. (2013). *Digital Disconnect: How Capitalism Is Turning the Internet against Democracy.* New York: New Press.

30.   Moore, A. (2003). "Interlocking Directorates and Megamedia." *Columbia Journalism Review.* Retrieved from http://cjrarchives.org/issues/2003/2/lists-moore.asp.

31.   Bagdikian (2004).

32.   Ibid.

33.   Lynch, A. (2005). "U.S.: The Media Lobby." *AlterNet.* Retrieved from http://www.corpwatch.org/print_article.php?id=11947.

34.   Ibid.

35.   Open Secrets.org: Center for Responsive Politics. (2013). "Communications/Electronics." Retrieved from http://www.opensecrets.org/industries/indus.php?Ind=B; Bender, A., and Warren, T. (2012). "Q4 2011 Lobbying Report Shows Google Spending Skyrocketed." *Consumer Watchdog.* Retrieved from http://www.consumerwatchdog.org/story/q4-2011-lobbying-report-shows-google-spending-skyrocketed.

36.   Schou, N. (2014). *Kill the Messenger: How the CIA's Crack-Cocaine Controversy Destroyed Journalist Gary Webb.* New York: Nation Books.

37.   Risen, J. (2014). *Pay Any Price: Greed, Power, and Endless War.* New York: Free Press.

38.   Bagdikian (2004) (p. 138).

39.   Rupert Murdoch, as quoted in McChesney (1999) (p. 74).

40.   McChesney (1999).

41. Moyers, B. (October 10, 2003), "U.S. Media Gets Bigger." *Now* with Bill Moyers on PBS. Retrieved from http://www.corpwatch.org/print_article.php?id=7836.
42. Bagdikian (2004).
43. Klinenberg, E. (2007). *Fighting for Air: The Battle to Control America's Media*. New York: Henry Holt.
44. Moyers, B. (2007). "Digital Destiny." Address to the National Conference on Media Reform in Memphis, TN, on Pacifica radio, *Democracy Now*, January 16.
45. Freire, P. (1968). *Pedagogy of the Oppressed*. New York: Seabury Press.
46. Moyers (2003).
47. Bagdikian (2004).
48. Lynch (2005).
49. Lowry Mays, as quoted in Lynch (2005).
50. Common Cause.org (2006). "Wolves in Sheep's Clothing: Telecom Industry Front Groups and Astroturf." Retrieved from http://www.commoncause.org/site/pp.asp?c=dkLNK1MQIwG&b=1499059; Center for Strategic and International Studies and the Massachusetts Institute of Technology (2004). "Astroturf: Interest Group Lobbying and Corporate Strategy." *Journal of Economics & Management Strategy*, Winter, 563.
51. Farsetta, D., and Price, D. (2006). "Fake TV News: Widespread and Undisclosed." *PR Watch*. Retrieved from http://www.prwatch.org/fakenews/execsummary.
52. Pew Research Center (September 2012). "In Changing News Landscape, Even Television Is Vulnerable: Trends in News Consumption: 1991 2012." Retrieved from http://www.people-press.org/2012/09/27/in-changing-news-landscape-even-television-is-vulnerable/.
53. Farsetta and Price (2006).
54. Soley, L. (1997). "The Power of the Press Has a Price." *Extra!* July–August. Retrieved from http://www.fair.org/index.php?page=1387.
55. Borjesson, K. (Ed.) (2005). *Feet to the Fire: The Media after 9/11, Top Journalists Speak Out*. New York: Prometheus Books.
56. McChesney (1999) (p. 271).
57. *Corpwatch* (n.d.). "General Electric." Retrieved from http://www.corpwatch.org/print_article.php?list-type&type=16.
58. 55 Shirky, C. (2008). *Here Comes Everybody: The Power of Organizing without Organizations*. New York: Penguin Group.
59. Huang, C. (June 2011). "Facebook and Twitter Key to Arab Spring Uprisings." *The National*. Retrieved from http://www.thenational.ae/news/uae-news/facebook-and-twitter-key-to-arab-spring-uprisings-report.
60. Beniger, J. R. (1986). "The Control Revolution: Technological and Economic Origins of the Information Society." In *Library of Congress Cataloging-In-Publication Data*. Cambridge, MA: Harvard University Press.
61. Shirky (2008); Temple, D. (2011), "Renaissance 2.0: The Web's Potential for Peaceful Transformation of Modern Society." In Pilisuk, M., and Nagler, M. (Eds.), *Peace Movements Worldwide. V3 Peace Efforts that Work and Why* (pp. 138-146). Santa Barbara, CA: Praeger ABC-Clio.
62. Chester, J. (2007). *Digital Destiny: New Media and the Future of Democracy*. New York: New Press.

63. Moyers (2007).
64. Edward Bernays, as quoted in Chomsky, N. (2005), *Imperial Ambitions: Conversations on the Post-9/11 World* (p. 20). New York: Metropolitan Books.
65. Nunberg, G. (2006). *Talking Right: How Conservatives Turned Liberalism into a Tax-Raising, Latte-Drinking, Sushi-Eating, Volvo-Driving, New York Times-Reading, Body-Piercing, Hollywood-Loving, Left-Wing Freak Show.* New York: Public Affairs.
66. Lakoff, G. (2002). *Moral Politics: How Liberals and Conservatives Think.* Chicago: University of Chicago Press; Fromm, E. (1964), *Escape from freedom.* New York: Holt, Rinehart, and Winston.
67. Pratkanis and Aronson, as quoted in McKay, F. (2006), "Propaganda: America's Psychological Warriors. " *Seattle Times.* Retrieved from http://seattletimes.nwsource.com/html/opinion/2002812441_sundayfloyd19.html.
68. Michael Parenti, as quoted in Snow (1998) (p. 10).
69. Farsetta (2006).
70. Ibid.
71. Ibid.
72. Associated Press (Feb. 2009), "Pentagon Spending Billions on PR to Sway World Opinion." Fox News. Retrieved from http://www.foxnews.com/politics/2009/02/05/pentagon-spending-billions-pr-sway-world-opinion/#ixzz2a6BP0wJC.
73. Blum, W. (2005). "The Anti-Empire Report: Some Things You Need to Know before the World Ends." *Dissident Voice.* Retrieved from http://www.dissidentvoice.org/June05/Blum0614.htm.
74. Billings, E. (2002). "Hearts and Minds: The Rendon Group's Top-Secret Spin Machine for the Pentagon Is Big Business." *Washington Business Forward.* Retrieved from http://72.14.253.104/search?q=cache:xUJGAujdlyAJ:www.bizforward.com/wdc/issues/2002; Sourcewatch (2007b). "Rendon Group." Retrieved from http://www.sourcewatch.org/index.php?title=Rendon_Group.
75. Bamford, J. (2005). "The Man Who Sold the War: Meet John Rendon, Bush's General in the Propaganda War." *Rolling Stone.* Retrieved from http://www.rollingstone.com/politics/story/8798997/the_man_who_sold_the_war/.
76. Ibid.
77. Ibid.
78. *New York Times,* as quoted in Chaterjee, P. (2006), "Information Warriors: Rendon Group Wins Hearts and Minds in Business, Politics, and War." Retrieved from http://www.corpwatch.org/print_article.php?id=11486.
79. Lincoln Group (n.d.). "Lincoln Group." Retrieved from http://www.lincolngroup.com.
80. Mazzetti, M., and Daragahi, B. (2005). "The Conflict in Iraq: U.S. Military Covertly Pays to Run Stories in Iraqi Press." *Los Angeles Times.* Retrieved from http://www.latimes.com/news/nationworld/world/la-fg-infowar30nov30,0,5638790.story?page=1&coll=la-home-headlines; Berkowitz, B. (2006), "Lincoln Group: Unethical Weapon of Mass Deception." *Working for Change.* Retrieved from http://www.workingforchange.com/printitem.cfm?itemid=2127; Sourcewatch (2006), "Planting Fake News in Iraq." Retrieved from http://www.sourcewatch.org/index.php?title=Lincoln_Group#Planting_Fake_News_in_Iraq.
81. Pessin (2005).

82. Roberts, K. (2006). "Iraq Propaganda Program Legal: Pentagon Report." Reuters. Retrieved from http://freepress.net/news/18536.

83. Department of Defense (2004). *Report of the Defense Science Board Task Force on Strategic Communication.* Retrieved from http://www.fas.org/irp/agency/dod/dsb/commun.pdf.

84. Rampton, S., and Stauber, J. (2003). *Weapons of Mass Deception: The Uses of Propaganda in Bush's War on Iraq.* New York: Tarcher/Penguin.

85. Hermann Goering (1946), as quoted by Kretzmann, D. (July 2012). "Hermann Goering: Explaining the Nature of War at the Nuremberg Trials." Retrieved from http://davidkretzmann.com/2012/07/hermann-goring-explaining-the-nature-of-war-at-the-nuremberg-trials/.

86. Lawrence, B. (Ed.) (2006). *Messages to the World: The Statements of Osama bin Laden.* New York: Verso Press.

87. Sourcewatch,org (2006). "Office of Strategic Influence." Retrieved from http://www.sourcewatch.org/index.php?title=Office_of_Strategic_Influence.

88. Douglas Feith, as quoted in Allen, M. (2002). "White House Angered at Plan for Pentagon Disinformation." *Washington Post.* Retrieved from http://www.washingtonpost.com/ac2/wp-dyn?pagename=article&contentId=A61716-2002Feb24&notFound=true.

89. Hersh, S. (2003). "Selective Intelligence." *The New Yorker.* Retrieved from http://www.newyorker.com/archive/2003/05/12/030512fa_fact?currentPage=1.

90. Dreyfuss, R., and Vest, J. (2004). "The Lie Factory." *Mother Jones.* Retrieved from http://www.motherjones.com/cgi-bin/print_article.pl?url=http://www.motherjones.com/news/feature/2004/01/12_405.html.

91. John Pike, as quoted in Borger, J. (2003). "The Spies Who Pushed for War." *Guardian.* Retrieved from http://www.guardian.co.uk/print/0,3858,4714031-103550,00.html.

92. Ibid.

93. Shulsky, as quoted in Hersh (2003) (p. 3).

94. Cheney, as quoted in Hersh (2003) (p. 2).

95. Caldicott, H. (2004). *The New Nuclear Danger: George W. Bush's Military-Industrial Complex.* New York: New Press.

96. Fetzer, J. (2007). *The 9/11 Conspiracy: The Scamming of America.* Chicago: Open Court/Catfeet Press.

97. Mandell, W. (2003). "The Press, the Press, The Freedom to Suppress." Retrieved from http://theoryandscience.icaap.org/content/vol004.002/11_letter_mandel.html.

98. Shane, S. (2005). "Vietnam War Intelligence 'Deliberately Skewed,' Secret Study Says." *New York Times,* December 2. Retrieved from http://www.nsa.gov/vietnam/index.cfm.

99. Herman, E. (2006). "U.S. Willing to Talk, with Conditions, and the Media Bites Once Again." *ZNet.* Retrieved from http://www.zmag.org/sustainers/content/2006-06/10herman.cfm.

100. Herman, E. S., and DuBoff, R. B. (1966). *America's Vietnam Policy: The Strategy of Deception.* Washington, DC: Public Affairs Press; Schurmann, F., Scott, P. D., and Zeinik, R. (1966). *The Politics of Escalation in Vietnam.* Boston: Beacon Press.

101. Herman (2006).

102. Ibid.

103. Schechter, D. (2005). *The Death of Media and the Fight to Save Democracy.* Hoboken, NJ: Melville House; Schechter, D. (2006). *When News Lies: Media Complicity and the Iraq War.* New York: Select Books.

104. Victoria Clarke, as quoted in Schechter (2006) (p. 173).

105. Wolff, M. (2003). "Live from Doha." *New York Magazine*. Retrieved from http://nymag.com/nymetro/news/media/columns/medialife/n_8545/.

106. Massing, M. (2003). "The Doha Follies." *The Nation*. Retrieved from http://www.thenation.com/doc/20030421/massing.

107. Robert Young Pelton, as quoted in Schechter (2006) (p. 193).

108. Rich, F. (2006a). *The Greatest Story Ever Told: The Decline and Fall of Truth from 9/11 to Katrina*. London: Penguin Press; Rich, F. (2006). "The Peculiar Disappearance of the War in Iraq." *New York Times*. Retrieved from http://select.nytimes.com/gst/abstract.html?res= F40E17FF385B0C738FDDAE0894DE404482&n=Top%2fOpinion%2fEditorials%20 and%20Op%2dEd%2fOp%2dEd%2fColumnists%2fFrank%20Rich.

109. Nichols, J., and McChesney, R. (2005). *Tragedy and Farce: How the American Media Sell Wars, Spin Elections, and Destroy Democracy*. New York: New Press.

110. McChesney (2004).

111. Nichols and McChesney (2005).

112. Ibid. (p. 26).

113. Hollar, J., and Hart, P. (2005). "When 'Old News' Has Never Been Told." *Extra!* Retrieved from http://www.fair.org/index.php?page=2612.

114. Ibid.

115. Ibid.

116. Klein, N. (2004). "You Asked for My Evidence, Mr. Ambassador: Here It Is in Iraq; the U. S. Does Eliminate Those Who Dare to Count the Dead." *Guardian*. Retrieved from http://www.guardian.co.uk/Iraq/Story/0,2763,1366349,00.html.

117. Roberts. L., Garfield, R., Khudhairi, J., and Burnham, G. (2004). "Mortality Before and After the 2003 Invasion of Iraq, a Cluster Sample Survey." *The Lancet* 364: 9445 Retrieved from   http://www.thelancet.com/journal/vol364/iss9445/full//llan.364.9445.early_online_ PUBLICATION.3113.

118. Ireland, D. (2006). "Why U.S. Media Dismissed the Lancet Study of 100,000 Iraqi Civilian Dead." *Common Dreams*. Retrieved from http://www.commondreams.org/cgi-bin/print. cgi?file=/views05/0127-23.htm.

119. Ibid.

120. David R. Meddings, as quoted in ibid.

121. Burnham, G., Lafta, R., Doocy, S., and Roberts, L. (2006). "Mortality after the 2003 Invasion of Iraq: A Cross-Sectional Cluster Sample Survey." *The Lancet*, 1–9.

122. Roberts et al. (2004).

123. *Time* magazine, as quoted in Anderson, R. (2003). "'That's Militainment!' The Pentagon's Media-Friendly 'Reality' War." In *Extra!* Retrieved from http://www.fair.org/indexphp?page=1141&printer_friendly=1.

124. Chinni, D. (n.d.). "Jessica Lynch: Media Myth-Making in the Iraq War." Retrieved from http://www.journalism.org/node/223.

125. London *Times*, as quoted in Anderson (2003).

126. Rush Limbaugh, as quoted in Remnick, D. (2004) "Hearts and Minds." *The New Yorker*. Retrieved from http://www.newyorker.com/printables/talk/040517ta_talk_remnick.

127. Hersh, S. (2004a). "Torture at Abu Ghraib." *The New Yorker*. Retrieved from http://www.newyorker.com/archive/2004/05/10/040510fa_fact?currentPage=1.

128. Hersh, S. (2004c). "The Grey Zone: How a Secret Pentagon Program Came to Abu Ghraib." *The New Yorker.* Retrieved from http://www.newyorker.com/archive/2004/05/24/040524fa_fact.

129. Hersh (2004a).

130. Ibid.

131. International Committee of the Red Cross (2004). *Report of the International Committee of the Red Cross on the Treatment by Coalition Forces of Prisoners of War and Other Protected Persons by the Geneva Conventions in Iraq during Arrest, Internment, and Interrogation.* Retrieved from http://www.globalsccurity.org/military/library/report/2004/icrc_report_iraq_feb2004.htm.

132. Human Rights Watch (2004). "The Road to Abu Ghraib." Retrieved from http://hrw.org/reports/2004/usa0604/.

133. Ibid.

134. Ibid.

135. Ibid.

136. Program on International Policy Issues (2003). "Study Finds Direct Link Between Misinformation and Public Misconception." *Truthout.org.* Retrieved from http://truthout.org/docs_03/printer_100403F.shtml.

137. Ibid.

138. Ibid.

139. Ibid.

140. Milbank, D., and Deane, C. (2003). "Hussein Link to 9/11 Lingers in Many Minds." *Washington Post.* Retrieved from http://www.washingtonpost.com/ac2/wp-dyn/A32862-2003Sep5?language=printer.

141. Solomon, N. (2003). "Linking the Occupation of Iraq with the 'War on Terrorism.'" *Media Beat.* Retrieved from http://www.fair.org/index.php?page=2385&printer_friendly=1; Solomon, N. (2005). *War Made Easy: How Presidents and Pundits Keep Spinning Us to Death.* Hoboken, NJ: John Wiley.

142. Rich (2006a).

143. David Brooks, as quoted in Bacon, J. (2005). "Saying What They've Been Thinking: Racial Stereotypes in Katrina Commentary." *Extra!* Retrieved from http://www.fair.org/indexphp?page=2795&printer_friendly=1.

144. Bill O'Reilly, as quoted in ibid.

145. Ibid.

146. Wolf Blitzer, as quoted in Yassin, J. O. (2005). "Demonizing Victims of Katrina: Coverage Painted Hurricane Survivors as Looters, Snipers, and Rapists." *Extra!* Retrieved from http://www.fair.org/index.php?page=2793&printer_friendly=1.

147. Allen Breed, as quoted in ibid.

148. *Washington Post,* as quoted in Yassin, ibid.

149. Yassin (2005).

150. Bacon (2005); Price, D. (2005), "Workers Get Hit Twice: Hurricane Katrina and Davis-Bacon Profiteering," *Counterpunch.* Retrieved from September, http://www.counterpunch.org/price09232005.html.

151. Ibid.

152. Bacon (2005).

153. Donaghy, T., Freeman, J., Grifo, F., Kaufman, K., Maassarani, T., and Shultz, L. (2007). "Atmosphere of Pressure: Report of Union of Concerned Scientists and Government Accountability Project." *Whistleblower*. Retrieved from http://www.whistleblower.org/storage/documents/AtmosphereOfPressure.pdf.

154. Ibid.

155. Revkin, A. (2005). "Bush Aide Softened Greenhouse Gas Links to Global Warming." *New York Times*. Retrieved from http://www.nytimes.com/2005/06/08/politics/08climate.html?pagewanted=1&ei=5090&en=22149dc70c0731d8&ex=1275883200.

156. PRW Staff (2011, December). "Upcoming American Petroleum Institute 'Vote 4 Energy' TV Campaign Disrupted by Undercover Activists." PRWatch.org. Retrieved from http://www.prwatch.org/news/2011/12/11196/upcoming-american-petroleum-institute-vote-4-energy-tv-campaign-disrupted-underco. See http://www.opensecrets.org/lobby/clientsum.php?id=D000031493&year=2011.

157. Center for Responsive Politics (2006). "Oil and Gas: Top 20 Recipients." Retrieved from http://www.opensecrets.org/industries/recips.asp?Ind=E01.

158. Suskind, R. (2004). "Without a Doubt." *New York Times*. Retrieved from http://query.nytimes.com/gst/fullpage.html?res=9C05EFD8113BF934A25753C1A9629C8B63; Lincoln Group, (n.d.). Retrieved from http://www.lincolngroup.com.

8. VALUES AND HABITS THAT MAINTAIN A VIOLENT SYSTEM

1. Parenti, M. (1995). *Democracy for the Few* (6th ed.). New York: St. Martin's Press; Chomsky, N. (1993), *The Prosperous Few and the Restless Many*. Berkeley: Odonian Press; Korten, D. C. (1995), *When Corporations Rule the World*. West Hartford, CT: Kumerian Press and San Francisco: Berrett-Koehler Publishers; Klare, M. T. (2002), *Resource Wars: The New Landscape of Global Conflict*. New York: Henry Holt.

2. Pilisuk, M., and Hayden, T. (1965). "Is There a Military-Industrial Complex which Prevents Peace? Consensus and Countervailing Power." *Journal of Social Issues* 21/3: 67–17.

3. Bello, W., Cunninghan, S., and Rau, B. (1999). *Dark Victory: The United States and Global Poverty*. London: Pluto Press.

4. Wolf, E. (1999). *Peasant Wars of the Twentieth Century*. Norman: Univ. of Oklahoma Press.

5. Pilisuk, M. (1982). "Games Strategists Play." *Bulletin of the Atomic Scientists* 38/9: 13–17.

6. Reiber, R. W., and Kelly, R. J. (1991). "Substance and Shadow: Images of the Enemy." In Reiber, R.W. (Ed.), *The Psychology of War and Peace: The Image of the Enemy* (pp. 3–39). New York: Plenum; Herman, E. S., and Chomsky, N. (1988), *Manufacturing Consent*. New York: Pantheon Books.

7. Pilisuk, M., and Wong, A. (2002). "State Terrorism: When the Perpetrator Is a Government." In Stout, C. (Ed.), *Psychology and Terrorism* (pp. 105–32). Westport, CT: Praeger.

8. Pillar, C. (2007). "Report: Gates Foundation Causing Harm with the Same Money It Uses to Do Good." *Democracy Now!*. Retrieved from http://www.democracynow.org/2007/1/9/report_gates_foundation_causing_harm_with.

9. Macy, J. R., and Brown, M. Y. (1998). *Coming Back to Life: Practices to reconnect Our Lives, Our world*. Gabriola Island, BC: New Society Publishers.

10. Avnery, U. (March 12, 2006). *Shhhhhh! Avnery on What Is Missing in the Election Campaign*. Jerusalem: Gush Shalom. Retrieved from http://zope.gush-shalom.org/home/en/channels/avnery/1142114960.

11. Chomsky, N. (1993). *The Prosperous Few and the Restless Many.* Berkeley, CA: Odonian Press.
12. Monbiot, G. (2006). *Heat: How to Stop the Planet from Burning.* New York: Doubleday.
13. Lewis, E. (1998). *The Buying of the Congress.* New York: Avon; Domhoff, G. W. (1990). *The Power Elite and the State: How policy Is Made in America.* Hawthorne, NY: Aldine de Gruyter.
14. Palast, G. (2004). *The Best Democracy Money Can Buy.* New York: Penguin.
15. Silverstein, K. (1998). *Washington on Ten Million Dollars a Day.* Monroe, ME: Common Courage Press.
16. Nossiter, B. D. (1970). *Soft State: A Newspaperman's Chronicle of India* (p. 32). New York, Harper & Row.
17. McChesney, R. W. (1997). *Corporate Media and the Threat to Democracy.* New York: Seven Stories Press; Webb, G. (2001). "The New Rules for the New Millennium." In Kick, R. (Ed.), *The Disinformation Guide to Media Distortion, Historical Whitewashes and Cultural Myths* (pp. 38–39). New York: Disinformation Company.
18. Goldberg, E., and Evans, L. (1998). *The Prison Industrial Complex and the Global Economy.* Berkeley, CA: Agit Press.
19. Kanner, A. and Gomes, M. (1995). The All-Consuming Self. In Roszak, T., Gomes, M. and Kanner, A. (Eds.), *Ecopsychology* (pp. 77–91). San Francisco: Sierra Club Books.
20. Pilisuk, M., McAllister, J., and Rothman, J. (1996). "Coming Together for Action: The Challenge of Contemporary Grassroots Organizing." *Journal of Social Issues* 52/1: 15–37.
21. Turnbull, C. (1962). *The Forest People.* New York: Simon and Schuster.
22. Pilisuk, M., and Joy, M. (2001). "Humanistic Psychology and Ecology." In Schneider, K., Bugental, J., and Pierson, F. (Eds.), *Handbook of Humanistic Psychology* (pp. 101–14). Thousand Oaks, CA: Sage Publications.
23. Misra, G.. and Gergen, K. J. (1993). "On the Place of Culture in Psychological Science." *International Journal of Psychology* 28/2: 225–43.
24. Pilisuk, M.,and Zazzi, J. (2006). "Toward a Psychosocial Theory of Military and Economic Violence in the Era of Globalization." *Journal of Social Issues* 62/1: 41–62.
25. Postman, N. (1992). *Technopoly: The Surrender of Culture to Technology.* New York: Alfred A. Knopf.
26. Seager, J. (1993). *Earth Follies: Coming to Feminist Terms with the Global Environmental Crisis.* New York: Routledge, Bredemeir & Toby.
27. Pilisuk, M., and Zazzi, J. (2006).
28. Norquist, G. (1994). *Rock the House.* Austin: Texas Policy Foundation.
29. Garfinkle, N. (2006). *The American Dream vs. the Gospel of Wealth: The Fight for a Productive Middle-Class Economy.* New Haven: Yale University Press.
30. Cox, H. (1999). "The Market as God." *The Atlantic Monthly,* March 1999, 18–23: McGloin, S. J. (September 1999), "The Market as God: Living in the New Dispensation." *Jesuit Center for Theoretical Reflection Bulletin* 41. Retrieved from http://www.jctr.org.zm/bulletins/market%20as%20god.htm.
31. Perelman, M., and Sandusky, S. (October 2006). "When Economists Didn't Buy the Free Market: An Interview with Michael Perelman." *Z Net.* Retrieved from http://www.zcommunications.org/when-economists-didnt-buy-the-free-market-an-interview-with-michael-perelman-by-michael-perelman.html.

32. Peterson, E. A. III, (2005a). "American Idols: From Petro-theism to Empire-theism." *The Peoples Voice.* Retrieved from http://www.thepeoplesvoice.org/cgi-bin/blogs/voices.php/2005/09/30/p2855#more2855.

33. Riebel, L. (2012). *The Green Foodprint: Food Choices for Healthy People and a Healthy Planet.* Lafayette, CA: Print and Pixel Books.

34. Voiland, A., and Haupt, A. (2012). "10 Things the Food Industry Doesn't Want You to Know." *U.S. News.* Retrieved from http://health.usnews.com/health-news/articles/2012/03/30/things-the-food-industry-doesnt-want-you-to-know.

35. Simon, M. (2006). *Appetite for Profit: How the Food Industry Undermines Our Health and How to Fight Back.* New York: Nation Books.

36. Lakoff, G., and Johnson, M. (2003). *Metaphors We Live By.* Chicago: Univ. of Chicago Press.

37. Dunlop, R., Van Liere, K., Mertig, A., and Jones, R. E. (2000). "Measuring Endorsement of the New Ecological Paradigm." *Journal of Social Issues* 56/3: 425–42.

38. Dunlop, R., Gallup, G. H., and Gallup, A. M. (1993). *Health of the Planet: A George H. Gallup Memorial Survey.* Princeton: Gallup International Institute.

39. Lace, Sosin and Snell Assoc. (1997). *US Opinion Poll Commissioned for the Abolition 2000 Network.* New York: Global Resource Action Center.

40. Pilisuk, M., Parks, S. H., and Hawkes, G. R. (1987). "Public Perception of Technological Risk." *Social Science Journal* 24: 403–13.

41. Chomsky (1993).

42. Perelman and Sandusky (2006).

43. Klein, N. (2007). *The Shock Doctrine: Rise of Disaster Capitalism.* New York: Macmiilan.

44. Klein, N. (2005). "The Rise of Disaster Capitalism." Retrieved from *The Nation* website: http://www.thenation.com/doc.mhtml?i=20050502&s=klein.

45. Beard, C. A. (1902). *The Industrial Revolution.* London: G. Allen & Unwin.

46. Zinn, H. (2006). "America's Blinders." *The Progressive.* Retrieved from http://progressive.org/mag_zinn0406.

47. Rogers, S. (2012). "Health Care Spending around the World, Country by Country." *The Guardian:* DataBlog. Retrieved from http://www.guardian.co.uk/news/datablog/2012/jun/30/healthcare-spending-world-country.

48. Mahon, M. (2010). "U.S. Ranks Last among Seven Countries on Health System Performance Based On Measures of Quality, Efficiency, Access, Equity, and Healthy Lives." *Commonwealth Fund.org.* Retrieved from http://www.commonwealthfund.org/News/News-Releases/2010/Jun/US-Ranks-Last-Among-Seven-Countries.aspx.

49. CIA Publications (2012). "Country Comparison: Infant Mortality Rate." CIA Publications: *The World Factbook.* Retrieved from https://www.cia.gov/library/publications/the-world-factbook/rankorder/2091rank.html.

50. Correctional News (2012). "U.S. Sees First Decrease in Prison Population in Nearly 40 Years." *Correctional News.* Retrieved from http://www.correctionalnews.com/articles/2012/02/22/us-sees-first-decrease-in-prison-population-in-nearly-40-years.

51. Garofalo, P. (2012). "US Has One of the Highest Child Poverty Rates in the Developed World." *Think Progress.* Retrieved from http://thinkprogress.org/economy/2012/05/29/491443/un-report-child-poverty/.

52. National Center for Children in Poverty (NCCP) (2012). "Child Poverty." Retrieved from http://www.nccp.org/topics/childpoverty.html.

53. Kiesling, J. B. (2006). *Diplomacy Lessons: Realism for an Unloved Superpower.* Washington, DC: Potomac Press.

54. Parenti, M. (1995).

55. Zinn, H. (2006). "America's Blinders." *The Progressive.* Retrieved from http://progressive. org/mag_zinn0406.

56. Alterman, E. (2004). *When Presidents Lie: A History of Official Deception and Its Consequences.* New York: Viking.

57. Carroll, J. (2005). "The Day after the Fireworks." *Common Dreams.org.* Retrieved from http://www.commondreams.org/views05/0705-24.htm; Peterson, F. A. III (2005b), "United States: American Militarism, Part 2: On Celebrating Militaristic Nationalism." *Axis of Logic.com.* Retrieved from http://www.axisoflogic.com/artman/publish/Article_19086.shtml.

58. Giles, as quoted in Andreas, J. (2004), *Addicted to War: Why the U.S. Can't Kick Militarism* (p. 3). Oakland, CA: AK Press.

59. Mander, J. (1996). "The Rules of Corporate Behavior." In Mander, J., and Goldsmith, E. (Eds.), *The Case against the Global Economy: And for a Turn toward the Local* (pp. 309–422). San Francisco: Sierra Club Books.

9. THE EVOLUTION OF CONCENTRATED CORPORATE POWER TO INFLICT VIOLENCE AND INJUSTICE: DANGERS AND HOPES

1. Wal-Mart (2012). Retrieved from http://corporate.walmart.com/our-story/our-stores.

2. Moreton, B. E. (2010). *To Serve God and Wal-Mart.* Cambridge MA: Harvard University Press.

3. Ibid.

4. Ibid.

5. Ibid.

6. WalMart Watch (2006a). "Tale of two WalMarts." Retrieved from http://walmartwatch.com/ blog/archives/tale_of_two_wal_marts_retailers_legacy_future_collide_in_transition_era/; WalMart Watch (2006b), "Betty v. Goliath: A History of Dukes vs. Wal-Mart." Retrieved from http://walmartwatch.com/blog/dukesWalMart backgrounder-1.#0.

7. Ibid.

8. Westheimer, J. (Ed.) (2007). *Pledging Allegiance: The Politics of Patriotism in American Schools.* New York: Teachers College Press.

9. Hedges, C. (2004). "The Christian Right and the Rise of American Fascism: The Rise of the Religious Right in the Republican Party." Public Information Project of the Center for Religion, Ethics and Social Policy at Cornell University. *Theocracy Watch.* Retrieved from http://www.theocracywatch.org/chris_hedges_nov24_04.htm.

10. Fernandes, D. (2007). *Targeted: Homeland Security and the Business of Immigration.* New York: Seven Stories Press.

11. Scott, P. D. (2006). "Homeland Security Contracts for Vast New Detention Camps." *Global Research.* Retrieved from http://www.globalresearch.ca/homeland-security-contracts-for-vast-new-detention-camps/1897.

12. Yassin, J. O. (2005). "Demonizing the Victims of Katrina." Fairness and Accuracy in Reporting (FAIR). Retrieved from http://fair.org/extra-online-articles/demonizing-the-victims-of-katrina/

13. Scott (2006); Fernandes (2007).

14.   Kennedy, D. (2007). "Chiapas: Reflections on Trade, Immigration, and the Global Economy." *Global Exchange.* Retrieved from http://www.globalexchange.org/tours/ChiapasReflections.html.

15.   Bacon, D. (2006). *Communities without Borders: Images and Voices from the World of Migration.* Ithaca, NY: ILR Press.

16.   Southern Poverty Law Center (SPLC) (2013). "Close to Slavery: Guest Worker Programs in the United States." Retrieved from http://www.splcenter.org/get-informed/publications/close-to-slavery-guestworker-programs-in-the-united-states.

17.   Britt, L. W. (2004). "Fascism Anyone?" *Free Inquiry* 23/2. Retrieved from http://www.secularhumanism.org/library/fi/britt_23_2.htm.

18.   Rosen, R. (2010). "The Tea Party and the New Right-Wing Christian Feminism." *50.50 Inclusive Democracy.* Retrieved from http://www.opendemocracy.net/5050/ruth-rosen/tea-party-and-new-right-wing-christian-feminism.

19.   Tomasky, M. (2009). "Something New on the Mall." *New York Review of Books.* Retrieved from http://www.nybooks.com/articles/archives/2009/oct/22/something-new-on-the-mall.

20.   Griffin, D. R., Cobb, J. B. Jr., Falk, R. A., and Keller, C. (2006). *The American Empire and the Commonwealth of God: A Political, Economic, Religious Statement.* Louisville, KY: Westminster John Knox Press.

21.   North, G. (1983). *Christianity and Civilization.* Tyler, TX: Geneva Ministries.

22.   Robertson, P. (1991). *The New World Order.* Dallas, TX: Word Publication.

23.   Fernandes (2007).

24.   Hedges, C. (2004).

25.   Flanders, L. (2007). *Blue Grit: True Democrats Take Back Politics from the Politicians.* New York: Penguin.

26.   Hartmann, T. (2006). "Reclaiming the Issues: Islamic Or Republican Fascism?" *Common Dreams.* Retrieved from http://www.commondreams.org/views06/0828-23.htm.

27.   Engelhardt, T. (November 2005). "Jonathan Schell, Welcome to Camp Quagmire." *TomDispatch.* Retrieved from http://www.tomdispatch.com/post/39141/

28.   Stone, O., and Kuznick, P. (2112). *The Untold History of the United States.* New York: Gallery Press.

29.   Pilisuk, M., and Parks, S. H. (1986). *The Healing Web: Social Networks and Human Survival.* Hanover, NH: University Press of New England.

30.   Lerner, M. (December 2012). "Banning All Guns Is Necessary but Not Sufficient: We Need a Transformation of Consciousness." *Tikkun.* Retrieved from http://www.tikkun.org/tikkundaily/2012/12/14/banning-all-guns-is-necessary-but-not-sufficient-we-need-a-transformation-of-consciousness/.

31.   Twain, M. (1889; 2007). *A Connecticut Yankee in King Arthur's Court.* Colorado Springs, CO: Piccadilly Books.

32.   Nader, R. (2014). *Unstoppable: The Emerging Left-Right Alliance to Dismantle the Corporate State.* New York: Nation Books.

33.   Alperovitz, G. (2013). *What Then Must We Do?* White River Junction, VT: Chelsea Publishing.

34.   Hawken, P. (2008). *Blessed Unrest.* New York: Penguin.

INDEX

A Note on the Cover Photograph

"I cannot really remember where this picture was taken. I travelled extensively along the Somalia/Eritrean and Sudanese border many years ago and probably snapped it then. It languished in a dark cupboard somewhere until I used it in an article a couple of years ago and it has prompted a host of requests to reuse it for book covers, posters, and the like.

"Those tired and pathetic souls in the image are in all probability deceased, in fact I would stake my life on it. The deprivation and human suffering in that drought torn and war infested area meant that the human suffering simply limped along being patently ignored by we in the West, leaving thousands of victims in its wake.

"I read somewhere that sometimes an image captured by the eye and not the camera should sometimes be the one we retain.

"At the time this shot was taken I was travelling with a well known photographer on assignment and to tell the truth as this was a shared assignment; we never really knew who pushed the shutter. There are several images that relate to that time, many of them just seconds apart but it was the haunted eyes that made this one stand out."

"If anything can stop the plight of these poor people then I suppose that is a good thing, however having visited Dafur a few years ago I note the pattern simply repeats itself."

—PAUL V. WALTERS, 20 October 2014